CW01083071

Liechtenstein · A Modern History

"Most men think that the happiness of a state depends on its being great. They may be right; but even if they are, they do not know what it is that makes a state great or small. They judge greatness in numerical terms, by the size of the population; but it is capacity, rather than size, which should properly be the criterion."

Aristotle, "Politics", Book VII, Chapter 4.

David Beattie

LIECHTENSTEIN
A Modern History

I.B. TAURIS

LONDON · NEW YORK

Exclusive co-publication and distribution by I.B. Tauris Ltd

Distributed in 2004 by I.B. Tauris & Co Ltd
6 Salem Road, London W2 4BU
175 Fifth Avenue, New York NY 10010
www.ibtauris.com

In the United States of America and Canada distributed by
Palgrave Macmillan a division of St. Martin's Press
175 Fifth Avenue, New York 10010

First published in 2004 by van Eck Publishers, FL-9495 Triesen, Liechtenstein
Copyright © 2004 Jeeves AG, FL-9494 Schaan, Liechtenstein

The right of David Beattie to be identified as the author of this work has been asserted by
the author in accordance with the Copyright, Design and Patent Act 1988.

All rights reserved. Except for brief quotations in a review, this book, or any part thereof,
may not be reproduced, stored in or introduced into a retrieval system, or transmitted,
in any form or by any means, electronic, mechanical, photocopying, recording or otherwise,
without the prior written permission of the publisher.

ISBN 1-85043-459-X

A full CIP record for this book is available from the British Library
A full CIP record is available from the Library of Congress

Library of Congress Catalog Card Number: available

CONTENTS

ACKNOWLEDGEMENTS

Many people have helped in the preparation of this book.

First and foremost, my thanks are due to Bryan Jeeves OBE, without whose unfailing support, encouragement and advice the book could not have been written. As Honorary British Consul in Liechtenstein (from 1992 to 2001) he rendered great assistance to me during my time as British Ambassador accredited to the Principality. To this should be added his public services, among many others, as President of the British-Swiss Chamber of Commerce, President of the Council of British Chambers of Commerce in Continental Europe and Chairman of the British Alpbach Committee. He has lived in Liechtenstein since 1962 and continues to make an active and many-sided contribution to British-Liechtenstein relations.

In Liechtenstein I have benefited from interviews with members of the Princely House, serving and former members of the Parliament and serving and former members of the Government. I have received much help and information from leading figures in local government, industry, financial services and the academic community as well as from personal friends. I should like to record my thanks to, among others, the Government Press and Information Office, the Foreign Ministry, the Office for the Public Economy, the Financial Services Authority, the Government Legal Services, the Attorney-General's Office, the Education Office, the Liechtenstein Bankers Association and the Archbishopric. The staff of the National Library (Landesbibliothek), the Liechtenstein Institute and the National Archives' (Landesarchiv) press cutting service have been unfailingly helpful.

In the United Kingdom I am grateful to officials of the Foreign and Commonwealth Office, other Government departments and the British Council for their help in various ways, as also to the staff of the British National Archives (formerly the Public Record Office), the British Library, the Foreign and Commonwealth Office Library, the Bank of England Archive and the Courtaulds Archive. The Swiss Embassy was generous in allowing me the use of its library and in answering my questions. A number of personal contacts have put their information, advice and papers at my disposal.

Elsewhere, the Swiss Bankers Association has responded helpfully to my inquiries. Dr Milan Kovac has very generously allowed me to consult and use his unpublished research on Czechoslovak-Liechtenstein relations.

As publisher, Frank van Eck has contributed much advice, local knowledge and assistance. Ian Rodger, "Financial Times" correspondent at Zurich from 1991 to 1996, kindly read the manuscript and made some valuable suggestions. My wife has shown constant and encouraging support and interest.

This book is not an official account of Liechtenstein. It is an independent study. None of those who have helped me is responsible for the presentation of the facts or for the views expressed.

David Beattie

ILLUSTRATIONS

Cartoon: Liechtenstein as seen from Switzerland before and after the two countries voted on the European Economic Area Treaty, December 1992

Maps:
1. The Principality of Liechtenstein
2. Liechtenstein and the surrounding region
3. Liechtenstein and Western Europe
4. The House of Liechtenstein's estates in 1914

The author gratefully acknowledges permission to reproduce the following photographs: Nos. 2, 3, 4, 5, 6, 7, Collection of the Sovereign Princes of Liechtenstein; Nos. 1, 11, 12, 13, the Liechtenstein Government Press and Information Office; No. 8, the Liechtenstein National Museum; Nos. 9, 10, 25, the Liechtenstein National Archives; Nos. 14, 18, Sven Beham; Nos. 15, 16, 27, 29, Paul Trummer; No. 17, Bryan Jeeves; No. 19, the Hilti Corporation; No. 20, the Ospelt Group; No. 21 Hilcona AG; No. 22, Ivoclar Vivadent AG; No. 23, the Liechtenstein University of Applied Sciences; No. 24, Klaus Schädler; No. 26, Christian Vogt; No. 28, Ruedi Walti.

Cartoon by courtesy of Chappatte
(© Chappatte, in L'Hebdo – www.globecartoon.com)

Maps drawn by beck grafikdesign

INTRODUCTION

Every country has its clichés. Sometimes they are useful as a handy point of reference. Sometimes they mislead rather than illuminate.

There are two clichés about Liechtenstein: it is often described, and dismissed, either as an anachronistic fairy-tale Alpine paradise or as a haven for dubious financial operators. The truth is more interesting. This is a study of a unique state whose small size has both helped and hindered it throughout its history. Repeatedly, and sometimes against all the odds, it has survived imminent political and economic disaster. Its lack of natural resources, its poverty and its comparative remoteness made it uninteresting to the big predators, yet in half a century the hard work and talent of its small population transformed it from a backward agrarian land into the most highly industrialised country in Europe. Many of its industries use and produce the most advanced technology. It owes much of its manufacturing success to its liberal tax policy, which in more recent years has allowed a flourishing financial services sector to develop.

Politically, it is a constitutional monarchy based on an advanced parliamentary democracy. The House of Liechtenstein acquired the government of the territory by peaceful purchase at the turn of the seventeenth century, gave it their own name and turned it into an independent Principality. There has sometimes been tension between Crown, people and politicians, as this study will show; but more often than not that tension has been creative. At its best, the constitutional partnership has been dynamic and productive.

Liechtenstein achieved full international sovereignty in 1806, which makes it one of the more senior European states. In the second half of the twentieth century it succeeded by trial and error, by doggedness and application, in asserting its sovereign identity at the international level. As a member of the United Nations, the European Economic Area, the Council of Europe and other international organisations it is now making its own contribution, admittedly small but always constructive and sometimes distinctive, to the wider community.

With all the caveats that caution, history and a turbulent world demand, Liechtenstein seems better placed now than at any time in its history to deal with the problems and to seize the opportunities that the future will bring.

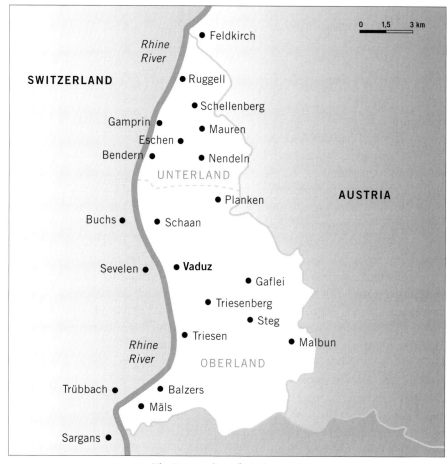

1. The Principality of Liechtenstein.

PART I
HISTORY

LIECHTENSTEIN'S EARLY HISTORY

The Land

The Principality of Liechtenstein lies on the right bank of the Upper Rhine. To the north and east is the Austrian Federal Land of Vorarlberg. To the west and south are, respectively, the Swiss cantons of St Gallen and the Grisons (Graubünden). It measures 24.75km (15.4 miles) from north to south and 10km (6.2 miles) from east to west at its widest point. Its area is 160 square km (62 square miles); that is, less than half the size of Rutland (England's smallest county) or the total size of Manhattan and the Bronx combined. About one third of this area is flat lowland along the Rhine, except for one long, whale-backed hill, the Eschnerberg, which rises towards the Austrian frontier in the north. The rest of the country is mountainous. Behind the screen of steep grey limestone mountains which the traveller sees on arrival lies a world of secluded Alpine valleys, pastures and (in winter) ski-slopes, reached by a road tunnel that pierces the mountain range. Further back again, another wall of peaks seals off the frontiers with Vorarlberg and the Grisons. The highest point is the Grauspitz (2,599m); the lowest is the Ruggeller Riet, a marshy area near the Rhine (430m above sea level).

There are virtually no natural resources apart from fertile agricultural land and some hydroelectric power. Nature has often been challenging. The Rhine has repeatedly burst its banks, causing much damage and hardship. The river's course was regulated in the nineteenth century, but the last and most disastrous flood, which owed much to human agency, occurred in 1927. Mountainside gullies ("Rüfen"), down which cascade torrents of rock and earth, have been a source of danger throughout the country's history and still call for constant vigilance and expensive precautions. A strong, warm and often unseasonable wind ("Föhn") from the south can fan forest and house fires even today or cause the snow to melt unexpectedly in the mountains.

Liechtenstein is not on one of the great north-south transit routes of Europe, but it offers the shortest and most direct passage from Milan and Como to Bregenz and Augsburg via the Splügen or San Bernadino passes. The Rhine gives an easy approach to Lake Constance. The road north leads to Feldkirch, just across the border in Austria, which historically was Liechtenstein's natural gateway to the wider German-speaking world. Liechtenstein is not a crossroads. In the nineteenth century the main east-west European railway to Vienna was built across its territory, but trains do not usually stop there. There is no airport.

Fortunately for itself, Liechtenstein has never been of great strategic importance, except briefly to Switzerland before and during the Second World War (page 95).

The Beginnings

The National Museum ("Landesmuseum") contains finds from the Later Stone Age (4000–1800 BC) which suggest that the Rhine plain was then inhabited by settled farming communities. The Bronze Age (1800–800 BC) and the Iron Age (800 BC onwards) have also left abundant traces, including some bronze figurines of very high quality found in the castle hill at Gutenberg (Balzers). In 15 BC Tiberius and Drusus, the stepsons of Augustus, led a well-planned and massive Roman invasion of Helvetia (modern Switzerland) to push the Empire's frontiers up to the Rhine and to a safer distance from the potentially weak spot of northern Italy. They finished the campaign in a single season. Military occupation gradually changed into peaceful development. Liechtenstein's present territory was included in the Roman province of Rhaetia. Villas and farms came into being along the south-north road through the Rhine valley. A Roman soldier's helmet from the first century has been preserved. It bears his name but not, unfortunately, the number of his legion. In the first half of the fourth century AD, as the Empire weakened internally and the pressure of invading tribes grew, the Romans built a strong six-towered fort at Schaan as a reinforcement point and a defence for their communication route.

In the fifth century AD Roman forces withdrew from Rhaetia. After years of raids the Alemanni, the Germanic ancestors of most of the people of Liechtenstein, were at last free to settle in the region. It seems, however, as if their more violent irruptions stopped short just north of Liechtenstein. The Latin-based Romansch language, five dialects of which are still spoken in the Grisons, was not completely replaced by German in the Liechtenstein area, Chur and South Vorarlberg until the twelfth and thirteenth centuries. Romansch has left many traces in the Liechtenstein dialect and place-names.

A second source of German-speaking immigrants was the Walsers, a tough and vigorous breed who colonised the wild valleys of the Upper Valais in Switzerland. Mediaeval lords in the Grisons and elsewhere imported them as settlers, but they kept their own dialect and traditions. Some Walsers arrived in present-day Liechtenstein in around 1300. The people of Triesenberg, perched in the mountains high above the Rhine valley (884 metres), remain proud of their distinctive Walser heritage.

Christianity

In the fifth century a church was built in Schaan on the foundations of the Roman fort. Christianity must have been present well before that. The later apostle of the area was St Lucius, whose name is commemorated by the road leading up to Liechtenstein from the Grisons, the St Luzisteig. It was long believed that he was a second-century British king who renounced his royal rank, became a missionary and founded the Diocese of Chur. His crowned reliquary bust is still to be seen in Chur Cathedral. However, this pleasing story has been disproved. It is now thought that St Lucius arrived in about 500 AD from the nearby heathen area of the Pritanni. Owing to the same confusion with the Pritanni, the same legend of British origin attached itself to St Florin, the patron saint of the parish church at Vaduz.[1] However, the Irish missionaries who evangelised eastern Switzerland, Upper Austria and Moravia may well have been active in the area. They are probably the earliest link between Liechtenstein and the British Isles.

Chur ("Curia", 40km south of Liechtenstein) was the capital of the Roman province of Rhaetia Prima. It became the seat of a diocese well before 451. In the Middle Ages it became a prince-bishopric whose incumbent exercised wide-ranging secular powers; the Emperor entrusted him with the guardianship of the Rhaetian passes. The diocese covered a large area, including parts of present-day Austria and Italy. The Liechtenstein area was ecclesiastically subordinate to it from the very beginning until 1997 (pages 268–270).

The Middle Ages

During the Dark Ages the Liechtenstein area was in a frontier zone on the fringes of several conflicting jurisdictions. Its inclusion in Charlemagne's empire gave it some temporary political stability, but murderous invasions from outside were a constant threat. The Hungarians robbed and burned nearby towns such as St Gallen in the ninth and tenth centuries, and the Saracens ravaged the towns from Chur to St Gallen in 940–950.

Nevertheless, some form of structure was maintained. The Emperor's senior officials gradually turned themselves into hereditary territorial lords. Charlemagne's third wife was of Frankish-Alemannic stock. From her brothers stemmed some of the local feudal magnates whose family relationships helped to hold the realm together despite frequent clashes of interest. From the Counts of Bregenz, who were powerful feudal lords in south-west Germany, descended Hugo, who inherited the county of Montfort (in Vorarlberg), Werdenberg and Sargans and established his residence in Feldkirch. His lands, therefore, extended across both banks of the Rhine. His territories were further divided when he died. His son,

---

[1] Tomamichel and Gröger, "Kathedrale Chur", NZN Buchverlag, Zurich 1972, p. 11

Rudolf I, inherited Werdenberg and Sargans, including the present-day territory of Liechtenstein.

In 1342 the county of Sargans was divided by treaty between two brothers, Hartmann and Rudolf von Werdenberg-Sargans. The lands on the right bank of the Rhine included the southern part of present-day Liechtenstein (the Oberland, or "Upper Country") and parts of Vorarlberg and the Grisons. The county of Vaduz was thereby established, and with it Hartmann's seat in the castle at Vaduz. In 1396 the Holy Roman Emperor Wenzel of Luxemburg, shortly before he was deposed, declared the county of Vaduz to be directly subordinate to the Emperor. This was important, for it meant that Vaduz was no longer subject to an intermediate overlord. The last of the Werdenberg Counts of Vaduz, Bishop Hartmann of Chur, assigned his possessions in 1416 to his kinsmen, the Barons von Brandis. In 1434 they acquired the lordship of Schellenberg (the present-day Unterland, or "Lower Country") from a descendant of the Montforts. Schellenberg, too, became an immediate fief of the Empire. The two parts of modern Liechtenstein thus came into the hands of the same ruler. Except for a brief interval, between 1699 and 1712, they have stayed together.

In 1515, the last von Brandis, Provost of Chur Cathedral, sold the county and lordship to his nephew, Rudolf von Sulz. A century of relative peace and order followed; but in 1613 Count Karl Ludwig von Sulz was forced by debts arising from obligations elsewhere to sell these possessions to his son-in-law, Count Caspar von Hohenems. The Hohenems were a distinguished military family. They also produced great patrons of the arts such as Markus Sittikus, nephew of Pope Pius IV and Archbishop of Salzburg from 1612 to 1619.

A Time of Troubles

Although there were several changes of ruling family, and although much depended on the individual personalities of the various lords, their common descent suggests a certain degree of continuity. Changes in and around the region, however, showed how vulnerable the tiny future Liechtenstein area was, both as a transit route and, once more, as a frontier zone. As the old feudal inheritances were sub-divided, their owners became poorer and more rapacious. Borders became more debatable.[2] On the far side of the Rhine, the Swiss cantons steadily expanded eastwards at the expense of the Habsburg lands and the possessions of the other magnates and the great monasteries. In 1499 the Swiss Confederates and the Grison Leagues invaded the Black Forest and Vorarlberg in their war against the Swabian League, which the Emperor had set up against them. On

[2] St Gallen and the Grisons did not become fully-fledged Swiss cantons until 1803. Habsburg territories in Vorarlberg (which was not so named until the eighteenth century) were not rounded off until 1765.

4

their way they burnt the castle at Vaduz and devastated the countryside. The Reformation and Counter-Reformation caused more instability. Count Rudolf von Sulz prevented the reformed faith from taking root in his lands and saved the country from a peasants' war. In nearby St Gallen, however, the town turned Protestant while the great abbey remained Catholic. It was much the same story in Chur. Of the three loose mediaeval leagues which made up the Grisons, the League of the Ten Jurisdictions (bordering on present-day Liechtenstein) and the League of the House of God turned Protestant while the Grey League remained Catholic. International political and military interest in the Alpine transit routes had meanwhile grown, since the Grisons territory formed a potential land link between the allied powers of Spain and Austria. Their opponents, France and the Venetian Republic, had a correspondingly strong strategic interest in denying them this link. Between 1607 and 1639 the Grisons territory was torn by the most atrocious savagery. For nearly fifteen years Austrian troops were billeted in the area of present-day Liechtenstein and marched up and down the country. There was repeated fighting around the fortress of Luziensteig. Hunger increased. In 1647, towards the end of the Thirty Years War, the Swedish army appeared at the border. The Swedes could be bought off only by an instant payment of 8,000 talers, which the impoverished population was obliged to borrow. It took the people more than a hundred years to pay off the principal and interest of the loan. Their miseries were made worse by outbreaks of plague.

The disasters from outside were aggravated by one of the worst outbreaks of witch-hunting in the German-speaking world. Out of a population of 3,000 some 300 men and women were tortured and executed. After appeals and complaints, legal experts in Salzburg declared the trials legally unsound and they were stopped.[3] The Emperor Leopold in Vienna, exercising his rights as immediate overlord, appointed the Prince-Abbot Rupert of Kempten to inquire into the matter. Rupert identified a sinister mixture of psychotic disorder in the ruler, Count Ferdinand Karl von Hohenems, a crisis in the public and the ruling family's finances and the count's vested interest in confiscating the property of the witch-trial victims. The count was deposed and Rupert took over the administration. The count's brother and successor, Jakob Hannibal III, was better intentioned but still unable to cope with the family's financial problems.

Rupert calculated the revenues of Vaduz and Schellenberg to be 4,500 and 2,500 florins, respectively: only three times the annual salary of a senior official in Vienna.[4] The debts of the Hohenems amounted to 200,000 florins. Rupert

---

[3] Witch trials were not abolished in Prussia until as late as 1714. The last alleged devil-worshipper was executed in Salzburg in 1750. The last witch burning in the Grisons was in 1760.

[4] Volker Press, "Die Entstehung des Fürstentums Liechtenstein", in "Das Fürstentum Liechtenstein", Konkordia, Bühl/Baden, 1981, page 74.

decided that the problem could only be solved by finding a buyer who was rich enough not to need the revenues from the two territories. He hoped that the sale of Schellenberg would settle the matter. However, the local Swabian nobility were too poor to bid. The Prince-Abbot of St Gallen showed interest, as had his predecessor in 1613, and so did the Prince-Bishop of Chur. But what the Emperor needed in the valley of the Upper Rhine, which was fraught with such political, military and confessional sensitivity, was a reliable, substantial and effective nobleman. This he found in Prince Johann Adam Andreas von Liechtenstein, nicknamed "The Rich". In 1699 the Prince bought the Lordship of Schellenberg for 115,000 florins (perhaps £1.05 million today), securing also a first option on Vaduz.[5] Count Jakob Hannibal's finances continued to worsen. In 1712 the county of Vaduz passed to Prince Hans-Adam I for 290,000 florins (69,000 in cash, plus the Liechtensteins' estate of Bistrau in Bohemia): perhaps £2.55 million today.[6] The Prince-Abbot of Kempten's long task was ended. On 25 January 1719 Emperor Charles VI granted the request of Hans Adam's successor, Prince Anton Florian, that the two territories be combined under the family name of Liechtenstein.

The nightmare of bankruptcy and witch hunts was over. The new Principality fell into the orbit of a great power which indirectly protected it from the turbulence of regional politics. On the other hand, while there were some family links between the Hohenems and the Liechtensteins, the Principality now passed for the first time in its history out of the power of local owners and became subject to an absentee magnate whose financial strength was rooted in Moravia and Bohemia and whose personal interests lay with the Court at Vienna. There were understandable misgivings in the Principality and grimaces among the Swabian nobles. However, with hindsight it is clear that no other solution would have secured the future of Liechtenstein as an independent entity. Ecclesiastical ownership would have led to absorption into Switzerland during or after the Napoleonic wars. Ownership by a local noble family would have ended in incorporation into Austria, as happened with so many other hereditary possessions in the area. (The Habsburgs themselves had contemplated purchase in 1613, but had lacked the money.) However, ownership alone was not enough to secure Liechtenstein's future: much skill, determination and luck were also to be needed.

---

[5] There was nothing unusual in this. The Habsburgs acquired most of their possessions in Vorarlberg by purchase between the fourteenth and eighteenth centuries.
[6] The sale enabled the Hohenems family to recover from the disaster. Jakob Hannibal's son Franz Rudolf became an Imperial Field Marshal. The male line of the family died out in 1759, after which the territory of Hohenems, which they had managed to keep, was incorporated into the Habsburg domains. The incognito visiting cards of Emperor Franz Josef (1848–1916) were inscribed "Le Comte de Hohenembs".

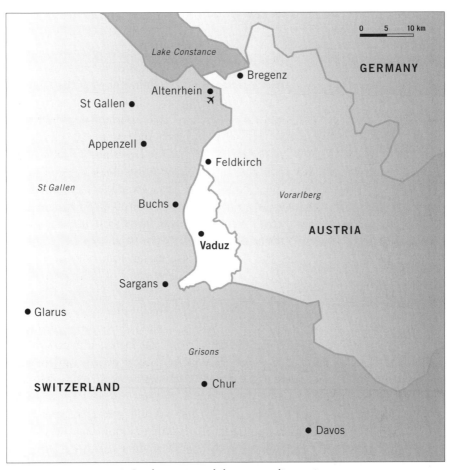

2. Liechtenstein and the surrounding region.

THE PRINCES OF LIECHTENSTEIN (TO 1723)

The House of Liechtenstein is now in its twenty-fifth recorded generation. It has produced a more than usually consistent line of tough, shrewd administrators, financiers, diplomats, soldiers and art collectors. Two or three of those talents have sometimes been combined in the same person. The family has taken some hard knocks in its history but has been remarkably resilient and adaptable. Its motto "Klar und Fest" ("Clear and Firm") rings true today.

The Beginnings

In the mid-twelfth century a nobleman called Hugo, who must already have been of some local distinction, built or bought a large castle on chalky white rock ("lichter Stein") near Maria Enzersdorf, not far south of Vienna.[1] This fortress's bleak silhouette is a reminder that Vienna was then very much on the outer frontier of Europe. In 1142 Hugo von Liechtenstein acquired Petronell, an important outpost on the Danube to the east of Vienna.[2] His grandson Heinrich (I) von Liechtenstein was prominent in the Teutonic Order's campaign against the Prussians. When Friedrich, the last of the Babenberg Dukes of Austria, was killed in battle with the Hungarians at the Battle of the Leitha in 1246, it was Heinrich who took command and ensured a decisive victory. He was on good terms with the rulers of Bohemia. In 1249 Przemysl Ottokar gave him an estate in the area of Nikolsburg (Mikulov), in Moravia to the north of Vienna. These lands were enlarged in 1370 when Johann (I) bought Eisgrub (Lednice) and again in 1395 when he acquired the neighbouring Feldsberg (Valtice) by marriage. So began the long connection between the Liechtenstein family and what is now the Czech Republic. Until the frontier changes of 1919 Feldsberg lay just inside Lower Austria, but was then incorporated into Czechoslovakia. The Eisgrub/Feldsberg estates remained the family's preferred seat until 1938.

---

[1] Harald Wanger, "Die Regierenden Fürsten von Liechtenstein" (Frank P. van Eck Verlagsanstalt, Triesen, 1995), page 14.

[2] There were some other families of the same name. Despite speculation, no relationship has ever been proved with the Styrian Liechtensteins, of Murau, who produced the Minnesinger Ulrich von Liechtenstein (c. 1200–c.1275), the poet of courtly love. That family died out in 1619.

Johann (I) started a tradition that was important for the family's future prosperity, even though it was not always observed in practice: in 1386 he concluded a family agreement on the indivisibility of its principal estates, which were to remain the common property of the family. The family's loyalties tended increasingly to lie with the rising dynasty of the Habsburgs. For example, Heinrich (II) was on the side of Rudolf von Habsburg when King Ottokar of Bohemia was killed at the Battle of Marchfeld in 1278. But Johann (I)'s political manoeuvrings with the Austrian and Bohemian nobility, and perhaps even his loans to the Habsburgs, led Duke Albrecht III von Habsburg to trap him in a castle together with a large part of the Liechtenstein family in 1394. They were not released until they had given up all their possessions south of the Danube (23 lordships and castles) and their property in Vienna. This blow deprived the family of their original seat, Liechtenstein Castle, and concentrated their landed interests even more than before in Moravia.[3]

Despite this episode various members of the family continued to serve the Habsburg dynasty and to hold high office under it in Austria. They also served the rulers of Bohemia and Moravia. Another family property agreement made in 1451 was soon followed by an amicable division in which the family split into branches named after Nikolsburg and Feldsberg, but the two branches seem to have worked together. Christoph (III), of the Nikolsburg branch, represented the Moravian nobility at the Imperial Diet (the Holy Roman Empire's equivalent of a parliament) in Frankfurt in 1455. He was appointed Land Marshal of Austria (King's representative) by Matthias Corvinus of Hungary and Bohemia in 1487 and campaigned against Emperor Frederick III of Habsburg. Nevertheless, after the death of King Matthias in 1490 Christoph was appointed counsellor to Frederick III and subsequently to his son Maximilian I. In 1504, shortly before his death, Christoph negotiated an agreement with his nephews that gave family members a prior right to buy any property that another member wished to sell and which made provision for the settlement of internal family disputes. One of those nephews, Georg (VI), played a leading part in the defence of Vienna during the first Turkish siege in 1529.

The record suggests that this family of landed, political and military magnates was too powerful to be ignored by its monarchs. The Liechtensteins had a solid territorial base, which they were determined to keep intact. However, their rather localised influence and their situation at the edge of conflicting realms meant that they had a difficult course to steer. The family generally showed a canny talent for survival. They tried not to burn their political bridges and were careful to keep their freedom of manoeuvre.

---

[3] Four centuries later, in 1808, Sovereign Prince Johann I re-purchased Liechtenstein Castle, whose restoration by the family was completed in 1903. Prince Johann I also built a new, neo-classical Liechtenstein Palace at the foot of the crag in 1820.

The Reformation

In 1517 Martin Luther nailed his 95 Theses to the church door at Wittenberg. In 1526 King Louis II of Hungary and Bohemia was killed in battle against the Turks at Mohács. Ferdinand of Habsburg, Archduke of Austria, husband of Louis' daughter Anna, was elected to the two vacant crowns. The Liechtenstein possessions were now enclosed within the realms of a single monarch. There was less room for manoeuvre. Decisions on religious allegiance had to be made.

At the Diet of Worms in 1521 the Emperor Charles V, for all his belief that the Church needed reform, made it clear that the House of Habsburg would stand by the traditional faith. However, Protestantism made quick and widespread inroads into Bohemia, Moravia and Austria. Leonhard von Liechtenstein (1492–1534), a younger son of Christoph (III) and himself a convert to the reformed faith, gave shelter at Nikolsburg to Anabaptist refugees in defiance of Ferdinand. Other members of the Nikolsburg branch continued in the military service of the Habsburgs until the line expired with the deaths of its last two male members on active service in 1688 and 1691. By that time, this branch's unlucky financial policies had led to the enforced sale of many important properties to outsiders despite the 1504 agreement. In 1560 Christoph (IV) sold Nikolsburg and in 1571 Wolfgang (II) sold Eisgrub. The family felt these disasters so deeply that in 1563 Christoph (IV) was obliged to assign the family seniority to his cousins of the Feldsberg branch.

The Feldsberg branch were strong Lutherans. Hartmann (II) (1544–1585) personally negotiated with the Emperor Ferdinand I as a member of the Committee of the Evangelical Estates. He was also well disposed to the Protestant sect of the Moravian Brethren. But he and his talented brothers were evidently indispensable to the Emperor as administrators, soldiers and diplomats. One brother served as envoy to the Sultan in Constantinople. As early as 1575 Hartmann was able to buy back the Eisgrub estate from the Emperor. Of Hartmann's five sons only three (Karl, Maximilian and Gundaker) reached maturity. It fell to them to administer the entire property of the family. They steered their house to new heights of power and prosperity in the most controversial and stormy circumstances.

Bohemia, 1620

By 1600 the Counter-Reformation, sponsored by Rome and led by the Jesuits, was in full flood. In 1599 Karl (1569–1627) converted to Catholicism. Maximilian (1578–1643) and Gundaker (1580–1658) followed him in 1600 and 1602, respectively. Their conversions made something of a sensation. How far their motives were spiritual and how far secular is unclear. In worldly terms, they took a risk: at the time, neither Habsburg success nor Protestant failure was at all certain. But once they had decided neither they nor their successors wavered, even though for some years Karl kept up his Protestant connections in Bohemia and Moravia.

Karl was a politician, Maximilian a soldier and Gundaker a courtier. They worked smoothly together in what seems to have been a systematic programme to build up the family's strength and standing. Karl and Maximilian married sisters through whom they acquired in 1597 the rich Boskowitz inheritance in Moravia. The next step was to correct the defects of the 1504 family agreement. This was done in 1606 when the brothers signed a fideicommissa, a device of private nobiliary law originating in Spain by which a perpetual entail was placed on the landed possessions that lay at the core of the family's wealth. Previously the oldest member had been head of the family, but henceforth succession was to be by primogeniture (the eldest son of the eldest line). The family head enjoyed the usufruct of the property for life. In addition, the head had responsibilities for settling family disputes. In this sense, Karl was the first Ruler ("Regierer") of the House. Fideicommissa became relatively common among the large noble land-owners in the Habsburg lands after 1600. Because they affected the monarch's rights they needed his approval, which Emperor Rudolph II confirmed to Karl in 1607. In the case of Moravia they also needed the approval of the Estates (repre-sentative assembly), which was forthcoming only after the Protestant nobles had secured the deletion of a clause binding the Liechtenstein family to the Roman Catholic faith.

Karl and his brothers showed themselves increasingly committed to the Habsburgs, in particular to Archduke Matthias, whose power grew as his brother Rudolph II (1597–1612) became an ever more eccentric recluse in Prague Castle. After the Boskowitz inheritance Karl's loans to the Emperor rose from 1,000 gulden in 1596 to 100,000 talers in 1597 and then to 410,000 gulden in 1605. Between 1603 and 1605 he was clearing Moravia of marauding Turks and Hungar-ians. In 1607 he secured a Catholic majority in the Moravian Diet, and in 1612 he was sent to Frankfurt to prepare the election and coronation of Matthias as Holy Roman Emperor. Amid all these strenuous activities, interspersed by occasional personal setbacks in the fluctuating politics of the time, he also devoted himself to administering his lands, a task requiring a small bureaucracy and constant supervision, and to collecting works of art.

Karl's accumulation of titles and functions began in 1600. In 1607 the Emperor bestowed upon him the privilege of coining money, building castles, approving markets, awarding titles, etc.[4] In 1608 he was raised to the rank of hereditary prince, which was also granted to his two brothers in 1623. Before 1600 no Habsburg subject enjoyed princely rank ("Fürst"), except for members of other

---

[4] Commemorative coins denominated in Swiss francs are occasionally issued under the superscription of the present sovereign, Prince Hans-Adam II.

ruling families who chanced to serve or settle in Austria. Karl von Liechtenstein was the first to be elevated to this title.[5] This high rank required suitable territorial jurisdiction. Karl would probably have liked this to be in a central location, but for reasons of financial or political prudence the Court Chancery thought it better to find him a more remote site. In 1613, against a payment of 159,000 gulden, he was assigned the Duchy of Troppau in Silesia. Karl now had his own Diet with four estates of prelates, gentry, knights and towns, together with a seat in the Silesian House of Princes. He received a mixed welcome there. The Protestant nobility objected; and, but for the events of 1620, the legal processes might have been lengthy. More honours were to follow: in 1622 the Order of the Golden Fleece, which brought the Liechtensteins into the top rank of the aristocratic families of the Empire, and in 1623 the grant of the Duchy of Jägerndorf. To celebrate the latter, Karl commissioned an elegant and richly jewelled ducal coronet which disappeared after his successor was forced to pawn it in 1677.

The first great crisis in the family's history came with the revolution in Bohemia. That country and its nobility had become largely Protestant. As in other countries, the centralising drive of the monarchy clashed with the desire of the estates and the nobility to assert themselves. Under the vague, irresolute and quarrelling brothers Rudolph II and Matthias the Imperial House lost direction. The Habsburgs' chosen heir, Archduke Ferdinand of Styria, was known to be a zealous Catholic. In 1617 the Bohemian Diet was induced by a political coup to elect Ferdinand the king-designate. The following year the Protestant Bohemian nobility reversed this decision and in effect set up a revolutionary government. The Jesuits were expelled. The death of the Emperor-King Matthias in March 1619 brought the crisis to a head. Even as Ferdinand was being elected Holy Roman Emperor in August, the Bohemian Estates were deposing him as their King and electing instead Frederick V of the Palatinate, a German Protestant prince married to the daughter of James I of England and VI of Scotland. In July 1619 a general diet of the Kingdom of Bohemia created for the first time a kind of confederation of Bohemia, Moravia, Silesia and Lusatia. In August 1619 the Estates of Upper and Lower Austria applied to join the confederation. The Hungarian Estates followed suit in 1620.

The stakes could not have been higher. Religious affiliations, the balance of power throughout Germany and the whole of Europe and the political existence of the House of Habsburg were in the balance. Karl von Liechtenstein kept Moravia quiet for as long as he could, then fled to Vienna. Ferdinand II's trust in God was rewarded by the appearance of the Catholic League's army under Tilly. In July 1620 Austria was re-conquered for the Counter-Reformation. On

[5] R. J. W. Evans, "The Making of the Habsburg Monarchy" (Oxford University Press, 1979), page 171.

8 November the League won the Battle of the White Mountain near Prague. Maximilian von Liechtenstein took part with 3,000 troops. Frederick V, who had never enjoyed either co-ordinated support within Bohemia or practical help from abroad, fled. Karl von Liechtenstein entered Prague as the Emperor's representative.

Karl was commissioned to lead an inquiry into the rebellion. This he did in close co-ordination with the Emperor. To set an example, twenty-seven alleged ringleaders were arrested and sentenced to death. Ferdinand II confirmed the sentences and Karl presided over the public executions on 21 June 1621. Three nobles, seven knights and seventeen burghers, including the German rector of the university, were put to death by the savage methods of the time. Where possible, Karl recommended clemency to keep the bloodshed to a minimum; and indeed the Emperor commuted death sentences passed on some others. In Moravia, under Cardinal Dietrichstein, there were no executions.

The properties of those executed, and of all who had collaborated with the revolutionary government, were confiscated either in whole or in part in both Bohemia and Moravia. The Crown, the Czech Roman Catholic nobility and the Roman Catholic Church were those who chiefly prospered in the first wave of expropriations, as did some important newcomers. By 1650 some three fifths of Bohemian and Moravian properties were still in indigenous hands, but the redistribution and upheaval had been radical.[6] Karl, who was appointed Governor and Viceroy of Bohemia in January 1622, was among those who made very large acquisitions. These were partly grants by the Crown in repayment of previous loans and partly purchases at advantageous prices. At the end of the nineteenth century it was estimated that 41% of the acreage of the then existing Liechtenstein family property had been acquired between 1620 and 1650.[7]

It was a time of economic slump and devaluation throughout Europe. The value of silver rose. Karl, who certainly showed ecumenical spirit in his financial affairs, presided over the debasement of the silver currency in company with his fellow-Catholic Wallenstein, the Dutch Calvinist economist Hans de Witte and the Jewish financier Jacob Bassevi. In consequence, those forced to sell their property for political or religious reasons did so at a considerable loss. The debasement eventually affected the Imperial Treasury. Once Karl was safely dead the full responsibility was assigned to him, and by 1660 the Treasury was claiming damages from his successor, Karl Eusebius, of 31 million gulden (including interest). However, there was no final proof against Karl. In 1665, after a contribution by

---

[6] New Cambridge Modern History, Vol. IV, page 519. But German as well as Czech landowners suffered; and the Bohemian nobility showed notable continuity (R. J. W. Evans, "The Making of the Habsburg Monarchy").

[7] Thomas Winkelbauer, "Die Verwaltung der liechtensteinischen Herrschaften und Güter im 17 und 18 Jahrhundert" in "Der Ganzen Welt ein Lob und Spiegel", ed. E. Oberhammer, Verlag für Geschichte und Politik, Vienna, 1990), p. 87.

Karl Eusebius of 275,000 gulden towards Emperor Leopold's military expenses, the Emperor formally granted an indemnity against any further claims by the Treasury and confirmed the Liechtenstein family in their possessions and privileges.[8] There were also questions concerning the legality of Karl's acquisition of the large Schwarzkostelets estate (nearly 10,000 hectares) which were settled in 1655 by the payment of over one million gulden.

It is difficult to assess the first Prince von Liechtenstein. Little is known of his personality. His likenesses in portraits and coins suggest a man crackling with energy and force. His intellectual interests were fashionably wide, to judge by his activities as a collector of works of art and curios. His actions indicate a man with an eye to the main chance, not overly scrupulous. But there are also signs of a wider vision, both for his family and his sovereign. Once his fundamental religious and political decisions had been made he stuck to them, despite the personal dangers and the very real pressures to trim. It is hard to disentangle the shared personal responsibilities for the events of 1620 and after. Such evidence as there is suggests that Karl's disposition was moderate, except for his relentless and shrewd accumulation of property. Given the crucial issues at stake, the standards then prevailing in western Europe and the atrocities that were to follow in Germany during the Thirty Years War, the public execution of the 27 leaders might be thought, for the times, a not exceptional retribution for what had occurred in Bohemia.

That, however, is not how it has been perceived. The executions and expropriations cast a long shadow. The Czech nationalist writers of the nineteenth century wove them into their people's story as a campaign of ethnic anti-Czech cruelty and tyranny by a German emperor and his servants.[9] Three centuries later, in 1920 and afterwards, their influence on the popular mood was to affect the fortunes of the House of Liechtenstein.

Consolidation and Recovery

Prince Karl died at 58, his strong constitution worn out by the exertions of a strenuous life. The education of his young son Karl Eusebius (1611–1684) was carefully completed by Prince Gundaker.[10] The economic depression and the

[8] Hannes Stekl, "Die Finanzen des Hauses Liechtenstein im 17 Jahrhundert", in "Der Ganzen Welt ein Lob und Spiegel", page 74.

[9] "…It is basically a nineteenth-century tale, contemporary events and attitudes heavily overlaid by the pathos of a late nationalism." (Evans, op. cit, page 196.) "This account is highly exaggerated and still worse shows a complete failure to understand what was possible in the seventeenth century." (New Cambridge Modern History, Vol. IV, page 518.)

[10] In 1633 Gundaker, who was very close to the Emperors Ferdinand II and Ferdinand III, founded a monastery at Wranau, near Brno, which was to serve until 1938 as the family's burial place. In the same year, the emperor elevated Mährisch Kromau and Ungarisch Ostra, which Gundaker had bought in 1622, into a Principality of Liechtenstein. It was not, however, directly subordinate to the Holy Roman Emperor.

Thirty Years War had caused much damage to the family lands. Karl Eusebius had to contend with the substantial claims against his late father. He probably did himself no good by keeping away from the Court, thus missing chances to argue his case. Leopold I, however, explicitly confirmed all previous grants to the Liechtenstein family. Strong in capital but weak in liquid assets, Karl Eusebius nevertheless managed to hold the estates together,[11] to found the famous stud at Eisgrub, to dabble in alchemy and to become the true founder of the family's collection of paintings. His policy of re-catholicisation in his lands was much more vigorous than his father's.

When his only surviving son Johann (Hans) Adam Andreas (1657–1712) succeeded, the European economy was enjoying an upswing. Hans-Adam inherited debts of 800,000 gulden (perhaps £7.71 million in 2002). A true manager-prince, he took his administration personally in hand, rationalised it, cut his staff by two thirds and reduced his level of debt from 38% to 22% by 1699.[12] He was soon able to embark on a campaign of land purchases costing more than his loans of 905,000 florins (perhaps £8.31 million today) to the government between 1687 and 1710.[13] Like his father he avoided as best he could the trouble and expense of serving the state. In 1699, however, he was appointed chairman of a committee to reform the imperial finances. He advocated large staff reductions, but also recommended the creation of a state bank. From 1703 to 1705 he presided over the newly founded Girobank. This was intended to raise money for the Imperial Treasury but was unsuccessful owing to the operating conditions imposed upon it.

Like other aristocrats of the Empire, his main efforts were devoted to raising the prestige of his ancestral house. One method was to collect works of art and to build palaces to house them. He acquired some of the greatest glories of the present Princely Collection, such as the works by Van Dyck and Rubens (including the Decius Mus Cycle). In 1706 work was finished on an imposing new town palace in the heart of Vienna, in what is now the Bankgasse: outwardly severe, inwardly splendid. The defeat of the Turks in 1683 made it possible to build outside the city ramparts; in a slightly more airy style he built the Garden Palace in the Rossau, which was finished in 1709.

The second method was harder: to gain a seat and a vote in the Imperial Diet ("Reichstag") at Regensburg. This was not merely a matter of show. The Diet had three houses: the Electors (9), the Princes (over 100) and the Imperial Free Cities (51). It had powers over coinage, military affairs and the raising of taxes for defence and other purposes. As the Habsburg emperors worked to regain the

---

[11] It is estimated that by 1650 the family owned 18.2% of the area of Moravia.
[12] Wanger, op. cit., pages 65–66; Stekl, op. cit., page 83.
[13] "New Cambridge Modern History", Vol. VI, page 601.

influence that they had lost at the Peace of Westphalia in 1648 it was important for them to have reliable and influential supporters in the Diet. Emperor Charles VI needed them even more as he worked for international acceptance of the Pragmatic Sanction which, in the absence of a male successor, was intended to guarantee the peaceful succession of his daughter Maria Theresa to the Habsburg lands. But admission to this exclusive club was not easy. Existing members were jealous of upstarts. Complex negotiations were needed. To be credible, a candidate had to possess a solid piece of territory directly subordinate to the Emperor.

The Liechtenstein family had been on the look-out for suitable territory from 1630 onwards.[14] In 1654 the Emperor reacted favourably to one request, but it fell foul of the Diet. Hans-Adam pursued a double policy. Not only did he buy Schellenberg in 1699, but he also sought, and finally at great expense obtained, a hereditary seat on the Princes' Bench of the Swabian Circle.[15] Hans-Adam I died immediately after the purchase of Vaduz in 1712. It fell to his successor Anton Florian (1656–1721), a grandson of Gundaker and very strong at Court owing to his having been the tutor of the new Emperor Charles VI, to merge the two territories into a single unit and to transfer to them the name of Gundaker's Liechtenstein principality of 1633. Thus, on 25 January 1719, Liechtenstein emerged as the 343rd state of the Holy Roman Empire.

Although Anton Florian had obtained a seat for life in the Diet in 1713, not even the creation of the new principality was enough to gain the family a permanent seat. It was not until 1723, after further tortuous negotiations and with firm support from the Emperor, that Anton Florian's son Josef Johann Adam (1690–1732) was able to crown more than eighty years of family policy with success.

[14] Press, op. cit., page 79.
[15] The Empire in Germany was divided into ten "circles". The Swabian Circle, despite having as many as 91 Estates, was effective in raising troops to defend the frontier with France. As a result, it and its minor princes were permanently short of money.

TOWARDS FULL SOVEREIGNTY (1806)

The Principality's First Century

People in the south of the German-speaking world including Switzerland, Liechtenstein and Vorarlberg tend to be traditional, conservative and intensely tenacious of their inherited rights and customs. The tidy-minded reformer Joseph II (1780–1790) was so exasperated by the Vorarlbergers' attachment to their ancient rights that he called them "The Impossibles". It would be an anachronism to describe this characteristic as "democratic" in the eighteenth century, but it underlies many democratic attitudes of present-day Swiss and Liechtensteiners.

The people of the Unterland (the Lordship of Schellenberg) swore fealty to Prince Hans-Adam I's representative on the Church Hill at Bendern on 16 March 1699. The people of the Oberland (County of Vaduz) followed suit under the lime tree at Vaduz on 9 June 1712. On 5 September 1718[1] the entire people of the newly reunited territories took the oath before Prince Anton Florian's representative at Vaduz Castle. On each occasion the Liechtensteiners requested assurances that their ancient rights, granted by the Brandis dynasty, and other rights written and unwritten, would be observed. These assurances were given "to the end of the world". According to these rights, the chief magistrate of each of the two districts (the "Landamman") was elected every two years by an assembly of all the men eligible to vote. He was chairman of the local court of law (composed of twelve magistrates), represented the people in their dealings with their overlords, had certain administrative duties and in time of war was responsible for calling up able-bodied men for military service.[2] The village communes also had certain liberties and duties.

The people had economic as well as political worries. The change of regime made the long-standing creditors in the Grisons more importunate in their demands. These were fended off by the Abbot of Kempten's representative, and

---

[1] The reason for the gap of six years is that Hans-Adam I, who disliked his successor, bequeathed the territories to his nephew Prince Joseph Wenzel. However, Joseph Wenzel and Anton Florian recognised their importance to the family's standing. Under the terms of an exchange of land, the territories were ceded to Anton Florian as head of the house and the titles to them were incorporated into the fideicommissa.

[2] "The Principality of Liechtenstein", a documentary handbook, ed. Kranz, 1973, page 9.

the financial future was assured. The people were well aware of conditions in the large domains in Bohemia and Moravia, where forced labour might occupy more than half of the serfs' normal working time and up to six days each week during the harvest period. They sought assurances on this point, too. Serfdom was not formally abolished in Liechtenstein until 1808, nearly thirty years after its abolition in Austria by Joseph II, but the agricultural labour practices of Bohemia were never introduced there. The way of life in Liechtenstein was too different, as were the economic conditions. For the Princely House, Liechtenstein was a political and not an economic investment. In 1914 their land holdings in the Principality comprised only 0.02% of their total agricultural land and 0.12% of their forests[3]. At the end of the seventeenth century they were responsible in Moravia for some 19,000 peasant families, whereas in 1784 the Principality's population amounted to only 4,228 persons accommodated in 983 houses. It is significant that until 1818 no member of the Princely House, and until 1842 no Sovereign Prince, visited the country.

The Liechtensteiners' first dealings with their new rulers were not happy. The Prince (or at least his unpopular Lutheran bailiff, Christoph Harpprecht) took the view that the creation of the new Principality in January 1719 marked a complete break with the old order. The two elected chief magistrates and the traditional courts were abolished, to be restored in diluted form only in 1733 after serious unrest among the population.[4] A dispute about tithes caused the Bishop of Chur to excommunicate an official of the Prince and to put the chapels in Vaduz and the Castle under interdict. Anton Florian retaliated by ordering the excommunication to be ignored and by blocking the clergy's incomes. Harpprecht also tried to force the village communities to give up land that they had acquired from the Count of Hohenems before 1699. In 1720 these problems went to the Emperor, who ruled that the clergy should keep two thirds of the tithes and that the communities should keep their land.

The tension in Liechtenstein between a remote, modernising and "enlightened" autocrat and a population devoted to its traditional rights and customs was characteristic of eighteenth century Europe. Until 1790 successive bailiffs lived outside Liechtenstein, in Feldkirch, which impaired their feel for the country. Their officials were foreign-born. No doubt the bailiffs had orders to make what they could out of an uneconomic investment. They may have believed that they were doing their best for a backward and obscurantist peasantry, which is how they described their charges in their reports to Vienna. Maize appeared in about 1700, potatoes were first mentioned in 1751. From 1790 the pace of reform and

---

[3] Franz Kraetzel, "Das Fürstentum Liechtenstein und der gesamte Fürst Johann von und zu Liechtensteinische Güterbesitz" (Brünn, eighth edition, 1914), pages 117–118.

[4] Prince Josef Wenzel was responsible for this. He also founded the parish of Triesenberg, to serve the spiritual needs of the mountain population.

modernisation speeded up, which showed that the Prince in Vienna was more mindful of his subjects than they may have supposed. But throughout the eighteenth century the arbitrary rule and secular reforms of the bailiffs were resented as insensitive and alien intrusions into a traditional agrarian way of life which, if precarious, was at least homely and familiar.

The Princes in the Eighteenth Century

In the eighteenth and early nineteenth centuries the House of Liechtenstein reached the height of its distinction in the Empire through two remarkable princes, Josef Wenzel Lorenz (1696–1772) and Johannes Josef (Johann I, 1760–1836).

In France, royal absolutism and bureaucratic reforms had long deprived the nobility of a role; but until 1848 the Habsburgs still depended heavily on their nobles for local government and judicial functions as well as for court, military and diplomatic services. The great estates were, on the whole, run efficiently and humanely. Churches were built and charities administered. The Liechtenstein family were active in all these areas, some of them devoting themselves to consolidation after a particular prince had undertaken a more than usually expensive term of public service. They married among their peers in the highest ranks of the aristocracy: the Auerspergs, the Dietrichsteins, the Esterhazys, the Harrachs, the Kinskys, the Lobkowitz, the Pálffys, the Schwarzenbergs. After the disruptive testament of Hans-Adam I they followed a policy of family reconciliation and prudent reorganisation of property. A daughter of Hans-Adam I, who inherited much from him and much from her husband (a Savoy-Carignan), left her large legacy to Prince Franz Josef I (1726–1781), who incorporated it into the fideicommissa. The family income helped daughters to marry and sons to pursue army careers; some achieved the highest military ranks. Almost all of the princes seem to have been ardent collectors. Josef Wenzel inherited 632 paintings from Hans-Adam I; Franz Josef I acquired 183 during the first eight years of his reign; Alois Josef (Alois I, 1759–1805) disposed of the second-class paintings and enlarged the library and print collection.

When Anton Florian's male descendants died out in 1748 his nephew Josef Wenzel became Sovereign Prince for the second time. In 1717 he fought as a captain under Prince Eugene of Savoy at the capture of Belgrade. By 1734, serving again with Prince Eugene, he was a lieutenant field marshal. A brief diplomatic mission to Berlin followed, to build on his newly made friendship with the future Frederick the Great. In 1737, after the War of the Polish Succession, Josef Wenzel was sent as ambassador to Paris to win France's support for the Pragmatic Sanction. He made his state entry into Paris and Versailles in the spectacular rococo Golden Coach that remains a unique jewel of the Liechtenstein collection. (It was used again in 1760 when the Prince escorted Isabella of Parma to Vienna for her marriage to the future Joseph II and in 1764 when he represented Austria at Joseph's election and coronation as King of the Romans at Frankfurt.) His efforts and personal expense at Versailles were in vain, for France joined Prussia and Bavaria in the general assault on Austria that followed Maria Theresa's accession in 1740. The Liechtenstein family steadfastly refused to recognise the Bavarian conquest of Prague despite their large holdings in Bohemia. In 1742 Josef Wenzel entered Bavaria as General of the Cavalry. In 1744 he was put in command of the Austrian artillery, where over many years he made important organisational and technical reforms. As General Field Marshal, he won a convincing victory over the French and Spanish armies at Piacenza in 1746. For all the baroque splendour which he loved and in which he lived, and for all his energy and imperiousness, Josef Wenzel was a religious and generous man. He was well known for his liberality to the poor and needy, expressed not only by his personal donations but also by his views on state policy towards the poor.

Johann I, a younger son of Franz Josef I, shared the military and diplomatic talents of his great-uncle Josef Wenzel. An energetic soldier, he won the army's confidence by his personal courage, his competence and his care for prisoners and the wounded. His appointments included those of Commandant of the City and Fortress of Vienna in 1806, General of the Cavalry in 1808 and Generalissimo of the Austrian Army and Field Marshal in 1809. In 1805, the year in which he succeeded as Sovereign Prince, he negotiated the truce with Napoleon after the Battle of Austerlitz and led the negotiations for the Treaty of Pressburg. Napoleon wanted him to be appointed Austrian Ambassador at Paris, but Emperor Franz I chose Metternich instead. In 1809 Johann I and his cavalry contributed to Napoleon's defeat at Aspern. After Napoleon's subsequent victory at Wagram, Johann I was the Austrian negotiator for the oppressive Treaty of Schönbrunn; and, when the state could not meet Napoleon's demand of ten million gulden in return for the evacuation of Vienna, it was he who gave a personal guarantee to the banks for that sum. Notwithstanding his conspicuous loyalty to the Austrian monarchy and state, Franz I's attitude to him cooled after the Treaty of Schönbrunn. Perhaps Napoleon's high regard for him contributed to this. Franz I once referred to him, with dry ambiguity, as "Prince Johannes Liechtenstein, who does me the honour of calling himself my subject".[5]

War and Sovereignty

The French Revolution made an immediate impact on Liechtenstein. As early as 1790 the country's military contingent (fifteen infantrymen and two cavalrymen) was called up for service in the forces of the Swabian Circle. In

---

[5] Prince Eduard von Liechtenstein, "Liechtensteins Weg von Österreich zur Schweiz" (Vaduz, 1946), page 46.

1796, 700 Austrian troops camped in the country, blocking the passes and hindering trade and movement. In 1798, as the French invaded Switzerland, 1,000 Austrian troops were quartered in Liechtenstein. In the following year Switzerland virtually fell apart. All the old political landmarks and most of the familiar frontiers were swept away. Eastern Switzerland became a battlefield for the Second Coalition against France. In March 1799 Masséna's cavalry overran Liechtenstein, looting and killing, before they were thrown back from their attack on Feldkirch. In October 1799 more than 16,000 exhausted Russian troops under General Suvorov passed through Liechtenstein on their way to Germany. They had arrived in Switzerland from Italy too late to join General Korsakov, who had just been defeated at Zurich. Thereafter they had made an epic march in terrible conditions across three snowbound Swiss mountain passes. Russian soldiers were not to set foot in Liechtenstein again until 1945.

After 1800 and 1801, when there were more French incursions, the country was largely left in peace, though not in a sense of security. The alternate billeting of troops from both sides, the looting, requisitions and disruption of the economy left the population of 5,000 with a debt of one million gulden at a time when public expenditure normally amounted to between 6,000 and 8,000 gulden.

At this point in history Liechtenstein ought logically to have vanished from the map of Europe. Revolutionary France's conquest of the left bank of the Rhine, the Peace of Lunéville (1801) and the need to compensate the dispossessed ("mediatised") German rulers led to a fundamental upheaval in the Holy Roman Empire. On 12 July 1806 Napoleon completed the work by setting up the Confederation of the Rhine. Fifteen German states, led by Bavaria, Württemberg and Baden, declared their independence of the old Empire and put themselves under Napoleon's protection. On 6 August Emperor Franz abdicated as Holy Roman Emperor, having two years previously assumed the title of Emperor of Austria so as to have an imperial title in reserve.

Liechtenstein, incongruous among these much bigger fish, was named the sixteenth member of the Confederation. It thus became a fully sovereign state, even though Johann I never signed the Confederation's founding act and never formally seceded from the Holy Roman Empire. He confined himself to sending a plenipotentiary representative to meetings of the Confederation's assembly ("Bundestag") in Frankfurt. Liechtenstein's membership of the Confederation was not an oversight. It is clear that Johann I was acutely conscious of the Principality's importance to his family. If he had been "mediatised", like so many other minor rulers, he would have reverted to the ranks of the upper aristocracy. A despatch from Talleyrand to the French envoy in Vienna suggests that he may have mentioned his principality's future during his negotiations in 1805; he certainly asked France and Bavaria for guarantees of independence soon after the Treaty of Pressburg. He paid the Duke of Nassau to supply forty soldiers in place of the Liechtenstein contingent, so that in case of war between the Confederation and Austria he should not find himself fighting against his own subjects.

For his part, Napoleon was surprisingly ready to accommodate Johann I's scruples of loyalty to Vienna. He enabled the Prince to accept membership of the Confederation by including in the act a clause stating that any ruler wishing to remain in the service of a power alien to the Confederation would have to abdicate in favour of one of his sons. Johann I took advantage of this by abdicating in favour of his third son Karl who, being only three years old, was in no position to exercise his sovereign powers or to sign the act. When the Bavarians occupied Tyrol and Vorarlberg in 1806 after the Treaty of Pressburg they tried to persuade Napoleon to give them Liechtenstein. Talleyrand rebuffed them with a clear statement of the French Emperor's intention "to keep the Prince of Liechtenstein among the sovereign princes".[6] They did not take this well and objected to the Prince of Liechtenstein being counted as a crowned head. In 1809, after Wagram, Bavaria again tried to seize Liechtenstein. A Bavarian general occupied Liechtenstein for one day, but was promptly withdrawn. His authorities later sought to pass it off as a "visit".

The three-sided relationship between Johann I, Napoleon I and Franz I is complex and not entirely clear. Perhaps there were matters that were not committed to paper. Napoleon seems to have liked and admired the Prince. He may have hoped to keep him as a powerful contact in Vienna; perhaps also as a pawn in reserve and a potential substitute for any ruler in his Confederation who might become troublesome. Franz I may have seen him as a source of information about events in the Confederation or even within Napoleon's circle.

It is unlikely that all these high politics were much noticed in the Principality. Bad harvests, the high price of fruit and poor prospects for the coming season were the theme of village chroniclers. Yet Liechtenstein's future was determined at this point by a chance combination of Johann I's determination and prestige, Napoleon's calculations and personal preferences and Franz I's patient watchfulness.

Johann I resumed his powers as Sovereign Prince upon the collapse of the Confederation of the Rhine in 1813. He no longer had an overlord following the demise of the Holy Roman Empire and could theoretically, if not practically, consider himself an equal of the Habsburgs. The Principality was represented at the Congress of Vienna in 1814–1815 and became one of the 39 member states of the new German Confederation. Liechtenstein's full sovereignty and its international recognition as an independent state were thus re-confirmed in 1815.

---

[6] Georg Schmidt, "Fürst Johann Josef I: Souveränität und Modernisierung Liechtensteins", in "Liechtenstein: Fürstliches Haus und Staatliche Ordnung" (ed. Volker Press and Dietmar Willoweit, Verlag der Liechtensteinischen Akademischen Gesellschaft, Vaduz, 1987) pages 388–394.

REFORM FROM ABOVE, PRESSURE FROM BELOW (1805–1858)

The Field-Marshal Prince took over his inheritance in 1805 in military style: he studied the situation, reconnoitred, defined his targets and issued his orders. An inspection of Liechtenstein by Court Councillor Hauer reported that deplorably archaic conditions prevailed: there were no skills and no training. A tough new bailiff, Johann Schuppler from Bohemia, was given detailed instructions. He set to work in 1808. His first act was to abolish the remains of the old elective magistrate system and the two local assemblies which represented the Unterland and Oberland. This caused enormous resentment.

Throughout this period, reforms came thick and fast. Compulsory elementary education was introduced in 1805, the village communes being obliged to build schools and appoint teachers. Sub-division of land and unregulated house-building were forbidden in 1806. Church and landlords' property tax privileges were abolished in 1807. Serfdom was abolished in 1808. New taxes were imposed on tobacco and salt consumption. Common land was privatised and a land register and new stamp duties were introduced in 1809. The village communes lost their autonomy in 1810. They were turned into local administrative units and people were allowed to settle freely in whatever commune they wished. The Austrian legal code was introduced in 1812; so was compulsory inoculation against smallpox. Many of these changes were beneficial, but they were imposed from above and against the grain. Popular and clerical resistance was strong. More than once Schuppler and his successor were faced with near-rebellion. The popular mood was made worse by French military exactions, indebtedness, the expense of maintaining a contingent of 80 soldiers, crop failures, hunger and flooding by the Rhine.

The 1818 Constitution

The treaty which established the German Confederation obliged the rulers to grant constitutions to their subjects. This Johann I did in 1818, the year in which his son and successor Alois first visited Liechtenstein. It was a short document in the spirit of the times. It contained no guarantees of basic rights. It envisaged only two Estates, of the clergy and peasantry; in Liechtenstein there were no nobility or towns to be represented. The clergy nominated three representatives to the Parliament ("Landtag") for life. The peasants (qualified male householders and widows) were represented by the mayors ("Vorsteher") and treasurers of their communes. The mayors were chosen by the Bailiff ("Landvogt") from among the three candidates who gained the most votes in each commune. The Austrian Emperor, who had sizeable land holdings in Balzers and Bendern, was also entitled to nominate a representative. The annual meetings of this well controlled assembly were limited to discussing and approving the Bailiff's taxation requirements and to making suggestions for the public well-being.

Alois II (1836–1858)

Johann I marked the end of an era. He was the last Sovereign Prince of Liechtenstein to play a central part in the public affairs of the Habsburg Monarchy. In his later years he confined himself to administering and enlarging his properties, which he did with great energy and efficiency, and to increasing the art collection. In 1807 he transferred the collection to the Garden Palace, where until 1940 it was one of the chief sights of Vienna. His son Alois Josef followed him in his agricultural interests, to which he added botany. He travelled widely, including to Britain, where he was impressed by the aristocracy's ability to hold on to its privileges without being a brake on progress. This interest inspired the remodelling of his residence at Eisgrub in a version of the English Gothic style, together with its English-style landscape gardens. The latter are now a UNESCO World Heritage site.

With such a Prince, it was natural for his subjects to hope for a more liberal approach to government. In 1840 a delegation including the future historian Peter Kaiser presented a petition to him at Vienna requesting, *inter alia,* a less restricted representation of the people in the Parliament and lower military costs. The Prince, who was not only conservative in his instincts but also had to keep in step with Austrian policies, refused. However, he quickly followed this up with a visit to Vaduz in 1842, the first by a Sovereign Prince, where he was given an enthusiastic reception on the meadow by the Castle. He underlined the Principality's significance to his family by promulgating at Vaduz a new dynastic code (the "House Law") which permitted female succession in the event of the extinction of the male line. In 1847 he was back again to see for himself the country's social and economic problems after the great flood of 1846. Measures to help the poor and orphans were put in place, relations with the Church were improved and work to regulate the Rhine, which had been started ten years previously in conjunction with Canton St Gallen, was intensified.

1848

Liechtenstein was quick to reflect the revolutionary mood of 1848. The foreign-born officials in the Prince's administrative office in Vaduz were first threatened, then chased out; but there does not seem to have been hostility towards the Prince personally. Village committees elected a representative assembly of more than 110 members to discuss the people's demands. This in turn appointed a three-member committee, chaired by Peter Kaiser, to draft petitions to the Prince. Representative committees were also elected to ensure order in the villages and the country as a whole. In June and July a five-member Constitutional Committee was elected under the chairmanship of Dr Karl Schädler. The Prince's Bailiff, Michael Menzinger, was one of its two advisers. After democratic discussion throughout the country, a draft constitution was submitted to the Prince which contained the then unusual idea that state authority was vested in Prince and people jointly. A Governor ("Landesverweser") was to be appointed by the Prince to be head of government but was to be responsible to Parliament (now to be called the "Landrat"). The Prince was to have a delaying veto only. All males aged 20 or over were to be entitled to vote. The Parliament was to have fifteen representatives from the Oberland and nine from the Unterland. (The current numbers are fifteen and ten respectively.) It was to elect a smaller body to conduct day-to-day business.

Alois II accepted most of these proposals on a provisional basis, preserving only his right of absolute veto, refusing the Parliament the right to impeach the Governor and insisting that there should be no distinction between the Oberland and Unterland. This proved a workable arrangement, and the first democratically elected parliament went to work between 1849 and 1850 with great moderation and maturity. Meanwhile, Kaiser and Schädler (as Kaiser's alternate) were popularly elected to represent Liechtenstein at the German National Assembly, which met at Frankfurt in May 1848 to draw up a constitution for a German nation state. The divisions within the assembly about the future structure of Germany, its lack of practical powers and the reassertion of monarchical authority in Vienna and elsewhere after revolutionary outbreaks caused it to peter out in the following summer. The Liechtenstein military contingent was sent to help re-impose the old order in Baden. Alois II refused his consent to the revised constitution when it was submitted to him in 1850. The Parliament was not re-convened and in 1852 the Prince restored by decree the constitution of 1818. Even if he had wished, he could not have stood aside from the new absolutism that temporarily prevailed in Vienna.

The Link with Austria

Alois II stepped up his programme of public investment, drainage and land reclamation. In 1852 he concluded a customs and tax agreement with Austria. This was intended to end Liechtenstein's economic isolation. The country was united economically with Vorarlberg. Austrian customs officials were stationed in the country, subject to showing due loyalty to the Sovereign Prince and his laws. Austrian weights, measures and currency were introduced. Revenues and transit duties were shared between the two states in fixed proportions, which gave the Liechtenstein state a dependable income. The Prince's and the country's sovereignty were carefully upheld in the formulae of treaties which Austria was to sign on Liechtenstein's behalf. Some Liechtensteiners would have preferred a customs treaty with Switzerland. However, Switzerland was then a relatively poor country, not to be compared as a market with the Danube Monarchy.

The achievement of full sovereignty in 1806 brought a subtle change of attitudes. The country gradually ceased to be seen, or to see itself, as a mediaeval manor that could be transferred at will from one feudal owner to another. Peter Kaiser's "History of the Principality of Liechtenstein" (1847) helped to create a sense of national identity. This awareness was never to be taken to the dangerous extremes seen in some other countries in Europe; the country's small size instils a sense of proportion in its inhabitants. Even the deficient 1818 Constitution helped to promote the concept of a Liechtenstein state. The debates of 1848–1850 and the provisional constitution showed that the people could handle responsibility and that the tradition of thorough, serious discussion in local assemblies was alive and productive. The economic reforms and the political experiences of the first half of the nineteenth century may have seemed sterile at the time, but they were to bear fruit in the second half.

JOHANN II (TO 1914)

Johann II succeeded his father Alois II in 1858 at the age of eighteen. He was brought up in the spirit of absolutism. Directly after his accession an adviser wrote to him, "The sovereign authority which Your Serene Highness has assumed the high vocation to exercise in the Principality of Liechtenstein is in truth by the Grace of God".[1] But he was also deeply influenced by the Christian Social thought of one of his tutors, Baron Carl von Vogelsang (a friend of Bishop Ketteler of Mainz), and took an interest in social reform and the renewal of Catholicism. He had wide intellectual interests, particularly in the fine arts. Persistent ill health and a generous, shy and retiring temperament kept him from imposing himself; but he took a close interest in Liechtenstein affairs, was invariably well informed and shrewd and could be sharply decisive at critical moments.

One of his first actions was to sign an education law, which extended compulsory schooling to the age of 14. In March 1859 he responded to the Parliament's increasingly insistent demands for a new constitution by summoning its two Estates to discuss the matter. He followed this up with a visit to the Principality in the autumn of 1859. Constitutional progress was made easier by developments in Austria. After the disastrous war in Lombardy in 1859, Emperor Franz Josef's February Patent of 1861 decreed a genuine constitution and gave very considerable powers to a central (but, in the event, Austrian-only) parliament. In Liechtenstein, there were negotiations throughout 1861 and 1862 between representatives of the Prince and the Parliament. The Prince signed Liechtenstein's first real constitution at Eisgrub on 26 September 1862.

The 1862 Constitution

This document drew on the constitutions of Vorarlberg (1861) and Sigmaringen (1833), although in certain respects it was significantly more liberal than they, and also on Peter Kaiser's ideas of 1848. In essence, it was a bargain between the Prince and the people. Sovereign power was vested in the Prince, with hereditary

---

[1] Elisabeth Castellani Zahir, "Die Wiederherstellung von Schloss Vaduz 1904 bis 1914" (Historischer Verein für das Fürstentum Liechtenstein, Stuttgart, 1993), page 78.

descent to be regulated according to the family's House Law of 1842. The Prince alone had the right to summon or dissolve Parliament, to appoint or dismiss officials and to represent Liechtenstein in international affairs. He had the right to take all necessary measures to ensure the safety of the country in an emergency. However, before he could receive the oath of allegiance the Prince had to pledge in writing that he would rule in accordance with the Constitution and the laws of the country.

For its part, the Parliament had its own unlimited right to propose legislation. No laws could be made, amended or repealed without its consent. No direct or indirect taxes or levies could be imposed without its approval, and it also had the right to approve the budget. It elected its own president and officers. It had to sit at least once a year between 15 and 30 May; in practice, it met more often. Since most of its members were preoccupied with their farms and businesses, sessions were short. Routine parliamentary business between sessions was conducted by a committee of three ("Landesausschuss") chaired by the president or his deputy. Suffrage was unusually liberal for the time: any gainfully employed male aged 24 or over had the vote. Voting was compulsory. The voters elected representatives in proportion to the population of their communes, and the representatives in turn elected twelve members of the Parliament. The Prince appointed a further three members. In practice, his Governor tended to choose respected previous members who had been passed over by the electoral representatives, with a view to finding a balance in the assembly. Since 1718 successive Princes had tried to efface the distinction between the County of Vaduz (the Oberland) and the Lordship of Schellenberg (the Unterland). The 1862 Constitution followed this line. However, in 1877, after a political crisis concerning the introduction of a gold-based currency, it was decided that the country should have two electoral districts. The Oberland was given seven parliamentary members and the Unterland five. The numbers have since been increased, but the principle endures to this day and continues, for example, to affect the composition of the Government.

The executive consisted of the Governor ("Landesverweser", the hated title of "Landvogt", or Bailiff, having now been abolished) and two Councillors ("Landräte"). These were appointed by the Prince. The Governor, as the head of government, reported to the Prince's Court Chancery ("Hofkanzlei") in Vienna. The Governor was usually an Austrian official in the Prince's service, while the two Councillors and their deputies had to be Liechtenstein citizens who were eligible to vote. Although controversy between Liechtensteiners themselves and between the Parliament and the Government was sometimes sharp, the small size of the country generally helped towards informal and easy co-operation. There were no marked social differences in the population and political parties were unknown until 1918.

The Constitution guaranteed personal freedom, freedom of religion, habeas corpus, the right of complaint and petition, the right of assembly, freedom from arbitrary house search, etc. The law courts were declared to be not responsible to the government. The lowest court was the Princely Court ("Landgericht") at Vaduz, responsible for civil and penal cases, assisted as appropriate by Austrian judges in Vorarlberg or Innsbruck. The Court Chancery in Vienna served as a court of appeal. It also supervised and swore in the Liechtenstein judges, who were appointed by the Prince. The final court of appeal was the High Court at Innsbruck. Decisions by the Liechtenstein Government could be contested in Vienna before three judges appointed by the Prince. Since the civil and legal codes in Liechtenstein were Austrian, there was no essential conflict; and the involvement of Austrian courts provided checks and balances which might not have been available within the Principality alone.[2]

The End of the German Confederation, 1866

Austria's defeat by Prussia in July 1866 and the dissolution of the German Confederation deprived Liechtenstein of an independent place within a wider Germanic body. Until 1918 the Principality's destiny was, to all outward appearance, increasingly submerged in Austria's.

The Austro-Prussian War was preceded by a curious episode. On 10 June 1866 Bismarck proposed a reform of the German Confederation, which, if adopted, would have meant the exclusion of Austria. Austria's reply was to demand of the Confederation's assembly in Frankfurt a general mobilisation against Prussia. The assembly gave its approval on 14 June by nine votes to seven. Bismarck accused Liechtenstein of being responsible for the mobilisation and, by extension, the war.

In the Confederation the larger and medium-sized states had one vote each. The smaller states were grouped together in "curias", which also had one vote each. A simple majority within each curia was decisive for the casting of that curia's vote. Bismarck alleged on 22 June 1866 that among the six members of the Sixteenth Curia only Liechtenstein had voted clearly for mobilisation but that the curia's vote as a whole had been wrongly recorded as being in favour. The implication was that Prussia was being unjustly attacked and that a confederation which could allow a mini-state with 7,000 inhabitants and an army of 80 to decide an issue of life and death was an absurdity. In fact, it appears that three of the states (including Liechtenstein) voted for mobilisation. Two voted against,

---

[2] Fuller details of the 1862 constitutional settlement are to be found in Raton, "Liechtenstein: History and Institutions of the Principality" (Liechtenstein Verlag, Vaduz, 1970), pages 37–41 and Paul Vogt, "125 Jahre Landtag" (Vaduz, 1987), pages 110–125.

and one for referring the matter back to the Committee for Holstein. This being so, the Sixteenth Curia's positive vote was valid. (If its vote had been negative, the overall result would have been a draw of eight against eight and the Austrian proposal would have fallen away.)[3] Bismarck's allegation was in fact a tactical device. He had taken a tremendous risk in engineering the war. Prussia's victory, to be crowned at Königgrätz a few days later on 3 July, was by no means a foregone conclusion. Bismarck had been preparing scapegoats in case of military defeat. It was not the last example of foreign politicians launching accusations against Liechtenstein for their own domestic purposes.

Liechtenstein did not sign the Treaty of Prague, which ended the war on 23 August 1866; but normal relations with Prussia, to the extent that they were necessary, were resumed almost immediately thereafter with no objection from Bismarck. However, the absence of its signature provoked a legend that Liechtenstein continued to be at war with Prussia. This gave rise to the joke that the Prussian Field Marshal von Moltke, when travelling to Bad Ragaz in Switzerland to take the cure, was careful to avoid passing through "enemy territory". In a more sinister vein, a Nazi organisation purporting to act for Germans abroad (the "Volksdeutsche Mittelstelle") ruminated in March 1938 on whether Liechtenstein's supposed continuing state of war with Prussia might not contribute to a pretext for imposing a National Socialist government on the Principality.[4]

The End of the Liechtenstein Army

On 2 July 1866 the Sixteenth Curia informed the German Confederation's assembly that Prince Johann II would place his military contingent at the Confederation's disposal to defend Tyrol. He did not wish to spill German blood. The contingent was therefore stationed on the Stilfserjoch (Stelvio Pass) to guard against an attack by Italy, with which Austria was also at war. The Prince paid for the campaign personally in order to relieve the public purse. The contingent saw no action and, indeed, no enemy. Eighty men set out; eighty-one returned in September to general rejoicing, having been joined by an Austrian soldier who was looking for work. The demise of the Confederation meant that the Principality was no longer under an international obligation to maintain an army. The Parliament seized its chance to refuse approval of further military expenditure. The Prince objected, since the Parliament's attitude touched on his constitutional prerogatives and would leave the country defenceless; but he gave way and on 12 February 1868 disbanded the contingent. The last surviving Liechtenstein soldier died in 1939 at the age of 95.

---

[3] Raton, op. cit., pages 45–46.
[4] Horst Carl, "Liechtenstein und das Dritte Reich" (in "Fürstliches Haus und Staatliche Ordnung") page 434.

Economic Progress

The establishment of a free parliament and access to the thriving Austro-Hungarian economy revitalised Liechtenstein. In 1861 the state-backed Savings and Loans Bank ("Zins-und Credit-Landes-Anstalt"), the precursor of the present Liechtensteinische Landesbank, was founded. For the first time farmers and house builders could obtain loans locally instead of going to the money-lenders of the Grisons or Vorarlberg. The country's thrifty savers began to accumulate solid deposits, which by 1900 amounted to twenty times the size of the state budget. The Austrian monetary system was introduced by treaty. After many years of operation in the country the Austrian postal service was regulated by treaty in 1911 and, after some opposition in Vienna, Liechtenstein began to issue its own stamps. These high-quality stamps soon gained prestige among philatelists and became a valuable source of income to the state.

The Redemption of Tithes Act removed burdensome dues from the farmers. The Communes Act of 1864 gave local autonomy to freely elected councils. The property register was reorganised. Compulsory fire insurance was introduced. Cattle breeding, alpine farming and forest management were improved by legislation. An energetic public works programme was put in hand. Roads were built. Four bridges (the first ever) replaced the Rhine ferries and Prince Johann II granted an interest-free loan of 175,000 florins for building a high embankment along the river. (To put this figure in perspective, the first state budget dealt with by the new parliament a few years earlier had amounted to only 39,000 florins, military expenses included.)

The total cost of the embankment works between 1855 to 1883 amounted to more than 1.2 million florins, of which four fifths was borne by the local government communities. The telegraph came in 1869 and the telephone in 1898. The first train crossed the country in 1872. The Liechtenstein Government had negotiated for many years for the rail connection between Austria and Switzerland to be built across the Principality, if possible via Vaduz. They did not achieve a connection to the capital, but when the line was built it included stations at Schaan and Nendeln. The line was part of the main east-west route across Europe. It continues to be operated by Austrian Federal Railways.

In 1865 a Trades Act regulated times of work, vocational training and qualifications. As a result, a skilled work force gradually came into being. A cotton-spinning industry was founded. As in nearby St Gallen and Vorarlberg, a home industry in machine embroidery developed.

By 1910 there were 186 machines in Liechtenstein, most of them in the Unterland. Agreements with Switzerland enabled the citizens of both countries to settle and work in either country and acquire land there, and Swiss doctors to practice in the Principality.

Emigration

The country's economic growth was encouraging, but it started from a relatively low base. Despite this growth and the improvements in public health measures, the population remained fairly static throughout the second half of the nineteenth century. From 8,162 in 1852 it declined to 7,394 in 1861, rose again to 8,095 in 1880, fell to 7,531 in 1901 and reached 8,693 in 1911.[5] Emigration was one of the causes. As in Scotland and Switzerland, many people needed to make their fortune (or simply a living) abroad, burdened as they were by low wages and the cost of the Rhine flood measures. Mercenary service offered one escape. 176 Liechtenstein soldiers are known to have died in foreign service between 1674 and 1857. Most of them enlisted in the Grison regiments or the Grison companies of Swiss regiments, in which they served in Italy (including the Papal States), Spain and the Spanish Netherlands.[6] In 1854 the British Army raised a British-Swiss legion for service in the Crimea, despite the Swiss constitution's ban on foreign recruiting. The legion never reached the Crimea because the war ended while it was on its way. It is not known whether any Liechtensteiners joined this force; a recruiting office was opened in Vaduz but was abandoned under pressure from the Austrian police.[7]

Throughout the nineteenth century about 10% of the population regularly left their villages between spring and autumn to work as labourers or chambermaids in Switzerland, Germany or France. In the earlier part of the century it was common for the poorest families to send their children to work in southern Germany for the summer. Permanent emigration was for all practical purposes forbidden in the first half of the nineteenth century, but some 250 people left for America after the Rhine flood of 1846 and another 200 during the slump of the early 1880s. Their main destinations were the largely German-speaking towns of Dubuque and Guttenberg in Iowa, where masons, bricklayers and carpenters were in demand. Economic depression in the 1920s was to cause further emigration to the industrial centres of Chicago, Cincinnati and Milwaukee.[8]

Social and Cultural Life

New societies were gradually added to the myriad activities of traditional village life such as the voluntary fire brigades, bands and choirs. An Agricultural Society was founded in 1885, a Gymnastic Society in 1886 and the Historical Society in 1901. Peter Kaiser (1793–1864) had already published his History of the Principality of Liechtenstein. Johann Baptist Büchel (1853–1927), a priest, was

---

[5] Statistisches Jahrbuch 1999, page 20.
[6] Heribert Küng, "Glanz und Elend der Söldner" (Desertina Verlag, Disentis, 1993), page 47.
[7] Bayley, "The Swiss, German and Italian Legions in British Service", London, 1977.
[8] Norbert Jansen, "Nach Amerika!", Vol. 1, (Chronos Verlag, Zurich, 1998), passim.

also a poet, teacher, historian, member of the Parliament and a strong patriot for Prince and country. Joseph Gabriel Rheinberger (1839–1901), later musical director at the Bavarian court in Munich, was a distinguished teacher, organist and composer. The centenary of his death was worthily commemorated in 2001 by the London Symphony Orchestra with concerts in Vaduz, Munich and London. These three men did much to form a public consciousness of Liechtenstein as a distinct society and state.

Liechtenstein's International Status

Liechtenstein's integration into Austria and the Princely House's close association with the Habsburg dynasty contributed to an impression abroad that the country was part of the Danube Monarchy. This was to cause misunderstanding during and after the First World War, just as the realignment with Switzerland was to do in later years. In fact, the country was careful to uphold its sovereignty. Its power may have been limited, but it kept its inner autonomy to act and to choose as it thought best.

Liechtenstein delegated certain functions to Austria, as she was later to do to Switzerland. If Austrian law courts were entitled in the last instance to overrule those of Liechtenstein, it was by agreement. An international treaty signed by Austria for and on behalf of Liechtenstein was binding on the Principality, but that did not mean that all Austrian treaties were automatically valid for Liechtenstein. Liechtenstein concluded numerous formal treaties with Austria during this period, including amendments to the customs union. It also concluded its own treaties with Switzerland and some other countries.

In 1880 Austria agreed to represent Liechtenstein's interests abroad, which no doubt misled some foreign observers concerning the Principality's status. The agreement formalised a practice which seems to have existed already. In 1860 the Austrian Minister at the Court of St James, Count Apponyi, put a formal request to the Foreign Secretary, Lord John Russell, for Queen Victoria to receive Prince Johann II. Apponyi made it clear that he was approaching the Foreign Secretary rather than the Royal Household precisely because the Prince was an independent sovereign.[9]

The close ties of service and relationship between the Liechtensteins and the Habsburgs could also be misleading. Alois II and Johann II kept some distance between themselves and the Court at Vienna. Other members of the family were not similarly constrained. Prince Franz (1853–1938), Johann II's younger brother

---

[9] British National Archives, PRO 30/22/44. Apponyi added to his letter to Lord John Russell, "J'ajoute pour votre information particulière que le Pce. L. est un jeune homme de 20 ans, "very good looking", qui n'a succédé à son père que l'année dernière."

and eventual successor, was the Austrian Ambassador at St Petersburg from 1894 to 1898. An energetic diplomat with wide vision, he helped to found the Chair of Eastern European History at Vienna University and endowed it with a library of more than 10,000 books. It is possible that Archduke Franz Ferdinand had him in mind as a potential Imperial Chancellor in the event of his own succession to the throne. A cousin, Prince Rudolf (1838–1908), was Court Chamberlain and Master of the Horse to Emperor Franz Josef. Prince Johannes (1873–1959) commanded a warship in the Austro-Hungarian navy. Prince Friedrich (1871–1959) served as military attaché at the Austro-Hungarian Embassy in London and reached the rank of major-general. Prince Heinrich (1877–1915) was killed fighting in Galicia in the Austrian army. Prince Alois (1846–1920) was active in Christian Social politics and served for a total of twenty years in the Austrian Parliament.

In 1882 Johann II's sister Therese (1850–1939) made a glittering marriage to a royal prince, Arnulph of Bavaria. In 1903 Prince Alois (1869–1955), grandfather of the present Sovereign Prince Hans-Adam II, married a Habsburg, Archduchess Elisabeth Amalie, half-sister of the heir-apparent Franz Ferdinand. Emperor Franz Josef attended the wedding. In order to avoid any misunderstanding about the status of this union the Emperor made it clear that he regarded his niece as marrying into a sovereign dynasty.

Sovereignty also found practical expression. From 1851 the Sovereign Prince enjoyed fiscal and legal immunity in Austria as a head of state, as did his immediate family. His principal palace in the Bankgasse in Vienna was granted extra-territorial status. Out of a sense of responsibility Johann II voluntarily paid the Austrian state six million kronen each year in income tax. Franz Josef extended immunity to his brother Franz and his sister Therese as a personal courtesy. (After 1918 the First Austrian Republic continued to respect Johann's privileges but not those of Franz because the latter were not justified by international law.) The estates of Lundenburg and Eisgrub were recognised as extra-territorial in 1880. All members of the House of Liechtenstein were Liechtenstein subjects; but, while Liechtenstein legislation permitted dual citizenship, the laws of the Austrian Monarchy decreed that an Austrian subject, in becoming the subject of another country, should lose his rights as an Austrian.

In 1887 the Austrian Foreign Minister declared that members of the House of Liechtenstein descended from the first bearer of the sovereign title (Johann I) were not subjects of the Austrian state "but only entitled to the rights of an Austrian subject, when they themselves or their descendants in direct line have obtained these rights independently".[10] It followed that service by a Liechtenstein

---

[10] FO 371/4653. Letter of 10 November 1920 from Prince Eduard, Liechtenstein Minister at Vienna, to The Hon. Francis Lindley, British Minister at Vienna.

prince in the Austrian Court, armed forces or Parliament did not of itself signify possession of Austrian nationality.[11]

These details may seem recondite in the twenty-first century, but they were to matter a great deal after 1918.

The House of Liechtenstein in 1914

The 1914 edition of Franz Kraetzl's survey of the Liechtenstein properties enshrines a world about to change for ever. In Vienna, the Court Chancery, headed by Court Councillor ("Hofrat") Dr Hermann Edler von Hampe, was responsible for all the business of the House. To him reported Karl von In der Maur, Governor in Vaduz. Two recourses for appeal from Liechtenstein, one political and the other judicial, were available in Vienna. The Private Office, the Picture Gallery, the Library, the House Archive, the Palace in the Bankgasse, the forests, lands, buildings, architects and other administrative departments each had its own staff. The 31 estates scattered across Moravia, Bohemia, Silesia, Lower Austria, Salzburg, Styria, Hungary and Liechtenstein, together with some smaller lands in Saxony and Prussia, were administered by 22 stewards' offices and 24 forest offices. The total area was more than eleven times that of the Principality. Some 75% was forest and some 24% was agricultural land. There were seven charitable organisations and ten hospitals. As a good employer, Prince Johann II voluntarily paid for accident insurance for his staff. He converted his castle at Mährisch Aussee into an important museum of forestry and hunting and established a horticultural school at Eisgrub.

The Liechtensteins do not seem to have followed the example of other great aristocratic families who invested the compensation received for the abolition of their seigneurial (feudal) rights after 1848 in industry, banking and the railways. Kraetzl's survey suggests that, apart from a long-established brewery, their first venture into industry was the purchase of a large fireclay factory in Bohemia in 1906. This employed between 800 and 1,000 people. There was also an earthenware factory in Austria, which employed 700 people.

Johann II enlarged and improved the art collection and gave the Garden Palace in which it was displayed a more welcoming atmosphere. He gave away and lent a great deal. For example, he gave more than fifty paintings to start the Vienna City Collection and also gave generously to museums in Prague, Troppau and Bolzano. Archaeology, medical research, geography and botany all benefited. So did young students from Liechtenstein: in addition to financial support, they

---

[11] The cosmopolitan Dual Monarchy was always relaxed about citizenship. Franz Josef employed a Saxon, Count Beust, as Austrian Chancellor. As modern parallels, citizens of the Republic of Ireland may serve in the British armed forces without becoming United Kingdom citizens and Hereditary Prince Alois of Liechtenstein has held a commission in the Coldstream Guards.

could live free of charge in the attics of the palace in Vienna and enjoy one free meal per day.

In Liechtenstein Johann II built the present churches in Vaduz, Schaan, Balzers and Ruggell. To help the growing tourist industry he sponsored the Prince's Path ("Fürstensteig") high up in the mountains. His enduring monument in the centre of Vaduz is the Government Building, to which he contributed 100,000 kronen. This spacious and elegant building was designed with an eye to the future. It is still able to accommodate an enlarged government and parliament as well as some civil servants. Earlier in its history it also accommodated the gaol (in the basement) and two banks.

On the cliff above Vaduz, the castle is another monument to the generous but reclusive prince. The monarch had nowhere suitable to live in Liechtenstein. The castle was in a poor state of repair; it had been used as a barracks by the Liechtenstein army and more recently as a tavern. In 1904 Johann II set up a commission to restore it, chaired by his brother Franz. Among the members was Count Hans Wilczek, who had recently restored his own large Kreuzenstein Castle in Lower Austria in romantic Gothic style. Such restorations were in vogue at the time: Cardiff Castle (restored by the Marquess of Bute) and Hochkönigsburg in Alsace (Kaiser Wilhelm II) are typical examples. Building began in 1905. By 1914 it was complete and the Liechtenstein collection of arms and armour had been installed. Until the 1950s it was possible to visit the castle as a museum. It is now very much a working palace and is closed to the public.[12] The reception rooms, designed in a timeless mixture of modified Gothic and Renaissance styles, are dignified but warm and welcoming.

The timing of the restoration was better than anyone could have guessed. Count Wilczek could not have foreseen that he was building a home for his great-granddaughter, Princess Gina. Johann II could not have predicted that he was building the future seat of his dynasty.

---

[12] Elisabeth Castellani Zahir, op. cit., gives a well-documented and well-illustrated account of the restoration.

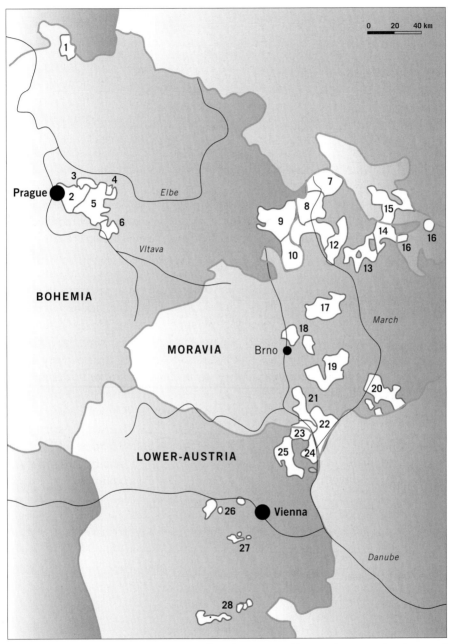

4. The House of Liechtenstein's estates before the First World War. The external and internal borders are those of 1914.

THE FIRST WORLD WAR

Between 1914 and 1924 three decisions were made which determined Liechtenstein's future for the rest of the twentieth century. With hindsight, they saved the country from extinction. These were the adoption of neutrality in 1914, the constitution of 1921 and the economic and political realignment with Switzerland.

Neutrality

On 12 August 1914 the United Kingdom declared war on the Austro-Hungarian Empire. On 28 August the British Home Office asked the Foreign Office whether Liechtenstein subjects were to be regarded as alien enemies. Foreign Office officials thought that this should probably be the case. However, since the United States (at that time neutral) were protecting Austro-Hungarian interests, the Foreign Office asked the American Ambassador on 9 September whether he was also protecting Liechtenstein's interests and inquired about Liechtenstein's position in the present war.

The US Embassy in Vienna consulted the Imperial and Royal Foreign Ministry; the Ministry consulted an astonished Court Chancery; and the Court Chancery consulted Johann II, who may in turn have consulted the diplomatic experience of his brother Franz. Johann II, considering his lack of an army, was certain that Liechtenstein must be neutral and wished this to be known. But he did not want to make too conspicuous a declaration, in view of the close treaty and other traditional relationships with Austria. He therefore decided to limit himself to replying to the US Embassy's request for information. The Austro-Hungarian Foreign Ministry had fewer scruples. Baron von Hold, a senior official, advised the head of the court chancery, von Hampe, to denounce the Customs Treaty so as to document Liechtenstein's full neutrality. When von Hampe said that the country could not manage without the annual customs income of 180,000 kronen which it derived from the treaty, von Hold went so far as to suggest that Liechtenstein might denounce it for external purposes but

---

[1] Prince Eduard of Liechtenstein, op. cit., page 56. Veronika Mittermair, "Die Neutralität Liechtensteins zwischen öffentlichem und fürstlichem Interesse", in "Bausteine zur liechtensteinischen Geschichte" (Chronos Verlag, Zurich, 1999), Vol. 3, pages 47–48.

retain the substance of the agreement.[1] Von Hampe and Johann II rejected this devious idea: they thought that it would be very damaging to the Principality's neutral status if such an arrangement were to leak out. They also feared that some future Austrian government might hold to the denunciation but not to the rest of the deal. On 30 September, therefore, the US Ambassador in London replied to the Foreign Office in the following terms:

"The Austro-Hungarian Government states that the subjects and interests of the Sovereign Principality of Liechtenstein enjoy the diplomatic and consular protection of Austria-Hungary and that they are therefore included in the functions transferred to diplomatic and consular officers of the United States.

I am further instructed to add that the Principality of Liechtenstein considers itself neutral in the present hostilities."[2]

On 17 November 1914 the matter was made public knowledge through a parliamentary question in the following terms:

"Sir John Jardine asked the Secretary of State for Foreign Affairs whether the Sovereign of the Principality of Liechtenstein is, by reasons of alliance with Austria or any other cause, in a state of war with this country; and whether any prohibition of commercial or other dealing with the subjects of the Prince has been published?

Sir E. Grey (Secretary of State for Foreign Affairs). I am informed by the United States Ambassador that the Sovereign Principality of Liechtenstein considers itself neutral in the present hostilities. No prohibition of commercial or other dealings with the subjects of the Prince has been published.

Sir John Jardine. Can publicity be given to this statement, seeing that one of the evening papers has published statements distinctly saying that this peaceable and friendly Prince is at war?

Mr Speaker. We do not pay any attention to evening papers here."[3]

In later years the Liechtenstein statement was to be criticised for not going far enough; von Hold had seen the danger at the time. Sir Edward Grey confined himself to repeating Liechtenstein's view of its position without endorsing it on behalf of the British Government. But at the time it seemed a happy compromise. Few people anywhere expected the war to last beyond Christmas. The Principality was spared military involvement, which some people there had feared or hoped given the strongly pro-Austrian public mood in the Principality.[4] In view of the

---

[2] FO 372/491
[3] FO 368/932
[4] The war memorial at Schaan records the names of a member of the Princely Family (Prince Heinrich, 1877–1915, a major in a dragoon regiment) and 27 others killed while fighting in the Austrian armed forces. However, of those 27 only two were native Liechtenstein volunteers. The rest were Austrians, Germans or Italians whose relations were living in Liechtenstein in the 1930s when the memorial was erected.

strong ties with Austria and the Habsburgs, it is perhaps surprising that Johann II should have taken as firm and far-sighted a position as he did.

For a time all went well. The British authorities gave permits for the export of spare parts and cotton to the Jenny Spoerry spinning mills in Liechtenstein, subject to undertakings that they would not be re-exported to Austria. However, on 8 June 1915 "The Times" printed a Reuters report that the Austrian Government had notified the Swiss postal service that the Principality of Liechtenstein had been placed under Austrian censorship. Reuters commented, "Austria has committed a positive breach of Liechtenstein's neutrality, which was declared when the war began." This led Sir John Jardine to ask another parliamentary question:[5] whether the State of Liechtenstein had remained neutral since the war began and whether pressure had been applied by the Austro-Hungarian Government to induce it to join the enemy powers in the war? Lord Robert Cecil replied, "His Majesty's Government was informed officially last September that the Principality of Liechtenstein considered itself neutral in the present hostilities. We have no other information on the subject".[6] The Russian Foreign Minister asked about the British attitude to Liechtenstein's neutrality in the light of the Reuters report. On 7 July the Foreign Office replied to the Russian Ambassador in the following terms: "The question of recognising this neutrality has not arisen in a concrete form so far as this country is concerned, and His Majesty's Government have not defined their attitude in the matter. They are however disposed at present tacitly to recognise the neutrality of Liechtenstein."[7]

Foreign Office officials were at first relaxed about the matter. ("This is not important.") They were aware that under the bilateral Postal Treaty of 1911 Liechtenstein was treated for postal purposes as part of Austria. Unlike Swiss officials at the time, Johann II and his government seem to have under-estimated the possible consequences; they made no effort to have the external censorship regime moved back from the Swiss-Liechtenstein to the Liechtenstein-Austrian frontier. Gradually the ripples spread. The result of Austria's imposition of external censorship was that the Allies came to regard Liechtenstein as a state under enemy control, unable to defend its neutrality and therefore as a hostile territory from the commercial and economic point of view. The non-committal attitude of the Foreign Office's reply to the Russian Ambassador turned to one of sharper scrutiny. Official papers began to describe Liechtenstein's neutrality as "fictitious" and "academic".

---

[5] FO 372/640
[6] Sir John Jardine Bt. KCIE (1844–1919) was Liberal MP for Roxburghshire from 1906 to 1918. Before that, he had a distinguished judicial career in India. His parliamentary interests included India and colonial questions, temperance reform, army questions and smallholdings. He had no obvious connection with, or interest in, Liechtenstein.
[7] FO 372/640

Economic Collapse

In October 1915 a small order for textile machinery from Jenny Spoerry caused hesitation in London. On 11 November 1915 the British Consulate-General in Zurich sent to London a report on Liechtenstein's foreign trade which seems to have been in preparation for some time previously.[8] It stated that the produce of the cotton spinning mills, which usually went to Switzerland, was now going to Austria, while the embroidered goods produced in Liechtenstein and Vorarlberg were usually marketed as "Swiss". Liechtenstein was in customs union with Austria and Swiss citizens could enter the country only with an Austrian visa. There was no list in Liechtenstein of goods which might not be exported to Austria, but Austrian lists of prohibited exports held good for Liechtenstein as well, which meant that Liechtenstein's exports were subject to Austrian control. If Liechtenstein wished to be an independent state and to continue to be free to import goods and foodstuffs from abroad it should align itself with the Swiss list of prohibited exports to Austria, allow Swiss and other citizens of neutral states to enter without an Austrian visa, and levy customs duties on the border with Austria. (All of which would of course have entailed a fundamental revision of the treaty relationship with Austria-Hungary).[9]

London and its allies now acted closely together, in the spirit of the recommendations from Zurich. In December 1915 the French Ambassador at Berne informed the Swiss authorities that goods manufactured in Liechtenstein were no longer to be stamped as being of neutral origin and that certain products intended for Liechtenstein were henceforth to be prohibited. The British Minister at Berne asked the Société Suisse de Surveillance Economique (SSS), which supervised Swiss foreign trade, how it proposed to treat Liechtenstein. A proposal by the SSS to treat Liechtenstein as a neutral country, subject to guarantees that any products imported from Switzerland would be consumed there, was considered and rejected by London, Paris and Rome; in their view, there was too much danger of leakage into Austria. There was some discussion in London as to whether to treat Liechtenstein as a hostile country for all purposes, but the Principality's wish to be neutral was acknowledged. The debate was summed up in the following words: "We do not want to declare war on Liechtenstein but we do not intend our consideration for its neutrality to harm us".[10]

In mid-February 1916 the British and French diplomatic missions in Berne,

---

[8] FO 368/1210

[9] Sir Francis Oppenheimer had predicted of the author of the report, "His views are sure to be extreme – to the disadvantage of every one concerned (Swiss, Austrian and Liechtenstein), except British interests". Sir Francis (1870–1961) devised and negotiated wartime blockade arrangements with The Netherlands in 1914 and Switzerland in 1915.

[10] FO 382/1080

acting on concerted instructions from their governments, sent formal notes to the Swiss Federal Political Department. The Italian mission took action with the SSS. The British note said that Liechtenstein was "subject to enemy control and authority" and "incapable of defending its rights or of fulfilling the obligations of a neutral state". It continued, "So long as Liechtenstein remains in the Austrian Zollverein…the Principality should, from a contraband point of view, be treated on the same lines as Germany, Austria, Hungary, Turkey or Bulgaria".[11] On 1 March the Swiss Government asked the three Entente Powers at least to allow it to supply Liechtenstein with foodstuffs and animal fodder within carefully controlled limits; Liechtenstein had asked for help several times in 1915. The Swiss argued that Liechtenstein gave no assistance whatever to Austria-Hungary and received none; it was scrupulous in observing its duties as a neutral; the situation in the Principality, a small and friendly state which was suffering through no fault of its own, was "disastrous".[12] The British and French governments were willing to agree on humanitarian and political grounds (i.e. in recognition of Swiss good offices elsewhere), but the Italians objected and the Swiss proposal was regretfully refused on 22 May. On 15 September the Prince's governor in Vaduz, following up a previous contact with the Embassy, made a direct appeal to the French Ambassador in Berne for Liechtenstein to be allowed to import a controlled quantity of foodstuffs and forage from Switzerland. He argued, as the Liechtenstein Government was to do in 1919, that the country had given numerous proofs of neutrality: it had, *inter alia,* imposed significant restrictions on exports to Austria (enforced by frontier guards); it had received a number of Entente nationals and escaped prisoners of war; it had refused to extradite conscientious objectors or deserters from the Austro-Hungarian Army; and Austrian censorship did not apply within the country.[13] The French Ambassador did not reply.

Meanwhile, individual Liechtenstein citizens were suffering. Some of those abroad were able to escape serious inconvenience. Others were less fortunate. The luckless Albert Hemmerle, a penniless sailor, was detained at Hartlepool in 1915. ("We look upon Liechtensteiners with suspicion", wrote one Foreign Office official.) He was interned at Reading for the rest of the war, not however as an enemy alien but because of hostile connections: he had served recently in a German merchant ship. Some were prevented from travelling, communicating with Liechtenstein or sending money home. Some had their property sequestrated. Where that property could still be identified in the United Kingdom, it was usually returned after the war in recognition that the country had, after all, been politically and militarily neutral.

[11] Text in Mittermair, op. cit., page 89, note 48.
[12] FO 382/1080
[13] FO 382/1080

At home, as the Swiss Government pointed out, the population of some 8,700 suffered serious privation. The Entente's economic blockade of the Central Powers caused the four spinning mills in Triesen and Vaduz to be closed down almost entirely and stifled the home embroiderers' business. (The mills employed 677 people, mostly women, out of a total work force of 747. The home embroidery machines gave work to 350.)[14] The openings for seasonal work abroad shrank. To unemployment was added hunger as normal food supplies from Switzerland were suspended, apart from special humanitarian deliveries A good harvest in 1917 gave only temporary respite. The formerly prosperous Austro-Hungarian economy broke down. In Vienna the cost of living multiplied fifteen times in four years. The Austrian currency collapsed at the end of the war. The Liechtenstein population's hard-earned life savings (the sixteen million kronen deposited in the country's only bank) vanished.

Liechtenstein and the Pope

The period of the First World War was marked in 1916 by one curious and short-lived proposal which became generally known only later. If it had been followed up it might have brought Liechtenstein into the centre of European affairs, but with no advantage to the country.

As the war dragged on, proposals for an international peace conference began to be mooted. The Pope was still "the prisoner of the Vatican", as he had been since 1871, and the Kingdom of Italy took steps to ensure that the Holy See should be excluded from any future peace conference. In the spring of 1916 Matthias Erzberger, a German Roman Catholic centrist politician and member of the Reichstag (the German parliament), began to promote the idea that the Pope might be given political sovereignty over Liechtenstein. The Pope would not have moved physically to Liechtenstein, but it was thought that sovereignty would give him more freedom of action in international politics, liberate him from Italian thrall and enable him to claim a seat at a peace conference. Pope Benedict XV, the Cardinal Secretary of State Gasparri and Mgr Pacelli (the future Pius XII) were enthusiastic, but declined to take the initiative; it must appear as a spontaneous gift to the Church.

Erzberger and others suggested various possibilities in their soundings of the Liechtenstein family, the Cardinal Archbishop of Vienna and the future Empress Zita. The Sovereign Prince might become the Pope's "hereditary regent" or "governor" in Liechtenstein; the Pope might become "Bishop of Rome and Liechtenstein"; in compensation to the family, the Emperor might create an

---

[14] Quoted by Peter Geiger, "Krisenzeit" (Verlag des Historischen Vereins für das Fürstentum Liechtenstein, Chronos Verlag, Zurich, 1997), Vol. 1, page 75.

independent principality out of the Liechtenstein estates in the Austrian Empire. When these ideas were floated with the family, one of Johann II's sisters objected that if they were demoted to the status of governors the family would no longer be able to marry into reigning houses as equals. The heir presumptive, Prince Alois, wondered whether the country might perhaps be split into two states, one for the Pope and one for the Sovereign Prince. Johann II said that he would gladly renounce his sovereignty but that he had to take account of the family. His brother Franz, the heir apparent, told Erzberger that he firmly intended to reign as Prince in his turn. He pointed out that the proposal would be of no practical use to the Pope, since if Italy had wished to recognise his sovereignty it could have done so already. Moreover, opinion in Liechtenstein would be against it. In an audience with the Cardinal, Franz spoke so bluntly that the Cardinal was left with "wounded feelings". No more was heard of the idea.[15]

---

[15] Maximilian Liebmann, "Der Papst – Fürst von Liechtenstein" in Jahrbuch des Historischen Vereins für das Fürstentum Liechtenstein (JBL) Vol. 85, 1985, pages 231–250. "Staat und Kirche" (Verlag der Liechtensteinischen Akademischen Gesellschaft, Vaduz, 1999), pages 187–191. "Fürstliches Haus und Staatliche Ordnung", page 74.

A DISCREET REVOLUTION (1918–1921)

Liechtenstein's national political and cultural consciousness was now well established. In 1914 the Triesenberg lawyer Wilhelm Beck, who had studied in Switzerland and worked there in a law office, founded a newspaper, the Upper Rhine News ("Oberrheinische Nachrichten"), with the aim of modernising the country's institutions and economy. Beck's thinking was heavily influenced by Swiss democratic practice and by the ideas of Swiss Catholic conservative politicians. As wartime conditions grew harder and the Habsburg Monarchy weaker, his slogan "Liechtenstein for the Liechtensteiners" attracted increasing support. Early in 1918 he founded the Christian-Social People's Party ("Christlich-soziale Volkspartei").[1] The party aimed for the end of rule by foreign officials, the filling of governmental and judicial posts by native Liechtenstein citizens and direct elections to the Parliament. It drew much of its support from the southern part of the Oberland, which had close ties with Switzerland, and from Liechtenstein citizens working in Switzerland.

Supporters of the existing order formed themselves, with great reluctance, into the Progressive Citizens' Party ("Fortschrittliche Bürgerpartei") in December 1918. They too were Catholic conservatives, but they abhorred political parties as divisive elements in what should be a harmonious and naturally developing state and society. Progress, they thought, should be reasonable and organic, not forced. They foresaw dangers to the Monarchy, the rule of law and the country's independence in what Beck and his followers were proposing. They drew most of their support from the Unterland, Schaan and Planken, whose economic ties with Austria were particularly close, and some support from Vaduz. Their newspaper was the "Liechtensteiner Volksblatt", which was first published in 1878 under clerical auspices.

The differences between the parties were, perhaps, a matter of psychological nuance rather than fundamental conflict. The Progressive Citizens were the more clerical; but both parties were essentially Roman Catholic and conservative. Modern liberalism and socialism were eschewed. The People's Party was not

---

[1] Called from now on "the People's Party" as a shortened title.

opposed to the Monarchy. Johann II's Austrian officials might be criticised, but the generous, high-minded and revered Sovereign Prince was above attack. There was no institutional or economic basis for organised party politics; there were no great aristocratic or ecclesiastical establishments and no proletariat. The People's Party was the more likely to advocate active reform, the Progressive Citizens to hold fast to well-tried values and institutions. Both were naturally concerned to win posts for their own supporters. Their similarities did not prevent the Progressive Citizens from labelling their opponents as dangerous "Reds" and the People's Party from denouncing their antagonists as reactionary and clerical "Blacks", labels which are still used today.

A Quiet Coup d'État

The old order was not set against all reform. For the parliamentary elections in March 1918, the 1862 Constitution was amended at the initiative of the Governor, Baron Leopold von Imhoff, so as to abolish the indirect electoral system and to introduce direct and secret elections. This accorded with modern Austrian practice and also with one of the wishes of the People's Party. However, through the autumn of 1918 that party kept up pressure for constitutional change, above all for a parliamentary government with a native Liechtensteiner at its head.

In October 1918 the Habsburg Monarchy ceased to exist as a political power and on 3 November, after the armistice at Padua, as a military power. On 30 October Beck, a member of the Parliament since 1914, was elected one of the two Secretaries of the Parliament. He and two close colleagues now concentrated intense pressure on von Imhoff behind the scenes. On 7 November, during a tense parliamentary debate whose minutes have never been found and whose results were briefly announced only on the following day, von Imhoff told the Parliament that he was resigning since there was no longer a basis for general confidence. According to Prince Eduard, he asked the Parliament to elect from its number a three-man provisional executive committee as an emergency and transitional measure pending a decision by Johann II. Beck became one of its members. The three members of Parliament appointed by Johann II declared that they could not recognise the committee as the new government and resigned from the Parliament. Johann II confined himself to taking note of the provisional committee's assumption of power "with reservation", in a telegram to the President of the Parliament, Dr Albert Schädler, on 22 November.

These developments were constitutionally dubious. Von Imhoff should have submitted his resignation to the Prince by whom he had been appointed, and provisional executive committees were unknown to the 1862 Constitution. Far away in revolutionary Vienna and not equipped with an army or police force, Johann II was in no position to impose himself even if he had wished to. On the other hand, there was general loyalty to the dynasty. It was felt to be a guarantee of continuity at a time of bitter party strife, and a support for the country's very existence in a turbulent period.[2] It was therefore in character that the proclamation of the new provisional committee should have ended with the words, "Long Live the Prince and the Fatherland!" Johann II invited Schädler to Vienna and nominated a close relation, Prince Karl (1878–1955), to take soundings in Vaduz to find a way out of the constitutional and governmental crisis.

On 10 December the Parliament unanimously voted a nine-point constitutional programme, to include the election of two Government Councillors by the Parliament and the appointment of (in principle) a native Liechtensteiner as Governor by the Prince in agreement with the Parliament. The Government was to operate on collegial lines and the Parliament could propose to the Prince the removal of a government member in whom it had lost confidence. This did not go as far as the People's Party would have wished, but it offered a starting point. For Johann II it was an acceptable basis for negotiation. On 13 December he legitimised the situation by appointing Prince Karl as Governor.

Negotiations began. Beck produced a draft constitution in January 1919, which made the Government too dependent on the Parliament for the Progressive Citizens' taste. The latter were, however, content with the principle of introducing popular initiatives and referenda. Another draft submitted by Prince Karl did not go far enough for the People's Party. The resulting deadlock was broken when Johann II held talks in Vaduz Castle between 10 and 15 September 1920 with the leaders of the People's Party. The proposals of 10 December 1918 were taken as the basis for a new constitution which was to be elaborated by Dr Josef Peer, an Austrian appointed by Johann II to succeed Prince Karl as Governor on 16 September 1920 for a period of six months. The formula which continues to be the basis of the Liechtenstein constitution was agreed: "The Principality is a constitutional monarchy on a democratic basis. The power of the state is inherent in the Prince and the People".

Peer's draft was considered by the Parliament in March 1921. He suggested that the Head of Government should be appointed by the Prince in agreement with the Parliament. He should be assisted by two State Councillors ("Landräte") elected by the Parliament. All three were to be responsible to the Prince and the Parliament and their terms of office were to be co-terminous with that of the Parliament. There were provisions for popular initiatives and referenda.

The Progressive Citizens considered that this draft made the Government too

---

[2] Although the parallel is not exact, it is interesting that another small country, Luxembourg, which had been in customs union with Imperial Germany, saved itself from French and Belgian designs in 1919 by a plebiscite vote in favour of the monarchy, continuing independence and a monetary union with Belgium.

dependent on the Parliament. The matter was referred to a constitutional commission of the Parliament. The commission, which had a majority of Progressive Citizens, proposed an unlimited term of office for the Head of Government (to be called "Regierungschef") and wanted to make him as far as possible a figure above party politics. The commission did not require that he should invariably be a native Liechtensteiner. The Parliament, in its turn, insisted on the birth qualification and proposed a compromise on the duration of office: it should be for six years (renewable) but independent of the Parliament's term.

At a very late stage in the proceedings, in August 1921, the Bishop of Chur (Georgius von Gruneck) intervened to protest at what he saw as neglect of the Church's interests and a lack of consultation by the drafters of the constitution. A few changes were made, but the bishop's last-ditch attempt to obtain a general reservation of the rights of the Church was rebuffed on grounds of the distinct roles of State and Church.[3]

The Parliament adopted the new constitution unanimously on 24 August 1921.[4] It was approved by Johann II on 5 October, his 81st birthday, and countersigned by Josef Ospelt, who since March 1921 had been the first native Liechtensteiner to hold office as Head of Government. When the new Parliament was opened on 2 March 1922 the Speech from the Throne was, for the first time, delivered by a member of the reigning house, Prince Franz, on behalf of his brother Johann II.

The 1921 Constitution is still in force and is therefore examined in greater detail below in Part II ("Constitution and Politics"). Although it has often been updated and amended, most recently in March 2003, its basic principles have stood the test of time. Its historic achievement was to repatriate the government of the country from Vienna to Vaduz and to put it firmly on a democratic and parliamentary basis. The Swiss Federal Council was to say, in 1923, that Liechtenstein enjoyed "such extensive popular powers as probably no other monarchy and few republics have". The constitution established the compromise, tailored to Liechtenstein's unique circumstances, of dualism between the Prince and the people.

The drafting process illustrated a characteristic of Liechtenstein people which is still very much in evidence. They take constitutional matters seriously. No matter how threatening circumstances may be (and they were very ominous in 1918–1921) they will continue to argue their points of view tenaciously, even fiercely, until the issues have been talked through and a common area of least objection

---

[3] Herbert Wille, "Verfassung von 1921" in "Das Fürstentum Liechtenstein" (Konkordia, Bühl/Baden 1981), pages 108–118

[4] For the history of the 1921 constitutional debate, see, *inter alia,* Wille (op. cit., pages 93–108), Rupert Quaderer, "Der historische Hintergrund der Verfassungsdiskussion von 1921" in "Liechtenstein Politische Schriften" Vol. 21, 1994, pages 107–139; Paul Vogt, "125 Jahre Landtag" (Vaduz, 1988), pages 128–131.

established. In the next two decades party strife was often to be bitter, but the hard-won consensus of 1921 held good. Strong in continuity, adaptable and flexible in application, the young constitution was to see the country through the internal perils generated by the as yet unforeseeable Nazi threat.

REALIGNMENT FROM AUSTRIA TO SWITZERLAND (1919–1924)

Having lost Austria as a political protector and economic partner, Liechtenstein needed another. Switzerland was the obvious choice and was willing. But Liechtenstein did not wish to be swallowed up by others; the slogan "Liechtenstein for the Liechtensteiners" shows that the country wanted to remain independent. Between 1919 and 1924 relations with Switzerland and the wider world were re-negotiated in a campaign of extraordinary vigour conducted (on the whole with reasonably good co-ordination) by a remarkably small team. The main actors were Prince Eduard (1872–1951) in Vienna, Prince Karl in Vaduz and Dr Emil Beck (a cousin of Wilhelm and a university lecturer) in Berne. Much depended on their energy and initiative, guided by the Government in Vaduz, Johann II and Prince Franz.

Relations with Austria

Prince Eduard, a senior official in the Austrian civil service, was descended from a younger son of Johann I. He was assigned the task of establishing diplomatic relations with the newly proclaimed "German-Austrian Republic". He obtained Austria's *agrément* to his appointment as Liechtenstein Minister at Vienna on 17 May 1919 and presented his credentials to the President on 24 May.

This arrangement suited both sides. It was Liechtenstein's diplomatic début in the post-war world.

For Austria, Prince Eduard was the first foreign diplomat to be accredited to the new republic, which had yet to conclude peace with the victorious powers. The Vienna legation temporarily became Liechtenstein's official link with the Swiss Government in Berne through the Swiss Minister at Vienna, Charles Bourcart. Prince Eduard had far-reaching ambitions for his legation, which he saw as a future Liechtenstein Foreign Office and as the link between the Government in Vaduz and the Sovereign Prince. These Vienna-centred plans ran counter to the "Away from Vienna!" line of the People's Party in Vaduz. They did not prosper.

The End of the Customs and Postal Treaties

Such plans apart, Prince Eduard had much work to do in managing the realignment of relations with Austria and in trying to shore up relations with Czechoslovakia. On 2 August 1919 the Parliament in Vaduz voted to denounce the 1852 customs treaty with Austria. The value of this agreement had fallen sharply: in 1907 the customs duties refunded by Austria covered 88% of the Principality's budget, whereas in 1918 they covered only 9%.[1] Reluctantly, because it feared that the denunciation of the treaty might encourage secessionist movements in the republic, the Austrian Government accepted this action on 30 August. Some administrative disorder on the frontier ensued. The commercial and customs relationship was put on a new but transitional footing by a treaty signed in Vienna on 22 April 1920. It was amended in the light of experience (and of inconvenience incurred) on 30 December 1921.

The Postal Treaty was ended at the wish of the Austrian side, which said in 1919 that it no longer wished to administer the Liechtenstein postal system as, in effect, a province of the Austrian postal system. A new, and also transitional, agreement was signed on 1 May 1920. This gave Vaduz complete freedom to issue and sell its own postage stamps. (Previously, this trade had been cornered by the Vienna stamp dealers.) The use of Austrian stamps in Liechtenstein was to be discontinued. Liechtenstein was no longer to pay an annual fixed lump sum to Austria, but would pay its own expenses as they arose. Austria undertook to continue to manage Liechtenstein's independent postal, telegraph and telephone services and the postal savings bank and to represent Liechtenstein at the Universal Postal Union.

The first stamps to be issued under the new agreement were produced by a Liechtenstein-Austrian consortium based in Salzburg. The consortium took advantage of the Liechtenstein Government's inexperience and abused its position. After two only years the Government cancelled the arrangement, which had been due to last for six years, not before some damage had been done to Liechtenstein's reputation among philatelists.

Enduring Features of the Liechtenstein-Austrian Relationship

Many features of the old relationship survived. Austria continued to manage the railway line through Liechtenstein. It continued to supply the services of certain judges, although the seats of the courts formerly located in Austria were transferred to Vaduz. Liechtenstein's criminal and private law is still largely on the Austrian model. Local trade continued, and the traditional frontier-crossing workforces in the Unterland and Vorarlberg needed an agreement to prevent

[1] Raton, op. cit., page 68.

double taxation. The Vienna legation's main work, however, was soon completed. The mission, whose costs had been borne personally by Johann II, was closed on 31 December 1921.

Relations with Switzerland

The first step with Switzerland was for Prince Karl, as Governor, to visit the Head of the Federal Political Department (the Swiss Foreign Minister) on 22 April 1919. He asked the Swiss Federal Council (government) to agree to the opening of a legation in Berne. He asked Switzerland to protect Liechtenstein's interests and citizens in foreign countries where Switzerland had diplomatic representation but Liechtenstein did not. Finally, he proposed that Liechtenstein should establish a close association with Switzerland through a series of treaties such as it had previously had with Austria. The Swiss agreed in principle; and Emil Beck presented his credentials as Minister at Berne on 13 August 1919. Within five years, Liechtenstein was to become realigned with Switzerland, economically and to a large extent politically.

Diplomatic and Consular Representation

On 21 October 1919 Emil Beck, on instructions from Vaduz, formally asked the Federal Council to undertake Liechtenstein's diplomatic and consular representation abroad. The Swiss handled this request quickly but circumspectly. On the following day the Swiss Legation in London asked Lord Hardinge (Permanent Under-Secretary of State at the Foreign Office) whether the British Government would be content for Switzerland to represent Liechtenstein abroad. On 30 October the Foreign Office informed the legation that the British Government had no objection. The Swiss sounded France, Italy and Germany as well. Meanwhile, on 24 October, the Federal Council conveyed its agreement to Emil Beck, adding, "We are very glad to be able to afford a country which is so near a neighbour another proof of our long-standing friendship". The way was now clear for the Swiss Legation in London, on 4 November, to request formal British agreement to its representing Liechtenstein in the United Kingdom, which was given on 14 November 1919.[2]

On 21 November 1919 the Swiss asked Beck for more detail about Liechtenstein's requirements. Beck provided this on 10 March 1920. The starting point was that representation should be without prejudice to the sovereign rights of the Principality or to the right of the Sovereign Prince to establish his own diplomatic representatives wherever he might see fit. The main emphasis was to be on the protection of Liechtenstein's economic interests: this was to include defending

[2] FO 371/3542.

property rights where these were threatened owing to citizens of Liechtenstein being regarded as nationals of the Central Powers, and intervening with foreign governments to ensure the supply of foodstuffs and coal to the Principality. Swiss missions were to be instructed to issue visas, to renew or issue fresh passports to Liechtenstein citizens and to help Liechtenstein citizens in distress, against reimbursement by the Principality. They were also to be requested to arrange for proper consideration, protection and assistance to be accorded to the Sovereign Prince and members of his family when travelling abroad, as had been the rule with Austro-Hungarian diplomatic missions.[3] (This last request was particularly necessary at a time when some countries were casting doubt on the Principality's sovereign status.) These arrangements were set out in diplomatic notes and were not made the subject of a formal treaty between the two countries.

The Postal Treaty

The new Postal Treaty was harder to negotiate. It came into effect on 1 February 1921 after a year of discussion. Much later, it was to serve as the model for the agreement between the USA and the United Nations Organisation for the establishment of a UN postal service in New York. It provided for the management of postal, telegraph, telephone and postal savings bank services by the Swiss PTT. Liechtenstein was to be allowed to issue its own stamps and sell them through post offices or to collectors through its own agency. Liechtenstein would bear any loss and enjoy any profit arising from the operation of the postal services, the monthly accounts to be prepared by the postal directorate of Canton St Gallen which was to administer them. The post offices were to bear the Liechtenstein emblems. On the other hand, Liechtenstein was to conform to Swiss PTT laws, regulations, norms and international postal agreements and might not change the number of post offices or postal routes without the agreement of the Swiss Government.

The Customs Treaty

If the Postal Treaty and the agreement on diplomatic representation could be regarded as examples of "out-sourcing", the Customs Treaty brought far more fundamental change: it reached into most areas of Liechtenstein's economic life and touched on some sensitive issues of sovereignty. It provoked controversy in both countries and it took far longer to negotiate. Liechtenstein proposed negotiations on 16 February 1920. The treaty was signed on 29 March 1923 and came into force on 1 January 1924. It was for a duration of five years and could

---

[3] The text was attached as Annex IV to the Secretary-General's Memorandum on Liechtenstein's application for admission to the League of Nations. (Assembly Document 105, November 1920, FO 371/4652.)

be extended automatically, subject always to one year's notice of cancellation by either side.

The preamble expressly reserved the Prince's (and therefore the Principality's) sovereign rights, but Liechtenstein was completely assimilated into Switzerland's customs area. All existing and future Swiss laws and regulations concerning customs matters and commercial, literary and artistic property were to be binding on Liechtenstein, which in these respects was to be in the same juridical situation as a Swiss canton. Trade and customs treaties negotiated by Switzerland with third countries were to apply to Liechtenstein; the Principality was not to negotiate any such treaty with a third country on its own initiative. Switzerland was to represent Liechtenstein at all negotiations with third countries for the conclusion of commercial and customs treaties, which would be automatically concluded for Liechtenstein as well; the only exception was that Liechtenstein was to be consulted before any such agreement with Austria was signed.

The customs border was moved to the Liechtenstein-Austrian frontier. The customs offices bore the arms of both Liechtenstein and Switzerland and were called "Swiss Customs Offices in the Principality of Liechtenstein". Swiss customs officers and Swiss border guards were to be appointed, paid and administered by the Swiss authorities only. In addition to customs matters, a large number of Swiss regulations affecting a very wide range of internal matters such as police supervision of foreigners, war material, trade, industry, agriculture and air traffic were to be applied.

For its part, Liechtenstein was to receive a share of the customs receipts and fees collected under Swiss law on its territory. This was initially fixed at 150,000 Swiss francs a year. (In 1925 the state's income was 602,253 francs.[4]) The sum varied over the years in the light of experience, prevailing conditions and the formula used to calculate it. It rose to 450,000 francs in 1936 but fell to 350,000 francs in 1944 and to 250,000 francs in 1945 and 1946. (The state's income was 2.4 million francs in 1945.) By 1963 the Swiss were repaying more than 3 million francs against a Liechtenstein budget of nearly 23 million francs. In 2000, Liechtenstein received over 31.9 million francs: only 3.8% of its revenue of more than 828 million francs.[5]

Agreement on the Control of Aliens

The package of bilateral arrangements was completed on 28 December 1923 by an agreement on the control of aliens. This flowed logically from the Customs Union Treaty, which implied an open border between the two countries. It stated

---

[4] Statistisches Jahrbuch 2001, page 274.
[5] Rechenschaftsbericht 2000, pages 360 and 361.

that Switzerland would relinquish police control at that border "if and as long as the Principality observes Swiss regulations on the sojourn, settlement, etc. of foreigners". It was for the Swiss Federal Council to judge whether Liechtenstein was in fact observing those regulations. If the Federal Council decided that it was not, it had the right to re-impose police control at the border. The agreement in practice gave the Swiss authorities the right to supervise the entry of all foreigners into Liechtenstein across the Austrian frontier. It meant that people expelled from Switzerland would not be able to settle in Liechtenstein and profit from Swiss economic conditions. It also gave the Swiss some power over foreigners who might wish to set up undesired commercial or political enterprises in Liechtenstein. For its part, Liechtenstein could ask the Swiss authorities to refuse to allow an expelled foreigner to reside in the neighbouring cantons of St Gallen and the Grisons. Liechtenstein's power to naturalise new citizens was unaffected, subject to keeping the Swiss authorities informed of any relevant measures.[6]

The Customs Treaty has been amended and updated many times. One of the biggest adaptations was when Liechtenstein joined the European Economic Area in 1995 (pages 163–173 below). The arrangements for the control of aliens have similarly been changed often; fresh agreements were negotiated in 1941, 1948, 1963 and 1981. Frontier controls were re-imposed along the Rhine during the Second World War, but except for that period the aim of both countries has been to keep their common frontier open. The trend has been to ensure equal treatment and, increasingly, equal employment and settlement rights for nationals of one country in the other. Liechtenstein set up its own Aliens and Passport Office in 1948, which is now also responsible for asylum-seekers and refugees. Like the Liechtenstein police, it works in close co-operation with its Swiss and Austrian counterparts.

Adoption of the Swiss Franc

The collapse of the Austrian krone made new currency arrangements necessary. The Sovereign Princes, although possessing the right of coinage since the mid-seventeenth century, did not issue coins for their Principality. A "Union Taler" was issued in 1862 and a gold coin issued by the Liechtenstein state appeared in 1898, to be followed by silver coins denominated in Austrian kronen in 1900.[7] The state-backed Savings and Loans Bank of the Principality of Liechtenstein ("Spar- und Leihkasse des Fürstentums Liechtenstein"), as the Zins- und Credit-Landes-Anstalt had been known since 1875, had the right to issue banknotes and indeed

---

[6] The Liechtenstein-Swiss agreements of this period are analysed in detail in Raton, op. cit., pages 73–90.
[7] Otto Seger, "A Survey of Liechtenstein History" (Government Press and Information Office, Vaduz, 1984), page 23.

did so for a short time in and after 1920 as an emergency measure. Between 1918 and 1920 the Government took expert advice from several quarters on whether to establish an independent Liechtenstein franc. Johann II was willing in principle to give partial cover for such a currency from his private fortune. In September 1920 the Government accepted that the country was too small to support its own currency and that the idea was unrealistic.[8]

Meanwhile, the Swiss franc was being accepted and used in the country. On 27 August 1920 the Parliament, without prior consultation with Switzerland, which at that time forbade the export of its banknotes, approved a law for the conversion of the krone to the Swiss franc at parity (a rate that can only be described as imaginative). On 26 May 1924, again without Swiss agreement, the Parliament declared the Swiss franc to be the Principality's legal currency. Curiously enough, this situation prevailed without a treaty or legal basis for more than fifty years. At that point a bilateral currency treaty, signed on 19 June 1980, became necessary because of upward pressure on the franc caused by the flow of foreign money into Switzerland and Liechtenstein and also because of weaknesses in the two countries' financial systems revealed by the Chiasso and Weisscredit affairs (page 144). However, between the world wars Liechtenstein and its relatively undeveloped economy posed no such problem to its bigger partner. During the 1920s the Savings and Loans Bank struck some silver coins denominated as Swiss francs, but these were withdrawn at the request of the Swiss National Bank after they had found their way into Switzerland. After 1930 only occasional issues of gold coins were made, but not for circulation.[9]

The Liechtenstein-Swiss Relationship

Switzerland knew very well that in becoming Liechtenstein's chosen partner it was mounting a rescue mission. It had been disturbed by the hardships suffered in Liechtenstein during the war; it had done its best to give material help and to intervene with the Entente Powers on Liechtenstein's behalf. The Federal Council told the Swiss National Assembly (parliament) that it was a "possibility to grant our help to a small neighbouring country which can regain its balance only with our aid". Liechtenstein was small enough not to be an impossible burden and, unlike the case of Vorarlberg, a closer connection with Switzerland was unlikely to cause the latter international or internal difficulties. The only immediate material benefit to Switzerland from the customs union was the guarantee that the Liechtenstein government's debts to a Swiss bank would be repaid. However, the

---

[8] Otto Seger, "50 Jahre Bank in Liechtenstein" (Vaduz, 1971), pages 6–7.
[9] Alexander Meili, "Geschichte des Bankwesens in Liechtenstein" (Verlag Huber, Frauenfeld, Stuttgart, Vienna, 2001), pages 25–26 and 121–122.

tough and invasive character of many of the provisions of the agreements signed in 1923 testifies to Swiss determination not to be exploited. In the longer term, the stabilisation of a small neighbouring state, which might otherwise have become a prey to adventurers, was clearly in Swiss interests. It was also in Swiss interests to preserve an independent buffer state, however small, opposite the strategically important Sargans Basin. The Swiss would have noted that the second paragraph of the declaration of the Austrian Republic on 12 November 1918 said, "German Austria is an indivisible part of the German Republic".

The new partnership brought great benefits for Liechtenstein. It gave the country a stable framework within which it could strive to put itself back on its feet by its own efforts. To casual observers, Liechtenstein sank into the status of a Swiss dependency. Swiss diplomatic representation, the automatic extension of Swiss commercial and customs treaties to the Principality and Liechtenstein's understandable deference to Swiss susceptibilities gave rise to the misconception that Switzerland was responsible for Liechtenstein's foreign policy. In fact, Liechtenstein continued to negotiate international treaties in the areas where it had not ceded autonomy to the Swiss. In the 1930s, and even more so after the Second World War, it pursued some markedly different lines in foreign policy. It was not included in Swiss military defence planning. Internally, its constitutional arrangements remained entirely distinct and it was free to legislate autonomously on, for example, company and private taxation and citizenship.

The Swiss have generally handled the relationship with generosity and tact. Their own complex internal linguistic, cultural and political balances make them sensitive to local susceptibilities. From the constitutional point of view the Swiss cantons were and remain (despite creeping centralisation) sovereign states which have delegated specified powers upwards to the Confederation. They are not regional administrative units which have been granted certain powers from above. This "bottom-up" brand of federalism made it easier for the Swiss to respect Liechtenstein's identity. Unlike a canton, however, Liechtenstein remained free to denounce any of the treaties with Switzerland by which it had ceded or delegated the exercise of certain sovereign powers, as had been the case with Austria-Hungary.

The Liechtensteiners responded to the Swiss with gratitude and enduring good will. Although the Customs Treaty has in many respects been overtaken by events, it remains a potent symbol of partnership and a reminder of help given at a difficult time. The partnership forged between 1919 and 1924 gave crucial and irreplaceable backing to Liechtenstein's efforts to remain free between 1933 and 1945.

THE CAMPAIGN FOR INTERNATIONAL RECOGNITION (1919–1922)

It is hard now to imagine the desolation in central Europe at the end of the First World War. Four years of death and destruction were succeeded by poverty, famine, disease and the psychological disorientation caused by the loss of familiar landmarks. Liechtenstein escaped the worst, but among its other problems it needed to assert its independence at the international level. This could best be done by securing formal recognition from other states and by admission to the Peace Conference and the League of Nations. Achievement of these goals would also help the Princely Family in their difficulties with the newly formed Republic of Czechoslovakia. There was an indirect threat from Vorarlberg's wish to unite with Switzerland. If that were to happen, Liechtenstein would become an enclave within Switzerland; all the more reason, therefore, to act quickly to establish itself internationally.[1] Diplomatic relations with Austria and Switzerland were established fairly soon; the rest was more difficult.

The Frontier with Austria

One immediate gain from wartime neutrality was that the victorious powers, whatever their foreign policy planners may have been calculating for the future, acknowledged Liechtenstein's present existence. When Austria's new frontiers were being discussed at the Peace Conference, the frontier with Liechtenstein seems to have been accepted without debate. Maps of the Austro-Hungarian Empire, prepared by the geographical section of the British General Staff in April 1919 as guidance for the British delegates, show Liechtenstein as an independent state.[2] References in British diplomatic correspondence indicate no disagreement with that position. Article 27 of the Treaty of St Germain, signed on 10 Septem-

---

[1] A British Foreign Office memorandum dated 30 December 1918 (FO 608/15) gives an insight into the potential dangers that faced a small country belatedly emerging from the shadow of the Central Powers. Casting about for ways to deal with the problems likely to arise from the new Austrian Republic's wish to unite with Germany, and from Italy's wish to annex South Tyrol, the paper speculated about the possibility of setting up "a perpetually neutral State consisting of North and Central Tyrol and perhaps Liechtenstein, and the Western German-speaking districts of Styria and Carinthia".

[2] FO 373/1/2

ber 1919, said: "The frontiers of Austria shall be fixed as follows…With Switzer-land and Lichtenstein [sic]: the present frontier." The Treaty therefore accepted and implicitly reaffirmed international recognition of the Principality.

The Paris Peace Conference

On 3 February 1919, two weeks after the formal opening of the Peace Confer-ence, Prince Karl suggested from Vaduz that Liechtenstein should try to be repre-sented among the neutral states; this, he thought, would be a good opportunity to have its sovereignty and neutrality confirmed internationally. Johann II approved. It was agreed that the application should be transmitted to the French Govern-ment through the Austrian Foreign Office and the Swiss Legation in Paris, which after some delay finally happened in April. The French Government insisted that the application should be sent to the Conference itself, which was done in mid-May.[3] In his note, Johann II told the Secretary-General of the Conference that the mission of his representatives, Prince Franz and Dr Emil Beck, would be to defend the Principality's interests, to gain its admission to the League of Nations and to obtain international recognition of the Sovereign Prince's rights. The latter included the extraterritorial status of the castle at Eisgrub, since the Czechoslovak Government made that question subject to the Conference's decision.[4] In another note, Johann II told the Secretary-General that he had accredited a diplomatic representative at Vienna and that the Austrian Foreign Office had officially wel-comed this step in view of the numerous historic, political and economic links existing between Austria and "the Sovereign Principality of Liechtenstein". Both notes were circulated to national delegations in early June.[5] Finally, in mid-June 1919 the Secretary-General circulated copies of a note dated 20 May from Prince Karl to Georges Clémenceau in his capacity as chairman of the Peace Conference, covering a ten-page memorandum.[6] The latter was the work of the indefatigable Prince Eduard. It set out, point by point, the evidence for Liechtenstein's wartime neutrality, which it said the country had observed as scrupulously as other neutral states such as Denmark, Holland, Sweden and Switzerland. The memorandum argued that the country's interests were likely to be drastically affected by the pos-sible political changes in Vorarlberg and the formation of new customs unions in the territory of the Austro-Hungarian Monarchy; Liechtenstein needed to be able to defend and promote those interests at the Conference and in the League of Nations.

In the Foreign Office in London A. W. A. Leeper minuted on 1 July 1919 that

---

[3] Mittermair, op. cit., pages 62–63.
[4] FO 608/18
[5] FO 608/18
[6] FO 608/18, FO 608/16

the Prince's note and the question of the future status of the Principality should be examined by the Supreme Council at a convenient moment. "It cannot of course be entirely divorced from the question of Vorarlberg".[7] On the same day Harold Nicolson wrote, "The Liechtenstein presents a knotty problem – especially if the Vorarlberg joins Switzerland. We cannot get away from the fact (1) that the Principality was neutral during the war (2) that, as such, it has every right to join the League of Nations."

On 21 July 1919 James Headlam-Morley[8] wrote a memorandum on the subject. Liechtenstein, he said, "is of no importance in any way except for the fact that the main line of railway from Zurich to Vienna passes through its territory". However, there seemed no doubt that it was a sovereign and independent state. Its treaties with Austria-Hungary had scrupulously maintained its sovereign rights in all matters of form. In the Treaties of Brest-Litovsk, so far as they dealt with customs matters, Liechtenstein had been specifically mentioned and not included in Austria-Hungary. It maintained successfully the position that it had observed neutrality. "There seems to me no doubt that Liechtenstein has in fact not been involved in the war and it remains therefore not only an independent, but also a friendly State." Headlam-Morley considered the Prince's claim to special privileges for his property in another sovereign state to be legally unfounded. However, a definite decision was needed as to the international status of Liechtenstein. If Vorarlberg remained with Austria, there was no reason why Liechtenstein should not continue as before. If Vorarlberg joined Switzerland, Liechtenstein either might choose formally to join the Confederation or might become like Monaco or San Marino, preserving merely the fiction of sovereignty. Headlam-Morley suggested that a courteous acknowledgement of the Liechtenstein notes should be sent, recognising that Liechtenstein was an independent and friendly state and expressing willingness that its relations with contiguous states should be determined by a friendly arrangement made with them. As for the League of Nations, he saw no reason why Liechtenstein should not be admitted, "provided it does not enter into any Treaty with another State by which it divests itself of the international status which it now possesses".[9]

In the end, no reply was sent. In the minds of the conference delegates the future of Liechtenstein became temporarily bound up with that of Vorarlberg.

Vorarlberg

Vorarlberg's wish to secede from Austria caused both sympathy and worry

---

[7] FO 608/18
[8] Later Sir James Headlam-Morley (1863–1929), appointed Historical Adviser to the Foreign Secretary in 1920.
[9] FO 608/16

in Switzerland and the Entente Powers. For Switzerland, it would have meant a large and potentially unsettling increase (130,000) in the German-speaking and Roman Catholic elements of the population. There were fears that Italy might claim territorial compensation in the Ticino, which Switzerland would have refused. There were suspicions that the Vorarlbergers' motives were only material: that they were not really attracted by love of Swiss institutions, but by the hope of economic advantage and of escaping their share of the Austro-Hungarian war debt. There were potential international complications to be weighed. The Swiss preferred that Austria should give prior consent to Vorarlberg's right to self-determination and considered that the Peace Conference would have to approve any territorial change.

On the other hand, Vorarlberg needed relief from its great material distress. The addition of a large number of conservative farmers to the Confederation would help to offset militant Bolshevist tendencies in the large Swiss cities such as Zurich and Basel and would further isolate revolutionary centres such as Vienna, Munich and Budapest. A union would guarantee Swiss control of an important sector of the main east-west railway line. From the strategic point of view, it would round off Switzerland's frontier with an enlarged Germany in the event of a union ("Anschluss") between Austria and Germany.

The Swiss Federal Council wavered between these considerations throughout the summer of 1919. In May, the Vorarlberg population voted for union with Switzerland by 47,727 in favour and 11,378 against. In Paris, the Allies' Supreme Council decided not to recognise any such separatist movements until Austria "as at present defined" had made peace.[10] By chance, it was at that moment that Liechtenstein applied to be represented at the Peace Conference.

On 1 June 1919 the French newspaper "Le Temps" reported that by its definition of Austria's western frontier (i.e. with Switzerland and Liechtenstein) the draft peace treaty indicated that the Vorarlberg plebiscite had no validity in Allied eyes and that the province would therefore remain Austrian. This caused indignation in Vorarlberg, whose people and parliament were to repeat their demand for independence from Austria on 10 August and 6 December respectively. The Swiss Federal Council viewed the report with mixed feelings: with some relief, perhaps, but also with annoyance that the Vorarlberg question should have been settled over their heads and with regret that their common frontier with Italy was to be extended into South Tyrol. They felt that the treaty gave encouragement to the claims of new nationalities and consequently contained the germs of future wars.[11]

---

[10] FO 608/27. Vorarlberg was not the only Austrian province where there was a secessionist movement.
[11] FO 608/27

In fact, it was not the end of the story. The Allies (or at least, the British) had not intended to foreclose the matter. At the end of July the Foreign Secretary, Arthur Balfour, was not in favour of dealing with the Vorarlberg question in the Austrian Treaty, but preferred "to avoid putting in the treaty any form of words which would preclude the entry of Vorarlberg into the Swiss Federation hereafter, if or when such a change might appear justified or desirable. The question of Liechtenstein would have to be considered in the light of such wording as may be adopted in the treaty."[12] On 19 August the Supreme Council approved a British proposal instructing the Central Committee on Territorial Questions in Europe to consider the questions of Liechtenstein and of Vorarlberg. The committee was asked to study the desirability of acceding to the requests which had been made that Vorarlberg should be permitted to join the Swiss Federation. It should also examine whether it would be desirable to insert in the treaty with Austria a clause to the effect that the international status of Austria and the frontiers as defined in the treaty should not be altered without the consent either of the Five Principal Allied and Associated Powers or of the League of Nations. On 23 August the committee decided to recommend that the Peace Conference should take no action concerning the union of Vorarlberg with Switzerland, a position which the Supreme Council endorsed on 29 August 1919. The committee also decided that it was not necessary to make a special recommendation concerning Liechtenstein.[13]

The question of Vorarlberg's future, with all its implications for Liechtenstein, was to be active throughout the rest of 1919 and beyond. Eventually, very much at French insistence, the province remained with Austria. In the British Foreign Office's view, "It was the shyness of the Swiss that killed the subject" (20 November 1919).[14] Meanwhile, Liechtenstein had shed the dangerous status of being a "question".

Relations with Czechoslovakia

In 1910 Bohemia, Moravia and Silesia contained more than three million German speakers and more than six million Czechs. The Germans were settled in the border areas and the larger towns. Under the Habsburg Monarchy they enjoyed *de facto* certain advantages, particularly linguistically and in local government. Czech national feeling revived in the nineteenth century under the influence of writers whose particular school of historical thought placed heavy emphasis on the Hussite tradition and the revolt of 1618–1620. This revival caused unease in

---

[12] FO 608/16
[13] FO 374/10
[14] FO 608/27

the German-speaking population. For their part, the Czech politicians were only too aware that they were surrounded on three sides by some 70 million Germans in the German and Habsburg Empires and on the fourth side by the Kingdom of Hungary, to which Slovakia belonged. They therefore concentrated on trying to achieve equality and as much autonomy as possible within the Habsburg Monarchy. This implied the preservation of the Austro-Hungarian Empire as the least unsatisfactory option open to them, as Thomas Masaryk, the Marxist Social Democrats and the right-wing nationalist Karel Kramar all made clear in 1909, 1913 and 1914, respectively.[15] Upon the outbreak of war in 1914 Masaryk, in exile in the West, was the first to work for an independent Czechoslovak state. Most other Czech politicians either clung to the Habsburg Monarchy or advocated autonomy, perhaps under a Russian Grand Duke, in some kind of Slav empire. This last hope was ended by the Russian Revolution.

It was only late in 1918, after many changes of attitude and policy during the previous eighteen months, that the Allied powers finally made up their minds that the collapse of the Habsburg Monarchy was both inevitable and should be encouraged. Czechoslovakia's independence was proclaimed in Prague on 28 October. Four geographically separated German-speaking areas, later to be given the common label of "Sudetenland", declared themselves part of German Austria. They were occupied by Czechoslovak troops. On 22 December 1918 President Masaryk, in a speech intended to be conciliatory, upset the Germans by describing them as "immigrants and colonists". In later years he regretted this expression. In his memoirs he was to write, "They were invited to come by our kings who guaranteed them the right to live their own lives in full measure... I for my part acknowledge and deliberately adopt the policy of our Premyslid kings who protected the Germans as a race".[16] (That, indeed, is how the Liechtenstein family first arrived in Moravia in the thirteenth century.) In the wake of an independence achieved suddenly and rather unexpectedly, feelings were euphoric on one side and resentful on the other. Czech nationalism led to the demolition of the baroque Column of Mary in the Old Town Square in Prague as a symbol of the post-1620 Habsburg Counter-Reformation. Gradually, however, tensions became less acute, and some Sudeten Germans began grudgingly to accept the new republic. In 1926 two of the German political parties provided ministers for the Czechoslovak national coalition government. It was the mass unemployment of the 1930s and the rise of Hitler which, in 1935, revived past resentments, inflamed current ones and tempted a majority of the Sudeten Germans into the path that

---

[15] "A History of the Czechoslovak Republic", ed. Mamatey and Luza, (Princeton University Press, 1973), pages 4 and 5
[16] Quoted in "Czechoslovakia Before Munich", J. W. Bruegel (Cambridge University Press, 1973), page 19.

led in 1938 to their incorporation into the German Reich. The disruption of the Czechoslovak Republic was followed by its destruction in 1939.

Land Reform

Masaryk's government programme of 18 October 1918 envisaged far-reaching reforms, including the expropriation of large estates, their distribution to small farmers and the abolition of aristocratic privileges. About 30% of the agricultural land and forests belonged to just over thirty aristocratic families and to the Roman Catholic Church. Fideicommissa were abolished as early as 10 December 1918. On 16 April 1919 the Land Control Act empowered the Government to expropriate all large estates exceeding 150 hectares (370 acres) of arable land or 250 hectares (618 acres) of land in general. Pending expropriation, the owners remained in possession of their estates and enjoyed their profits. Compensation was based on the average price during 1913–1915, calculated in Austrian kronen which had long since lost most of their value, and was paid largely in bonds; even British land-owners had cause to complain about this arrangement to their legation in Prague.[17] The German and Hungarian minorities complained that the Czech majority was favoured in the redistribution. The reform was carried out gradually and with many modifications as internal political balances changed and foreign policy considerations evolved. However, between 1920 and 1936, in the second great crisis in the family's history, the Liechtensteins lost more than one half of their land: 91,000 hectares out of 160,000. This included almost all their agricultural land and about half of their forests. By their calculations, the compensation offered was about one-fifth of the true value. At the end of October 1938 they were still owed one third (43 million korunas) of this compensation.[18]

In the first flush of independence the newly constituted Land Office gave particular attention to the Liechtenstein family. It commissioned expert opinions about the possibility of "reparations" for Prince Karl's activities between 1620 and 1627 and about the international status of the Sovereign Prince. The Professor of International Law at Prague University concluded that the new republic was under no obligation to recognise him since he was not fully sovereign and "as an annex of Austria the Principality of Liechtenstein is in a state of war" with Czechoslovakia. However, if France, Great Britain and Italy expressly stated that Liechtenstein was indeed sovereign and neutral, measures aimed directly against the Prince for confiscation without compensation would be contrary to international law.[19]

---

[17] FO 371/5782
[18] Peter Geiger, "Krisenzeit", Vol. 2, pages 246–247
[19] Mittermair, op. cit., pages 61–62.

The Government in Vaduz gave full support to Johann II's efforts to save his family's property, not least because they saw it, with good reason, as unofficial backing for the Principality's finances. In November 1919 the Prince directed a personal appeal to the British Government, warning that the threatened confiscation of his and other landowners' property showed that Czechoslovakia was in danger of being engulfed by Communist revolution. Masaryk and Benes, he said, were well aware of the peril, but advice from the British Government would give them the strength they needed to stand up to Bolshevist and anarchist tendencies. The Foreign Office told the British Legation in Prague that it was not possible for His Majesty's Government "in any way to interfere in matters of this nature, which are of a purely internal character".[20] Although the appeal was self-serving, it no doubt genuinely reflected the personal views of Johann II and his brother Franz. They no doubt expected that the strong Marxist tendency in the powerful Social Democratic Party and the general political confusion inside and around Czechoslovakia at the time would give it added plausibility internationally.[21]

The next moves were more formal. In February 1920 Prince Eduard, in Vienna, asked that the British Minister in Prague should be instructed to inform the Czechoslovak Government that the British Government recognised Liechtenstein as a sovereign independent state. This presented no problem and London duly sent instructions.[22] One year later the French Ambassador in London, no doubt in connection with the same matter, asked about the British Government's position and was told that it had recognised Liechtenstein as independent since before the war.[23] In the summer of 1921 Prince Franz went to Paris and asked the Directeur-Général of the Quai d'Orsay to reaffirm that the French Government considered Liechtenstein to be both sovereign and neutral. Berthelot promised to instruct the French missions in Prague and Vienna accordingly. (He first again checked the British Government's position.)[24] The Foreign Office told the British Minister in Prague in June 1921 that the fact that the British Government recognised Liechtenstein as a sovereign and independent state implied the recognition of the reigning Prince as an independent sovereign. The Government "have never regarded themselves as at war with Liechtenstein and have certainly not made peace with her, and the same applies with at least equal force to Czecho-Slovakia". Therefore, in the Government's view the Prince's property in Czechoslovakia could not be confiscated as enemy property, nor as property of the former Austrian Empire or of the former Royal Family of Austria under Articles 208 and 249 of

---

[20] FO 371/3542
[21] Other land-owners in Czechoslovakia also appealed for foreign support.
[22] FO 371/3542
[23] FO 371/5781
[24] Mittermair, op. cit., page 79.

the Treaty of St Germain, nor as property of an Austrian national. However, "it seems to be a generally accepted principle that real property belonging to the head of a foreign state personally is subject to the laws and jurisdiction of the state in which it is situated. If so, there would seem to be no reason why the provision of any Czecho-Slovak law of general application dealing with the expropriation of large estates should not be applied to the Prince's property. The action taken would not be directed at him in particular, and he would merely not be able to claim more favourable treatment than other foreign land-owners in Czecho-Slovakia. This aspect of the question is, of course, not one in which His Majesty's Government are in any way concerned, and must clearly be dealt with either in the Czecho-Slovak courts or by diplomatic correspondence between the Prince and the Czecho-Slovak government." Sir George Clerk was warned not to get into detailed discussion with the Prince's representative, who did indeed approach him soon afterwards.[25]

Meanwhile, the Prague Government stonewalled. It refused to accept a permanent Liechtenstein diplomatic mission. The Swiss Government declined to defend the Sovereign Prince's property interests but was willing to undertake general representation of Liechtenstein's interests in Czechoslovakia through its Consul-General. The Foreign Minister, Benes, refused even this in early 1921. He said that representation of Liechtenstein's interests by Switzerland could be accepted only after the land reform had been completed. The Prince, in his Government's view, was an Austrian citizen and his sovereignty could not be recognised.[26] The Czechoslovak Government finally agreed to representation by Switzerland on 30 July 1938, two months before Munich. This decision signified its full recognition of Liechtenstein as a sovereign state, as did a subsequent exchange of formal letters between Franz Josef II and President Benes upon Franz Josef's accession.[27]

The League of Nations

In 1919 the Parliament in Vaduz declared in favour of applying to join the League, which began its existence on 10 January 1920. On 14 July 1920 Prince Karl, as Governor, signed a formal application. On the following day the Swiss Legation in London gave notice of the application to Sir Eric Drummond, the

---

[25] FO 371 5781 and FO 371/5782.

[26] Mittermair, op. cit., page 78.

[27] I am grateful to Dr Milan Kovac for his generosity in allowing me to consult his unpublished research on Czechoslovak-Liechtenstein relations. The Liechtenstein Government made its approach to Prague through the Swiss Government on 5 April 1938. In a letter to the Czechoslovak Legation in Berne, dated 30 July 1938, the Foreign Ministry in Prague explained that the decision on recognition had been postponed until land reform in connection with the Liechtenstein estates had been completed and various tax matters had been settled; there were now no more objections from this standpoint. According to Dr Kovac, it is believed in Liechtenstein that as part of the settlement Prague also promised to return 700 sq. km. of land together with some monetary payment. If so, events overtook the arrangement.

Secretary-General of the League, which was then meeting in London. Liechtenstein's application was based on Article 1, paragraph 2 of the Covenant of the League, by which any self-governing state might become a member if its admission were agreed by two-thirds of the Assembly.[28] Emil Beck supplied additional information directly to Drummond during the autumn at the latter's request.

The matter was referred to the Fifth Committee of the Assembly, which was charged with the admission of new members. On 1 December 1920 the committee endorsed a sub-committee report that the application was in order; that the Government of the Principality had been recognised *de jure* by many states; that it possessed fixed frontiers and a stable government; and that juridically it was a sovereign state. However, by reason of its very limited area, small population and geographical situation it had chosen to depute to others some of the attributes of sovereignty. Furthermore, it had no army. Therefore, "We are of the opinion that the Principality of Liechtenstein could not discharge all the international obligations which would be imposed on her by the Covenant".[29] (Article 16 of the Covenant envisaged the enforcement by members of international economic and military sanctions against offending states.)

The Swiss Foreign Minister, Motta, had previously suggested to the sub-committee that if Liechtenstein could not become a member Switzerland might represent its interests in the League. The sub-committee saw no objection to that if it could be managed in conformity with the Covenant. At the meeting on 1 December Motta said that it would be very undesirable for sovereign states that were too small to be admitted to find themselves shut out of the international community. He proposed that the committee appointed to consider proposals for amendments to the Covenant should also consider whether, and in what manner, it would be possible to attach such states to the League. This was agreed unanimously.[30]

On 17 December 1920 the Assembly voted against Liechtenstein's admission by 27 to 1 (Switzerland), with 14 abstentions.[31] The recommendation to consider ways of involving small states was adopted. After ten months of circular debate, during which several proposals were aired and shot down and the perils of amending the Covenant were invoked, the Assembly consigned the matter to permanent diplomatic limbo on 4 October 1921.

Lord Robert Cecil told Emil Beck in September 1920 that the only difficulty about membership was Liechtenstein's small size.[32] Prince Eduard reports, in page

---

[28] Assembly Document 105, FO 371/4652.
[29] Assembly Document 178, FO 371/4652.
[30] FO 371/7048.
[31] On 3 December 1920 a British official minuted, "Our delegates will vote against the admission of Liechtenstein. It is too small to be of any use to the League." (FO 371/4652)
[32] Raton, op. cit., page 61.

415 of his memoirs, that Comte Clauzel (the successor to Sir Eric Drummond as Secretary-General) told him that the real reason for the rejection of Liechtenstein was the Allies' fear that it might vote in the political and economic interests of the defeated Central Powers. The surviving British records are silent on this point.

Striking a Balance

In February 1923 the Liechtenstein family took steps to provide for the future. In addition to the past and impending losses caused by land reform in Czechoslovakia, there was a danger of a series of crippling death duties. Johann II was 82 and childless. His brother Franz was 69 and also unmarried. The next heir, Franz ("the Younger"), was 65 and unmarried and Alois was 53. The family therefore decided to skip an entire generation and to transfer the administration of the property to Alois' eldest son Franz Josef (born in 1906) upon Johann's death. They would have liked to appoint Prince Franz Josef the political heir as well. Franz ("the Younger") and Alois resigned the succession to the throne, but Franz ("the Elder") insisted on the right to reign in his turn.

The results of the hectic efforts of the last few years must have seemed meagre at that time. The Principality was successfully building a new relationship with Switzerland; and one may doubt whether the Liechtenstein family, any more than most Liechtensteiners, would have felt much lingering enthusiasm for an Austria now so diminished and insecure. On the other hand, while the worst had not yet happened to their properties in Czechoslovakia, the prospects there were gloomy. The attempts to get seats at the Peace Conference and the League of Nations had failed. However, the Conference and the League had recognised the Principality's sovereignty and independence[33]. It was not too bad a starting point. Useful experience had been gained for the future.

---

[33] Johann II and Franz (the Elder) were sons of Alois II (reigned 1836–1858). Franz (the Younger, 1868–1929) and Alois (1869–1955) were grandsons of Alois II's next younger brother Franz de Paula.

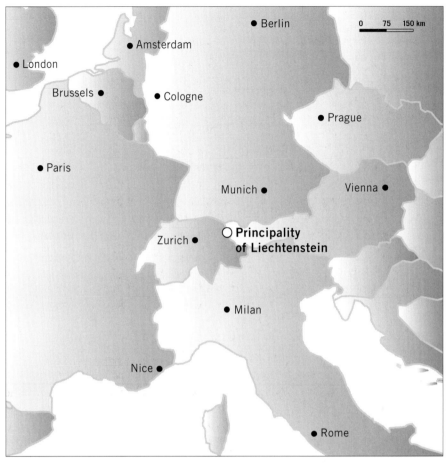

3. Liechtenstein and Western Europe.

THE NINETEEN TWENTIES

In the elections of 1922, the first under the new constitution, Wilhelm Beck's People's Party won a convincing victory: they gained all nine Oberland seats and two in the Unterland, leaving the Progressive Citizens with only four. Beck reserved for himself the influential position of President of the Parliament and, together with his cousin Emil, devoted himself to working on legislation to develop the country's economy. The Government, consisting of a journalist as its head, a retired schoolmaster and two farmers, was untrained, inexperienced and over-burdened. Events were to undermine and destroy it. But before that happened, it enacted measures which proved to be the foundations of the country's later prosperity.

Plans for Economic Development

In 1921 the State's income was 246,209 Swiss francs, its expenditure 468,301. At the end of the war Liechtenstein owed the Credit Suisse bank 437,349 francs for wartime food purchases. In July 1920 Johann II raised 550,000 francs (perhaps some £492,000 in 2002) partly from the sale of family jewels, which he gave to the State as an interest-free loan to settle this debt. He cancelled the loan in 1923, on the 65th anniversary of his succession. In August 1920 he gave another interest-free loan of 500,000 francs (£447,000) to cover the country's most urgent credit needs, and further sums for food purchases and the payment of officials' salaries. He also continued his philanthropic activities in Austria. The Government meanwhile commissioned expert advice from Professor Jakob Lorenz about long-term ways to revitalise the economy and from Professor Julius Landmann (Basel University) about ways to attract foreign capital through tax-efficient legislation. At that period, out of a population of around 9,000 more than one third of the workforce of around 4,400 people was engaged in agriculture, mostly on an extremely small scale.[1] Industry had shut down.

The great economic hinterland of the Habsburg Monarchy was disrupted

---

[1] 1,721 in 1930, according to the Statistisches Jahrbuch 1999. By 1990 the number of people working on the land (including forests) had fallen to 239.

and largely closed. The Government had no capital and the Principality was not attractive to serious foreign investors.

There was no lack of proposals from adventurers and speculators of all kinds. One suggestion was to found a casino, with the aim of turning Liechtenstein into a land-locked Monte Carlo. Johann II opposed this on grounds of morality; in November 1919 he expressed the hope that the Swiss Government would back him up.[2] A British lottery company was granted a concession in 1925, but did not last long. More successful was a lottery based on horse racing in the Anglo-Saxon world, the Mutual Club, which started discreetly in 1925 and employed about 30 people until the Swiss authorities forced it to close in 1934. Its elegant 1930s-style building in the centre of Vaduz, still known as the Engländerbau, is today an art gallery and museum.[3] Some more fanciful (and dangerous) ideas were quickly dismissed; for example, a proposal from a foreign consortium for the cession of a piece of land on an extraterritorial basis from which would be launched a new international currency, the "Globo".[4]

It was clear that if industry were ever to develop, the country's infrastructure would have to be improved. The first step was to complete the Lawena power plant, work on which had been started in 1914 but interrupted because of the war. This project was approved by the Parliament and by a referendum in 1925. Since it involved a State loan of one million francs it was a big act of faith. Johann II contributed a credit of 200,000 francs. A small number of factories started up, with varying success and often with no great profit to the Liechtensteiners because of their inexperience in business negotiations. By 1929 the factories employed 152 men and 359 women; but this total of 511 was still far below that of 747 recorded for 1912.

The Bank in Liechtenstein

In August 1920, less than a year after Prince Eduard had started discussions about it in Vienna, the Government granted a concession to a consortium with Dutch, Liechtenstein, Austrian and Swiss participants to establish a new bank (the second in the Principality), to be as known as the "Bank in Liechtenstein" (BiL). It was largely owned and led by the Anglo-Österreichische Bank in Vienna, which had been founded in 1863 with predominantly British capital but whose shares had over the years mostly come into Austrian ownership. The BiL opened

---

[2] Swiss Diplomatic Documents, Vol. VII, Document 138, page 311.
[3] After 1934 it served successively as a cinema and a factory. It then became the headquarters of the Stamps Administration and the Tourist Office and until 2000 was also the home of the Liechtenstein State Art Collection and major art exhibitions. It then underwent a major refurbishment. A short history of the building is given in "Liechtensteinische Staatliche Kunstsammlung", Vaduz, 1995.
[4] Raton, op. cit., page 120.

in 1921 with a staff of ten, accommodated in the Government Building. It concentrated on foreign banking. Its aim was to provide a centre in a neutral and independent country where firms from the old Austro-Hungarian and German Empires, now divided between a number of states, could concentrate the management of their assets under single holding companies.[5] From the Liechtenstein point of view, it was intended to bring in foreign capital and to generate industry, employment, taxable objects, tourism and hotels.[6] Until the idea of a Liechtenstein franc was given up it was also thought of as a possible future central bank. The British Legation in Vienna reported as early as March 1920 that there was some thought of using the bank to introduce a new Liechtenstein franc, to be valued at half a Swiss franc or gold franc. The legation acknowledged its potential contribution to Liechtenstein's development but thought that it would not be in the interest of the Allies for assets from former enemy territory to be placed out of reach of taxation and so made inaccessible for reconstruction and reparations.[7]

Johann II gave the bank a funding guarantee of 500,000 Swiss francs. The bank's business started well enough but later stagnated, partly because of the general economic climate and partly because the Anglo-Österreichische Bank had its own troubles owing to the general disruption of economic life in what remained of Austria. In 1930 the Princely House acquired a majority of the shares, with the dual aim of inspiring confidence in the bank and saving it from the possible influence of German speculators.[8] A generation later, this turned out to have been a masterly decision. It may not have seemed so at the time.

Tax and Company Legislation

The Taxation Law of 1923, the Persons and Company Act of 1926 and the Trust Enterprises Law of 1928 are still in force, subject to many adaptations over the years to bring them up to date and to prevent abuses.

The 1923 law envisaged special incentives for holding companies and domiciliary companies (companies registered in the Principality but not doing business there). Such companies paid a low capital tax but no wealth, income or profits tax. The 1926 legislation offered the widest possible range of instruments for business people and financiers to manage their funds and investments, including various forms of companies and trusts. Side-by-side with the two banks there grew up a number (at first quite small) of trustees and fiduciaries ("Treuhänder"). Their function was, and remains, to channel foreign capital into tax-favourable arrangements such as holding and domiciliary companies. Some, like Wilhelm Beck and

---

[5] Meili, op. cit., pages 22–23.
[6] Prince Eduard, op. cit., page 472.
[7] T1/12526. Memorandum by O. S. Philpotts, British Legation, Vienna, 11 March 1920.
[8] Otto Seger, "50 Jahre Bank in Liechtenstein", Vaduz, 1971, page 18.

Ludwig Marxer, were also politicians and lawyers. There was not enough business to make it a full-time job.

The number of holding and domiciliary companies grew rapidly: fewer than 100 before 1925, 333 by the end of 1927, 524 by the end of 1928, 747 in 1930. In 1927 they brought in 205,000 francs in taxation and in 1928, 275,000 francs: more than the refunds of customs duties from Switzerland under the Customs Treaty.[9] State income rose from 602,253 francs in 1925 to 1,335,589 francs in 1930.

An example of the use of such holding companies is provided by Courtaulds, then a world-famous British textile company. In the 1920s it made some major overseas investments for strategic commercial reasons. These included the acquisition of sites and the construction of factories at Calais and Cologne. Courtaulds centralised the financing of these two investments and legally reduced its English and foreign tax liabilities on the resulting profits through two Liechtenstein companies. (It eventually owned three.) Later in the decade, in response to new American tax legislation, Courtaulds chose to use the original two Liechtenstein companies for a different purpose: legal share transactions designed to reduce the big surpluses being made by the American Viscose Corporation, Courtaulds' large and very profitable subsidiary in the United States.[10]

Like the Lorenz plan, the taxation and companies legislation was slow to bring a fundamental improvement to the country's finances. Meanwhile, it caused occasional difficulty with Switzerland and no little annoyance to Hitler when he took action to turn Germany into an economic fortress. One important beneficial consequence was that it created an indigenous body of business, financial and legal expertise, which had hitherto been lacking. This, too, was an essential precondition for the country's later prosperity.

The Rhine Disaster, 1927

The railway bridge across the Rhine was too low. Despite acknowledging warnings from Liechtenstein of the potential danger, the Austrian Federal Railways did nothing to raise its height. On 25 September 1927 a dam of floating tree trunks formed against the bridge during unusually high water. The river rose higher and burst through the dike near Schaan. The whole of the Unterland plain and some land in Vorarlberg was flooded. Only two people were drowned,

---

[9] Geiger, Krisenzeit, Vol. 1, page 79. Meili, op. cit., page 31.

[10] In 1934 this move provoked a tax claim by the US Treasury for over $13.6 million. By 1938 the claim had risen to nearly $40 million, but the US Treasury settled out of court for only $5 million. However, it was probably no accident that in 1941 US Treasury Secretary Morgenthau insisted that the American Viscose Corporation should be the first British asset to be sold (as it happened, at a figure much below its true worth) as a token of British good faith in connection with the Lend-Lease and Appropriations Acts. (D. C. Coleman, "Courtaulds: an Economic and Social History", Oxford 1969, Vol. II, pages 279–281, 304–305 and 460–491.) Courtaulds wound up its Liechtenstein companies in about 1951.

but the damage to property and farming land was immense. Austrian and Swiss troops gave immediate help. The Austrian Federal Railways had the bridge back in operation by 17 November, but it was not until Christmas that the Liechtensteiners were able to close the gap in the dike. Johann II donated a million francs (perhaps £1.2 million in 2002). Switzerland gave 1.5 million francs as an advance payment under the Customs Treaty. The total cost of works to repair and raise the dike amounted to 3.5 million francs over six years. The flood was a bitter blow to the country's morale as well as to its finances.

Much sympathy was felt throughout Europe. One result of the disaster was the organisation of what must have been one of the first international relief operations in peacetime. In April 1928 163 volunteers from nine nations, aged from 18 to 69, arrived to start clearing the sand and gravel from the farmlands. The work continued throughout the summer. In all, 632 people took part, of whom 301 were Swiss, 103 from the United Kingdom (including two Indians and one South African), 41 from Austria, 38 from Czechoslovakia, 32 from Germany and the rest from various European countries, the Soviet Union and even Mexico.[11] The relief work was co-ordinated by a retired Swiss military officer under the patronage of two Swiss Federal Councillors, and the Swiss gave much practical help besides. This greatly strengthened popular affection for Switzerland, especially in the traditionally pro-Austrian Unterland where the Progressive Citizens Party had its roots.

According to Liechtenstein accounts of the operation, everyone worked in harmony. However, on 24 June 1928 the London "Observer" described it as "an experiment in Communism" launched by pacifist, socialist and anti-militarist organisations. "The Berlin Communists and Paris anarchists are active in these discussions. At one of the first gatherings they protested against compulsory washing and going to bed, and against discipline in general, on the ground that those were odious reminders of military service." But for the supervision of the Swiss Federal Military Department, it said, the whole experiment would go to pieces. This view was supported by a letter from an Oxford undergraduate, who contrasted the "cordial and large-hearted" attitude of the Liechtenstein population with the insolence and left-wing propaganda of the Swiss and German activists.[12] The Foreign Office was sufficiently disturbed to ask the British Minister at Berne to comment. His reply was reassuring. He reported that the organisation of the relief work was purely charitable, some useful work had been done and it was co-operative philanthropy in action.[13]

---

[11] "Rheinnot in Liechtenstein", Schaan, 1977, page 148.
[12] FO 371/13446
[13] FO 371/13446

Prince Franz was impressed by the part played by the Scouts in the relief operation. At his initiative, the Liechtenstein Scout and Guide movement was founded in 1931 and was given Princely patronage. The movement was soon to play an important moral and psychological part in countering attempted inroads from abroad by the Hitler Youth.

The Sparkasse Affair, 1928

The Savings and Loans Bank (generally known as the "Sparkasse") was, like Swiss cantonal banks, guaranteed by the State. Like the Bank in Liechtenstein it was housed on the ground floor of the Government Building in Vaduz. Early in 1928 the Bank in Liechtenstein and the Prince's estate management began to receive reports about a number of Savings Bank bills which were in circulation. It was soon revealed that since 1926 the manager and three young businessmen had been using the Savings Bank as backing for a series of loss-making speculations without the knowledge of any of the supervisory organs including the board, the Government and the Parliament. The direct losses were feared to be at least four million francs, perhaps more. They turned out to be 1.8 million francs: twice the national budget.

The speculators' main objective was to rescue the failing Liechtenstein lottery by extending it to Romania; but the Romanian concession never came, despite many expensive business trips to Bucharest. Other projects, which also entailed expensive travel, included an arc-light business, land speculation, landscape architecture and artificial fertilisers. The three Liechtenstein citizens involved were arrested in June 1928 and the fourth speculator, a Swiss, was extradited from Budapest to Vaduz a year afterwards. They were later given prison sentences.

Prince and Government moved swiftly to rescue the country and the bank from ruin. The bank provisionally ceased payments and was put under the interim administration of the BiL. Johann II gave a personal guarantee to cover the losses and the Government publicly stated that it bore primary responsibility for the bank. The Government took out a short-term credit of 300,000 francs with the Swiss banks and then a loan of two million francs from the Swiss Government as an advance on payments under the Customs Treaty. Johann II and the BiL made large sums of money available; Johann II also gave one million francs to the country (perhaps £1.2 million in 2002) to mark the 70th anniversary of his accession.

In an era of feverish financial speculation throughout Europe and America, the affair was by no means unique; but it was a sobering warning to the country. It also produced a political earthquake. Wilhelm Beck bore heavy political and administrative responsibility as both President of the Parliament and chairman of the board. Overburdened by political duties and not least by the Rhine disaster, he, the board and the Government had in practice given a naïve and under-qualified manager, Franz Thöny, too much latitude. Everyone, and therefore no-one, had been in charge. Competences had been exceeded, basic controls had been neglected. The prime mover in the affair was Anton Walser, chairman of Beck's own party and a member of both the Parliament and the body responsible for checking the bank's operations. He, *inter alia*, had founded a bank, an advertising company and a film company in Romania. The third Liechtensteiner was Niko Beck, brother of Emil Beck in Berne (who was not involved).

On 10 June 1928, immediately after the arrest of the three Liechtensteiners, the Progressive Citizens Party launched a popular vote for the dissolution of the Parliament under Article 48 (3) of the constitution. It soon gained the necessary 1,000 signatures. On the same day the Head of Government, Professor Gustav Schädler, went to Vienna, where the morally outraged Johann II refused to see him. The Prince summoned a delegation from the Progressive Citizens, who requested the dissolution of the Parliament, new elections, the resignation of the Government and, as in 1918, the installation of a prince as temporary Head of Government. Johann II demanded and received the Government's resignation under threat of ruling by emergency decree (Article 10 of the Constitution). All this happened within one week. Prince Alfred acted as Head of Government from 24 June to 6 August and a parliamentary election was called.

At the elections of 15 July 1928 the Progressive Citizens gained a crushing victory: all six seats in the Unterland (as in the 1926 elections) and in addition five of the nine seats in the Oberland. It was to be 42 years before Beck's party regained a parliamentary majority. The new government was better balanced and more experienced than its predecessor. The new head, Dr Josef Hoop, was an Orientalist by education and a diplomat and customs official by profession; he had also experienced personally the hardships of unemployment in Vienna. He was to serve until 1945. His deputy, Dr Ludwig Marxer, was a lawyer and trustee. As often happens in Liechtenstein, they were a young team, in their early thirties. The other two were older: a farmer and a forest overseer. The new President of the Parliament was Fr Anton Frommelt (33), an energetic and artistically minded priest, a robust Christian rather than a party-political figure. He combined that office with those of Deputy Head of Government from 1932 to 1938 and Minister ("Regierungsrat") from 1938 to 1945.

The People's Party felt aggrieved by its treatment. Its coolness to the Throne persisted until Franz Josef II rebuilt political bridges in the wider national interest in 1938. The Sparkasse affair was followed by impeachments and civil actions for some years. It was a wretched end to the career of Wilhelm Beck, whose contribution to the country had been so great.[14]

---

[14] For this summary account of the Sparkasse affair and its consequences, I am heavily indebted to Peter Geiger's "Krisenzeit", Vol. 1, pages 86–111.

The Death of Johann II

Johann II died on 11 February 1929 after one of the longest reigns in European history. His life spanned the ages of Metternich, Bismarck, Mussolini and Stalin. Active but remote, restrained but benign, his aura in Liechtenstein must have been as potent as that of Queen Victoria, Franz Josef and Louis XIV in their more extensive realms; the more so since he came to represent the standards of, and continuity with, a vanished era. It has been calculated that to Liechtenstein alone he gave more than 75 million francs during his long life.[15] His memorial at the church in Schaan reads, "To the Father of the People, the Helper of the Poor, the Friend of Peace, the Shepherd of Art, Prince Johann the Good".

---

[15] Otto Seger, "A Survey of Liechtenstein History", page 35.

THE SHADOW OF HITLER

The 1930s slump hit Liechtenstein hard. Prices of the main exports, cattle and milk, fell. Unemployment and hardship grew. Liechtensteiners could no longer find seasonal jobs abroad. Unlike in the nineteenth century, emigration was not possible because most other countries were in the same plight. The population rose from 9,948 in 1930 to 11,094 in 1941. The State's income grew from 1,335,589 francs in 1930 to 1,711,597 francs (roughly equal to £2.7 million in 2002) in 1940. It is difficult to establish the number of unemployed because there was no unemployment insurance and therefore no statistics. The number employed in industry fell from 511 in 1929 to 359 in 1935. Geiger estimates that in 1933 between 11% and 23% of the population suffered long-term unemployment. (In 1931 it was about 23% in the United Kingdom.) In 1933 there were 2,749 applications at the newly founded Labour Office; by 1936 there were 3,121. Some of these may of course have been multiple applications by the same persons in the same year.[1]

In the absence of a welfare state the local government commune was the first port of call for someone in need, but many appeals were also made to the Government, which in 1933 dealt with between 30 and 70 per week, and to the Prince. There were various state, Princely, charitable and insurance funds available for people in need; but the system, such as it was, was put under strain. The resulting hardship aggravated the political bitterness that followed the change of government in 1928. Although trade unions as such were never deeply rooted in Liechtenstein, there were peaceful strikes and demonstrations between 1930 and 1934. Some "self-help" movements appeared, with varying anti-capitalist and (later) fascist tendencies. The country's largely agrarian economy and structure offered no scope for social democracy or communism. The social damage, although considerable, was nowhere near as catastrophic as in Austria and Germany.

The people's spirit of self-reliance was strikingly shown in a referendum on 22 November 1931 when, by 1,152 votes to 653 and with a turnout of 84.9%, they rejected a government proposal for unemployment insurance which was sup-

---

[1] Geiger, "Krisenzeit", Vol. 1, pages 153–159. I am, again, indebted to Geiger for much of the material in this chapter.

ported unanimously by the Parliament and by both parties. The voters believed that the State's scarce resources would be more productively used in creating work rather than supporting the unemployed in enforced idleness.[2]

The Government had already embarked on a heroic programme of public works. Chief among these was the Inner Canal ("Binnenkanal"), which had been mooted as long ago as 1894. Despite reservations in some of the communes about the diversion of resources from their own needs, the people voted for the project on 14 December 1930 by 1,469 to 616, with a turnout of 91.2%. The canal was dug along the whole length of the Rhine from the southern frontier to the northern. The objective was to close the three gaps in the Rhine dikes by which Liechtenstein's streams issued into the river. These closures would cut off ever-present entry points for Rhine floodwater and promote the drainage of land, which could then be used for arable farming. Much of the work was done by hand. It was hard and wages were low: an unskilled labourer might earn eight francs (about £16.65 today) for ten hours of work in summer, 6.40 francs for eight hours in winter.[3] The canal was finished in 1943, a year ahead of schedule, at a total cost of nearly 4.6 million francs. It provided twelve years of employment. It also brought justified pride and new optimism to the country.

Much work was also done to tame the landslide gullies. The elegant Town Hall ("Rathaus") was built in Vaduz. Roads were improved. Schools, post offices and chapels were built. As a result, Liechtenstein was endowed with a modern infrastructure that was to serve it well when the economic upturn began.

At the same time, the State did what it could to economise. Official salaries were frozen or reduced. Government jobs were cut where possible. The legation in Berne was abolished in 1933, mainly as an economy measure but not without an element of point-scoring against Emil Beck. Thereafter, the Government dealt directly with the Swiss authorities in Berne or in the cantons. This was quicker and more efficient when decisions had to be made, but it deprived Liechtenstein of a permanent international listening post, a means of influencing Swiss policies as they were being considered and a symbol of sovereignty. In certain economic respects, Liechtenstein wished to be treated as a Swiss canton; but, unlike the cantons, it did not have a voice in the legislative process and now no longer had a permanent official voice in Berne.

The State's Sources of Income

Direct and indirect taxation of the population could contribute only between one fifth and one quarter of the Principality's revenues, even though a special

---

[2] Paul Vogt, "125 Jahre Landtag", page 239.
[3] Geiger, "Krisenzeit", Vol. 1, page 242.

"crisis tax" was imposed for a short time. A further 15% or so could reliably be counted on from the Swiss remittances under the Customs Treaty. The remainder (from sales of postage stamps, taxation of holding companies and charges for naturalisation) was unpredictable and unreliable, since it depended so much on external circumstances beyond the Principality's control. The Government therefore budgeted extremely cautiously. Nevertheless, in most years revenues from these sources exceeded the plan. The surpluses were ploughed into public works, reduction of the national debt and building up the reserves.

The German Hermann Sieger developed the postage stamp industry so successfully that (with ups and downs from year to year according to international economic conditions) sales rose from 105,000 francs in 1925 to 750,000 in 1937: a substantial contribution to the State's revenue.[4]

Between 1921 and 1931 the number of companies, foundations and trusts registered in Liechtenstein rose from ten to 1,035.[5] As the decade advanced the number fluctuated; by 1939 it was below 1,000. Tax income from this source fell from 430,438 francs in 1931 to 217,230 in 1939, but related receipts such as coupon tax and foundation and liquidation fees rose to around 750,000 francs per year in the late 1930s, partly because of the growing number of liquidations. Total revenue from this sector rose in size between 1929 and 1937, but declined in importance from 35.15% to 30.70%.[6] These enterprises were no doubt uneven in size and importance. But as the Great Depression and public hardship began to bite in continental Europe following the collapse of the Credit Anstalt in Vienna in 1931, the search for scapegoats began.

Liechtenstein inevitably became a target for German and Austrian press attacks. In 1933 Hitler's press was quick to describe Liechtenstein as a nest of racketeers and Jewish emigrants. One German newspaper suggested that 15 thousand million francs worth of fugitive capital was invested in Liechtenstein. In fact, the total sum invested in holding companies, foundations and trusts seems to have been around 280 million francs.[7] It was at this time that the Liechtenstein Government began to be more discreet concerning the statistics published about this sector of the economy.[8]

Immediately after the First World War Liechtenstein's neutrality made its citizenship attractive. The Depression and Hitler's persecution of the Jews added to the number of applicants. As in Switzerland, naturalisation involves an element

---

[4] Geiger, "Krisenzeit", Vol. 1, page 206.
[5] Ibid., page 204. Horst Carl ("Liechtenstein und das Dritte Reich" in "Fürstliches Haus und Staatliche Ordnung", page 422) says that the number of holding companies rose from 333 to 747 between 1928 and 1930.
[6] Geiger, "Krisenzeit", Vol. 1, pages 202–203
[7] Ibid., page 205.
[8] In 1934 the Swiss bank secrecy legislation was brought into force. This, *inter alia*, helped to protect the Swiss accounts of victims of Nazi Germany.

of popular election and there is a presumption that the new citizen will bring something to the community. Citizenship has always been a sensitive subject in a country with such a small territory. In the 1930s the procedure was that an application for naturalisation (with references and proofs of financial standing) was voted on at a meeting of a commune's assembly. If it was approved at that level, it went to a vote in the Parliament and then to the Prince for final approval. In 1934 the total cost to an adult male would have been 16,000 francs: 10,000 for the commune, 5,000 for the State and 1,000 for administrative expenses.

Over the years the price rose. In 1938 the British Consul-General at Zurich reported that the fee for Liechtenstein citizenship was 40,000 francs (more than £57,000 in 2002) plus a deposit of 30,000 francs to guarantee fulfilment of obligations to the State such as the annual tax of 800 francs if the new citizen chose to live outside the country.[9] Between 1920 and 1932 there were 123 cases of naturalisation totalling 341 persons, of whom two thirds were from Germany. Between 1933 and 1937, 126 persons were naturalised, of whom some two thirds were Jewish.

Naturalisations were, therefore, an important source of income for the State and the local authorities: just over 10% of the state revenue in 1937. Only the rich could afford them. Most of the new citizens did not live in the country. For them, Liechtenstein was either a staging post on the way to a more distant land or a place to which they came for one day, to make their oath of allegiance and receive their new passport before returning to their homes in Switzerland, France, Belgium or The Netherlands. Some immigrants did stay. They were mostly Jewish, but not rich enough to afford naturalisation. No doubt they felt insecure and would have preferred to move on, but could not. Some of them founded small businesses, which created jobs for some Liechtenstein people. They were therefore welcome and were granted the right to stay.

Taken together, the new businesses helped to overcome the consequences of a certain reluctance in some circles in Switzerland to see Liechtenstein develop industries of its own.[10] Liechtenstein's exports were helped by the 30% devaluation of the Swiss franc in 1936.

The communes also made some money from granting permits to foreigners to buy plots for building their own houses. The British Consul-General at Zurich reported in 1939 that Vaduz was not, after all, a "big peasant village" as it had been described to him. There were many prosperous looking villas belonging to Jews, of whom considerable numbers had, he said, lived there until very recently[11].

---

[9] FO 371/22472.
[10] Liechtenstein's first high-technology company, Ramco, which produced false teeth, was founded by a German immigrant, Dr Friedrich Bock, in 1932. He was a Nazi sympathiser.
[11] FO 371/23859

Prince Franz I (1929–1938)

The Sovereign Prince might also have been described as a source of income to Liechtenstein. In the last decade of the old way of life of the aristocracy of central and eastern Europe, the tradition of paternalist generosity still prevailed. Upon his accession Franz I sprang a surprise by formally marrying Elsa von Gutmann, the daughter of an ennobled Moravian Jewish industrialist and widow of the Hungarian Baron von Erös von Bethlenfalva. They seem to have been married secretly some years previously. It is possible that Johann II opposed the marriage as a *mésalliance*; it was known to very few. Princess Elsa, 22 years younger, petite, pretty, lively, and a devout Catholic, was well received in the country. Together they visited the Principality annually and spent time there. The "Franz and Elsa Foundation for the Youth of Liechtenstein" was endowed with 100,000 francs (about £120,000 in 2002). The "Princess Elsa Foundation" was endowed with 40,000 francs for the hospital in Vaduz. Franz gave the country 100,000 francs on his eightieth birthday in 1933. Many other donations followed for churches, public works, the Scouts and people in distress. Franz had always taken an active interest in Liechtenstein. He was on good terms with Hoop and never had to deal with a serious government crisis during his reign. The rise of Nazism and Communism in Europe distressed him, the more so since anti-Semitic utterances touched him personally.

Party Politics

Although the Principality had not suffered the loss of its institutions like other countries in central Europe, its constitutional arrangements were still bedding down at a time of unprecedented external and internal stress. Despite the strains, they weathered the storm more successfully than those of many other European countries.

The four People's Party deputies walked out of the Parliament in 1930 over a dispute about the date of elections. A few weeks later, the party's proposal for proportional representation was roundly defeated in a referendum. Frustration led to poisoned and very personal attacks in the press, which the Hoop government tried to moderate with a press law. Both parties managed to induce the Swiss press to take sides in the matter, which inadvertently led to a distorted picture of the country abroad. The voters took an independent view, rejecting Hoop's proposed press law by 1,008 to 1,005 votes even though they voted solidly for all the other government proposals at that period (apart from unemployment insurance). The 1932 elections returned only two People's Party deputies, leaving the Progressive Citizens even more entrenched in power. In the same year, the rising tensions inside and outside the country led to the establishment of the Principality's first professional police force: seven trained men. Order had until then been maintained by four untrained national constables and a beadle in each village.

The Rotter Affair

Liechtenstein felt the rise of Hitler instantly. Two Jewish brothers, Alfred and Fritz Schaie, had been naturalised in 1931. They owned a number of theatres in Berlin, where they moved in high social circles. For professional purposes they used the surname Rotter. Their business went bankrupt, a hostile press campaign started and they moved to Vaduz in January 1933 when Hitler came to power. The Nazi press denounced Liechtenstein for not sending them back to the Reich. So strong was the external and internal pressure that Dr Ludwig Marxer, the lawyer who had arranged their naturalisation, felt obliged to resign as Deputy Head of Government. On 5 April 1933, four Liechtenstein extremists, aided by five Germans from Konstanz, tried to kidnap the brothers with the intention of returning them to Germany. They bungled the attempt. Alfred Rotter and his wife escaped, but fell to their deaths over a cliff. Fritz Rotter and a woman companion survived with injuries. The four Liechtensteiners were arrested. This unprecedented crime in a hitherto peaceful country aroused horror, but also a feeling in some quarters that new citizens like the Rotters could bring only trouble. The four Liechtensteiners were found guilty of attempted kidnapping and were sentenced to terms of imprisonment of up to one year. Four of the five Germans were sentenced to three months imprisonment by a court in Konstanz. Naturalisations stopped. International confidence in Liechtenstein's stability was affected. The number of holding company registrations fell, to the detriment of the public finances and of work creation schemes.

A further immediate consequence was the enactment on 30 May 1933 of a law on the lines of recent Swiss legislation, empowering the Government to take all necessary measures to preserve peace and order and to protect the reputation and economic interests of the country. The law could have been oppressive, but was invoked only a few times in the 1930s and 1940s. It was used against provocative actions by pro-Nazi elements and so contributed to the defence of democracy.

Hoop's Visit to Berlin, October 1933

On 9 April 1933, only four days after the attempt on the Rotter brothers, the Liechtenstein Government sent an astonishingly sharp protest to Hitler's government through Swiss diplomatic channels. The note denounced the attacks in the Nazi press as "the crudest slanders, untruths and false accusations" and asserted Liechtenstein's right to defend itself against lying campaigns abroad. It concluded with a hint of readiness for a meeting, which finally took place in the German Foreign Office on 6 October in the presence of Swiss diplomats. At that meeting Hoop insisted that Liechtenstein and its banks were not awash with foreign capital; its tax laws were comparable with those of other countries; it was preferred by many companies because it was neutral, centrally located, stable and used a reliable currency; and it was not a haunt of swindlers because it had the same entry policies as Switzerland. These arguments had some effect. The Nazi press campaign stopped. The Germans dropped an unofficial hint that it would be helpful if the two kidnappers remaining in gaol could be amnestied, which happened six weeks later.

Hoop was obliged to promise the Germans that Liechtenstein would review its naturalisation laws. New legislation was enacted on 14 November 1933. This stipulated, *inter alia*, that applicants for naturalisation must have three years previous residence in the Principality, other than in exceptional cases. In practice, every subsequent case was found to be "exceptional"; there were 126 such between 1934 and 1937, of which two-thirds concerned people of Jewish origin.[12] The demand for naturalisation grew after the enactment of the Nuremberg race laws in 1935. In a parliamentary debate in 1936 Dr Otto Schaedler (People's Party) denounced one application in anti-Semitic terms. Hoop warned against anti-Semitism as a danger to the country, not least to its economy, while Fr Frommelt criticised anti-Semitism as contrary to Christian morality. The internal controversy continued. Naturalisation policy remained unchanged throughout the Second World War. Meanwhile, despite occasional complaints from Berlin, part of the Liechtenstein press continued to criticise the actions and philosophy of the Nazi regime.

The "Liechtenstein Homeland Service"

The Liechtenstein Homeland Service ("Liechtensteiner Heimatdienst") was founded in October 1933 as an authoritarian movement to put an end to party strife, establish a corporate state and found a harmonious social and economic order. The driving forces, who soon ousted the more naïve founding members, were Otto Schaedler (a medical doctor), Dr Alois Vogt (a lawyer) and Carl Baron ("Freiherr") von Vogelsang (grandson of the Christian Social thinker, an unsuccessful journalist, a former member of the right-wing German volunteer corps ("Freikorps") and a crypto-Nazi). A noisy recruiting campaign gathered about 300 members, of whom many were young people in the movement's storm troop ("Sturmtrupp"). There was sharp criticism of the ruling party and especially of Fr Frommelt. This culminated in a noisy, fascist-type demonstration on 9 December 1934 outside the Government Building to demand a complete restructuring of the State. Hoop avoided confrontation. He sent only one policeman to observe the demonstration, which fizzled out. Once again, however, public opinion was horrified. Capital flowed out of Liechtenstein. Hoop took the opportunity to impose a ban on the wearing of party uniforms and to require permission for demonstrations in the open air. (For the same reasons, Switzerland and Britain introduced similar legislation in 1935 and 1937 respectively.)

---

[12] Geiger, "Krisenzeit", Vol. 2, page 96.

The NSDAP Local Group

Another potential source of trouble was the local foreign Nazi Party group ("NSDAP Ortsgruppe") founded in 1933 for German and Austrian residents in the Principality. It was subordinate to the group founded in Switzerland in 1932, which after 1936 was run by the German Legation in Berne. It did not recruit more than 40 out of the 455 German residents before 1938. The Liechtenstein Government, like the Swiss, decided to tolerate it rather than risk driving it underground as happened in Austria.

Hoop's Visits to Berne, 1934: Defence of the Frontier with Austria

The Liechtenstein government had its disagreements with the Swiss Federal Council and problems with sections of the Swiss press (including the influential "Neue Zürcher Zeitung", which drew on reporting by Hoop's political opponents).[13] Hoop tried to deal with these difficulties directly. At the end of January 1934 he also asked the Swiss Government to strengthen the force on the Liechtenstein-Austrian frontier in view of the danger of kidnappings and of incursions by refugees and armed gangs.

For a short time the frontier guard was increased from 45 to 118. However, these guards were mainly intended to enforce the customs regime on the frontier. The Federal Council did not wish to be dragged into internal disputes in Liechtenstein, still less into international disputes in the event of a seizure of power by Nazis in Liechtenstein or Austria, or both. Swiss policy was to withdraw the frontier guards to the Swiss-Liechtenstein border in case of serious disorder or military operations.

Later in 1934, Hoop inquired about the possibility of military defence by Swiss forces. This revived a question first considered in 1924 by the Swiss General Staff, who for strategic reasons would dearly have liked to integrate Liechtenstein into the Swiss defensive system. Among themselves, the Swiss decided that it would make no military sense to fortify Liechtenstein unless the latter became almost permanently attached to Switzerland. Politically, it would not have been easy for them to undertake the protection of an unarmed neutral state at a time when they were trying to reaffirm internationally their own unique brand of armed neutrality, which had been endorsed by the European powers since the Congress of Vienna. So, while in practice Liechtenstein and Swiss neutrality walked hand in hand and the Swiss worried about their neighbour's future, Hoop was given no guarantee.

---

[13] In reply to criticism of the alleged lack of democracy in Liechtenstein, Hoop pointed to the shooting of 13 demonstrators in Geneva in 1932 and the banning of processions and certain newspapers in Switzerland.

The Formation of the Fatherland Union

The People's Party and the Liechtenstein Homeland Service, each despairing of gaining power on its own, now began to work together. A joint referendum proposal, on proportional representation and the introduction of a corporate popular representation, came to the vote on 30 May 1935. It was defeated by 1,319 votes to 1,182 with a turnout of 95.5%.[14] After this setback the two organisations dissolved themselves and decided to fight the parliamentary elections of January 1936 as a single party, the Fatherland Union ("Vaterländische Union"). (From now on this party will be referred to as the VU and the Progressive Citizens Party as the FBP, in accordance with their German initials.)

The elections were not a success for the VU: it won only four seats, and the FBP eleven. The VU was an uneasy coalition. From the Homeland Service Otto Schaedler took over as party president, Alois Vogt as secretary and Carl von Vogelsang as editor of the new party paper, the "Liechtensteiner Vaterland". Their pro-Nazi and authoritarian views sat uneasily with the pro-Swiss and liberal stance of Wilhelm Beck's People's Party.

Isenberg and Vogelsang

In June 1936 the German Nazi paper "Stürmer" published a defamatory article about a naturalised citizen of German origin, Sally Isenberg, who had lived with his family in Vaduz since 1931. Vogelsang approvingly reprinted the article in the "Liechtensteiner Vaterland". Isenberg, remarking that this time they had attacked the wrong Jew, sued Vogelsang in the Liechtenstein courts for libel. The political repercussions grew. Despite all their efforts Vogelsang and his colleagues were never able to obtain evidence from Germany to support their allegations. Then, suddenly, the case collapsed. Hoop obtained written evidence that Vogelsang had secretly been collecting and sending to Germany information about Jews and leading personalities in Liechtenstein. On 23 January 1937 Hoop ordered a police search of the "Liechtensteiner Vaterland" office and Vogelsang's flat. Vogelsang fled to Germany and his party disowned him. In March 1937 Hoop brought in legislation on the Swiss model of 1935 and 1936 to punish kidnapping, espionage for foreign states, parties or organisations and the importation of communist, anarchist or anti-religious written material. The law also imposed controls over public speakers. In May, 20 auxiliary policemen were recruited.

The "Spy Affair" marked a watershed. The people smelt real danger and demanded internal peace. Not before time, a mood of political compromise began to set in. It is worth remembering that despite the turbulence at home

---

[14] The Swiss voters, who had their own pro-fascist "Front" movements to contend with, also rejected a referendum proposal for a corporate state in 1935.

and abroad, when constitutional order in some other European countries broke down, Liechtenstein managed to preserve its democratic rights, the political process, independent courts, free debate and a free press. No newly naturalised citizen was stripped of his rights and expelled.[15] It could have been very different.

The Death of Franz I, 1938

On 25 July 1938 Prince Franz I died. He had spent much of his life in the service of the Austro-Hungarian Empire. Shortly before his death the Austrian Republic ceased to exist. Two months after his death the Czechoslovak soil in which he was buried was annexed by Hitler's Reich. His small and unarmed Principality now had to steer through dangers that had destroyed Austria and disrupted Czechoslovakia: two countries which, unlike his own, had seemed to enjoy the support of powerful allies and binding international treaties.

---

[15] There was one partial exception. When the VU joined the Government in 1938 it demanded, in a mean-spirited act of revenge, that Isenberg should be expelled. This did not happen, but Isenberg decided to leave voluntarily and with dignity. He went to the USA. (Geiger, op. cit., pages 222–223.)

THE AUSTRIAN ANSCHLUSS;
MUNICH; A NAZI PUTSCH; PATRIOTIC UNITY

Franz Josef II's shy and courteous style was deceptive; he knew when and how to be firm. While still young, he gained experience in managing the Liechtenstein properties in Czechoslovakia. From 1930 he represented Franz I abroad and in Liechtenstein, when necessary. Through frequent visits he knew the Principality and the politicians of both sides, but he evaded attempts to draw him into party politics. He had no illusions about the Nazis. Hitler for his part despised Franz I for his Jewish wife and Franz Josef II for his Habsburg ancestry; he looked forward to the day when all the old noble families from the former Empire would be dispossessed.[1]

The Nazis' pagan, urban and populist creed did not appeal morally to the devout, agrarian and conservative mentality of the people of Liechtenstein. On a practical level, the threat of the suppression of free speech and democratic rights, of compulsory labour and military service and of higher taxes was equally unpalatable. Hitler's main allure was the relief of unemployment and poverty. Some Liechtensteiners were tempted by the prospects of personal power and of "modernising" the country. For the Prince and most of the people, however, the main concern was to hold on to what they could (politically as well as economically) and to try to weather the coming storm in the knowledge that beyond the Principality's borders they had no power to influence events.

The Fall of Austria

As a last desperate measure against Hitler, the Austrian Chancellor Schuschnigg announced a plebiscite on Austrian independence to be held on 13 March 1938. On the night of 11/12 March German troops occupied Austria. On 15 March Hitler appeared in Vienna. The persecution of Austrian Jews, Social Democrats, monarchists and others began. German uniforms appeared on Liechtenstein's border. Feldkirch was awash with swastika banners.

Most Liechtensteiners reacted with shock. In Berne and further afield there were rumours that Liechtenstein, too, had been occupied. Jewish immigrants,

---

[1] Goebbels' diary for 15 June 1938, quoted by Geiger, "Krisenzeit", Vol 2, pages 225 and 226.

holding companies and capital fled. The two Liechtenstein banks were rescued by a loan from Count von Bendern.[2] In London, Courtaulds asked the Foreign Office on 22 March whether any third power was committed to defend Liechtenstein against unprovoked aggression, to which the answer was negative.[3] Courtaulds' inquiry prompted the Foreign Office to ask in the City about the extent of British financial interests in Liechtenstein. Mr Nigel Law's[4] reply, on 16 April, estimated total British assets at between £10 and £20 million (perhaps £312–£624 million in 2002). Law advised that if the Germans took over and a company's directors were Liechtenstein citizens, the Germans could impose any legal obligations they thought fit, take possession of assets domiciled in Liechtenstein and abroad and appoint new company officers whose instructions foreign banks would be forced to obey. "Conclusion. Liquidate and get out as soon as possible."[5]

The British Consul-General at Zurich on 18 March produced a more nuanced analysis. On balance, he thought it likely that Germany would not annex Liechtenstein. Its population was negligible. He pointed out that its wealth stood or fell with independence, since the holding companies' assets were outside the country. The country itself was not rich. It would not be worth Germany's while to be blamed by the whole world and to run into diplomatic trouble even with Switzerland. Furthermore, "The whole spirit of the citizens of Liechtenstein is one [of] patriotic unity, as it is also in Switzerland, and this is the great difference between Switzerland and Liechtenstein on the one hand and Austria on the other. Internal political disagreement is a kind of invitation or provocation which should be carefully avoided by those who wish to remain independent."[6]

The Consul-General's analysis, had he but known it, was much in line with that of Hitler and Ribbentrop on the same day; but he was premature concerning patriotic unity.

Closing the Ranks

On 15 March 1938 the Parliament held a closed session. It passed a unanimous

---

[2] Born 1878, died 1968. An adopted son and heir of Baron Hirsch, the Austrian financier and friend of King Edward VII. As Baron de Forest he owned land in Moravia. A naturalised British subject. As a member of the British House of Commons, his Liberal politics were so radical that George V warned Prime Minister Asquith during the House of Lords constitutional crisis in 1911 that among all the possible candidates for peerages he would absolutely refuse to consider de Forest's name. (Kenneth Rose, "King George V", page 129.) Naturalised in Liechtenstein in 1932 and ennobled by Franz I in 1936 as Count von Bendern. He was a generous benefactor to Liechtenstein. The Liechtenstein State Art Collection was founded in 1968 with ten paintings donated by him.
[3] FO 371/22472
[4] Nigel Walter Law (1890–1967). HM Diplomatic Service 1913–1922. Partner (later director) of Jessel, Toynbee 1922–1956 and in charge of all of his firm's foreign business. In the 1930s the Foreign Office occasionally consulted him discreetly about German economic affairs.
[5] FO/371/22472
[6] FO 371/22472

resolution in support of Liechtenstein's continuing independence and the main-tenance of the treaties with Switzerland. This had a good effect abroad. However, the resolution was unanimous only in the sense that Otto Schaedler (president of the VU) had left the room before the vote was taken. Schaedler had set out a seven-point ultimatum, which included the reconstruction of the Government, proportional representation, an amnesty for political offences and the introduc-tion of various anti-Semitic measures. The parliamentary resolution was helpful enough to Hoop when he went to Berne the next day with Fr Frommelt to discuss economic and defence matters; but the Swiss, although encouraging, demanded more clarity and they returned to Vaduz without any very concrete result. On Friday 18 March the two political parties hammered out a provisional agreement based on Liechtenstein's autonomy and independence, to include the reconstruction of the Government and proportional representation. The anti-Semitic proposals were not pursued.

On the same day Franz Josef, alerted to the party crisis by a Liechtenstein businessman and VU supporter, arrived unexpectedly from Vienna. Although at that point he had no constitutional standing he held a series of separate interviews with the party leaders, putting pressure on them to clinch the agreement. Over the weekend, this was achieved. On 30 March Josef Hoop (FBP) was reappointed Head of Government. His deputy was Alois Vogt (VU): pro-Nazi, but his local political ambition now satisfied. Fr Frommelt (FBP) and Arnold Hoop (VU) were appointed Government Councillors ("Regierungsräte"). The two-party coalition thus formed was to last until 1997. Also on 30 March, Franz I handed over to Franz Josef the exercise of his sovereign powers as his representative. The Parliament (this time truly unanimously) rose to its feet to express its support for independence, loyalty to the dynasty and adherence to existing treaties. By the latter was meant the relationship with Switzerland as opposed to any change in favour of Germany. Thus fortified, Franz Josef and Josef Hoop paid a formal visit to Berne on 4 April. Before long, Franz Josef moved his official residence from Vienna to Vaduz and, with the visible support of his coalition government, began a series of visits to every commune in the Principality to rally support for independence and the Monarchy.

Hitler's Policy

The "Volksdeutsche Mittelstelle" was a Nazi organisation. Its purpose was to organise covertly political agitation by members of the German race living abroad. It was run by a senior SS officer in Berlin. On 16 March 1938 it submit-ted plans for Nazi sympathisers in Liechtenstein to use the forthcoming elections to bring a National Socialist government to power, to be followed by a gradual union ("Anschluss") with the Reich. Ribbentrop, the Foreign Minister, and his staff were wary of possible foreign policy complications and thought the proposal "not feasible". Hitler was consulted on 18 March. He seems to have ruled that there should be no German intervention in Liechtenstein.[7] So at any rate, Ribbentrop urgently informed Goebbels when the latter appeared to be planning a coup which would have led to a pro-Anschluss referendum in Liechtenstein on 10 April, the same day as the Anschluss referendum in Germany and Austria. (The Nazi sympathisers already had plans to replace the crown in the Liechtenstein flag with the swastika.[8]) German policy was crystallised in a draft approved by Ribbentrop on 25 March 1938. In short, Germany would not get involved in Liechtenstein internal politics. Germany had nothing against the continuation of an independent Principality with its current status. If Liechtenstein chose to draw closer to the Reich, "that could only be welcome to us"; but any attempt to draw Liechtenstein closer to Switzerland, and especially into the Swiss military defence system, would be viewed as an anti-German move.[9] The "non-intervention" line was repeatedly affirmed in German public statements. Few took these at face value, but it was also repeated to Liechtenstein politicians of either party who for whatever reason made official or private journeys to Germany. The public version gave some hope to those who wanted to keep Liechtenstein free, but the policy as a whole also encouraged Nazi sympathisers who wanted to work for change.

Hitler's policy towards Liechtenstein was not accidental. His planned course of political and military aggression still had some way to run. There was no point in alarming those foreign politicians who still chose to wear blinkers. After his triumphant reception in Vienna, he might have been exposed to ridicule if he had acted against a tiny and impoverished country where he was known to have few supporters. Relations with Switzerland would have been seriously disturbed. There was therefore no advantage, and some disadvantage, in a forced Liechtenstein Anschluss. But psychology may also have played a part. In November 1938, admittedly at second hand, a report reached Berne of a conversation between the German State Secretary von Weizsäcker and a Liechtenstein citizen who had raised with him the subject of an Anschluss with Liechtenstein and Switzerland. Von Weizsäcker said that there was no question of it. He himself had recently touched on the matter with the Führer. Hitler had snapped at him: he said that he never wanted to hear the words Liechtenstein and Switzerland again "because the people there hate me".[10]

[7] Geiger, "Krisenzeit", Vol. 2, page 144.
[8] The crown had been inserted as recently as 1937, to distinguish Liechtenstein's blue and red flag from those of the Swiss Canton Ticino and the Republic of Haiti. (Goop, "Liechtenstein Gestern und Heute", page 289.)
[9] PRO: GFM 33/533, page Nos. 331739–331745
[10] Swiss Diplomatic Documents, Vol. 12, No. 446

The National German Movement in Liechtenstein (VDBL)

The FBP/VU coalition left the more extreme VU members, including many who had joined from the Homeland Service, disappointed and dissatisfied. They immediately broke away to form a National German Movement in Liechtenstein ("Volksdeutsche Bewegung in Liechtenstein", or VDBL), the aim of which was to work for a customs union with Germany and then a total Anschluss. It operated on standard Nazi lines: youth and sports activities, noisy meetings, beating of opponents, anti-Semitism, graffiti, fiery swastikas at night, etc. At this pre-war stage the movement was not large: about 200 members. Its youth wing had about two dozen boys and a few girls, compared with 650 Scouts and Guides and 200 members of the Catholic Youth.[11] But the VDBL enjoyed moral and material support from the Reich. It could act as a fifth column when needed. It supplied dangerously misleading information to Berlin.[12] It could also clamour for "protection" from Germany if the Liechtenstein Government were to take action against it.

The Growth of the German Presence

The fall of Austria caused a large growth in the Reich's presence in Liechtenstein. To the original 400-strong German community were now added between 900 and 1,000 formerly Austrian residents. The new total of 1,400 amounted to 12% of the population. However, they seem on the whole to have kept out of local politics. Dr Bock, one of the leaders, was against an Anschluss because Nazi taxation and the loss of Swiss credits would have hurt the interests of his company, Ramco. The railway was now run by German National Railways (the "Reichsbahn"). This caused the Swiss frontier station at Buchs to become a nest of espionage, but the change of management had little effect in Liechtenstein and was to turn out to be unexpectedly helpful in 1945. The Austrian judges were now German citizens. Some were replaced by the new regime, but those remaining were allowed to take the oath to the Sovereign Prince and the old Austrian legislation remained unchanged in the Principality.

Continuing Worries

There was a fresh invasion scare in July 1938, to the detriment of Liechtenstein's financial standing;[13] but once again the German authorities assured the Swiss and Liechtenstein governments that the Reich had no designs on Liechtenstein as

---

[11] Geiger, op. cit., pages 196, 197, 215
[12] For example, a report by Dr Stier of the Volksdeutsche Mittelstelle to the Auswärtiges Amt dated 7 April 1938, denied that Franz Josef had been welcomed enthusiastically and said that everyone in Liechtenstein saw an Anschluss as inevitable. (GFM 33/533, No. 331751)
[13] Between March and July 1938 149 holding companies with a total capital of 185 million francs were liquidated, which caused the state a loss of 113,000 francs in tax receipts. (Geiger, op. cit., page 292)

long as Switzerland's neutrality was respected. The head of the Division for Foreign Affairs in Berne, Pierre Bonna, told the British Minister on 12 July that he personally was satisfied that the Reich had no plan to absorb Liechtenstein. "The danger is unemployment and steps are being taken to prevent any considerable unrest from arising on that account."[14]

Munich

The Munich Agreement of 30 September 1938 forced Czechoslovakia to cede the Sudeten areas to the German Reich. This raised immediate problems for Franz Josef II. His most valuable lands were now in Reich territory: eight estates comprising 46,000 hectares, as against three estates and 23,000 hectares in what was left of Czechoslovakia.[15] However, the central administration of the property and the bank accounts were located in Czechoslovakia. Working capital was needed in the new Reich territory for management purposes and the payment of death duties for Franz I, and the Czechoslovak state still owed him money. This entailed a complicated triangular negotiation with Berlin and Prague. Josef Hoop played an energetic part, in keeping with the Liechtenstein family property's importance to the Principality's finances. The money began to move in 1939. Because of Nazi currency restrictions much of it stayed in the Reich rather than going to Vaduz.

Franz Josef was concerned to take a "loyal" attitude to Czechoslovakia in its agony.[16] At the same time, some thought began to be given to a reorganisation of the property and to a partial restitution of what had been expropriated. Franz Josef appears to have envisaged the return of about a quarter of the lost land, on which he would have continued the social and charitable traditions of the family and for which he would have repaid the compensation received. These plans continued to be pursued after Hitler's destruction of the Second Czechoslovak Republic on 15 March 1939, but it is not clear to what extent, if at all, they bore fruit.

Radio Liechtenstein

This radio station was one of the first casualties of World War II, albeit bloodless.[17] Under the Postal Treaty of 1921 Switzerland was responsible for

---

[14] FO 371/22472. Swiss Diplomatic Documents Vol.12, No. 343.

[15] Geiger, op. cit., pages 242–248.

[16] Liechtenstein never recognised the Munich Agreement nor (unlike Switzerland) the regimes imposed on Czechoslovakia by Hitler in 1939. According to Hans-Adam II, the Liechtenstein family may have given financial support to the Czechoslovak Government in Exile. (Authorised interview made available to the author by Dr Kovac). In November 1943 Franz Josef's cousin Prince Ferdinand, allegedly with Franz Josef's full approval, published an article in the Swedish paper "Dagens Nyheter" about the importance of Czechoslovakia's coming post-war role in central Europe. (FO 371/34467)

[17] The story has been told by Norbert Jansen, in "Jahrbuch des Historischen Vereins Liechtenstein" (JBL), Vol. 73, 1973, pages 111–201.

Liechtenstein's radio arrangements. From 1935 onwards several business concerns, impressed by the commercial success of Radio Luxembourg, inquired about the possibility of acquiring a radio concession in Liechtenstein. For its part, the Hoop government was only too keen to diversify the sources of state revenue. The Parliament granted a concession on 28 July 1937 to Roditi International, London, and Mills and Rockley Ltd, Croydon, who were represented by William Kenmore.[18] After a long tussle the Swiss postal authorities, who were worried about preserving their monopoly and about the potential dangers from commercial advertising and political propaganda, granted permission on 26 September 1938. The transmission equipment was bought from Berlin and the first trial broadcasts began in October 1938. However, the gathering war clouds made the financial and commercial conditions unfavourable. The Germans viewed with disfavour a British-owned radio station only a few kilometres from the former Austrian frontier. The station fell silent soon after 1 September 1939; a heavy German hint that it might fall victim to a bomb may have contributed to its demise. The equipment was dismantled and sent to Switzerland in November 1942.[19]

Tensions with Switzerland

In the autumn of 1938 the VDBL generated unease by various provocations including small but noisy bomb attacks against Jewish property. The authorities retaliated with arrests and house searches. On 11 December Hoop tried to stabilise morale by a speech to a crowded audience in which he stressed that Liechtenstein had nothing to fear from German intentions. The relationship with Switzerland was, he said, both firm and fruitful. He compared conditions and prospects in Germany with the happy state of Liechtenstein surprisingly bluntly, to the annoyance of the VDBL and the pained regret of the German Consul-General in Zurich.[20] On 14 December the Government renewed the ban on unlicensed demonstrations, adding to it a prohibition of military-style marches and provocative assemblies.

---

[18] Born Willi Kahnheimer in Hong Kong. Active in the German film industry. Emigrated from Berlin to London in 1935. Naturalised as a British subject in 1940. Roditi was an international finance house.

[19] Kenmore tried to revive the project in 1951 by offering it to the BBC in the first instance for "propaganda purposes", with the Voice of America and the United Nations as alternatives. The BBC was unable to make use of it for financial and technical reasons but was "highly alarmed at the prospect of the Voice of America moving in and undertaking indiscriminate broadcasting, causing chaos in the ether in that part of the world." The US Information Service, when finally consulted by the Foreign Office, also foresaw problems for itself through lack of complete control. The Swiss would only tolerate completely neutral transmissions. So the project lapsed. (FO 953/1208 and FO 953/1209)

[20] Dr Voigt wrote sadly from Zurich of the Liechtensteiners' "dwarf- and snail-like" attachment to low taxes, material well-being and free expression of opinion compared with Nazi Germany's "vibrant life, discipline, readiness for self-sacrifice and great national goals". (Geiger, op. cit., page 269.) He also lamented that, "In this pure German little land, all-German thought is so stunted that it is still alive to some extent only in a small circle". (GFM 33/533, page No. 331776)

For some time the Swiss authorities had privately become increasingly worried about Liechtenstein for both political and military reasons. They felt that the government was too passive against the internal Nazi threat and that Franz Josef's stake in Austria and Czechoslovakia gave the Reich a hold over him.[21] For its part, the Swiss General Staff continued to worry that a German annexation of Liechtenstein would pose a serious military threat to the strategically vital Sargans communications junction, which the Swiss were now busily fortifying. (The Swiss Head of Military Intelligence was rather more open to the British Legation about this fear than was the Chief of General Staff.)[22] The Swiss had already made it clear to Hoop on 16 March that the continued presence of Swiss frontier guards would depend on the maintenance of calm and order in the Principality, for which the Liechtenstein authorities were responsible. The Swiss had further insisted that Liechtenstein should make up its mind about the inclusion of the Principality into Swiss neutrality (which Hoop would have welcomed) and about military protection by Switzerland of Liechtenstein's neutrality (which would have been much more problematic, since perpetual fortification and military stationing rights would have meant virtual annexation by Switzerland.) The Germans learnt about this matter on the same day and were quick to oppose any inclusion of the Principality into the unique Swiss brand of armed neutrality.

The Swiss authorities made a series of helpful gestures throughout the summer of 1938. The labour market was opened to 150 Liechtenstein building workers, the interest rate on the loans of 1928 and 1934 was reduced to 3.5%, Liechtenstein workers in Switzerland were made eligible for social assistance (to be refunded by Vaduz) and permission was granted for Radio Liechtenstein (page 94 above). Liechtenstein was given permission to take part in the forthcoming Swiss National Exhibition and to organise its own National Day there on 16 July 1939. In October 1938 the Swiss allowed goods exported from Liechtenstein to be designated as goods of Swiss origin. In December the Swiss granted a credit of two million francs to tide the government and the Savings and Loans Bank over their post-Anschluss liquidity problems, under conditions which bound Liechtenstein more closely than ever before to Switzerland.

Meanwhile, Swiss military planning had been proceeding in secret. In December 1938 the Swiss unofficially proposed to Hoop in Berne that, in return for monetary compensation, Liechtenstein should give up the Ellhorn, a 200 metres high outlying mountain which dominates the Sargans Basin from across the Rhine. Hoop's anxiety to steer Liechtenstein through its perils sometimes made

---

[21] However, the Federal Political Department, in conversation with the British Minister at Berne, deplored the spreading of pessimistic rumours about Liechtenstein in London and elsewhere and speculated about the motives of those behind them. (14 February 1939. FO 371/23859)

[22] FO 371/22472, FO 371/22969, FO 371/22970.

him promise more than he could perform, and too ready to tell his interlocutors (whether Swiss or German) what he thought they wanted to hear. This was one such occasion. He contrived to give the impression that there would be no fundamental problem. In fact neither Franz Josef, nor the rest of the Government, nor the commune of Balzers to which the Ellhorn belonged, was willing to cede the land, for a variety of reasons.

When this reluctance became known on 19 January 1939 Swiss irritation at Liechtenstein's apparent ingratitude was intense. The Federal Council expressed its frustration in a stiff note despatched to Vaduz on 30 January. The note complained about Liechtenstein's failure to track down the perpetrators of the attacks against Jewish property and to prevent Nazi propaganda against the Jews and the Swiss-Liechtenstein relationship. In future, the Swiss customs officers would take much stronger measures against the importation of such propaganda material, which could all too easily find its way into Switzerland. The note called on Liechtenstein to take serious measures against Nazi subversive activities. It recalled Hoop's public statements that there would be no more naturalisations of Jewish citizens. Naturalisations had in fact continued. This caused problems for the Swiss authorities: it was difficult for them to prevent such new citizens from entering Swiss territory, and Swiss missions abroad were obliged to protect their interests as Liechtenstein citizens. Naturalisations of Jews gave fuel to Nazi propaganda and risked creating incidents, which would only do further damage to Liechtenstein's financial interests. Until Liechtenstein had clarified its position, delivery of the second half of the two million francs credit would be suspended.[23] The note was, in fact, a diplomatic version of a much fiercer internal Political Department report. Unlike the report, the note did not mention the Ellhorn, nor Swiss suspicions of Franz Josef, nor Swiss fears that in the event of a German annexation of Liechtenstein the newly naturalised citizens might become a burden on Switzerland.

The Liechtenstein government had already taken some measures on its own account. Hoop's speech of 11 December had been followed by a renewed surge of noisy and violent VDBL activity.

On 27 January, following the model of a Swiss public order decree issued the previous month, the Liechtenstein Government announced that the production and distribution of leaflets would in each and every case require official permission and prior submission of the text to the authorities. The lighting of fires in the open air would need official permission. Insults to foreign states and the carrying of unlicensed weapons including steel rods and rubber truncheons were made punishable offences. This decree had a helpful effect, both internally and

---

[23] Swiss Diplomatic Documents, Vol. 13, No. 16, pages 32–38.

in Switzerland. Meanwhile, the naturalisations continued: 23 cases and a total of 48 persons in 1939.[24]

The State Visit to Berlin, 2–3 March 1939

At the same time as his courtesy visit to Berne as Prince Regent in April 1938 Franz Josef asked for an equivalent visit to Berlin. Hitler was not interested, but once Franz Josef had become a head of state it became awkward for the Germans to put it off indefinitely. It was at last arranged for 2–3 March 1939. The full ceremonial of a State Visit was deployed (wreath-laying, guards of honour, official lunch, the opera, etc). Accompanied by Hoop, Vogt and two of his own officials, Franz Josef had separate meetings each lasting half an hour with Hitler, Ribbentrop, Frick (Minister of the Interior) and Göring.

Three years later the British Consul-General at Zurich reported Franz Josef's own account of the visit to him, which was evidently delivered with some irony:

"The Fuhrer had apparently impressed him as being a jovial Austrian, and had held forth, while not looking at him but staring at the opposite wall, for a considerable time on how misunderstood he was by certain people who believed that he was preparing for war, whereas all he was interested in was to build hospitals, schools and roads, and to turn Berlin into a beautiful city. Goering had been even more jocular but had lost no opportunity of expressing his veneration for, and his blind faith in, the greatness of his Fuhrer. Ribbentrop had taken a seat in the corner of his office, closed his eyes, and in the coldest of voices soliloquised on his views of international politics, salient points among which were that America would never enter the war and would have nothing of importance to contribute to a war as concerned Europe."[25]

Franz Josef briefed the Swiss Minister at Berlin after the talks. It had been intended that the Minister should accompany him throughout the visit, but he was dropped from the programme. Ostensibly this was because of German protocol rules. In fact, Franz Josef himself may have been reluctant to have a Swiss presence; von Weizsäcker hinted to the Swiss Minister more than three weeks later that "the wish of the Prince or his entourage" [to be accompanied by him] "had been less positive than he perhaps believed".[26] Coming on top of the Ellhorn affair and the independent arrangement of the visit itself, this episode did nothing to reduce Swiss annoyance with Liechtenstein.

The State Visit was a bold move. Luckily the Nazi leaders, and Hitler in

---

[24] Geiger, op.cit. pages 316–319.
[25] Letter of 25 June 1942 from Mr Eric Cable to HM Minister, Berne. (FO 371/31312)
[26] GFM33/533, No. 331811.

particular, were somewhat abstracted at the time. The visitors could not know that they were in the last stages of planning the final destruction of Czechoslovakia less than two weeks later. Hosts and guests had a common interest, for different reasons, in asserting the sovereignty and independence of Liechtenstein, which were symbolised by the very fact of a State Visit. There was no other interest for the German side, which does not seem to have put pressure on the visitors. For the Liechtenstein side, it was a once-for-all opportunity to gain access to the top leaders and to gauge their personalities and intentions. Franz Josef was able to assess which of them might be susceptible to flattery in future. (He seems to have fixed on Ribbentrop and Göring.) The preparatory work for the visit deepened personal knowledge of important but less senior German contacts; it would be that much easier in future to pick up a telephone in case of need. It was important for Hoop, whose VU colleague Vogt enjoyed German contacts and confidence as a result of his Homeland Service period, to build up his own standing. It was important for the Government as a whole to be able to outflank the pernicious influence of the Volksdeutsche Mittelstelle and the VDBL. These were areas where the Swiss Government could not help them.

The Liechtenstein Government had announced beforehand that it would be purely a courtesy visit and that no negotiations would take place. Inevitably, the visit provoked international speculation which was made all the more feverish by the absence of tangible results. Much of the speculation centred round the idea that Franz Josef might have done a deal to save his properties in Czechoslovakia, possibly at the expense of Liechtenstein itself. The British Minister at Prague reported a story that the Prince had told Hitler that he knew that his country could be taken over at any moment, but he thought Hitler would probably prefer that a request to be embodied in the Reich should come voluntarily from Liechtenstein itself, a request that he would be willing to make, subject to certain unspecified conditions. On this the British Minister at Berne commented that Franz Josef had only recently "emphasised the desire of the people and authorities of Liechtenstein to maintain the independence of the country and its economic conventions with Switzerland."[27] The speculation is best judged in the light of what actually happened.

The Attempted Nazi Putsch, 24 March 1939

Following the agreement of March 1938 between the two main parties, proportional representation was introduced in January 1939. To hinder the VDBL's

---

[27] Letters of 21 March 1939 from Sir Basil Newton, Prague (FO 371/22967) and 19 April 1939 from Sir George Warner, Berne (FO 371/22970). Newton does not name his informant, whom he describes only as "gossipy but perhaps well informed". The atmosphere in Prague six days after the Nazi entry must have been fraught, and all kinds of rumours must have been rife. Sir George Warner's note of caution seems reasonable.

chances the new electoral law provided that no party could claim a seat unless it had secured 18% of the votes eligible to be cast. To hinder them further, and to avoid disrupting the newly won political peace, the two main parties agreed to share out the seats so that the parliamentary elections on 6 April should not be contested. The Parliament was dissolved on 11 March.

Frustration, awareness of the electoral deadline, the illusion that the Prince and his government "must" have made fundamental concessions in Berlin, and Hitler's drive into Prague and Memel combined to force the VDBL into the frame of mind that "something must be done". The plan was to stage a demon-stration in Vaduz, provoke clashes with their opponents and then call on Nazi organisations across the border in Feldkirch for "help". The latter would come to the aid of their oppressed brothers, occupy the country and so enable a newly formed VDBL government to declare Liechtenstein's union with the Reich. By Wednesday 22 March an SA battalion and an NSKK company (600 armed men altogether) and 150 vehicles stood ready in Feldkirch as a result of local initia-tive. A hard core of about 100 VDBL activists was scattered in groups around Liechtenstein, prepared to block the Rhine bridges and to march on Vaduz.[28] The coup was postponed to Thursday and then to Friday, to take advantage of both Franz Josef's absence in a clinic in Zurich and a long weekend by Hoop in Lugano. At that point things began to go wrong. The advantage of surprise was lost. Rumours and warnings began to trickle in.

Alerted by telephone calls from people in Liechtenstein and the Federal Political Department in Berne, Vogt went to Feldkirch at noon. The authorities there finally admitted that they knew that an "unauthorised initiative" was being planned. Vogt threatened them with personal consequences and pointed out that in Berlin the Reich Government had guaranteed Liechtenstein's independence to Franz Josef. On his return to Vaduz at 5pm Vogt briefed the other members of the Government, asked Berne to alert the Swiss Legation in Berlin, called the chief of police and summoned the VDBL leader, Theodor Schädler, to the Government Building.

On hearing later that evening that threatening movements seemed to be start-ing in Feldkirch, Vogt again contacted the Feldkirch district head, Dr Tschofen, this time by telephone. Tschofen was evasive. Vogt threatened to get in touch directly with the government in Berlin. Tschofen asked him not to do that and promised to do something about the matter. Vogt said that he would come to Feldkirch again to check up, and if he were not home in good time the Swiss Federal Political Department would be in touch with Berlin. With Schädler and his associates Vogt took an uncompromising line. They left the Government

---

[28] The story has for the first time been fully analysed and recounted by Geiger, op. cit., pages 346–408.

Building determined to carry out the putsch, but they knew that Vogt, contrary to their hopes, would not be with them.

Meanwhile VDBL supporters were assembling in Nendeln, Schaan and Triesen, having been told by their leaders that the Germans would cross the border at 10.30pm. In Schaan, the house where about 20 of them had met (now including their leader Schädler) was surrounded by an angry crowd numbering about 100. The mood became ugly. The group in Nendeln (about 40 strong) marched off to rescue them, closely observed by the police. On the frontier, Nazi Party officials took up positions at about 10pm to stop any further advance by the SA, NSKK and Hitler Youth detachments. Vogt arrived in Feldkirch at about that time. He found nobody in authority to speak to, but learnt that the SA had just been told that "the march was off" and saw them drinking in their usual tavern.

Acting independently and on his own initiative, Fr Frommelt forced his way through the crowd at Schaan and into the house, where he argued unsuccessfully with the VDBL leaders. One of them threatened him with Dachau. He then drove to the frontier to see what was happening, stopping at Nendeln to have the conspirators' telephones cut off. Having met the marchers on the way, he asked the mayor of the Schaan commune to do what he could to stop them. The mayor and the Scouts barred the road, armed with sticks, scythes and a fire hydrant. On his way back from the frontier Fr Frommelt halted 100 metres in front of them and, standing quite alone in the dark, waited for the marchers. He stopped them, argued with their leader and asked them to wait while he took the leader into Schaan to reassure him about the wellbeing of those besieged in the house. After that, he said, they should turn back. Vogt appeared by chance at the house on his return from Feldkirch. The march leader saw enough in Schaan to convince him that his column had no chance of success and ordered it to withdraw. At 4am the occupants of the house (now numbering 18) were arrested. The group at Triesen melted away. The night of fear and tension ended.

Of the hundred conspirators, 36 fled to Feldkirch. 22 stayed abroad and many of them fought in the war. Others returned. In all 76 people were questioned; eight were accused of high treason and rebellion. Lesser charges were brought against more than 40 others. The charge of high treason against the five leaders remaining in Vaduz portended problems. It carried the death penalty; it would have created martyrs and caused friction with Germany; and the president of the Liechtenstein criminal court was himself a German judge. The solution found was to release the five from arrest against a written undertaking to leave the country immediately together with their families, to abstain from any political activity affecting Liechtenstein and to return when required for further criminal proceedings. Four did indeed return for trial in 1945.

In other respects, too, it was necessary to play down the affair in public and in private. The attempt had been contrary to Hitler's policy. It is likely that Hitler himself was informed of it through two separate channels (one of them an official on Ribbentrop's staff whom the Liechtenstein Government had been cultivating for some time). It is even possible that Hitler himself gave the order to stop the march.[29] That being so, German face had to be saved and the Germans personally involved had to shift the blame onto others. Liechtenstein itself had nothing to gain from living with a humiliated and resentful Gauleiter of Tyrol-Vorarlberg. So, in a formal note to Berlin, the Liechtenstein Government thanked the Vorarlberg authorities for their part in preventing SA and NSKK units from helping the plans of a "small Liechtenstein group" and asked the German Government to ensure that similar incidents would not be repeated in future. Von Weizsäcker was happy to confirm this explicitly to the Swiss Minister in Berlin. Hoop and Vogt took a similar line with the neighbouring German authorities, including those at Feldkirch and the Volksdeutsche Mittelstelle, in some cases at the Germans' own request. In Berlin, the leader of the Volksdeutsche Mittelstelle, SS Obergruppenführer Lorenz, was brazen enough to boast in a report to Ribbentrop that thanks to his organisation's efforts the foreign policy consequences of the undertaking had been completely averted.[30]

Hitler's disdain for Liechtenstein's insignificance, the existence of the Swiss connection and good luck helped the Principality to escape. Yet matters could easily have gone the other way on that dark March night. Vogt's prompt use of his German contacts and his firmness (the latter unexpected by some but perhaps reinforced by his belief that Berlin was not interested in a coup) saved the day in Feldkirch and Vaduz. Fr Frommelt's moral and physical courage (without knowledge of Berlin's policies) enabled him to dominate the critical situation in Schaan. He kept the two sides apart, whereas violence or bloodshed might have precipitated a Nazi onslaught. The local people's spontaneous rally proved that the bullies were outnumbered. Without all this quick thinking and active opposition in Liechtenstein, the unauthorised invasion might easily have gone ahead and succeeded. If so, it is hard to see how the German Government could have disowned it without looking unacceptably foolish or out of control of its own forces. Switzerland would not have intervened. The world would have accepted the *fait accompli*. The disappearance of Liechtenstein, either immediately or in the near future, would have been noted but quickly forgotten in the international tumult. As Sir Alexander Cadogan minuted to Lord Halifax at the Foreign Office on 22 April 1939, "I am sorry if its annexation should cause inconvenience and alarm in Switzerland, but I really don't see what we could do about it."[31]

---

[29] Geiger, op. cit. pages 365–368
[30] Akten zur deutschen auswärtigen Politik, Serie D, vol. VI, pages 146–147
[31] Respectively, Permanent Under-Secretary of State and Foreign Secretary (FO 371/22969).

The importance of what had happened was instantly recognised in Switzerland. The Neue Zürcher Zeitung, not always well disposed to Liechtenstein, wrote on 27 March 1939, "We can be proud to have a neighbour that despite its smallness is ready, without an army, to sacrifice its last drop of blood for its existence, true to the saying 'God helps those who help themselves' ".[32] Over the next few months, and especially after the outbreak of war, the Swiss Government took some practical steps to help Liechtenstein workers and exports. On 5 July the Liechtenstein Government replied to Berne's note of 30 January and obtained reluctant Swiss acceptance of its naturalisation policy, albeit with restrictions on the extent to which Switzerland would accept or represent its newly naturalised citizens. The remaining credit of one million francs was unblocked on 8 September 1939.

Patriotic Unity

The collapse of the putsch unleashed a mood of fervent patriotism, all the stronger because of the pent-up frustration caused by the politicians' hesitations and intrigues. On 25 March the Liechtenstein Loyal Union ("Heimattreue Vereinigung Liechtenstein"), an anti-Nazi, non-party organisation formed in January 1939, launched a spontaneous petition in support of the sovereignty and independence of Liechtenstein under the Monarchy, the maintenance of the treaty relationship with Switzerland and the renunciation of any other new political or economic orientation. Within one week 95.4% of all eligible voters (men) had signed; a similar collection of women's signatures was made. There could be no stronger sign to Switzerland or Germany. It gave added force to Franz Josef's call for the "serious co-operation" of the parties in his Speech from the Throne at the opening of the new Parliament on 4 April.

The Act of Homage

On 29 May 1939, after High Mass in the parish church at Vaduz, a formal lunch for foreign official guests in the castle and a popular procession through the streets,[33] the new Sovereign Prince swore the oath of loyalty to his people on the Castle Meadow.

In return the people (many thousands of them) swore loyalty to him. In his speech as Parliament President Fr Frommelt said that the Liechtenstein people had survived the era of the Romans, the era of the national migrations, the era of the Thirty Years War and the era of the Great War, and it could therefore be

---

[32] Quoted by Horst Carl, "Liechtenstein und das Dritte Reich", page 441.

[33] In his report of 30 May 1939 to the British Minister at Berne (FO 371/23859) the British Consul-General at Zurich, Mr John Bell, noted that Franz Josef's mother (Princess Elisabeth, born an Austrian Archduchess) showed visible distaste when the German and Italian representatives greeted the procession with Fascist salutes.

expected with certainty that they would stay faithful to their age-old traditions in the future. This was applauded by all the Liechtensteiners present.

The ancient symbolism of this day of dedication and celebration turned into a powerful affirmation of national loyalty and unity.[34]

The Approach of War

On 14 April 1939 President Roosevelt sent an open letter to Hitler and Mussolini calling on them to guarantee that they would not attack a long list of nations, beginning with Finland in the north and ending with Iran in the south. Liechtenstein's inclusion in the list was at least an assurance that its existence was not overlooked.[35] Three months later, on 16 July, Franz Josef II went to Zurich to represent Liechtenstein at the Swiss National Exhibition. This was a great demonstration of solidarity. He was accompanied by members of the Princely Family, Hoop, Fr Frommelt, various members of Parliament, 300 Scouts and 2,300 Liechtensteiners (about one fifth of the population), who travelled in three special trains. The exhibition was intended to boost Swiss unity and morale. It was all the more significant, therefore, that the Swiss speakers emphasised the close links between the two countries and Hoop replied that Liechtenstein intended to stick by this close connection.[36]

Switzerland guaranteed the supply of wartime provisions and included Liechtenstein in its food rationing system. The Parliament and the Prince passed emergency and empowering legislation to keep the country in step with Swiss wartime economic measures. On 30 August Liechtenstein declared the "strictest neutrality" (thus avoiding the mistake of 1914), which Swiss diplomatic missions transmitted to other countries together with the Swiss declaration of neutrality of 31 August. Hitler invaded Poland on 1 September. Swiss military police were posted on the Swiss-Liechtenstein frontier to provide an additional check on transit by foreigners. On 25 March 1940, the anniversary of the attempted coup, while Hitler was preparing to open the western front, Franz Josef II went to the pilgrimage chapel at Dux to commend himself and his country to the Virgin Mary's protection. Well he might.

---

[34] The war caused a rallying to ancient symbolism in several countries. In June 1940 General Guisan proclaimed a policy of military resistance to Swiss officers assembled on the Rütli Meadow, where the oath that founded the Swiss Confederation was sworn in 1291. Stalin was to revert to Tsarist military insignia and reach an accommodation with the Russian Orthodox Church. In 1944 there was a proposal, which George VI rejected, to parade the English Coronation regalia before the British troops as they prepared for D-Day. Liechtenstein, with its Act of Homage, seems to have been first in this field.

[35] FO 371/22970.

[36] FO 371/23859.

THE SECOND WORLD WAR

The full history of Liechtenstein's role during the Second World War has been studied for several years by Dr Peter Geiger, whose comprehensive book on the subject is due to appear in November 2004. An independent historical commission, chaired by Geiger, was established by the Government in 2001 and will report in 2005. The commission's role is to examine whether any assets plundered by the Nazis ended up in Liechtenstein or passed through it; Liechtenstein's policy towards refugees; and production by Liechtenstein industry for the German war effort. Pending Geiger's book and the commission's report, any assessment can only be provisional.

From June 1940 Switzerland and Liechtenstein lost direct contact by land or water with the Allied states. The last indirect land link through Vichy France was cut in November 1942. They depended almost entirely on Germany for coal and iron, imported fertilisers and seeds, machinery, tools and postal communications. They feared unemployment as a possible cause of internal unrest. Switzerland, whose traditional sources of income such as tourism and luxury goods were hard hit, had to live more than ever from its exports of manufactured goods. Both sides in the war needed Swiss war material such as technical instruments, machinery, guns, ammunition, watches and fuses in addition to Swiss financial services. The traditional Swiss good offices and humanitarian services were naturally in demand.

German political and economic pressure was intense. In the summer of 1940 there was a debate in London as to whether it was possible, or even worth trying, to maintain relations with Switzerland. The British Minister in Berne, David Kelly, argued that Switzerland could not be compared with, or treated like, the Vichy regime: it was the oldest and most solidly established democracy in the world. He was, moreover, convinced (not least by General Guisan personally) of its will to resist any attempt at military invasion. The Swiss themselves showed

---

[1] The late Lord Brimelow (Permanent Under-Secretary of State at the Foreign and Commonwealth Office), in conversation with the author, paid tribute to the skill with which the Swiss managed to supply the United Kingdom with important military components despite German blockade measures. See also Sir John Lomax, "The Diplomatic Smuggler" (Arthur Barker, London, 1965) pages 147–160.

that they were keen to continue to trade with the United Kingdom, despite the obstacles.[1] London therefore decided that as long as Switzerland struggled to preserve some degree of independence it should be offered the encouragement of carefully regulated imports.[2]

The Liechtenstein Economy in Wartime

This was the background against which Liechtenstein had to exist from the fall of France in June 1940 until France's liberation in August 1944. The impact on daily life was immediate. Liechtenstein followed all the Swiss rationing and censorship measures and regulations, most of which were applied automatically. Strict food rationing began on 1 November 1939. The German offensive in the West in May 1940 caused the Liechtenstein Government to organise emergency measures for the possible evacuation of the population into the mountains. In October, all households that were able were ordered to keep themselves supplied with the basic vegetables. In November, a complete blackout was imposed during the hours of darkness. In 1941 collections of empty toothpaste and cosmetics tubes were organised and firewood was rationed. The food rations were reduced from 500 to 250 grams of rice, from 750 to 500 grams of flour and from 2 to 1 decilitre of oil. Wednesdays and Fridays became meatless days. In 1942 a tax on "luxuries" was imposed. Food rationing continued until July 1948.

The economy was still in a precarious state, but the country had to be made as self-sufficient as possible. The Inner Canal, although not yet finished, had already increased the area of cultivable land. This was immediately exploited. In November 1940 workbooks were introduced and the unemployed were obliged to report to labour offices. In 1942 compulsory one-year service on the land was introduced for 17-year olds and in 1943 general labour service was started. These measures reduced the insidious economic and psychological effects of unemployment and, in consequence, the potential appeal of pro-Nazi propaganda. A new aliens control agreement with Switzerland in January 1941 opened the Swiss labour market more widely to Liechtenstein workers.

As the war continued, so industry began to grow. In 1939, industry employed 372 persons; in 1940, 477; in 1942, 704 (almost the same number as in 1912); and by 1946, 1,063.[3] The number of apprentices rose from 91 in 1941 to 193 in 1950.[4] Even more important than these figures was the qualitative change. For the first time, Liechtenstein began to have an indigenous, technologically high-quality industry. This began to take off in 1941, when firms in Switzerland were

---

[2] Official History of the Second World War: "The Economic Blockade" by Professor W. N. Medlicott, Vol. I, pages 585–594. "The Ruling Few" by Sir David Kelly (Hollis and Carter, London, 1952) pages 276–278.
[3] Horst Carl, op. cit., page 451 and Adulf Peter Goop, "Liechtenstein Gestern und Heute" (Liechtenstein Verlag, Vaduz, 1973), page 310.
[4] Statistisches Jahrbuch 2001, p. 92.

experiencing a labour shortage owing to the mobilisation of the Swiss Army. The upswing coincided with Hitler's invasion of the Soviet Union.

The companies founded at that time were the Swiss-owned Press und Stanzwerke AG (Presta) at Eschen (which produced empty 20mm cannon shell cases for the Swiss armaments firm Oerlikon Bührle); Hilti Maschinenbau (mechanical engineering, including axle bearing components for tank engines); and Präzisions-Apparatebau (precision tools). Presta employed 300 workers in 1943, and the Germans gave it a direct power link from Feldkirch. Hilti employed 80–100 workers. All of these firms' exports from Liechtenstein had to be approved by the Swiss War Material Department ("Kriegstechnische Abteilung").

The Bergier Report has established that Switzerland's economic relations with the Third Reich did not help to prolong the war.[5] This verdict must also apply to Liechtenstein, in view of the customs union with Switzerland and its own minute size as a production centre.

However, Liechtenstein's post-war reputation was not helped by a couple of far-sighted German figures in the arms industry who took the precaution of settling in Liechtenstein while the going was good. One was Alexander Rahm, the Berlin representative of the Geneva fuse-manufacturing company Tavaro, who discreetly moved to Vaduz in 1942.[6] More spectacular was Rudolf Ruscheweyh, who represented Oerlikon Bührle in Berlin and succeeded in persuading the reluctant German armed forces to buy the company's products after it proved impossible to deliver them to Britain and France in 1940. Having owned a firm which had produced bullet-proof tyres in The Netherlands since 1936, he transferred the patent to a Liechtenstein firm called Patva in 1940. He worked for the German Army arms procurement office in Paris from 1940 to 1943. He exchanged his German diplomatic passport for a Liechtenstein one in 1944 and settled in Schaan. This did not protect him from interrogation by the Allies in 1946.[7]

The Internal Front

A Swiss Federal Council report on anti-democratic activities by Swiss citizens and foreigners between 1939 and 1945, published on 26 January 1946, illustrated the internal and external pressures in Switzerland during the war.[8] National Socialist organisations were first founded in Switzerland in 1932. By 1942 Nazi-

[5] The Swiss Federal Council's statement of 22 March 2002 on the publication of the final report of the Independent Commission of Experts on "Switzerland – Second World War" (the Bergier Report).
[6] "Schweizer Rüstungsindustrie und Kriegsmaterialhandel zur Zeit des Nationalsozialismus", by Peter Hug (published by the Bergier Committee, 2002), p. 721.
[7] His career is outlined by Hug, op. cit., pages 618–624.
[8] FO 371/60841.

style organisations had 25,000 members, including 2,400 members of the Nazi Party itself. Aspiring Swiss Gauleiters were quarrelling among themselves about the future division of the spoils.

The situation in Liechtenstein was similar. The VDBL was re-launched by a new and academically better qualified group of leaders. Its membership and followers never exceeded 500 but it remained a threat until 1942, not least because of support from Germany. On 5 October 1940 there appeared the first number of its newspaper "Umbruch" ("Revolution"), modelled on the German "Stürmer". Its programme was clear: "the ordering of German life and economy in the sense of National Socialism".[9] Like "Der Stürmer", it was violently anti-Semitic. In 1942, for example, it called for Jews in Liechtenstein to be made to wear yellow stars and for work camps to be established for them.[10]

The Liechtenstein government was in no position at that time, any more than the Swiss government, to ban this activity. Instead, it built up the country's moral resistance as best it could. In 1940 it declared 15 August (the Feast of the Assumption and the eve of Franz Josef's birthday) as the National Day. The annual tradition was established of a Mass in Vaduz parish church followed by formal congratulations to the Sovereign Prince by the Government and officials. A non-party "National Movement" continued the work of the Loyal Union of Liechtenstein ("Heimattreue Vereinigung"). Vogt frustrated efforts by the Volksdeutsche Mittelstelle, who thought of him as "our man", to tempt the VU into political co-operation with the VDBL. Fr Frommelt succeeded in keeping Nazism out of the schools and Liechtenstein cultural organisations. The State subsidised the Scouts, despite "Umbruch's" violent criticism of that movement. After the fall of Paris, the Scouts, who represented 67% of the country's organised youth, showed defiance by organising bicycle rides through the whole Principality.

Franz Josef II took on a unifying role within Liechtenstein, above party politics. His public stance was one of diplomatic reticence. He articulated his Government's policy as one of national independence, a continuing close relationship with Switzerland in every way, good neighbourly relations with the Reich and internal peace. On 18 February 1943, at the joint wish of the Government, the Parliament and the two main parties, he extended the Parliament's mandate for an indefinite period under Article 10 of the Constitution (measures for the security and welfare of the state) in order to avert the internal tensions that elections might have produced. His wedding to Countess Georgina (Gina) von Wilczek in Vaduz parish church on 7 March 1943 raised the people's morale amid the gloom of the war. It was seen as a pledge of hope for the future. The Scouts, representing

---

[9] "Liechtenstein 1938–1978", page 54.
[10] JBL Vol. 95, 1998, Peter Geiger, "Am Rande der Brandung", page 64.

the youth of the country, formed the guard of honour. The Prince and his consort were quick to visit every commune and then to pay an official visit to Berne in April 1943.

The External Front

In December 1940 Hoop made a speech in Stuttgart. His tone was superficially friendly, but in keeping with his personal and official views he was careful not to praise the Nazi regime, mention Hitler or make any commitments. The tone, however, was later remembered against him. In 1941 a summer camp for sons of Germans and former Austrians living in Switzerland who belonged to the German Reich Youth ("Reichsdeutsche Jugend", the external arm of the Hitler Youth) was permitted in the alpine area of Steg, away from inhabited areas. It passed almost unnoticed by the Liechtenstein public at the time. In October 1940, meanwhile, Switzerland had allowed the reopening of NSDAP offices, which had been closed after the assassination of the local Nazi leader Wilhelm Gustloff in 1936. Gradually, a better balance was struck in both countries. By December 1942 Berlin was worried enough about Switzerland to be considering ways of combating the anti-German mood in Swiss official circles, the population and the press.[11]

Throughout the war Franz Josef II, Hoop and Vogt kept up their own separate contacts with various personalities in the Reich. Liechtenstein of course had no state diplomatic or intelligence apparatus at its disposal. Hoop withdrew from contacts on German soil in 1941. Vogt had the widest networks within the various Nazi bureaucracies, including the Foreign Office, the SS, the SD and (not least because of his governmental responsibilities for the economy) the local authorities in Vorarlberg including the Gestapo. Franz Josef used him from time to time, for example in his efforts to recover his art collection or to counteract impressions in Berlin that might have threatened Liechtenstein's interests. Vogt undoubtedly operated on his own account as well. He was a Nazi sympathiser. Had the war ended in the Reich's favour, which he expected from 1939 until at least 1942 or 1943, he would have been well placed with the victors. His party, the VU, might then have taken the leading role in Liechtenstein rather than the VDBL. In the event of a German victory he would have favoured an economic, but not a political, Anschluss with the Reich.

The German Foreign Office advised him to cultivate the SS, pointing out that attitudes to Liechtenstein there were not as benign as in the Wilhelmstrasse. Vogt

---

[11] In return for German concessions, the Swiss would have to had to remove General Guisan from office, impose stricter press censorship and permit a Swiss "German-conscious" political movement. These unrealistic proposals were not, it seems, ever put to the Swiss. (GFM 33/12, B004778).

found that even the SS was divided. Some factions wanted a quick Anschluss, while others wanted Liechtenstein to stay independent for their own intelligence and contact-making purposes. Vogt therefore had some room for manoeuvre. One practical effect of his activities was largely to neutralise German support for the extremists in the VDBL, although the constant intrigues never quite died down.[12]

In 1942 the German Foreign Office began to receive anonymous reports about the allegedly pro-Jewish attitude of the Liechtenstein government. In November 1942 Vogt, on a visit to Berlin, found it necessary to contest rumours that Franz Josef was pursuing an anti-German policy. According to Otto von Erdmannsdorff, Head of the Political Department of the German Foreign Office, Vogt argued that the Prince "was certainly no National Socialist but thoroughly German-conscious"; Vogt said that Franz Josef's Habsburg descent might have caused the mistrust existing in "certain German circles". The other, perhaps more personal, purpose of Vogt's visit was to test the attitude of the Reich government to the possible establishment of a Liechtenstein Legation or other representation in Berlin, an idea which he said had not been broached during the State Visit in 1939 for fear of possible objections by Switzerland.[13] He received no answer on the spot.

By early 1943 Hoop felt strong enough to ban the VDBL's paper "Umbruch" for one month on the grounds that it had demanded an immediate Anschluss with the Reich in a bullying manner. The director of Franz Josef's office in Vienna, Josef Martin (a former Lieutenant-Colonel in the Austro-Hungarian Army and a Nazi Party member) told Berlin on 16 February that this decision had been taken during the Prince's absence; the Prince, he said, regretted it and the ban had since been lifted. He added that the Prince intended to visit Berlin in the near future and wished to be received at the Foreign Office.[14] Franz Josef did indeed visit Berlin on 15 July 1943, when he called for half an hour on Baron von Steengracht, von Weizsäcker's successor as State Secretary. Steengracht's record of the meeting indicates that apart from giving some elementary background information about the Liechtenstein economy and the relationship with Switzerland,

---

[12] The relations of Alois Vogt (1906–1988) with Nazi Germany, including with the intelligence authorities and the Gestapo, have been analysed by Jürgen Schremser. ("Der einzige Mann, der die Sache auf sich nehmen könnte", JBL Vol. 98, 1999, pages 49–108.). After the war, when interrogated by the Swiss security police, this enigmatic man tried to put those relations in the best possible light as defensive tactics. Whatever his ultimate loyalties, he made a provable contribution to Liechtenstein's national interests on several occasions. But the Nazis also exploited the relationship.

[13] GFM 33/284, 192037–192038. The idea of a legation in Berlin was however considered in Liechtenstein circles in 1939, not least as a way of gaining further token recognition of independence by the German side. It was raised informally with German contacts. It got nowhere. (Geiger, op. cit., Vol 2, pages 340–342.)

[14] GFM 33/284, 192039. Martin added that the pro-German sentiments of the Liechtenstein population were proved by the fact that 4% (!) of eligible males had volunteered for service in the German armed forces.

Franz Josef confined himself to listening to Steengracht's account of the political and military situation.[15] There was no mention by either side of a legation or of "Umbruch", even though a week previously the Liechtenstein Government had again banned "Umbruch", this time until further notice, ostensibly because of its criticism of Switzerland and its Government.[16] On 27 June 1944 Vogt was again in Berlin, this time to say that he had spoken out in Vaduz against plans to re-establish a legation in Berne, on the grounds that it would look one-sided not to have a legation in Berlin as well. He and von Erdmannsdorff agreed (sensibly enough, in the circumstances) that the question of a Berlin legation had better be postponed until the end of the war.[17]

Relations with Switzerland and the Allies

Anxiety about Liechtenstein among the Swiss military never completely died down during the war. A secret inter-departmental conference in Berne debated the matter on 24 March 1943.[18] The military and the police expressed the usual fears about the alleged passivity of the Government, the paucity of the police and the mobility of the work force (250–300 Liechtensteiners working in the Reich, 120–150 in Switzerland and 40–50 Reich citizens working in Liechtenstein). There was concern about illegal frontier crossings (not numerous, but some "dubious elements" were involved). The economic ties with Germany were close and the dynasty and the Government were considered very dependent on the Reich. Sentences for espionage were too light in Liechtenstein.[19] There were 300 "unreliables" in the country. There was espionage by foreign officials at Buchs railway station. Dr Stucki, Head of the Foreign Affairs Division, countered these arguments by pointing out that the Liechtenstein Government was not afraid of the National Socialist minority and had shown courage in banning its newspaper. But Liechtenstein, he said, had to manoeuvre since its neutrality was not recognised by the great powers (i.e. in the same way as Switzerland's). The presence of foreign (i.e. German) officials was to be expected at an international railway station. The conference concluded that better counter-espionage coordination was needed on the Swiss side, and it agreed on measures for that purpose. There was no proposal for a démarche to the Liechtenstein Government. In a subsequent message to the Swiss Army Command, the Foreign Affairs Division said that nothing should be done which would make Liechtenstein's political and economic position more difficult.

[15] GFM 33/284, 192045–192047.
[16] Despite the ban it made a final appearance on 19 February 1944, when it was promptly confiscated.
[17] GFM 33/284, 192048.
[18] Swiss Diplomatic Documents Vol. 14 No. 413.
[19] During the war, the Swiss authorities passed 33 death sentences for military treason, on 22 Swiss citizens, 7 Germans, 3 Liechtensteiners and 1 Frenchman. Of these, one Liechtensteiner was executed. (Peter Geiger, "Landesverrat", JBL Vol. 98, 1999, pages 109–142.)

During the second half of the war Franz Josef II cultivated close relations with the British Legation in Berne.[20] He mentioned more than once to the British Minister, Mr Clifford Norton, his feeling that the Swiss Federal Political Department did not always give Liechtenstein's affairs the prompt attention that they merited; he would have liked to be able to deal direct with foreign legations, for instance on commercial or business matters. Norton advised him to speak to M. Pilet-Golaz, the Head (Minister) of the Department, which he did. Pilet-Golaz later told Norton that he had no objection to the Liechtenstein Government dealing direct with foreign missions on minor matters, but he did not wish the heads of mission in Berne to feel that they were accredited to Liechtenstein.[21]

A paper sent by Franz Josef to Pilet-Golaz to summarise and confirm the line that he had taken during a personal discussion on 18 August 1943 gives a clearer indication of his thinking.[22] Franz Josef noted that after the war America and Britain would have the main say in world affairs. In America, Liechtensteiners' interests were not always being taken into account in accordance with Liechtenstein's wishes. It was possible that the interests of both the country and its citizens might suffer severe disadvantages. No other country in the world had (proportionately) such extensive holdings abroad as Liechtenstein. His own interests and those of his House might be affected. He therefore wanted to establish direct contact with the two governments in good time through their official representatives, with Pilet-Golaz's agreement. He already knew personally their Ministers and Consuls-General in Switzerland. Franz Josef emphasised that he would not touch on Liechtenstein-Swiss relations in his discussions with them. He would keep Switzerland informed of his exchanges, "which will come always from me according to the Constitution". Franz Josef represents Pilet-Golaz as having agreed in principle to his request.

The paper illustrates a recurring constitutional and political dilemma in Liechtenstein. Franz Josef was keen to exert more influence over foreign affairs. Taking the long view, he was anxious to assert his country's independence and to anticipate and if possible influence events that were bound to have an important effect on his country and family. His Government on the other hand had established working channels with Switzerland and Germany that met the country's immediate needs. They were reluctant to embark on more far-reaching enterprises.

In December 1944 the Liechtenstein Legation in Berne was reopened at Franz Josef's personal decision under the charge of his younger brother Prince Heinrich, in the teeth of united opposition from Government and Parliament. The tussle

---

[20] FO 371/49709. The Legation's Leading Personalities Report for 1945.
[21] FO 371/49709. Despatch of 26 January 1945 from Norton to the Foreign Secretary, Anthony Eden.
[22] Swiss Diplomatic Documents, Vol. 14, No. 410. It is not clear whether this meeting preceded or followed the conversations reported by Norton.

over this matter contributed perhaps more than anything else to Hoop's resignation in the following year. It was Hoop, after all, who had closed the legation in 1933. Franz Josef and the Government reached an understanding that the existing close and informal working arrangements between Vaduz and the Swiss federal and cantonal authorities would continue, while the legation would concern itself with broader foreign policy and diplomatic questions. Franz Josef paid personally for the legation until August 1952, when the Liechtenstein state took over responsibility for its costs and expenses. Successive Liechtenstein Ministers and (since 1969) Ambassadors to Berne have to date always been members of the Princely House.

Liechtenstein's Policy towards Refugees

In accordance with successive bilateral agreements, Liechtenstein's immigration and refugee policies were those of Switzerland and were carried out by Swiss border guards. Switzerland's policies before and during the Second World War have been examined in detail by the Bergier Commission.[23] The Liechtenstein aspects, as noted above, are still being studied.

Between 1920 and 1941 Switzerland, which then had a population of 4.1 millions, reduced its foreign component from 10.4% to 5.2%.[24] This policy was prompted by the wish to protect jobs during the Great Depression, fear of being flooded by foreigners, worry that foreign-born immigrants might not share the native Swiss loyalty to national security and concern that they might become an economic burden, especially in wartime. Switzerland was in principle ready enough to grant asylum to the oppressed, but saw itself as a transit country. Like the United Kingdom,[25] it did not contemplate a large permanent presence of refugees.

From 1933 onwards the growing threats against Jews and other minorities, violence, expropriation and murder led to increasing emigration from Germany. This turned into a flood after the Nuremberg Laws of 1935, the annexation of Austria in March 1938, the "Reichskristallnacht" on 9/10 November 1938 and the aggression against Czechoslovakia in 1938–1939. By September 1939 some 350,000 people had escaped. Few, if any, countries were willing to open their gates widely to these dispossessed people. In consequence Switzerland's self-envisaged role as a transit station was not workable. President Roosevelt's conference on Austrian and German refugees at Evian in July 1938 did not lead to a liberalisation of US immigration laws. In 1939 Belgium took 12,000 Jewish refugees and Switzerland

---

[23] "Switzerland and Refugees in the Nazi Era", Berne, 1999.
[24] Its current foreign population stands at more than 18%.
[25] "Refugees in an Age of Genocide", Kushner and Knox (Frank Cass, 2001), page 128.

10,000. In that year, there were 14,649 refugees from Germany, Austria and Czechoslovakia in the United Kingdom[26] (0.03% of the population).

By 1945 the Nazi regime had murdered some six million Jews and several hundred thousand gypsies. Information about their fate began to reach the West in the summer of 1941. Meanwhile, in January 1942 the Nazi regime finally decided on the administrative machinery for the total physical destruction of the Jews By February 1942 over two million Soviet prisoners had perished.[27] Such was the scale of the growing massacre across Europe.

From March 1938 Swiss border controls became stricter in the face of the Nazis' wish to expel as many Jews as they could. This was the origin of the "J" stamp, which was introduced at Switzerland's request and which was binding for Liechtenstein also. German citizens continued to be allowed to enter Switzerland without visas (as since 1926), except for those whose passports were marked "J". In their case, the German authorities were to prevent them from entering unless the passports showed entitlement to enter Swiss territory which had been granted by the Swiss authorities themselves. (The Swiss Federal President Villiger formally apologised for the J stamp in 1995.) The Swiss borders were completely closed to refugees from August 1942 until September 1943, when there was some relaxation. From July 1944 the Swiss decreed that all in mortal danger (among whom Jews were reckoned), but not Nazis, Fascists and collaborators, were to be accepted.

There are some 24,500 documented cases of refugees being turned away from the Swiss frontiers between January 1940 and May 1945; the true figure was no doubt higher. During the war nearly 170,000 persons (over 4% of the Swiss population) were admitted. Nearly 104,000 of these were military personnel. Some 55,000 civilian refugees were admitted, of whom more than 21,000 were Jewish. Temporary asylum was given to more than 126,000 other adults and children.[28]

Our knowledge of what happened at the frontier between Liechtenstein and post-Anschluss Austria will depend on the forthcoming studies. So far as pre-war attitudes to refugees were concerned, the Liechtenstein authorities had their own worries about jobs and possible burdens on the economy. Even more than Switzerland, they had to reckon with both possible Nazi German reactions and domestic opinion should there be a marked increase in numbers. The restrictions on longer- and shorter-term foreign residents became tighter. Some were expelled. Other potential residents were refused entry. Preference was given to

---

[26] Whitaker's Almanac for 1940, page 723.

[27] "Switzerland and Refugees in the Nazi Era", p. 12 et seq.

[28] The United Kingdom accepted about 55,000 refugees from Nazism in Germany, Austria and Czechoslovakia between 1933 and 1939; 60,000 non-military European refugees between 1940 and 1943; and between 2,000 and 3,000 children from concentration camps between 1945 and 1946 ("Refugees in an Age of Genocide", page 184 and map).

those who could bring economic benefit to the country. But there were also instances of turning a blind eye, out of humanity, just as happened with Swiss officials. A count of foreign Jews in November 1938 showed that there were 118 in the country (about 1% of the population). In May 1940 the number was much the same[29] and it remained steady throughout the war. As in Switzerland there were people in Liechtenstein willing to help refugees to cross the frontier from the Reich either as individuals or in organised groups, sometimes from humanitarian, sometimes from mercenary motives. They used quiet roads in the Mauren area or sometimes rough mountain tracks. Once in Liechtenstein the refugees would usually be taken by taxi to Switzerland, to chance their luck with the authorities there.

So far as naturalisation policy was concerned, Liechtenstein was not bound by treaty with Switzerland. However, Switzerland was not satisfied with Liechtenstein's policy and from 1940 onwards there was an understanding with Switzerland that Liechtenstein would naturalise only a handful of people. The number of naturalisations fell considerably during and after the war.

Liechtenstein's naturalisation policy was established in the 1920s. It was both restrictive in character and profitable to a state which had few other resources. Naturalisations continued in the changed circumstances after 1933. Could more have been done for those who were less privileged? Certainly, some people were allowed to stay in Liechtenstein without going through this costly process. What can be said is that the naturalisations that did take place during the 1930s and 1940s saved the lives of some hundreds of people, mostly Jews, who might otherwise have perished.[30] To be stateless and paperless in the Europe of the time was to lose all official protection, the power to travel legally and, in too many countries, one's liberty or life.

---

[29] Geiger, op.cit., Vol 2, pages 430 and 439.
[30] Geiger, op. cit., Vol. 2, pages 102–103. In 1938 the United Kingdom issued new grants of naturalisation to 293 German and 53 Austrian citizens, in 1939 to 390 and 129 respectively and in 1940 (1 January–16 September) to 200 and 34 respectively (Whitaker's Almanac for 1942, page 604).

THE END OF THE WAR

The German defeat at Stalingrad in February 1943 and the capitulation of Italy in September pointed to Hitler's inexorable defeat. The approaching end of the war brought new uncertainties and dangers. There were strong reports that Nazi forces would fight to the last in an Alpine redoubt. No-one could predict how they might lash out, nor the consequences of the impending chaos in Europe. The Swiss city of Schaffhausen was badly damaged by an accidental American air attack in April 1944. Stein am Rhein, and even a village deep inside the Grisons, suffered in February 1945. So did Zurich and Basel in March 1945. Feldkirch, just inside Austria, was bombed by US aircraft in October 1943 with the loss of almost 170 lives. In fact, Feldkirch had not been the intended target; but the raid made Liechtenstein feel vulnerable, not least because of the Presta factory.[1]

In December 1944 William Kenmore, now a captain in Special Operations Executive, reappeared in Liechtenstein. His mission was to study ways of smuggling people, money and objects into and out of the Reich across the Swiss and Liechtenstein frontiers. He reported favourably on the possibilities. These seem not to have been followed up, since there was no German last stand in the Alps and the end of the war came more quickly than expected. However, when Kenmore called on Hoop he found him worried about the future attitude of the victorious Allies to Liechtenstein. Hoop said that Liechtenstein would open its books to the Commercial Counsellor of the British Legation at Berne so that he could see whether the Germans had been hiding money in the country and, if so, what the sums were and who had been involved. Kenmore reported to London that the government's co-operation could be counted on, if only for reasons of self-interest.[2]

It seems that Liechtenstein did co-operate. A Berne Legation telegram of 10

---

[1] One curious by-product of the general uncertainty was a reported plan by Hitler to kidnap Pope Pius XII "for his own safety" in the face of the Allied advance on Rome in the autumn of 1943 and to intern him according to the military situation either in Germany or in neutral Liechtenstein. The Waffen SS General Karl Wolff, who was ordered to plan the operation, said after the war that he had persuaded Hitler that it was unworkable. (Horst Carl, "Liechtenstein und das Dritte Reich", pages 447–448.)
[2] HS6/911, /910 and /909.

July 1945 reported that a full list of holding companies in Liechtenstein had been sent to London.[3]

The Allies were, nevertheless, clear about Liechtenstein's status. The draft of Operation Freeborn, for the liberation of Austria, said, "Liechtenstein is an independent state whose neutrality has been respected by all belligerents throughout the war". The plan provided for Allied travel controls on the Liechtenstein-Austrian frontier as well as on the Swiss-Austrian frontier in order to avoid any complications with Switzerland.[4]

The Rescue of the Prince's Art Collection

In March 1945 the surviving members of the Liechtenstein family were assembled in the ruins of Vienna and delivered safely to Vaduz after a road journey of fourteen days across Austria.

More complex, and far more prolonged, was the operation to save the Princely collections. After the annexation of Austria the Germans declared the whole gallery in Vienna to contain "inalienable works of art". The art collection was thus in effect nationalised and confined to Reich territory. The Nazis ignored objections that their law was not applicable to the private property of a foreign head of state. During the Sudeten crisis the collection was stored in the palace cellars in case the Czechoslovaks bombarded Vienna. (A reminder of the strength of the Czechoslovak armed forces before Munich.)

When war broke out the Nazi authorities refused every request to have the collections moved to Vaduz. The print and porcelain collections, the tapestries, furniture and archives were stored in various castles. The pictures went to Gaming Monastery in Lower Austria alongside the collection from the Vienna Kunsthistorisches Museum. By the end of 1942 the collections had been distributed between five centres: Gaming, Feldsberg, Eisgrub, the Garden Palais in Vienna and the palace beneath the old Liechtenstein Castle outside the city. Even the baroque stucco ornamentation of the City and Garden Palaces was dismantled and stored safely. The problem was, to guess from what side and by whom the Reich would be invaded. As a result, the collections were in constant movement across Austria. Their curator, Gustav Wilhelm, wisely declined a suggestion that they should be stored alongside Hitler's collection.

From the autumn of 1943 Wilhelm began surreptitiously to take the smaller items to Vaduz. In June 1944 Baldur von Schirach, Gauleiter and Reich

---

[3] Berne telegram No. 508 ARFAR. (FO 371/49709) Unfortunately, neither the list nor any other relevant material seems to have been preserved in London.

[4] FO 1020/288. Paragraph 13 (f) of the fourth draft, issued under the name of Field Marshal Alexander on 22 February 1945. The draft repeated the common error that Switzerland conducted Liechtenstein's foreign affairs.

1. Karl von Liechtenstein (1569–1627).

2. Johann (Hans) Adam I Andreas (1657–1712). Portrait by Peter van Roy.

3. Josef Wenzel (1696–1772). Portrait by Hyacinthe Rigaud.

4. Johann Josef I (1760–1836). Portrait by Johann Baptist Lampi, about 1816.

5. Josef Wenzel in the Golden Coach. Detail of painting by Martin van Meytens of the entry of Isabella of Parma into Vienna, 1760.

6. Johann II (1840–1929), "The Good". Portrait by John Quincy Adams.

7. Franz I (1853–1938). Portrait by Victor Scharf.

8. Eisgrub (Lednice), in Moravia (the Czech Republic). Remodelled in the English Gothic style by Alois II (1796–1858).

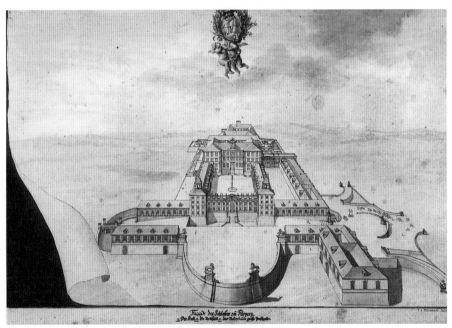

9. Feldsberg (Valtice), in Moravia.

10. Franz Josef II (1906–1989).

11. Hans-Adam II (born 1945, Sovereign Prince since 1989).

12. Private visit by Queen Elizabeth II and the Duke of Edinburgh to Liechtenstein in May 1980. Here shown with Franz Josef II (between them) and Princess Gina (left).

13. Visit by Pope John Paul II to Liechtenstein on 8 September 1985. Behind him are Princess Gina and Franz Josef II.

14. Hereditary Prince Alois and Princess Sophie with their children (from left to right) Nikolaus, Josef Wenzel, Marie Caroline and Georg, 2000.

15. The National Day celebrations, 15 August. Procession to the Castle Meadow.

16. Vaduz Castle.

Commissioner for Vienna, agreed to Franz Josef's request that the entire collection should be shipped to Vaduz; but he was over-ruled from Berlin. Franz Josef and Vogt used their various German contacts, but the Nazi refusals were repeated to the end. Gradually a large part of the collections was concentrated at Count Wilczek's Schloss Moosham, near Salzburg. From August 1944 Franz Josef began discreetly to take pictures and tapestries to Vaduz from Sternberg, Feldsberg and Eisgrub in his car. Eventually it became possible, in the growing chaos, to use some Reichsbahn and Swiss railway wagons to transport the bigger items, including even Josef Wenzel's Golden Coach, from Feldsberg. Wine, cigarettes and plenty of guile helped. So did the fact that the Austrian provincial railway staff knew that Schaan was a station on the Reichsbahn but not that it was in a foreign country. The items from Gaming arrived in mid-February 1945 and the very last consignment, from nearby Reichenau, on 19 April, six days after the fall of Vienna.

By no means everything was rescued, but all the major items were brought to safety. Without the dedication and ingenuity of the relatively few people involved, and above all of Gustav Wilhelm, one of the world's greatest private collections of masterpieces might now be dispersed in ashes or adorning the walls of Russian museums.[5]

Tension on the Frontier

Nazi power held out on the Liechtenstein frontier until the very last. It was not until the end of April 1945 that French troops approached Vorarlberg. The battle for Bregenz began on 1 May. German troops withdrew from the Liechtenstein frontier on 3 May but sporadic fighting continued until 4–5 May. The occupation of Vorarlberg was completed only on 7 May, the eve of VE Day.

In August 1943 the Liechtenstein Government increased to 50 the auxiliary police force established in 1939 to help the Swiss border guards. The Swiss authorities' position was unchanged: their border guards would be allowed to respond to requests from the Liechtenstein police for help against violent intrusions by gangs, but in the case of military attack or invasion they would withdraw to the Swiss frontier. The Federal Council confirmed this position on 4 January 1945 after reviewing the possibility that German operations in defence of the Alpine redoubt might spread into Liechtenstein territory. In mid-February the Liechtenstein Government felt worried enough to ask Berne for the presence of Swiss armed forces on the former Austrian frontier. The Swiss Foreign Affairs Division's reply was evasive. When this was reported to the Federal Military Department,

---

[5] The story is told in detail (but posthumously) from Wilhelm's diary notes, in JBL, Vol. 95 (1998), pages 5–48.

the latter rebuked the Division for possibly having left Liechtenstein with illusions: in no circumstances would Swiss armed forces get involved in armed resistance outside Swiss territory, and the Liechtenstein Government must be left in no doubt about the matter.[6] The message was duly conveyed.[7]

German Assets

Article VI of the Final Act of the Bretton Woods Conference in July 1944 called on neutral states to take immediate measures to prevent the transfer of enemy assets to their territories. The Allies set up the "Safehaven" programme to deprive the enemy of his assets abroad. After negotiations with British and American representatives in Berne in February 1945, the Federal Council blocked German assets in Switzerland on 16 February. On 8 March the Federal Council signed an agreement with the Allied governments which, *inter alia*, committed it to take measures to ensure that Swiss territory should not be used as a cache for looted assets and to conduct a census of German assets in Switzerland. Negotiations on the liquidation of German assets in Switzerland began in Washington on 18 March 1946 and an agreement was signed on 25 May 1946.[8]

By agreement with Vaduz, the Swiss Government represented Liechtenstein in all these dealings and Liechtenstein's territory was covered by them.[9] The Swiss themselves had to overcome a number of technical difficulties in organising a census of assets.[10] The formidable Dr Stucki had to put great pressure on the Liechtenstein Government, including threatening suspension of the Customs Treaty, before Liechtenstein could be brought to agree.[11] In the political and military tension of the time the Liechtenstein Government feared that the blockage of assets might provoke armed revenge by the Germans; hence the anxious but vain request for Swiss military protection immediately after the decree of 16 February. Franz Josef wanted the Allies to be asked to guarantee compensation for any damage done by the Germans, but Hoop and Vogt thought that this would not be negotiable.

The Forcing of the Floodgates

On 22 April 1945 the Swiss closed the Rhine Valley frontier. On the following

---

[6] Swiss Diplomatic Documents, Vol. 15, No. 375. Memorandum of 22 February 1945 from Federal Councillor Kobelt (Head of the Federal Military Department) to Federal Councillor Petitpierre (Head of the Federal Political Department.) This thunderous message incorporated the views of General Guisan.

[7] FO 371/49709. Norton's telegram No. 331 from Berne, reporting a conversation with Stucki on 23 February 1945.

[8] FCO History Note No. 11, second edition, January 1997. "Nazi Gold: Information from the British Archives".

[9] Swiss Diplomatic Documents, Vol. 15, Nos. 367 and 391.

[10] Swiss Diplomatic Documents, Vol. 15, No. 360. Note of a Federal Council discussion on 9 February 1945.

[11] Peter Geiger, "Am Rande der Brandung", JBL, Vol. 95, page 56

day the Liechtenstein frontier with Austria was blocked with 10,000 reels of barbed wire in a strip five metres wide. 150 Swiss frontier guards were now on duty in Liechtenstein. In the first months of 1945 some 27,000 refugees passed through the Swiss frontier post at St Margrethen. Between 25 April and 2 May 7,369 people (the equivalent of 60% of the then population of the Principality) passed through the Liechtenstein frontier post at Schaanwald[12]. Most of them were people released or escaped from forced labour, prisoner of war and concentration camps. The majority were sent on to Switzerland. Moved by their suffering, Princess Gina established the Liechtenstein Red Cross on 30 April and took an active and practical part in its work. The Scouts and Guides built and serviced soup kitchens for the refugees. The situation was still so uncertain that as late as 3 May the Government announced emergency and evacuation measures in case of an armed invasion.

A military invasion did indeed seem imminent on the night of 2/3 May, when a column of 462 armed but exhausted Russian soldiers, 30 women and two children, the remains of the First Russian National Army of the German Wehrmacht, forced its way through the wire at a closed frontier post at Schellenberg. After a warning shot fired by a Swiss frontier guard, they laid down their arms and were interned. They were accompanied by the Russian Grand Duke Vladimir,[13] who had recently come across them by chance after his release from German internment at Sigmaringen, and the Austrian Archduke Albrecht. Franz Josef received the Grand Duke at the Castle in Vaduz and then ensured his safe return to Austria. The other Russians remained in Liechtenstein, to become the object of difficult negotiations. None was sent to the Soviet Union by force (pages 129–132 below).

On 8 May the church bells announced the end of the war. In his Speech from the Throne on 12 May Franz Josef ascribed Liechtenstein's preservation to the loyalty of the great majority of the people and to the relations with Switzerland, "which can never be forgotten and which in the eyes of all of us have become indissoluble". He did not omit to go to the pilgrimage chapel at Dux to return thanks.

---

[12] Geiger, "Am Rande der Brandung", page 60, gives a figure of about 10,000 for the period 25 April–3 May.
[13] Vladimir Kirillovich Romanov (1917–1992), Head of the Russian Imperial House from 1938 until his death. Buried at St Petersburg.

THE AFTERMATH OF WAR

Liechtenstein ended the Second World War in much better condition than the First. Its neutrality and independence were not disputed (except by Czechoslovakia, for its own reasons). The population was adequately nourished. A manufacturing base and a good infrastructure existed. Although the political pressures before and during the Second World War had been much more vicious than during and after the First, the 1921 Constitution had stood the test despite being not yet 25 years old. The rule of law and democratic principles had been maintained against all the odds.

Post-War Politics

The first requirement was to return to normal political life as soon as possible. Despite the fighting in nearby Austria and Germany, parliamentary elections were held on 29 April 1945. For the first time the proportional system was used. The results were identical to those of the uncontested elections of 1939: eight seats for the FBP, seven for the VU. At Franz Josef's wish the parties continued to govern in coalition.

There was a vocal movement for reprisals against the VDBL. On 21 May, the day when Franz Josef gave thanks in the chapel at Dux, mock gallows were erected in Schaan. The houses of the VDBL's leading members were daubed with swastikas and they were named as traitors in placards which read, "Now it's *our* turn to make demands". In 1946 the trials of the 1939 putsch leaders were resumed. Of those who returned, three were sentenced to 5 years of imprisonment, one to 2½ years and three to lesser terms. Five were acquitted. The leader of the VDBL, Dr Alfons Goop, took upon himself entire responsibility for its newspaper "Umbruch" and was imprisoned accordingly. The editorial staff and their activist leader, the engineer Martin Hilti, went free. No doubt the sentences could have been harsher and more people could have been tried. Personal memories lingered long in the villages and in the Castle. But, after twenty-five years of party strife and thirteen years of nerve-racking danger, there seems to have been a mood not so much of reconciliation as of determination not to relapse into internal conflict. In 1949 a new law for the protection of the State was enacted. This not only brought together existing provisions against espionage and the wearing of party uniforms but also prohibited service in foreign armed forces, which had not previously been an offence.

Directly after the war, a campaign against Liechtenstein was started in parts of the Swiss and British press. On 3 July 1945 the London "Daily Telegraph" printed what looks like a carefully briefed report under the headline "Trouble in Nazis' Paradise. Clean-up Demand in Liechtenstein. Hunted Men's Life of Luxury." It said that during the war Liechtenstein had been a centre of Axis espionage and a useful auxiliary to the German military effort. It was still a haven for profiteers, a refuge for Nazis and a hiding place for German funds. It alleged that most of the Germans whose accounts had been blocked on 16 March had been warned two days beforehand, possibly with official connivance. The names of some individual Liechtensteiners and Germans were mentioned, including Hoop, Vogt and Ruscheweyh. Among the cases cited was that of Hermann Sieger, curator of the Liechtenstein Postal Museum, philatelic adviser to the Government for many years and a prominent Nazi official in Württemberg. According to the report, he had returned to Liechtenstein from Germany and Prince Heinrich had used his personal influence to have him expelled.[1]

Sieger had in fact rendered great service to the Liechtenstein philatelic industry for many years and had also been Hoop's main link-man in Germany. Hoop may have felt that Liechtenstein owed him a debt. However, his attempted return was damaging and unwelcome. Franz Josef, much though he appreciated Hoop's achievements before and during the war, had for some time been convinced that in the new circumstances a complete change of government was needed.[2] The question of the Berne legation had in any case been causing friction for some months. He confronted Hoop about Sieger. Hoop resigned on 20 July together with the entire government. A new coalition was formed under Alexander Frick (FBP), a former tax official and Chief Scout. Fourteen undesirable foreigners were expelled, with permission given to take their property. Others outside the country were forbidden to return.

The Russians in Liechtenstein

The story of the handing over of more than two million Russians, Ukrainians, Cossacks and others by the Western Allies to the Soviet Union between 1944 and 1947 has been told by Nikolai Tolstoy in "Victims of Yalta". The events in Liechtenstein are recounted there in pages 489–497[3]. They have also been analysed

---

[1] FO 371/49709
[2] FO 371/49709. Despatch of 17 September 1945 from Clifford Norton (Berne) to the Foreign Secretary (Ernest Bevin), reporting a conversation with Prince Franz Josef on 13 September 1945.
[3] Revised and updated Corgi Books edition, 1979.

in detail by, among others, Claus Grimm,[4] Henning von Vogelsang[5] and Peter Geiger and Manfred Schlapp.[6]

When Hitler invaded the Soviet Union on 22 June 1941 his forces were greeted by some as liberators. Stalin's regime, with its collectivisation, famines, purges, destruction of churches and general climate of terror, had given many people good cause to detest it. For three centuries the Germans had been regarded in Russia as an advanced and cultured people, efficient (if sometimes grating a bit on the Russian mentality) and as having done much to develop the country. Soviet propaganda criticised the Hitler regime (at least, until the Ribbentrop-Molotov pact), but experience had taught most Soviet citizens to be sceptical about their own authorities' propaganda. When the invasion came, hundreds of thousands of deserters and prisoners of war were willing enough to fight against Stalin. These people discovered that the new Germans were different from the old. They found themselves caught between two tyrannies. Luckily for the Allies, Hitler's racial theories and his plans to exploit the conquered territories prevented him from making much use of this potent weapon.

Of the millions of Soviet citizens at Hitler's disposal, labour camps and concentration camps swallowed up many. The Nazi regime allowed the largest anti-Soviet force, General Vlasov's Russian Liberation Army, to exist only on paper until 1945. A quite separate unit was the German Wehrmacht's Special Division R (for "Russia") under the White Russian émigré and German army intelligence officer Count Boris Smyslovsky, who latterly used "Holmston" as a cover name. He was the first Russian officer to be allowed to form a Russian unit for operations on the Eastern Front. It started as a training unit but grew from one to twelve battalions. 85% of it consisted of prisoners of war and deserters. The officers were a mixture of White Russian émigrés and former Red Army personnel. It was used for intelligence and anti-partisan activities and had links with anti-Soviet partisans fighting in the rear of the Red Army. Smyslovsky himself maintained that Russia could be liberated only with foreign help. In December 1943 he was arrested by the SS Security Service and his division was dissolved, but he and the division were rehabilitated in April 1944. A year later, he was a major-general in command of the "First Russian National Army", the remains of which he led in a desperate march south, keeping between and ahead of the advancing American and French forces. A Swiss journalist in Warsaw had advised him in about 1943 to make for neutral Liechtenstein in case of need. This he did, keeping his "army's" destination secret until the last moment. Once arrived, he requested and was granted asylum.

---

[4] JBL Vol. 71, 1971, pages 43–100.
[5] "Kriegsende – in Liechtenstein". (Herderbücherei, 1985)
[6] "Russen in Liechtenstein 1945–1948". (Vaduz and Chronos Verlag, Zurich, 1996)

The Swiss, who had 9,000 Russians of their own to deal with, refused to accept Smyslovsky's force. On 18 May the Liechtenstein Government formally dissolved it as a military unit and, after five weeks' quarantine, those who wished were allowed to do paid work on the land. In that small country, people in distress soon become known as individuals rather than as faceless categories. Personal sympathies began to develop. Nevertheless, the Russians were a burden. Their numbers equalled more than 4% of the population of 12,141. Food and accommodation cost 30,000 francs a month, against an annual state budget of some 2.5 million francs. Policing their camps consumed most of the manpower of the auxiliary police. Concerned about this, and also about the possibility of international complications, Franz Josef told his government at the end of June that they must negotiate. For some time Liechtenstein, like Switzerland, put pressure on the interned Russians to leave for "repatriation" to the Soviet Union, but compulsion was never used.

From 14 August 1945 a succession of Soviet delegations came to Liechtenstein to persuade the interned Russians to return voluntarily. Many did so; little was heard from them again. By the end of August the Soviet army and NKVD officers were losing patience with the remaining interned Russians and with the two governments. By this time also news was seeping in of the shootings of Vlasov's men in Bohemia, the forced repatriations of Russian prisoners by British and US forces and the despairing suicides of many. When the Liechtenstein internees were summoned to a meeting in the Vaduz gymnasium on 30 August many of them feared that their turn had come. The Bishop of Chur and the International Committee of the Red Cross appealed against any forced repatriation. The Swiss Government told a Soviet delegation in Berne on 31 August that they would not help to repatriate "their" Russians by force; the Government and Parliament in Vaduz followed suit on 3 September. This led to a Soviet hint that "Liechtenstein can be glad that Soviet troops are not on its border, otherwise there would be order" and to a suggestion that a Swiss battalion or the arming of the Liechtenstein population might finish the job. The rations, they said, should be reduced; the only reason why the internees were refusing to return was that they were eating too well. The Soviet delegation demanded that Smyslovsky and his staff should be handed over as war criminals, but refused Liechtenstein's request for evidence on the grounds that it was a purely Russian affair. The Soviet Government, they threatened, would take measures (unspecified) against the Liechtenstein Government.

The pressure continued into 1946. Successive Soviet delegations made themselves steadily more unpopular in the country. In 1947 a solution was found: Argentina agreed to take the remaining internees. Over 100 travelled there at a cost to the Liechtenstein government of 160,352 francs. The Government took this decision not knowing where it was going to find the money.

The whole episode cost Liechtenstein 449,298 francs (20% of one year's budget at the time). There was no expectation that the country would ever see that money again. As it happened, the Federal German Government reimbursed it in 1956 as part of its post-war financial settlement with Switzerland. For Franz Josef personally the affair brought considerable risks since the fate of his properties in Czechoslovakia was in the balance and his properties in Austria were in the Soviet zone of occupation. To some Liechtensteiners the story has become a national legend; others have pointed to Liechtenstein's manoeuvrings in the matter. It is fair to say that by showing compassion and by sticking to the principle of refusing forced expulsion the authorities and people of Liechtenstein saved 494 people from summary repatriation in May 1945, with all its likely consequences. In the end they saved the lives of the 134 Russians, including 20 women, who refused to leave voluntarily.

The Liechtenstein Properties in Czechoslovakia

If decisions at Yalta forced difficult decisions on Liechtenstein, decisions at Potsdam also weighed heavily upon it.

During his wartime exile in London President Benes brooded on how to undo the Munich Agreement with all its legal, territorial and political consequences for his country. His solution included the expulsion of the minority German population from Czechoslovakia. He won the agreement of the British Government in 1942 and of the US and Soviet governments in June 1943.[7] At the Potsdam Conference (17 July–2 August 1945) the Allies formally recognised that "the transfer to Germany of German populations or elements thereof, remaining in Poland, Czechoslovakia or Hungary, will have to be undertaken. They agree that any transfers that take place should be effected in an orderly and humane manner."[8] By that time, however, the mood in Czechoslovakia was so radical that many violent reprisals, confiscations and expulsions had already taken place.[9] Benes had originally hoped to save the democratically minded Germans, but even 100,000 anti-Nazi Germans were eventually expelled. In the end there remained about 165,000 registered Germans out of a former population of 3,231,688.[10]

The Czech and Slovak political parties agreed in Moscow in March 1945 that, pending the convocation of a National Assembly, Benes should have the power to make decrees with the force of law. He issued ninety-eight between May and October. At the same time Benes made far-reaching concessions to the Czech and

---

[7] "A History of the Czechoslovak Republic 1918–1948", ed. Mamatey and Luza: Chapter 11, by Edward Taborsky, p.323 et seq.
[8] Documents on British Policy Overseas, Series I, Vol. I, 1945, page 1275.
[9] See, for example, "Armed Truce" by Hugh Thomas (Hamish Hamilton, London, 1986), pages 265–267.
[10] "A History of the Czechoslovak Republic 1918–1948", pages 40 and 422.

Slovak Communists and their fellow-travellers, with the result that when the country was liberated the administration was taken over at local level by "people's committees". It was these bodies that in many cases occupied the big estates, including those of the Liechtensteins. The way ahead was pointed by Zdenek Fierlinger, the Social Democrat Prime Minister of the National Front Government, who said on Prague Radio on 13 June 1945 that after the First World War not all "injustices" had been put right. The large estates of the Liechtensteins and other persons had still been preserved; they were "bulwarks of feudal order".[11] An intense nationalist and left-wing press campaign pictured the Liechtenstein family as having been invited to settle in the country after the Battle of the White Mountain in 1620, as conquerors and despoilers of the Czech landowners and patriots.

Several of the Benes Decrees affected the Liechtenstein properties. Decree No. 5 of 19 May 1945 stipulated that all factories and properties should be placed under national administration where that was necessary for the smooth functioning of production and economic life, especially those which had been abandoned or were owned or controlled by persons with an unreliable attitude to the State. Among the categories of persons considered to be unreliable to the State were persons of German and Hungarian nationality. The Decree of 2 August 1945, *inter alia*, declared all Sudeten Germans to be citizens of the German Reich, obliged to prove their loyalty to Czechoslovakia before being allowed to apply for Czechoslovak citizenship. The Decrees of 19 May, 21 June and 25 October declared all German- and Hungarian-owned property to be confiscated without compensation.[12] The Decree of 21 June specified that this was regardless of the owners' citizenship. "Germans" were defined according to the 1930 census as those who had German as their mother tongue: "All persons of German or Magyar race, as entered in any census after 1929".[13]

On 26 June 1945 the Ministry of Agriculture, acting on the basis of Decree No. 5, announced that the assets of Franz Josef of Liechtenstein in Czechoslovakia were to be put under national administration. These included some 70,000 hectares of agricultural land and forests. The Ministry said that these assets were not centrally administered and had become subject to influence by local and district national committees even though previously they had always been administered centrally, so that their smooth running and production were in danger. The lands, it said, had been gained by robbery of the Czech owners after 1620. The Ministry implied that Franz Josef remained an enemy of the nation. It alleged that during

---

[11] FO 371/47163. Enclosed in a Chancery letter from the British Legation, Prague. Fierlinger led his party into the embrace of the Communists. His popular nickname was "Quislinger". (Mamatey and Luza, op. cit., page 394.)

[12] "A History of the Czechoslovak Republic 1918–1948", page 420

[13] FO 371/47163. Chancery letter dated 16 July 1945 from the British Legation, Prague.

the Occupation the administration and senior management of the properties had been almost exclusively in the hands of Germans who were more often than not members of the Nazi party and had helped the Occupation forces.[14]

Further notices followed at local level, extending to other members of the Liechtenstein family. One such notice, issued by the Olomouc National Committee on 30 July 1945, and also by other committees, included the point that if Franz Josef had taken an active part in the fight for the territorial integrity and liberation of the Czechoslovak Republic he might have some claim to prevent the confiscation of his agricultural property. However, the tone of these notices was set by their preambles: "Meeting the requests of the Czech and Slovak peasants and landless persons to carry out consistently a new land reform, and at the same time inspired by the aim to remove Czech and Slovak land once and for all from the hands of interloping German and Hungarian farmers and landowners as well as from the hands of the traitors to the Republic"… etc., etc. A Czech Foreign Ministry official explained the expropriations to the Swiss Consul in Prague as "acts of social justice which had been in the making for generations and finally materialised as a part of a national revolution… Public opinion cannot be ignored when the Decrees are applied".

This third crisis in the House of Liechtenstein's history found it in an unusually difficult position. About thirty other Liechtenstein citizens were in the same plight. There were three issues: the nationality of the Liechtenstein family, the legality of the confiscations and the international status of the Principality of Liechtenstein.

The Liechtenstein family had lived in Czechoslovakia for almost four centuries before the Battle of the White Mountain; longer, perhaps, than the families of many contemporary Czechoslovak citizens. Their mother tongue was German, not Czech; but the House of Liechtenstein had no historic, political or legal connection with Germany except perhaps as Sovereign Princes in the Confederation of the Rhine and then the German Confederation between 1806 and 1866, before Bismarck's unification of Germany in 1871. Its members had not been involved in Sudeten German politics and had never possessed German citizenship. They could not, therefore, be described as German in any but the most general ethnic or linguistic sense.[15]

In September 1945 Franz Josef II appealed to the Czechoslovak Supreme

---

[14] Here, as in some of the succeeding paragraphs in this section, the author has drawn on unpublished factual information kindly supplied by Dr Milan Kovac. Any emphases, comments or conclusions are the author's alone.

[15] In Hugh Thomas's apt phrase (op. cit., page 265): "German-speaking aristocrats whose loyalties were above national origins". In his view, these aristocratic families contributed, along with the German-speaking bourgeoisie and farmers, to making Bohemia "the most successful part of the old Empire".

Administrative Court against the Ministry of Agriculture's decision. He pointed out that he had not been consulted about it. He had never declared German nationality, but only Liechtenstein nationality.[16] Most (he at first said "all") of the land acquired by the House of Liechtenstein after the Battle of the White Mountain had been surrendered in the post-1918 land reform. The lands had in any case been acquired by purchase and it was absurd to describe him as an enemy of the nation more than 300 years after the event. During the Occupation there had been no major changes in the composition of the personnel working for the Liechtensteins: in April 1945, 131 out of 215 employees had been Czech, including Dr Svoboda, the director, and 24 had been German. He had sympathised with the Czech nation during the war and had supported it as much as possible in the circumstances.

At the end of August 1945 the Liechtenstein Government, through the Swiss Government, formally protested against the imposition of national administration, the confiscations and the actions of the Czechoslovak Ministry of Agriculture. Liechtenstein, it said, had learned with astonishment that the first citizen of the State was suddenly considered to be German. Liechtenstein's autonomy was internationally recognised, including by Czechoslovakia. The fact that Liechtenstein was not involved in the war proved its independence and neutrality. The Prince was a constitutional head of state and, as such, could not take an active part in resistance movements in other countries. An unprovoked attack on the Prince and his estates by a foreign power was an act against Liechtenstein. The confiscation of all his estates without compensation was a breach of international law.

Certain Czechoslovak official and academic legal experts seem to have had doubts about some of the formal aspects (at least) of the Ministry's edict and of the public announcement by the District National Committee in Olomouc. Franz Josef II fought on, even after the Communist coup in February 1948. Legal action in every possible Czechoslovak court continued until the last appeals by Franz Josef and members of his family were rejected in 1951.

The diplomatic exchanges from 1945 onwards revealed that the Czechoslovak Government's attitude towards Liechtenstein had changed since 1938. Switzerland, unlike Liechtenstein, recognised the German-created entities of the Protectorate of Bohemia and Moravia and the Slovak Republic in 1939. As a result, its relations with the Republic of Czechoslovakia lapsed. On 28 February 1945 Switzerland proposed to the Czechoslovak Government in Exile in London that diplomatic relations should be re-established, to which the Czechoslovak Government agreed on 21 March 1945. When Switzerland then proposed that it should represent

---

[16] Hans-Adam II has said that he has seen a copy of the 1930 census form, which was obviously filled in by a local official, not by a member of the Liechtenstein family.

Liechtenstein interests as before, the Czechoslovak Foreign Ministry chose to argue (on 25 June 1946) that through the interruption in Swiss-Czechoslovak relations during the war the relations with Liechtenstein had also fallen away. The exchange of notes in London in 1945 by which Swiss-Czechoslovak relations had been re-established had made no mention of Liechtenstein; consequently, it said, relations between Czechoslovakia and Liechtenstein had not been re-established.

On 3 February 1947 the Liechtenstein Government pointed out, through the Swiss Legation in Prague, that relations had never been legally severed during the war. Liechtenstein had never recognised the Protectorate of Bohemia and Moravia, nor the independent Republic of Slovakia. It had always recognised the validity of passports issued by the Czechoslovak Government in Exile in London. The interruption of Czechoslovakia's relations with Switzerland could have no effect on relations with Liechtenstein since the latter was a separate sovereign state whose union with Switzerland was purely economic. The same legal situation therefore existed as on 30 July 1938, when Czechoslovakia had agreed that the Swiss Legation might represent Liechtenstein's interests in that country.[17] The Swiss Government added that it had been unnecessary to mention Liechtenstein in the exchange of notes in February and March 1945 since the relations between Czechoslovakia and Liechtenstein could have been interrupted only through an act by either side which might have led to that result; but so far as the Swiss Government was aware, no such event had taken place. The Czechoslovak Government did not reply to these arguments. A Czech Foreign Ministry official noted in May 1947 that if Czechoslovakia complied with the request it would open the door for compensation claims for confiscated Liechtenstein property, but that compensation was out of the question for domestic policy reasons. The Swiss Government continued its efforts to represent Liechtenstein's interests in Czechoslovakia until 1949.

A relationship of seven centuries appeared to have ended. In 1945, as in the land reforms of 1918, the Czechoslovak authorities' aim was to seize as much of the Liechtensteins' land as they could; the Liechtensteins' aim was to hold on to it. On both occasions the authorities exploited nationalist historical emotions. In 1945 anti-Sudeten feeling and growing communist influence were added to the brew. Even if the Liechtenstein family had succeeded in warding off the Benes Decrees, their estates could not have survived long into the communist era.

The family's unavoidable dealings with the Occupation and Protectorate authorities concerning the estates inevitably caused speculation about collaboration. Seven years of the management of 70,000 hectares must have generated a lot of paper. In view of the animosity, real or artificial, against the Liechtenstein

---

[17] "Liechtensteiner Vaterland" for 1 March 1950, quoted in "Liechtenstein 1938–1978", pages 124–125.

family the files must have been combed in the heat of the Liberation and later under the more systematic rule of the communists. Yet no accusation or charge seems to have ever been brought. The family's continuing court actions after February 1948 would have provided the communist regime with a perfect theatre for such a counter-attack had evidence against them been available. In the end, the only basis for their expropriation without compensation seems to have been the argument that their mother-tongue happened to be German.

The Loss of the Ellhorn

The Second World War had ended. The Cold War, however, was in full swing and a Soviet army of occupation was only 250 miles away in Austria. The Swiss General Staff resumed the unfinished business of the Ellhorn. On the Swiss side the negotiating tactics were brisk and blunt, in ultimatum style. On 23 December 1948, with great reluctance, Liechtenstein surrendered 45 hectares of land worth 80,000 francs in exchange for an equivalent area worth 120,000. Liechtenstein's debt to Switzerland for wartime supplies was reduced from 2.6 million francs to 800,000.[18] The British Minister in Berne noted that the Federal Council had, most unusually, stated that the treaty had been concluded for "considérations d'ordre militaire".[19]

The International Court of Justice

On 6 March 1949 Liechtenstein applied to become a party to the Statute of the International Court of Justice. Under Article 93 of the UN Charter all UN member states are automatically parties, but non-members may become parties on conditions to be determined in each case by the General Assembly upon the recommendation of the Security Council. In Liechtenstein's case the conditions followed the precedent established for Switzerland in the previous year, including an undertaking to contribute to the expenses of the Court.

On 8 April 1949 the Security Council discussed the application. The Soviet Permanent Representative (Malik) said that since Liechtenstein was not a free and independent state there was "no need to manufacture conditions" on which it could become a member of the ICJ.[20] The Security Council voted to refer the matter for an opinion to the Committee of Experts, where the representatives of the USSR and the Ukrainian SSR argued that parties to the Statute had to be independent and sovereign states; Liechtenstein, they said, "had yielded important parts of its sovereignty to another State" and was therefore not eligible.

---

[18] Arthur Brunhart, "Der Verlust des Ellhorns 1948", in "Balzner Neujahrsblätter" 1999.
[19] FO 371/79829. Despatch of 29 March 1949 from Mr T. M. Snow to the Rt. Hon. Clement Attlee MP.
[20] Security Council Official Records, Fourth Year, 423rd meeting, 8 April 1949.

The majority argued that Liechtenstein possessed all the qualifications of a state. They considered that the ICJ's jurisdiction should be extended as far as possible. Furthermore, Liechtenstein's accession to the Statute "was all the more useful for it since it was a small State and protection of law was most necessary in such a case."[21] The committee voted in favour of Liechtenstein by nine votes with two abstentions. On 27 July the Security Council recommended in favour to the General Assembly by nine votes to none. The USSR did not exercise its veto; the Ukrainian SSR also abstained. The General Assembly's Sixth Committee (Legal Affairs) reported in favour on 1 November; only the Byelorussian SSR's representative expressed opposition in a remarkably inaccurate speech. On 1 December 1949 the General Assembly voted in favour by forty votes, with two against (the USSR and Czechoslovakia) and two abstentions (one of them the Ukrainian SSR). Liechtenstein became a party to the Statute on 29 March 1950.

To Liechtenstein, this was an important vindication of its sovereignty and independence after the war.[22] The Cold War tensions in the UN debates are striking. The communist camp's arguments against Liechtenstein no doubt owed something to the USSR's recent memories of the Smyslovsky affair and its reluctance to add another moderate and democratic western voice to a UN forum, and to Czechoslovakia's long-standing unwillingness to see Liechtenstein's international standing enhanced. The western camp seems to have had no doubt about Liechtenstein's entitlement both to participation in the ICJ and to the protection of international law.

[21] Report of the Chairman of the Committee of Experts, 23 June 1949, S/1342.
[22] Having accepted the jurisdiction of the ICJ, Liechtenstein brought a case against Guatemala in 1951 on behalf of Friedrich Nottebohm. He had lived in Guatemala since 1905 and had lost his native German nationality when he acquired Liechtenstein nationality in 1939. He was removed from Guatemala in 1943 as a result of war measures. The ICJ held in 1955 by a majority (eleven to three) that the Principality was not entitled to present an international claim on his behalf against Guatemala because his links with Liechtenstein were so tenuous that he could not be regarded as having "effective nationality" of that country. (Professor D. J. Harris, "Cases and Materials on International Law", Sweet and Maxwell, London, 1998, pages 588–594.) The notion of "effective nationality" was an important, although in Liechtenstein's case unintended, contribution to ICJ case law.

THE ECONOMIC MIRACLE (1950–1990)

For some years after the war Liechtenstein largely vanished from the head-lines.[1] This was, however, a period of peace: the first for fifteen, perhaps even for thirty-five years. It was also the country's first experience of general prosperity.

In 1947 a referendum approved the building of the Samina hydroelectric power plant, which remains the largest project in the country's history. After it had started production in 1949, Liechtenstein was for two decades a net exporter of energy. The road network was modernised. New bridges over the Rhine were built. In 1951 Liechtenstein became the first country in Europe to have a fully automated telephone system. Its modern telecommunications gave its banks and companies a head start when first the telex and later information technology were introduced. Its comparative isolation from air and rail transport ceased to matter.

The Marshall Plan and the rebuilding of Western Europe led to a strong demand for manufactured goods and financial services. Liechtenstein benefited from its central location, its neutrality, its political and social stability, its bank-ing and tax privacy, and the strong and stable Swiss franc. Its inclusion in the Swiss economic area and the Swiss banking system opened wider international dimensions to its economy. It was further helped by the gradual liberation of world trade and currencies from wartime restrictions. It had no costly state bureaucracy. Taxes were held low, the budget was almost always kept in prudent surplus and the tax receipts from holding and domiciliary companies (estimated to number around 4,000 in the mid-1950s after the fluctuations of the 1920s and 1930s) lightened the burdens on the public purse. Although the Customs Treaty subordinated many aspects of the economy to Swiss regulations and taxes, Liech-tenstein kept its autonomy in, for example, direct taxation and the regulation of financial services.

---

[1] In 1959, for example, the British Foreign Office found it necessary to ask the Embassy at Berne how far the Principality ran its own affairs (FO 371/145558: Miss J. J. d'A. Collings' letter of 28 August 1959 and Mr R. S. Scrivener's reply of 18 September 1959.)

The changing economic scene is illustrated in the following table:[2]

	1950	1960	1970	1980	1990
Employed in agricultural sector	1,315	962	646	525	239
Employed in industrial sector	3,074	4,349	5,797	6,641	5,387
Exports (in millions of francs)	15.2	82.8	332.6	887.0	2,213.1
Employed in services sector	1,602	2,260	3,770	5,720	8,742
Employed by banks	24	96	272	485	1,144
Banks' balance sheet strength (in millions of francs)	67.7	244.4	1,478.8	4,364.0	17,347.9
Completely unemployed	14	4	29	3	29

The Growth of Industry

Liechtenstein's manufacturing companies are discussed in greater detail below (pages 286–293). From a small beginning, they grew with remarkable speed. They benefited from low taxation, but they enjoyed no state subsidies or export credit guarantees. The domestic market was minute: they had to export 95% of their products. The hard currency meant that imports were cheap, but that the products had to be technically advanced if they were to enjoy a competitive edge abroad. The firms were left to sink or swim. They swam. The British Consul-General in Zurich commented in 1971 on the country's exceptional economic vigour and the "intelligent planning, good service and expert marketing which have kept these industries running so profitably". He also commented on the high calibre of Dr Hilbe, the then Head of Government, compared with the average Swiss cantonal politician. He had the international facts at his fingertips. He looked to be "of the stuff of which Ministers are made".[3]

Industry's reliance on advanced niche products (automated central heating plants, dental prosthetics, high vacuum products, high grade building and fixing tools, precision machinery, pharmaceuticals) was vindicated during the "Oil Shock" in the early 1970s and the upwards revaluation of the franc. Despite these difficulties, Liechtenstein's exports suffered little and growth continued. Participation in EFTA in 1960 increased the export opportunities. Liechtenstein companies began to expand abroad; for example, Hilti (building tools) and Hoval (heating equipment), opened factories in the United Kingdom. Liechtenstein participated in a foreign exhibition for the first time in 1950, in Luxembourg. Its stand at the Brussels World Fair in 1958 attracted much attention.

[2] Figures taken from Statistisches Jahrbuch 1999, pages 96, 111, 190, and 235
[3] Despatch of 8 July 1971 from Mr P. D. Stobart to the Foreign and Commonwealth Secretary, entitled "Liechtenstein – An Economic Miracle in a Teacup". (FCO 33/1651)

Low-Tax Companies and Trusts

Figures for the companies and trust offices at this period are not available. One guess is that by 1980 the number had grown to about 50,000 registered companies.[4] The number of lawyers doubled between 1950 and 1978 and the number of trustees quadrupled between 1960 and 1978.[5] Taxes on domiciliary and holding companies produced 48.6 million francs in 1980 and 68.9 million in 1990 (33% and 25% of total tax receipts respectively)[6]. These figures point to the growing volume of financial business handled, although this sector became less important as a pillar of the Liechtenstein economy and of state finances during the last third of the twentieth century compared with other sources of revenue.[7] (See pages 278 below.)

Banking

At the very beginning of the economic miracle the role of the Liechtenstein banks was less dominant than that of industry, the low-tax companies and the trusts. Whereas the number of Swiss banks rose during the 1950s by about fifty to a total of 441,[8] Liechtenstein's banking policy was restrictive to the point of protectionism.

It remained so until the prospect of entry into the European Economic Area in 1995 forced a change. After the war, there were still only two banks: the Sparkasse (the state-guaranteed bank which in 1955 was renamed the Liechtensteinische Landesbank (LLB) and whose role was not unlike that of a Swiss cantonal bank) and the Bank in Liechtenstein (BiL).

Both were still fledglings. From 1921 the BiL was housed on the ground floor of the Government Building, until it moved in 1933 to the newly built Vaduz Town Hall and then in 1960 to its own building. The LLB was also housed on the ground floor of the Government Building from 1923 until it moved into its own building in 1953.

For the first few years, until 1967, the LLB let one of its floors to the National Museum and the Stamps Museum. In 1951 the LLB had a nominal balance of 56.6 million francs (1980: 2,169.2 million, 1990: 5,981.4 million). In 1950 it had a staff of 12 (1980: 181, 1990: 349). In 1950 the BiL had a nominal balance of 15.2 million

---

[4] Meili, op. cit., page 150. The British Consul-General, Zurich, suggested a figure of 15,000 in 1971. Such companies are not unique to Liechtenstein. They are to be found, *mutatis mutandis*, in Swiss cantons such as Zurich and Zug.

[5] Meili, op. cit., page 152.

[6] Statistisches Jahrbuch 2001, pages 284 and 288.

[7] In his Speech from the Throne on 4 April 1963 Franz Josef II emphasised the need to plan ahead for sources of income which could still be counted on in the event of a great European economic area coming into existence, and advised against reliance on sources which might one day cease to exist. ("Die Thronreden", Government of the Principality of Liechtenstein, Vaduz, 1986, page 82)

[8] Meili, op. cit., page 54.

francs (1980: 1,563.3 million, 1990: 6,967.0 million) and in 1951 a staff of 13 (1980: 200, 1990: 466).[9]

Both of these banks had had their problems in the past, the LLB especially in 1928. The BiL, orientated as it was towards international finance, managed to survive during the Second World War, but not much more than that. In 1937 it changed its international orientation from eastern to western Europe. Hitler's restrictive financial measures hurt its Austrian business after 1938. It began to compete with the LLB in the domestic market for savings and loans, but with little success until after the war. With recent and painful memories of the pre-war economic and financial stresses, the Liechtenstein Government was extremely anxious to protect these two native institutions from competition. Its philosophy, as expressed in the Banking Law of 1960, was that no new bank should be established unless there were a proven need for it.[10]

The restrictions connected with the State's financial backing made the LLB unable to provide the full range of services needed by the growing trustee and fiduciary sector. In 1955 Guido Feger, who in 1929 had founded what was to become one of the oldest and biggest trust offices, the Allgemeines Treuunternehmen, applied to set up a private bank where his clients could deposit their assets. The Government, advised by the LLB, refused the application on grounds of likely damage to the LLB's interests. Feger then undertook to restrict himself to dealing in securities and foreign currency. His new "Verwaltungs- und Privat-Bank" (VPB) opened for business in April 1956 with two rooms, a staff of two and a nominal balance of 2.9 million francs. It was not until 1975 that it acquired a full banking licence, to include savings and loans activities. By 1980 it had a nominal balance of 634.4 million francs and a staff of 105. By 1990 these had grown to 3,865.1 million francs and 329 staff.[11]

These constraints, together with the small size of the country and its lack of a stock exchange and similar institutions, meant that Liechtenstein could never become a financial centre in its own right like Zurich, London and New York. However, since the domestic market was so small the banks and trust firms, like Liechtenstein's manufacturing industry, became globally minded. The LLB, BiL and VPB became members of the Swiss Bankers' Association in 1947, 1948 and 1965 respectively. This was a tribute to their solidity; it also made their day-to-day conduct of business with Swiss banks easier. On their side, the Swiss banks no

---

[9] Meili, op. cit., pages 139 and 141; Seger and Nuener, "50 Jahre Bank in Liechtenstein", Vaduz 1971, page 21; "Die Liechtensteinische Landesbank 1861–1986, Vaduz", 1986, page 105; the Liechtenstein Bankers' Association (LBA).

[10] The Swiss philosophy was quite different: the Swiss Banking Commission would normally grant permission for the establishment of a bank provided it met the professional and legal criteria.

[11] Meili, op. cit., pages 55–58, 139 and 141; and the LBA.

doubt welcomed readier access to the funds attracted to Liechtenstein by low taxation, which it was the function of the Liechtenstein banks and trust offices to recycle more widely. The Liechtenstein Bankers Association was founded in 1969 to represent the sector's interests to the government and to the Swiss National Bank. The three banks founded a school for apprentices in 1978, but relied heavily on Switzerland and the USA for higher training. During the 1980s the banks began to acquire representational offices, then subsidiaries, abroad. The volume of their activities should be kept in perspective. In 1980 the nominal balances of all three Liechtenstein banks taken together amounted to less than one quarter of that of the Zurich Cantonal Bank, although the Liechtenstein banks' rate of growth since 1945 had been far more rapid than that of their Zurich colleague.[12]

The breakdown of the Bretton Woods system in the 1970s, the floating of currencies, the spread of information technology and the demand for deregulation and innovation contributed to the growth of "offshore" centres such as Liechtenstein, Luxembourg, the Channel Islands, the Isle of Man and some of the Caribbean islands. Financial and political instability in the wider world, especially at the time of the Oil Shock in the early 1970s, led to an unusually rapid inflow of dollars and other foreign currencies into Switzerland. In order to reduce this flow, which was having an inflationary effect and making Swiss exports uncompetitive, Swiss institutions for a time charged "negative interest" on foreign clients' accounts; the clients had to pay for keeping their money in Switzerland. In 1972 Liechtenstein passed a law to bring its money, capital market and credit systems into line with those of Switzerland in order to avoid being classified by Switzerland as a foreign country for currency purposes.

As sometimes happens in times of economic turbulence, the authorities of more highly taxed countries began to turn a critical eye on Liechtenstein and to enact measures to make the use of companies and other legal entities there more difficult for their own citizens. Inside Liechtenstein, responsible voices began to argue that while it was, as always, legitimate for foreigners to reduce their tax liabilities by legal means, it would do Liechtenstein no good in the longer term to appear to be helping those who were breaking their own countries' laws. From the middle of 1976 the Government began to close down companies and other entities which were clearly abusing their status or which were not being properly supervised by their local partners and lawyers[13].

The Chiasso Affair

In his Speech from the Throne on 24 March 1977 Franz Josef II emphasised

---

[12] Meili, op.cit., page 146.
[13] Meili, op. cit., pages 108–109.

the need to maintain foreign investors' confidence by responsible behaviour. He added, "Perhaps the future will show that in a number of cases supervision and the regulations should be more severely applied".[14] Only three weeks later the "Chiasso Affair" broke out. The head and deputy head of the Credit Suisse branch office at Chiasso, on the Swiss-Italian frontier, had over some years built up their own financial empire without the knowledge of their head office. (The affair has its parallels in banking history elsewhere.) The Chiasso bank officials transmitted smuggled Italian currency to a Liechtenstein finance company, from which it was reinvested into the Italian economy. The fall of the lira and a slump in the Italian tourist industry led to the company's bankruptcy. Owing to a guarantee which had been given contrary to Credit Suisse's regulations and in the ignorance of the bank's senior management, the bank was faced with a loss of 1.2bn francs. The Liechtenstein trustees responsible for administering the finance company argued successfully that they had had neither the legal obligation nor the legal power to scrutinise the company's affairs. Another Liechtenstein company turned out to have been involved in a similar but separate scandal in 1977 (the Weisscredit affair in Lugano).[15]

Company Law Reform and the 1980 Currency Treaty

The damage to the reputation of Swiss banking was bad enough; but the Swiss authorities were also incensed that their legislation to protect the franc's stability against the importation of foreign currency had been circumvented. Liechtenstein was worried about harm not only to the standing of its financial services but also to the reputation of the country in general, including its manufactured exports. The Government speeded up its work on reforming company law. In his Speech from the Throne on 21 April 1978 Franz Josef II reminded the Parliament that if the country's industry, trades and standard of living were to continue to benefit from the low taxation which depended on the financial services sector, the latter (notwithstanding the efforts already made) would have to be run in an orderly way with more attention paid to due diligence.[16] In June 1978 the President of the Swiss National Bank, Fritz Leutwiler, went to Vaduz to propose a formal treaty on the inclusion of Liechtenstein into the Swiss currency area and to demand that Liechtenstein companies and legal entities should be subjected by his bank (which was independent of the Swiss state) to the same norms and controls as Swiss companies.

Although no particular complaint had been made against the three

---

[14] "Die Thronreden", op. cit., page 140.
[15] Meili, op. cit., page 109–112.
[16] "Die Thronreden", op. cit., page 144.

Liechtenstein banks, they had already committed themselves in June 1977 to stronger measures to know their clients and to check the origin of assets entrusted to them. The revised Company Law of April 1980 provided for proper accounting procedures and the annual submission of balance sheets by companies conducting commercial activities. The obligatory Liechtenstein representatives in the companies were given the right to check the companies' activities in detail; this carried with it responsibility for any abuse committed. The Government set up a compulsory supervisory authority for the majority of companies. After examining the desirability of introducing an independent Liechtenstein currency the Government decided in favour of a currency treaty with Switzerland, to regularise the situation which had existed since 1924 (page 56 above). The treaty came into force on 25 November 1981. It gave the Swiss National Bank greater control over, and insight into, the workings of Liechtenstein banks, companies and persons and improved its dialogue with the Liechtenstein Government. The Liechtenstein banks, for their part, could now expect uninterrupted access to the Swiss capital market whatever the state of currency markets in the wider world. They benefited from greater exposure to modern Swiss banking practices. In addition, the Swiss National Bank became their lender of last resort in the event of liquidity problems of the kind that had bedevilled them in the 1920s and 1930s.[17] The Parliament voted unanimously for the treaty, not without some individual expressions of regret for the further restrictions on national sovereignty which it implied. In fact, the treaty is one between two sovereign states, either of which is free to denounce it, and it left Liechtenstein autonomous in many areas of financial activity.

Social Changes

As in other Western European countries at that time, the social changes were vast. The peasant society ended. In 1946 30% of the working population was employed on the land; in 1950 it was 22% and in 1990 only 1.5%. As early as 1970 the value of exports per head was said to be the highest in the world and income per capita was the third highest. The annual budget rose from 3.3 million francs in 1950 to 201 million in 1980 and then to 400 million in 1990. As indicators of prosperity, the number of cars rose from 472 in 1950 (35 per thousand of the population) to 12,569 in 1980 (487 per thousand) and 16,891 in 1990 (594 per thousand). Energy consumption rose from 37,628 megawatt hours in 1960 to 145,620 in 1980 and 221,915 in 1990.[18]

Even more important for society was the fact that Liechtenstein changed

---

[17] Meili, op. cit., pages 118–124.
[18] Statistisches Jahrbuch 2001, pages 274, 204 and 222.

from being an exporter of labour to an importer of skilled industrial and financial workers. The population grew from 13,757 in 1950 to 25,215 in 1980 and to 29,032 in 1990. Of these, 2,751 were classified as foreigners in 1950, 9,302 in 1980 and 10,909 in 1990. The native population had become too small to sustain the country's economic growth. In addition to resident foreigners,[19] the number of commuters from Switzerland and Austria rose from 1,700 in 1960 to 3,279 in 1980 and to 6,885 in 1990. By 1970 the number of foreigners employed (6,240) was more than half of the total workforce (11,569). By 1990 the number of foreigners employed was 11,933 out of a workforce of 19,905.[20]

Fears of being swamped by foreigners ("überfremdung") began to be expressed. The effects of these fears were cushioned by the general prosperity and by the fact that the great majority of foreigners, some 78% of them in 1970, were of similar cultural background. These were Swiss, Austrians and Germans: but that similarity counted for little in a country where identity is deeply rooted in the individual communes. One practical consequence was that the price of building land rose to the point where it was feared that young Liechtensteiners might no longer be able to set up home in their own country. In 1963 Franz Josef II suggested that the communes might buy and set aside land which might later be assigned, against a loan, to Liechtensteiners who wanted to build their own homes.

Throughout these decades the legislation on citizenship remained very restrictive, despite Franz Josef's insistent calls for a more liberal policy and his reminder in 1977 that if foreign residents of long standing were not allowed to be naturalised, native-born Liechtensteiners might find themselves a minority in their own country. One practical consequence of the large foreign population (many of them non-Roman Catholic) was that legislation for compulsory civil marriage and for the possibility of divorce and remarriage was passed in 1974. When, in 1980, the number of foreigners passed 10,000 for the first time, the Government took measures to ensure that they should not exceed one third of the population. These measures did not at first apply to Swiss citizens, but some restrictions were applied even to them by agreement with the Swiss Government in the following year. The method chosen was to impose ceilings on employment in certain occupations. It did not work very effectively.

A new era in social welfare began in 1952 with the narrow victory in a referendum of a proposal for old age pensions and survivors insurance. This was followed in 1957 by family allowance benefits (paid for by the employer), in 1960 by disability insurance and amended legislation for health insurance of workers

---

[19] The British Consul-General in Zurich wrote in 1968 that the British colony was increasing to the stage where "Mr Bryan Jeeves, a dynamic businessman resident at Vaduz, is…on the point of forming a British Club there". (Mr A. C. Maby's report of 12 June 1968 to HM Ambassador, Berne: FCO 9/97)

[20] Statistisches Jahrbuch 2001, pages 31, 33, 98 and 90.

and employers, in 1965 by social insurance, in 1966 by labour legislation, in 1970 by unemployment insurance and in 1971 by compulsory health insurance. The philosophy underlying this social legislation was to help those in need, but with the aim of levelling up rather than by levelling down through punitive taxation.

Votes for Women

Female suffrage in Switzerland was achieved at federal level only in 1971 after a long and difficult campaign. Progress in Liechtenstein was even slower. A consultative referendum in 1968 showed 887 men in favour and 1,341 against, while the women were almost equally divided. (The sexes voted separately.) In 1971 the two parties and the Parliament united in favour of women's suffrage, which was defeated in a referendum by only 81 (male) votes in a turnout of 85.6%. A repetition of this process in 1973 provoked a higher turnout and a more decisive rejection, by 451 votes. Franz Josef II spoke up for women's suffrage in 1974, reminding the male population that in the critical days of 1940 it had been the Liechtenstein women who launched a petition in support of the country's independence and partnership with Switzerland.[21]

Although there was vehement opposition to women's suffrage from part of the population, the British Consul-General in Zurich thought in 1973 that there was a lack of strong pressure for it from the women themselves at a time of general prosperity and unexciting politics.

He speculated that liberal-minded men might have voted against women's suffrage out of fear that women, if given the vote, might be responsible for defeating the current proposals to introduce divorce.

Supporters of women's suffrage advanced their cause by a flanking movement at commune level. In 1976 Vaduz was the first commune to introduce the right of women to vote and to be elected in local matters. The first women were elected to local councils in Vaduz and Gamprin in 1983.

It is tempting to speculate that the women's cause may have been helped by Hanni Wenzel's spectacular skiing victories, which put Liechtenstein on the international sporting map at that time (gold and silver medals at St Moritz in 1974, the World Cup in 1978 and two Olympic gold medals in the giant slalom and slalom at Lake Placid in 1980). However that may be, the cause gradually gathered speed until, in 1984, a referendum approved voting and election rights for women at national level. Once again, the parties and the Parliament were united in supporting the proposal. It succeeded by the narrow margin of 119 votes (2.6%) in a turnout of 86.19%.[22] The Unterland was much more in favour than

---

[21] "Die Thronreden", page 129 (27 March 1974).
[22] "125 Jahre Landtag", page 251. (Pages 247 and 248 for the 1971 and 1973 referenda respectively.)

the Oberland. It was not until 1986 that all the communes had voted for women's suffrage at their local level.

The first woman member of the Parliament (a FBP candidate) was elected at the very next parliamentary elections in 1986. In 1993 the first woman (Cornelia Gassner, FBP) was appointed to the five-member coalition government. She was joined later that year by Andrea Willi (VU) as holder of the Foreign Affairs portfolio, among others. Andrea Willi continued in the subsequent single-party VU government. In 2001 Rita Kieber-Beck was the first woman to be appointed Deputy Head of Government, in the current single-party FBP government. In that government three of the five alternate ministers, including the Head of Government's alternate, are women.

LIECHTENSTEIN'S FOREIGN POLICY IN THE 1970s: CSCE AND THE COUNCIL OF EUROPE

From the 1960s onwards Liechtenstein joined a number of international organisations in areas which affected its interests but which were not covered by the Customs Treaty with Switzerland. These included the Universal Postal Union (1962), the International Telecommunications Union (1963), the International Atomic Energy Agency (1968) the World Intellectual Property Organisation (1972), UNIDO, UNCTAD, INTELSAT and (as a consultative member) the UN Economic Commission for Europe. The EFTA Convention of 1960 was merely extended to Liechtenstein by a special Protocol. (Switzerland was a founding member of EFTA but not all EFTA matters were covered by the Customs Treaty.) Rather more satisfactory to Liechtenstein than this arrangement was the supplementary agreement signed by the European Economic Community, Switzerland and Liechtenstein and appended to the Swiss-EEC Treaty of 22 July 1972. This entitled Liechtenstein to have its own representative in the Swiss delegation to the Swiss-EEC Joint Committee, to promote its interests.

By the early 1970s foreign observers were reporting a growing internal consciousness of Liechtenstein's sovereignty and of the country's different character from Switzerland, and a reluctance to be seen as an adjunct to eastern Switzerland however helpful and considerate the Swiss authorities might be.[1] The tone was set by a speech by Hereditary Prince (Crown Prince) Hans-Adam on 12 September 1970 in which he likened Liechtenstein to a political Sleeping Beauty.[2] To the extent that the metaphor was justified, there was a prince at hand to wake her up.

Hans-Adam said that it was time for Liechtenstein to start working out its own foreign policy. Matters were unlikely to continue for the next fifty years in the same comfortable way as in the past fifty. Switzerland had been, and continued to be, a good friend and support. But the feeling was growing there that Liechtenstein was now economically strong enough to do more for itself. The

---

[1] See, for example, the "Financial Times" for 31 January 1974.
[2] "Liechtenstein 1938–1978", page 394.

1920s treaties were in need of revision, which was already under way in the case of the Postal Treaty. Sooner or later Switzerland would, with reason, demand that Liechtenstein should either learn to walk on its own two feet or largely give up its independence. Hans-Adam went on to outline a further stark choice in characteristically vivid language: if in a future united Europe Liechtenstein were to have only the status of an observer (as it did in the case of the Switzerland-EFTA relationship), it would be the end of its independence. In that case, it would be better to ask to join Switzerland as a new canton. The people would be directly represented in the Federal Parliament at Berne and Switzerland could intervene in Brussels for Liechtenstein's interests with much more right and weight. "Perhaps we could even continue to issue postage stamps to finance our budget and keep a Prince in the Castle as a tourist attraction." But Hans-Adam was convinced that the great majority of Liechtensteiners did not want such a solution. If that was so, they should pay more attention to foreign policy and to long-standing domestic issues such as the naturalisation of foreigners and women's suffrage, which needed to be settled for the sake of the country's standing abroad.

This unsparing analysis was to hold good for the rest of the century.

CSCE

It was the Conference on Security and Co-operation in Europe that gave Liechtenstein an unexpected breakthrough. For many years the Soviet Government had been pressing for a pan-European conference. It hoped that such a conference would ratify the consequences of the Second World War in the absence of a peace treaty, confirm for ever the division of Germany and, at least implicitly, endorse the so-called Brezhnev Doctrine ("limited sovereignty for the Warsaw Pact members"). In the event, the provisions in the CSCE Final Act about human rights and the freedom of movement of people, information and cultural contacts contributed mightily to the dissolution of the Soviet empire and of the Soviet Union itself.

East and West agreed that participation in the conference and its preparation should be open to all European countries, plus the United States and Canada. Liechtenstein made its interest known. At the Finnish Government's invitation Liechtenstein, together with 34 other states including San Marino and the Holy See, took part in multilateral preparatory talks which began in Helsinki on 22 November 1972. The Liechtenstein delegation played an active part in the conference until it fell to Walter Kieber, as Head of Government, to sign the Final Act in Helsinki on 1 August 1975.

The Head of the United Kingdom delegation reported to the Foreign Secretary in June 1973, "It was a stimulating experience for Western delegations to find the Russians, in the hearing of representatives of all their satellites, obliged to give a detailed defence of their domestic policies on, for example, the increase of human and cultural contacts, in order to answer criticism by Liechtenstein. For the Soviet spokesmen themselves the experience cannot have been so refreshing. It is no wonder that the Soviet leadership are still pressing for an early end to the Conference."[3]

The United Kingdom delegation described the Liechtenstein delegation as, *inter alia,* admirably robust on questions of freedom and extremely pedantic on legal and financial questions. Although technically belonging to the "Neutral and Non-Aligned" at the CSCE, the Liechtenstein delegation made it very clear where its sympathies lay. For example in October 1973 its leader, Prince Heinrich, was critical to a British diplomat of some proposed Swiss negotiating tactics which in his view might prejudice western objectives.

Diplomatic Representation Abroad

The CSCE experience was sobering. It was perhaps no surprise to find the Soviet delegation at Helsinki "patronising and implicitly bullying". But Liechtenstein had not realised how demanding of time, manpower and administrative resources such marathon meetings could be. It was not merely a matter of appearing and speaking at formal sessions; one had to negotiate in committee rooms and there were voluminous background papers to master.

Count Gerliczy-Burian, Head of the Office for International Relations, began to devote increasing thought to the practical problems of running an independent foreign policy. He mused over the future pattern of foreign representation in various press interviews. In 1973 he wondered whether the Swiss and the Austrians might accredit ambassadors at Vaduz.

There might be Liechtenstein ambassadors at Bonn, the Council of Europe in Strasbourg and the EC in Brussels, perhaps in the latter two cases the same person. There might also be an observer at the UN. In 1974 he pointed out that he ran his office virtually single-handed, but was abroad on average for three fifths of each year at international meetings, including the CSCE. He was aware of the heavy cost of creating a proper Foreign Affairs Department at home and more diplomatic posts abroad, but he regarded separate representation in Brussels, Paris, London, Vienna and Bonn as desirable. With the exception of Paris and London, the pattern of Liechtenstein's diplomatic representation abroad was to develop very much on these lines.

---

[3] Despatch of 13 June 1973 from Mr T. A. K. Elliott to the Rt. Hon. Sir Alec Douglas-Home MP, entitled "CSCE: The First Two Hundred Days" (Documents on British Policy Overseas, Series III, Volume II, HMSO 1997, pages 144–145.)

The Council of Europe

Liechtenstein's admission to the Council of Europe was less straightforward than participation in CSCE. The initial soundings were between Prince Heinrich (Liechtenstein's Ambassador in Berne) and Sir Peter Smithers (Secretary-General of the Council of Europe, 1964–1969). The advice from Strasbourg was to take the matter step by step and to start by ratifying some of the main conventions.

From as early as 1962 Liechtenstein officials had attended meetings of experts at the Council of Europe. From 1971 members of the Parliament were invited to attend sessions of the Parliamentary Assembly, *ad hoc*. In 1974 Liechtenstein was granted observer status, after which its representatives took an active part in various Parliamentary Assembly committees. Liechtenstein joined the Resettlement Fund and acceded to nine other Council of Europe conventions.

In January 1977 Gerard Batliner (Head of Government 1962–1970 and President of the Landtag 1974–1978) invited Georg Kahn-Ackermann (Secretary-General of the Council of Europe, 1974–1979) to pay a private visit to Vaduz. After discussions during that visit the Liechtenstein Government decided to apply for full membership.

The application met some resistance. Liechtenstein was helped by the consistently constructive and moderate attitude it had already shown at international gatherings.[4] Germany, which was its staunchest supporter, remembered Liechtenstein's help in CSCE on Berlin and all-German matters. It was also keen that Liechtenstein should join the recently concluded European Convention on the Suppression of Terrorism. France was the country most strongly opposed, on the grounds that it was not fitting for mini-states to be members of the Council of Europe. France also wanted a legally binding agreement to restrict Liechtenstein's power of voting on budgetary matters, which Liechtenstein was most unwilling to give. Italy, too, was reluctant, fearing that a vote for Liechtenstein might later oblige it to vote for San Marino. The other states floated between, with various degrees of enthusiasm or resistance. Kahn-Ackermann's strong personal support for Liechtenstein was not endorsed by everyone.

The first reactions of British officials were negative. However, at the political level the Foreign and Commonwealth Office was clear that membership of the Council should always be open to any democratic European state, Liechtenstein included, which was able and willing to uphold the principle of the rule of law and to grant its people the basic human rights and freedoms. The main British worries (shared by others) were about how far Liechtenstein would be able to

---

[4] In another context, a British Foreign and Commonwealth Office legal adviser said in 1973 about Liechtenstein's performance in 1968 and 1969 at the UN Conference on the Law of Treaties at Vienna, "We were very thankful to have Liechtenstein's vote on particularly difficult issues at that Conference."

make a reasonably effective contribution to the work of the Council, and whether it might argue and vote for controversial and expensive proposals for which it would not in practice have to pay. These concerns were spelled out to Prince Nikolaus (brother of Hans-Adam) and Count Gerliczy-Burian as they carried out two energetic lobbying tours of European capitals in the spring and summer of 1977. British support for Liechtenstein's admission stayed firm from June onwards.

One suggestion put to Liechtenstein was that the Principality might become an associate member with restricted rights and obligations like the Federal Republic of Germany and the Saar in 1950, before the former gained full statehood in 1955 and the Saar rejoined Germany. Liechtenstein rejected this idea out of hand, for obvious reasons.

In his formal letter of application, dated 4 November 1977, Kieber dealt with the objections by saying, "In the decision-making of the Council of Europe, Liechtenstein would exercise her vote as a member in a manner appropriate to her size". Liechtenstein would co-operate actively in the Council's various bodies and would ratify the so-called closed agreements such as the Human Rights Convention. In a letter to the British Foreign Secretary dated 5 November 1977 (versions of which were no doubt sent to other Foreign Ministers) Kieber went slightly further: "It will therefore be the policy of the Liechtenstein Government not to use the vote of Liechtenstein so as to be decisive in support of proposals entailing major budgetary allocations". Liechtenstein made it clear that it would establish a permanent mission at Strasbourg.

From the Committee of Ministers, where support was eventually unanimous, the debate moved to the Parliamentary Assembly. Mr Toby Jessel MP (UK) was commissioned to make a fact-finding visit to Liechtenstein on 26–29 July 1978. His report favoured Liechtenstein's admission. In the debate on 28 September opinions were quite sharply divided. Mr John Roper MP (UK) proposed that the matter be shelved while the principle of membership by mini-states was examined. (He may in fact also have been aiming at the question of women's suffrage.) His motion was defeated. In the ensuing discussion objections were raised on the grounds of Liechtenstein's size, sovereignty, tax laws and women's suffrage. The question of size was dealt with on the grounds that the Council of Europe had no criteria on the subject and each application had to be decided on its own democratic merits. A French Socialist parliamentarian said that Europe was a mixture of large and small nations and it was not always the large ones who provided the best examples. The argument about sovereignty was quickly settled. A British parliamentarian said that existing member states such as Luxembourg, Malta and Switzerland were also described as tax havens (indeed, Great Britain and France were themselves in certain terms tax havens), but that no-one was suggesting that these members should be expelled on that account. A German parliamentarian said that tax oases could only exist if there was a surrounding tax desert, and the fact that there was a desert was perhaps due to member countries' own legislation. On women's suffrage (the most thorny of the objections) several speakers pointed out that Swiss women had not had the vote when their country was admitted in 1961 and that in Liechtenstein's case the Government, the Parliament and the political parties were solidly in favour of women's suffrage.[5] Furthermore, the main women's organisation in Liechtenstein had written to Jessel to say that they would welcome their country's admission to the Council as a way of helping their cause.[6]

The vote in the Parliamentary Assembly was strongly in favour of Liechtenstein's admission. Shortly before the debate the new Head of Government, Hans Brunhart, wrote to Kahn-Ackermann on 19 September to say that if elected Liechtenstein would immediately sign the European Convention on Human Rights and Fundamental Freedoms. He wrote again on 8 November to say that Liechtenstein's admission to the Council of Europe would greatly help towards achieving votes for women and that the Government would make every effort towards this.

These efforts brought results. On 13 November 1978 the Committee of Ministers invited Liechtenstein to join the Council of Europe as its 21st member. On 23 November Brunhart deposited the Instrument of Accession at Strasbourg.

Admission to the Council of Europe was welcomed in Liechtenstein as an important landmark in its history. It was not merely a fresh acknowledgement of its independence and sovereignty, important though that was, but it also gave an opportunity to show what a small country could contribute to a major international organisation. Liechtenstein has remained an active member. It has run an efficient presidency when its turn has come round. Membership has given it a much-needed East-West vantage and contact point in a new and increasingly complex Europe.

High Level Visits

A more active foreign policy and easier international travel generated a flow of important visits, both outward and inward. Many of these have been unofficial, such as the private visit by Queen Elizabeth II and the Duke of Edinburgh after their State Visit to Switzerland in 1980. The first official visit by a foreign head of government was by the Austrian Federal Chancellor Bruno Kreisky in 1975. Others began to follow. For Liechtenstein as a whole, the most moving and symbolic visit of all was that paid by Pope John Paul II in 1985.

---

[5] Report of the Council of Europe Parliamentary Assembly, 28 September 1978, AS (30) CR 11.
[6] Council of Europe Parliamentary Assembly Doc. 4211, 13 September 1978 (Mr Jessel's Opinion on Liechtenstein's accession to the Council of Europe).

THE ACCESSION OF HANS-ADAM II (1989)

Franz Josef II became the longest serving monarch in Europe. His later years were marked by a series of celebrations of his major birthdays, jubilees of his reign and national anniversaries. These became occasions for people to look back in gratitude (and perhaps in surprise) at what had been achieved since 1938 and to weigh up the country's prospects.

Franz Josef often referred to Liechtenstein as a "big family". He was revered as its father. He was anxious to maintain the human dimension of the State and the coherence of society as a whole. He showed particular care for education and housing, so that younger people might have the greatest possible opportunity to advance their careers and to found families. His speeches at the annual opening of the Parliament tended to concentrate on internal matters. However, he also took a close interest in foreign affairs. He did not live to see the final collapse of communism in Europe, but he had predicted the date with remarkable accuracy. His friendly but shy personality was well complemented by Princess Gina's warm and outgoing manner.

Franz Josef's concern for harmony, social progress and the disadvantaged did not mean that he was disposed to compromise at any price. *In extremis*, he was ready to use his constitutional prerogatives. On his 75th birthday in 1981 the President of the Parliament Dr Karlheinz Ritter said, like other commentators, that Franz Josef had "the courage to say and to decide the uncomfortable".[1]

Prince Hans-Adam as Franz Josef's Representative

On the 45th anniversary of his accession, in 1983, Franz Josef announced his intention to transfer the exercise of his sovereign powers to his eldest son Prince Hans-Adam, while himself remaining titular Head of State and Head of the House of Liechtenstein. This decision took effect in 1984 after an amendment to the Constitution.

Hans-Adam's reign is studied in greater detail below (pages 178–188). When he became his father's representative he was already well known for his questioning

---

[1] "Liechtenstein 1978–1988", page 111.

style and his direct, informal approach to people and problems. His message from the start was that he would take a personal and active part in foreign policy, which would include visits and personal contacts. He did not feel a need for special advisers. Like his father he would deal directly with the Head or other members of the Government and he would in general make himself as accessible as possible.[2]

The change of style is noticeable in Prince Hans-Adam's Speeches from the Throne. Like his other speeches and press interviews they are more detailed and analytical than his father's, more concerned with foreign policy, perhaps more urgent in tone. It was Hans-Adam who made the National Day ceremony more accessible to the public by transferring the religious service from the Vaduz parish church to the Castle Meadow and by opening the Castle gardens afterwards for a reception for all who wish to attend. On this, as on many other occasions, he is open to anyone who wishes to speak to him.

Franz Josef's Death

In the year after Franz Josef II's Golden Jubilee, Princess Gina died on 18 October 1989. Franz Josef followed her on 13 November 1989. This double loss was felt in Liechtenstein as the end of an era. Although Franz Josef had ceased to take part in affairs of state, he and his wife had remained active in the country's social life until their last few weeks. The country felt that it and they had been companions on a long historical journey. They were deeply mourned.

The Succession

On 5 December 1989 Prince Hans-Adam II made the prescribed declaration to the Parliament to the effect that he had assumed the government of the country and would rule according to the Constitution and the other laws. The Parliament formally accepted this declaration and undertook to recognise Hans-Adam as the country's Prince, to respect his honour and dignity and to promote the wellbeing of the Princely House to the best of their ability and in good faith.

A law was passed to make 15 August the country's permanent National Day. On that day in 1990, at an open-air ceremony modelled on his father's accession ceremony in 1939 but on a larger scale, Hans-Adam II promised the assembled people to work for their welfare and that of the country according to the Constitution. His eldest son Alois made the promise with him. Hans-Adam explained that this was because he was already taking important decisions jointly with the Hereditary Prince. He intended to appoint him as his representative from time to

---

[2] "Liechtenstein 1978–1988", sections on 1983 and 1984. See also his extensive interview published in the "Liechtensteiner Volksblatt" for 14 August 1990 and reprinted in "Thronfolge" (Verlag der Fürstlichen Regierung, Vaduz, 1990), pages 82–85)

time on particular occasions. He would in due course follow Franz Josef's example by entirely handing over to him his own duties as Head of State. "Neither sickness nor death should decide when the functions of the Head of State shall pass to the successor".[3]

---

[3] "Thronfolge", pages 91–94. At the National Day ceremony on 15 August 2003, Hans-Adam II announced that he would hand over the exercise of his powers to Prince Alois on 15 August 2004, while remaining Sovereign Prince.

ADMISSION TO THE UNITED NATIONS (1990)

The Problem of Small States

Article 4(1) of the United Nations Charter states, "Membership in the United Nations is open to all other[1] peace-loving states which accept the obligations contained in the present Charter and, in the judgment of the Organization, are able and willing to carry out these obligations". The word "all" implies universal membership. Unlike the League of Nations, the UN has never refused an applicant on grounds of lack of size.

Size was, however, a problem for the larger Western member states as decolonisation advanced in the 1960s. This process produced a number of small, militarily vulnerable and potentially unstable states. Some of them were impoverished and economically dependent on metropolitan economies. The turning point was probably the admission of the Maldives (population 90,000, area 298 square miles) in 1965. By mid-1971, 85 of the UN's 127 members accounted for only 10% of the world's population and 5% of its economic wealth, but they had the power to commit the UN to serious actions and expenditure by a two-thirds majority vote.

In August 1969 the US Ambassador Yost proposed a UN study of the micro-state problem, fearing that the UN could "die of creeping irrelevance". In that year the US proposed a status of Associate Membership, without the power to vote or to hold office but with exemption from the obligation to pay financial assessments. The United Kingdom followed in 1971 with a variant that would have involved voluntary renunciation of certain rights (in particular voting and election rights in certain UN bodies) and only a nominal financial assessment. But these ideas foundered on the fact that the right to vote was an expression of the sovereign equality of all member states. It would have required an amendment of the Charter to accommodate them; and, in the Cold War, Charter amendment was not an attractive proposition. The United States began to find that the votes of small states could in fact be helpful. For their part, small states with limited resources found the UN headquarters an essential clearing house for their diplomatic, security and economic needs.

[1] That is, states other than the 52 original members.

Preparations for Liechtenstein's Application

Liechtenstein was not comparable with the newly decolonised countries, but an application for UN membership was not possible until the international climate was right and the UN's older and bigger members had reconciled themselves to the participation of very small states.

There was much opposition among domestic public opinion, too. Many people feared that UN membership would drag the country into international disputes, prejudice its neutrality, lock it into an international bureaucracy and cause needless and unforeseeable expense. Above all, there was great psychological reluctance to part diplomatic company with Switzerland. Although Switzerland belonged to many organisations in the UN "family", Swiss public opinion was known to be hostile to UN membership, as was to be proved again in the referendum of March 1986.

With membership of the Council of Europe assured, Franz Josef II, Hereditary Prince Hans-Adam and the Government began an insistent campaign to win over public opinion. In his Speech from the Throne on 31 March 1982 Franz Josef pointed to the need for Liechtenstein, in an economically interdependent world, to develop its contacts and co-operation with other states. In 1985, in a stroke of cultural diplomacy, Hans-Adam organised a spectacular exhibition of the Princely art treasures at the Metropolitan Museum of Art. This attracted more than 500,000 visitors and put Liechtenstein on the map in New York. In June 1985 Hans Brunhart paid an official visit to London as Head of Government and Foreign Minister during which he was received by Mrs Thatcher. Baroness Young (Minister of State at the Foreign and Commonwealth Office) recalled in her speech at a dinner in his honour that in 1983 Liechtenstein, together with its fellow neutrals, had rescued the Madrid CSCE talks from deadlock. She said that the British Government would welcome Liechtenstein's membership of the UN as "the addition of a responsible voice to the highest levels of international debate and decision-making. We would do so because we recognise the potential of a nation to which we are bound by a common commitment to individual freedoms and democratic values."

From 1985 onwards, in successive speeches from the throne, Hans-Adam returned again and again to the need for UN membership. Liechtenstein, he said, needed to fight for its existence through an active foreign policy, but "any diplomacy must fail if one is not on the diplomatic stage".[2] Liechtenstein's historical experience was different from Switzerland's. Switzerland had always defended its existence by armed neutrality and possessed an excellent diplomatic machine. Liechtenstein, on the other hand, had always worked for its existence and inde-

---

[2] Speech from the Throne, 27 March 1985.

pendence by participating in international organisations and conferences. Hans-Adam admitted that the UN was not very popular and sometimes got a bad press, but he hoped that the Parliament would judge the matter in the light of Liechtenstein's long-term interests.[3]

European integration was much more directly relevant to Liechtenstein's foreign policy interests than was the UN, but world-wide recognition of Liechtenstein was vital for the country's European policy.[4] If, one day, the Liechtenstein people decided to give up their sovereignty so as to merge into a democratically united Europe, well and good; but it would not be acceptable for the people to lose their sovereignty by default, through not having taken sensible foreign policy decisions. Independence brought great economic advantages, which far outweighed the trivial costs of UN membership. Liechtenstein exported goods and financial services all over the world; if only for that reason, it needed to have its sovereignty internationally recognised. The treaty relationship with Switzerland might not last for ever. It would certainly change if Switzerland were to join the European Community. Liechtenstein would then need to be in a position to negotiate international trade and other arrangements for itself as a sovereign state.[5]

Success of the Application

Although the Prince and the Government were of the same mind on this question, their arguments made slow progress with the population. In May 1987 the Government for the first time issued a report on foreign policy, but a public opinion poll in 1988 suggested that only one quarter were in favour of UN membership and two thirds against. The affair provoked sharp controversy. Inevitably, it acquired a constitutional dimension. The Government commissioned two expert opinions on whether a popular referendum about UN membership was constitutionally necessary. They contradicted each other. It was decided that Article 8(2) of the Constitution would suffice and that the Parliament had sufficient competence to decide.

The Parliament held a discussion in closed session in 1988 (its first on the matter). After soundings in New York, the Government was able to report in October 1989 that an application would be treated favourably. The Parliament voted unanimously in favour. Liechtenstein's application was submitted to the Secretary-General. The Security Council voted for it unanimously and the General Assembly accepted it by acclamation. On 18 September 1990 the national flag

---

[3] Speech from the Throne, 16 April 1986.
[4] Speech from the Throne, 8 March 1988.
[5] Speech from the Throne, 18 March 1989.

was hoisted in New York to denote Liechtenstein's admission as the 160th member of the United Nations.[6]

Since 1990 the Liechtenstein delegation, led until 2002 by Ambassador Claudia Fritsche, has been as active as its small resources have allowed.[7] It has to be selective. Its priorities have been international law, human rights, social and humanitarian questions including the advancement of women, and the environment. The Liechtenstein Initiative on Self-Determination occupies a special place in its activities (see pages 359–360 below.) Probably no-one in Liechtenstein now harbours doubts about the value of UN membership.

The Referendum on State Treaties

Article 8 (1) of the 1921 constitution says that the Sovereign Prince "shall represent the State in all its relations with foreign countries, without prejudice to the necessary participation of the responsible government". This gives him a strong position in the conduct of foreign affairs. Article 8 (2) of the Constitution says, "Treaties by which national territory is ceded, national property alienated, rights of sovereignty or State prerogatives disposed of, any new burden for the Principality or its citizens imposed or any obligation to the detriment of the rights of the People of the Principality contracted shall not be valid unless they have received the assent of the Parliament".

Knowing that hard and controversial decisions on foreign policy lay ahead, Prince Hans-Adam said in March 1988 that it did not seem consistent with the spirit of the constitution to exclude the people from all foreign policy decisions, especially if some future move to join the EC might (unlike UN membership) impinge on direct democracy.[8]

In 1989 the small radical political party "Freie Liste" argued that a popular vote was necessary for so controversial a matter as UN membership. It proposed an initiative for the right of holding popular referenda on Liechtenstein's adhesion to international treaties. Both parties in the Parliament voted unanimously against the proposal, arguing that the Government's hands must not be tied when handling internationally and domestically sensitive matters such as these. The people voted against the proposal by 3,644 to 4,787 (turnout 64.9%).

In 1992 the initiative was repeated, this time by the Liechtenstein Chamber of Commerce and Trade, possibly with the intention of frustrating Liechtenstein's entry into the European Economic Area. Once again the Government and all but three members of the Parliament voted against it, for the same reasons as before.

---

[6] Switzerland joined only in 2002 as the 190th member.
[7] The Ambassador was quoted by "Newsweek" in December 1990 as saying, "For next year's General Assembly I will buy a pair of roller skates".
[8] Speech from the Throne, 8 March 1988.

On this occasion the proposal won a convincing victory. By 6,281 votes to 2,513 (turnout of 64.7%) the people approved an additional constitutional Article (66 bis), under which any resolution of the Parliament concerning assent to a treaty must be submitted to a referendum if the Parliament so decides or if no fewer than 1,500 citizens or four communes submit a petition to that effect.

Diplomatic Representation in Vaduz

By 1990 Liechtenstein had established permanent diplomatic missions at ambassadorial level in Berne, Strasbourg and New York. However, with the exception of Austria, which conducted relations with Liechtenstein through a Foreign Ministry official based in Vienna, most foreign countries transacted business with Vaduz through consular officials based in Zurich or honorary consuls in Liechtenstein. The Liechtenstein Government considered consular representation alone to be inconsistent with its UN membership, and insufficient in view of the looming European negotiations.

Early in 1991 the Liechtenstein Ambassador in Berne, Prince Nikolaus, requested that the EC member states should accredit ambassadors to Liechtenstein. He said that Vaduz was prepared to accept the accreditation of ambassadors on a non-reciprocal and non-resident basis from states with which it had substantive dealings, i.e. Council of Europe members and CSCE participants. Liechtenstein would not appoint non-resident ambassadors in return; it had neither the resources nor the staff to do so. Vaduz suggested that normally the ambassadors should be resident in Berne; consular services might also be based in Berne, or else in Zurich or St Gallen. Vaduz said that the Swiss authorities had been sounded and had no objection.

The EC ambassadors in Berne reported to Brussels that Liechtenstein's motivation to establish diplomatic relations with third countries was to underline its sovereignty and identity, but also that it was a practical priority for Liechtenstein in the light of the European Economic Area negotiations then in progress. On the EC side, the ambassadors considered that the fact that member states were represented only at consular level hampered political dialogue. The EC's Political Committee agreed on 13 September 1991 with their recommendation to appoint non-resident ambassadors to Liechtenstein. Other countries such as the USA and the Russian Federation took the same decision.

THE EUROPEAN ECONOMIC AREA (1988–1995)

By 1988 the European Free Trade Area (EFTA) consisted of Austria, Finland, Iceland, Norway, Sweden and Switzerland. Liechtenstein was an appendage to EFTA by virtue of the Special Protocol to the EFTA Convention signed on 4 January 1960: it was not a member of EFTA but the EFTA Convention applied to its territory. Liechtenstein also had a seat in the Switzerland-European Economic Community Joint Commission by virtue of the Swiss-EEC Treaty of 22 July 1972.

Under Jacques Delors' presidency of the European Commission the process known as "the construction of Europe" gathered speed. The EFTA states were the EEC's biggest trading partner. In 1984 ministers of the EEC and EFTA countries stated in the Luxembourg Declaration their political intention to create a "dynamic European economic space" which would go beyond the realm of pure trade policy. After years of negotiation the EEC member states signed in 1986 the Single European Act which, starting from 1 July 1987, was intended to bring the European Single Market into existence on 1 January 1993. In January 1989 Delors spoke to the European Parliament of a search for new forms of EC-EFTA association, with common organs for decision-making and administration on the basis of the "two pillars" of the EC and EFTA. In the following months ministers and officials from the countries concerned, including Liechtenstein, considered the way forward, the opportunities and the obstacles.

The Commission made it clear that it wanted to negotiate with EFTA as a whole, not with its individual members in parallel. This was unwelcome to Switzerland, which however accepted in November 1990 that bilateral co-operation *à la carte* or at varying speeds would no longer be possible. As a result, the nature of EFTA changed: it became necessary for its member states to speak with one voice after consultation and consensus among themselves. The matter became more urgent as the Single Market approached completion, communism collapsed, Germany reunited peacefully within NATO, the Maastricht Treaty was signed and the prospect appeared of a new wave of central European applicants for EU membership.

The Perspectives for Liechtenstein

Isolation was economically impossible for a small country depending on its worldwide export trade and its financial services. Some form of association with the EC was therefore inevitable; but in what form? Prince Hans-Adam and his government were agreed that full membership of the EC would be a practical impossibility. The economic and political demands would be too great and a country as small as Liechtenstein could hardly hope, for example, to run a six-months presidency whose demands were taxing even for much bigger states.[1] It was natural to hope that Liechtenstein would, as in the past, be able to swim in Switzerland's wake. Switzerland had a powerful economy and strong links with the EC. The open border between the two countries that was symbolised by the Customs Treaty was essential for Liechtenstein. Although the Customs Treaty itself dated from a bygone era, historical and personal memories made it a totem that people were reluctant to tamper with.[2] But Switzerland's own future path was unclear. It was not certain that Switzerland would be able to extract from the negotiations all that it and Liechtenstein needed. It was not certain that the joint EC-EFTA European Economic Area (EEA) would come into being or, if it did, that Switzerland would become a member. If Switzerland were to join the EC, part of the Customs Treaty would be overtaken by that new relationship and the successor arrangements might not suit Liechtenstein's interests. It therefore became clear that Liechtenstein would have to strike out as a negotiating partner in its own right or risk disappearing as an independent political force.

Late in the day, therefore, (but not too late) the Liechtenstein Government began to make official and unofficial contacts with Brussels. At an EC-EFTA ministerial meeting in Brussels in February 1988 Liechtenstein signalled its interest in participating in its own right in areas of co-operation not covered by the Customs Treaty (for example, services). In October 1988 Hans Brunhart (Head of Government and Foreign Minister) paid an official visit to Brussels to become better acquainted with the EC's thinking. At a meeting in Berne in January 1990 the Swiss Government showed much understanding. It had no wish for Liechtenstein to atrophy, even if privately some Swiss may have doubted Liechtenstein's stamina to see the story through. Liechtenstein began gradually to raise its profile with the EC and EFTA, receiving an open and frank welcome in both quarters. On 1 March 1991 it applied to join EFTA as the seventh full member. It was accepted on 22 May. This step was preceded by a Supplementary Customs Treaty

---

[1] Speech from the Throne, 18 March 1989. Liechtenstein Government's Report No. 45/1989 of 7 November 1989 on European Integration, pages 81–82. Liechtenstein Government's Supplementary Report No. 92/1992 of 13 October 1992 on a Possible Application for EC Membership, pages 14–15.

[2] Prince Hans-Adam caused a stir when he suggested in a speech at Feldkirch in January 1987 that the Customs Treaty with Switzerland was not indispensable to Liechtenstein.

with Switzerland, signed on 26 November. The new treaty adapted the 1923 relationship by allowing Liechtenstein to become a party to treaties or international organisations with economic objectives provided that Switzerland was also a party to them.

The way was now clear for Liechtenstein to embark on the most ambitious and complex negotiations in its history. Its inexperienced negotiators had to learn quickly.

The Purpose of the EEA

The Liechtenstein Government set the scene domestically on 7 November 1989 with a first report to the Parliament on its European integration policy. It dawned on everyone that this would be no ordinary international negotiation: its results would touch many aspects of economic and daily life.

The purpose of the EEA was to give freer access to an integrated Single European Market of 380 million people. To this end, the EC insisted that the EFTA states should accept the principles of free movement of persons, services, goods and capital. It also insisted that they should accept the whole of the *"acquis communautaire"* (the sum of EC legislation and rules) in these areas. This amounted to some 1,500 measures in about 12,000 pages, which had to be taken over into Liechtenstein's legislation. Associated with the four freedoms was a range of "horizontal" and "flanking" measures. The horizontal measures were designed to promote more equal competition. They included social policy, health and safety, health insurance, employees' rights, consumer protection, the environment, statistics, company law and sex equality. The flanking measures consisted of looser co-operation in the form of programmes in such areas as research and development, further education, information services, small and medium enterprises, the audiovisual sector, civil protection and tourism. They also included contributions to the economic and social "cohesion" funds for the benefit of the EC's less prosperous regions, which the EFTA states said they were willing to make.

Far-reaching though it was, the EEA fell a long way short of EC membership. It was not a customs union abolishing borders between EC and EFTA states. It did not entail common trade, agricultural or fishery policies. EFTA states were left free to negotiate their own foreign trade treaties with third countries. There was no monetary union and no co-operation in foreign and security policy, justice and home affairs. It did not cover taxation. There was no ultimate objective such as the "ever closer union" enshrined in the Treaty of Rome. It could be denounced by any of its parties, unlike the Treaty of Rome and its successors.

The Problems and Opportunities for Liechtenstein

Having a highly-developed industry but a minute domestic market, Liechtenstein needed its access to the Single European Market to be as free and unrestricted as possible. The 1972 Swiss-EEC Agreement alone was not sufficient for this. Neither was GATT (soon to be replaced by the World Trade Organisation), which Liechtenstein joined in 1994. The physical export of goods presented no great problem. What was more important was the elimination of discrimination and the harmonisation of standards and regulations (the so-called "technical barriers to trade"). Liechtenstein needed to participate, where possible and necessary, in that harmonisation. This would reduce the risk of Liechtenstein's manufacturing industry's transferring its research, development and production abroad, which was thought more likely to happen should Liechtenstein find itself in isolation. Conversely, while the opening of the country's financial sector would expose the three Liechtenstein banks to domestic competition, it would make it easier for them to expand their operations in the other eighteen EEA member states. Liechtenstein industry's participation in EU research programmes would help to secure the 400 highly qualified research jobs in the country and to enhance its own competitiveness. It would become easier for Liechtenstein citizens to find employment elsewhere in the EEA. Programmes like ERASMUS and COMETT would offer young people better chances to study abroad and at home, while the diplomas of the Liechtenstein Engineering School would be recognised throughout the EEA.

Individual EFTA member states had particular bilateral problems; for example, fisheries in the case of Iceland and Norway and Alpine transit traffic in the case of Switzerland. All shared a concern for environmental standards, which were higher in EFTA states than in the EC. For Liechtenstein, the biggest among many other problems were those connected with the free movement of persons, which was a crucial component of the *acquis communautaire*. The indigenous workforce was small. The economy needed foreign workers, particularly skilled workers. By 1988 the proportion of resident foreigners in the country had risen to 34.5% (9,711), despite attempts to hold it at 31.4%. Of 19,103 registered jobs, 11,433 (59.8%) were held by foreigners (both residents and trans-frontier commuters).[3] However, completely free access as required by the EC would lead to intolerable pressure on the economy, political identity and character of the country. The right to acquire land would go hand in hand with the right of EEA persons and businesses to establish themselves freely, seek employment and transfer capital. But Liechtenstein's land area was small. It could not be enlarged. Overcrowding and over-building would have serious environmental consequences. Like Austria and Switzerland, Liechtenstein imposed severe restrictions on the purchase of real estate by foreigners. However, in Liechtenstein, unlike in its two neighbours,

---

[3] Liechtenstein Government Report of 7 November 1989 to the Landtag, page 71.

there was a general requirement for official permission to purchase real estate which applied equally to everyone, including Liechtenstein citizens.[4]

The Negotiations

From 1989, even before it became a full member of EFTA, Liechtenstein took part at all levels in the EEA exploratory talks and later in the negotiations. At the same time, the Government embarked on thorough programmes of domestic consultation and information.

EFTA and the EC intended that the negotiations should be concluded by the end of 1990, so that the EEA Agreement might come into force simultaneously with the Single European Market. At that stage EFTA was aiming for a structured partnership in which the decision-making and administrative machinery would be genuinely joint in both substance and form, so that neither side could present *faits accomplis* to the other. The *acquis communautaire* would be taken as the standard against which any exceptions and transitional arrangements should be measured. There should be independent joint surveillance authorities and a joint EEA Court for the settlement of disputes. However, in his speech of 17 January 1990 to the European Parliament Delors said that while a certain "osmosis" would be necessary between the EC and EFTA pillars of the EEA, it would not be possible to permit joint decision-making on matters which were reserved to the EC member states.

There was, therefore, no agreement on institutional matters. EFTA's bargaining hand was weakened by differing perspectives among its members. Austria applied for EC membership in July 1989 and therefore no longer had any strong interest in pressing hard in the EEA negotiations. The Swedish Government's decision in October 1990 to consult about EC membership (perhaps influenced by Delors' tough stand and the related drive of the Twelve towards the Maastricht Treaty on European Union) was a turning point. In 1991 the Swiss Federal Council declared EC membership to be "a strategic goal". Finland applied to join the EC in 1992.

Formal negotiations began in June 1990. The question of exceptions became another sticking point. Positions hardened. In October the Commission made new demands for concessions on agriculture. Disagreements on environmental protection deepened. The EC Council of Ministers, however, gave a political signal of continuing interest in the negotiations. EFTA tabled a new offer: it would withdraw its demand for permanent exceptions provided that there was a satisfactory solution on the legal and institutional structures, that transitional periods

---

[4] Liechtenstein Government Report to the Landtag No. 1995/1 of 7 February 1995, page 158. Fifth Supplementary Report No. 48/1991 of 26 June 1991, page 14.

for the adaptation of national legislation could be introduced and that safeguard clauses and mechanisms for specific circumstances would be possible. This last point was of crucial importance to Liechtenstein.

By December 1990 progress had been made on a number of points, including safeguards. But the institutional, legal and certain other problems remained. The Commission was not much disposed to make substantive concessions; it saw the opening of the Single Market to the EFTA states as sufficient concession in itself.[5] By May 1991 the negotiations had reached crisis point across a range of issues. Successive deadlines for initialling the EEA Agreement were missed. In December the European Communities Court rejected the proposed EEA Court even in the diluted form which had been agreed. A further solution agreed in February 1992 was met with objections by the European Parliament. After more negotiations, the agreement was initialled in Brussels by the negotiators on 14 April 1992 and signed by EC and EFTA ministers at Porto on 2 May 1992.

Referenda in Switzerland and Liechtenstein

After a tough and in some respects disappointing negotiation the Swiss and Liechtenstein governments were nevertheless able to commend the results to their voters.

Through the summer of 1992 a rather tense and bad-tempered campaign was fought out in Switzerland. The entire "establishment" favoured the agreement, but part of the public (how big, no-one could tell) was sceptical. On 18 May the Federal Council, encouraged by a referendum vote in favour of Swiss entry into the Bretton Woods institutions, formally applied for membership of the EC. This move had the advantage of putting their application on the table while it was still politically possible: if the EEA referendum went badly, it could always be reactivated at some future date. But it stiffened the opposition of those Swiss who suspected that the Federal Council saw the EEA not as a goal but only as a stepping stone to EC membership.

In Liechtenstein, the Government admitted that the EEA would not have the same power of co-decision as EFTA had originally intended. But it argued that the country's vital interests (freedom of movement and land ownership) had been protected and that new opportunities would be opened up. In answer to objections, it said that the smaller businesses were unlikely to suffer too much from greater foreign competition since they were already exposed to competition from Switzerland and Austria. Wage levels were unlikely to fall. The EEA Agreement neither included tax harmonisation nor affected bank client secrecy.

The timing of the referendum in Liechtenstein in relation to that in

---

[5] Liechtenstein Government Report No. 46/92 of 15 June 1992, page 13.

Switzerland proved troublesome; it led to the constitutional crisis of 28 October 1992 (pages 197–198 below).

The Swiss people voted first. On 6 December 1992 they decided by 50.3% to 49.7% to reject the EEA Agreement. The majority was slim (23,105), but the turn-out was nearly 80%. Only seven out of the twenty-three cantons showed a majority for the treaty. By Swiss standards, this was decisive. The Federal Council embarked on the long and stony road of bilateral negotiations with an irritated Brussels on a package covering seven separate sectors. There was much domestic acrimony.

On 13 December the Liechtenstein people voted firmly for the treaty by 6,722 in favour and 5,322 against. The turnout was 87%. The atmosphere after the vote was one of mild bemusement at their own boldness, but much optimism. The Swiss cartoonist Chappatte noted the irony that tiny Liechtenstein was now more closely integrated than his own country into Europe and the international community.[6]

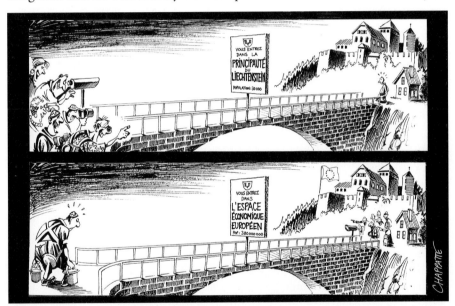

Liechtenstein viewed from Switzerland, before and after the two countries' differing votes on entry into the European Economic Area, December 1992.

Negotiations with Berne and Brussels

The Swiss people's refusal to ratify the treaty unleashed a wave of interna-tional renegotiations and adaptations. The EC and EFTA had to remove those provisions which were specific to Switzerland. This was done by an Adaptation Protocol signed on 17 March 1993, and the EEA came into existence on 1 January

---

[6] His cartoon is reproduced above, by kind permission.

1994. Liechtenstein's membership, however, was delayed owing to the need to adjust its own treaty relationship with Switzerland in the light of the new circumstances.

Liechtenstein now had to square the circle of conforming to its EEA obligations while keeping the open border with Switzerland. Throughout 1993 and most of 1994 the Liechtenstein Ambassador in Berne, Prince Nikolaus, led negotiations with the Swiss authorities. They found that while there were a myriad technical problems to be solved, the Customs Treaty and other agreements threw up no insuperable obstacle of principle. The Swiss authorities were helpful. In December 1993 Liechtenstein was able to present the outlines of a solution to its EEA partners. The Commission expressed itself content after talks in 1994. After further negotiations, a treaty with Switzerland was signed in Berne on 2 November 1994 and was unanimously approved by the Swiss Parliament the following month. Approval by the various EFTA, EEA and EU bodies followed in the next few weeks.

The central point was that Liechtenstein's territory was so small that flows of goods could easily be monitored. There was only one customs post in the country (Schaanwald, on the Austrian frontier). It was easy to adapt that and its Swiss counterpart at Buchs to the new requirements. Liechtenstein took over responsibility for policing EEA requirements. For that purpose it set up its own Customs Office and created some new posts in other government departments (thirteen extra people in all). It had to ensure that unauthorised goods did not flow into the EEA from Switzerland, and vice-versa. In practice this was unlikely to be a great problem since Swiss and EU standards were increasingly coming into line. EEA and Swiss goods were left free to circulate in Liechtenstein in parallel. The Customs Treaty was further modified to say that if Liechtenstein wished to become a party to a treaty or international organisation to which Switzerland did not belong, but whose subject matter was within the framework of the Customs Treaty, a special agreement between the two countries would be necessary. The Postal Treaty was made EEA-compatible. Provision was made that Swiss citizens should not be at a disadvantage compared with EEA citizens in terms of residence, land purchase or public procurement in Liechtenstein.

The Government commended all this work (ten agreements with Switzerland and six EEA documents) to the Parliament, which approved it. A popular referendum in Liechtenstein on 9 April 1995 gave consent by 6,412 votes to 5,062, with a turnout of 82%. Liechtenstein formally became a member of the EEA on 1 May 1995.

Safeguards

Crucial to the Liechtenstein people's approval was the understanding in Brussels of the country's inability to accept an unlimited number of new residents from other EEA countries (or, indeed, from anywhere).

Article 112 (1) of the EEA Agreement contains a general safeguards provision to the effect that "If serious economic, societal or environmental difficulties of a sectorial or regional nature liable to persist are arising, a Contracting Party may unilaterally take appropriate measures under the conditions and procedures laid down in Article 113". Protocol 15 (Articles 5–7) allowed Liechtenstein to keep its restrictions on freedom of movement from other EEA countries in force until 1 January 1998, while Article 9 (2) said, "At the end of the transitional period for Liechtenstein the transitional measures shall be jointly reviewed by the Contracting Parties, duly taking into account the specific geographic situation of Liechtenstein". The Liechtenstein Government made a unilateral declaration that it "Expects that due regard will be paid under the EEA Agreement to the specific geographical situation of Liechtenstein". It considered that a situation relevant to Article 112 would be considered to exist if capital inflows from another contracting party were liable to endanger the access of the resident population to real estate, or if there were to be an extraordinary increase in the number of EC and EFTA residents or in the total number of jobs compared with the number of the resident population.[7] The European Community made no comment on this unilateral declaration, unlike most other countries' unilateral declarations attached to the Agreement.

After the successful completion of Liechtenstein's negotiations with Switzerland, the EEA Council decided on 10 March 1995 that "the good functioning of the Agreement is not impaired by the regional union between Switzerland and Liechtenstein". Among other separate declarations, the EEA Council specifically recognised that "Liechtenstein has a very small inhabitable area of rural character with an unusually high percentage of non-national residents and employees. Moreover, it recognises the vital interest of Liechtenstein to maintain its own national identity."[8]

The transitional arrangements were formally reviewed between 1997 and 1999. The EEA Joint Committee maintained the principle of freedom of movement but concluded that Liechtenstein's situation continued to justify the maintenance of certain conditions on the right of taking up residence there. The granting of residence permits to EEA nationals was slightly eased and restrictions on seasonal workers were relaxed, but the Principality's needs were met in general. The next review is to be completed by 31 December 2006, again with Liechtenstein's "specific geographical situation" being taken into account.[9]

---

[7] Official Journal of the European Communities, 3 January 1994, pages L/28, 176–178 and 562.
[8] EEA Council Decision No. 1/95, Official Journal of the European Communities, 20 April 1995, pages L 86/58 and 86/80.
[9] Decision No. 191/1999 of the EEA Joint Committee of 17 December 1999, Official Journal of the European Communities, 15 March 2001, pages L74/29–31.

Liechtenstein's New Standing in Europe

The accession of Austria, Finland and Sweden to the EU on 1 January 1995 left only three EFTA states as members of the EEA (Iceland, Liechtenstein and Norway). This lopsided arrangement raises questions about the EEA's future in the longer term. However, the popular votes of 1992 and 1995 left Liechtenstein as well positioned as it could hope to be. The country was integrated into European structures but the relationship with Switzerland was kept intact. Liechtenstein created room for manoeuvre for itself. It was no longer politically dependent on whether Switzerland joined the EU, or the EEA, or stayed outside. It was free to decide for itself how best to adapt to the further changes that were bound to come in Europe. This freedom, and the international recognition from which it sprang, were no foregone conclusion. They were the result of foresight, determination and hard work.

The institutions of the EEA consist of a Council, a Joint Committee, a Joint Parliamentary Committee and a Consultative Committee, each under a rotating presidency. The EEA Council's role is to give political impulse to implementation and amendment of the Agreement. It consists of members of the Council of the European Communities (Ministers), the Commission and one member of the government of each of the EFTA states. It normally meets twice a year. It is supported at official level by the EEA Joint Committee, which meets in principle at least once a month and which takes decisions by agreement between the EU on the one hand and "the EFTA states speaking with one voice" on the other. The EEA Consultative Committee represents the social partner bodies of the two organisations. There is an independent EFTA Surveillance Authority, which monitors fulfilment by EFTA states of their obligations under the Agreement in co-operation with the Commission. There is also an EFTA Court with competence for surveillance matters within EFTA.[10]

As a result of these arrangements Liechtenstein has the right to be informed and consulted by the Commission, both through the Joint Committee and at the level of experts, about proposed legislation that may affect it. It thus has the opportunity to influence decisions within the sphere of the Agreement before they are made. It can raise questions at any stage and at any level. It can raise political concerns at meetings of the EEA Ministerial Council. It can veto an EEA development at the point of acceptance, and open negotiations for a generally acceptable solution. It can take part in EU committees dealing with programmes in which EEA states have a financial stake. It also of course has continuing rights in the EFTA pillar of the EEA.

On joining the EEA Liechtenstein made a substantial contribution to a

---

[10] Official Journal of the European Communities, 3 January 1994, pages L1/22 to 28.

Cohesion Fund loan programme for the benefit of Greece, Portugal, the whole of Ireland and certain Spanish regions, back-dated to 1 January 1994. As a separate measure, it also joined the European Bank for Reconstruction and Development in 1991, to help the newly liberated countries of central and eastern Europe.

As Hans Brunhart said to EFTA and EC Ministers in May 1991 about their common European objectives, "You may be sure that Liechtenstein… will make its modest (but, for a small country, big) contribution".[11]

---

[11] Liechtenstein Government Fifth Supplementary Report No. 48/1991 of 26 June 1991, page 11.

PART II
THE CONSTITUTION AND POLITICS

THE 1921 CONSTITUTION

Pierre Raton summed up Liechtenstein's constitutional arrangements in 1949 as "a semi-direct governmental system combined with a representative system characterised by a Parliament, a referendum and a popular initiative".[1] This complicated definition holds good today.

The following pages set out to survey Liechtenstein's constitutional order, and how it operates in practice, as follows:

– the basic principles of the 1921 Constitution;
– the reign and policies of Hans-Adam II;
– the political parties and pressure groups:
– the constitutional controversy between 1992 and 2003;
– the powers and constitutional roles of the Prince, Parliament, Government, direct democracy, the courts and local government, including the changes that will result from the popular vote of March 2003;
– the relationship between State and Church;
– a summing-up.

The Basic Principles of the Constitution

Like any written constitution, Liechtenstein's is a product of its time. The preamble presents it as a modification of that of 1862. In fact, the 1921 revision was fundamental. Since then it has been adapted many times to changing circumstances, but the basic principles of 1921 have remained unaltered. In 1938 its working environment changed when, in place of an old and absentee monarch, a young and active Prince took up permanent residence in Vaduz.

The 1921 Constitution is usually described as a compromise between Prince and people. That is correct, in that Johann II was prepared (or obliged) to take account of the wishes of the leaders of the People's Party on the basis that they represented those of the majority of the people.[2] But it was also a compromise between the politicians themselves. If Wilhelm Beck and his colleagues were the

---

[1] Raton, op. cit., page 114.
[2] Wille, "Die Verfassung von 1921", op. cit. page 101.

174

driving force of change, the more conservative and monarchist FBP also influenced the work of the Constitutional Commission and the Parliament, partly but not entirely as a braking force.

As in 1862, the 1921 Constitution was negotiated between the Prince and the Parliament. It was not "granted". From henceforth it could be changed only with the approval of the Parliament or the people. The most important innovations were:

- Whereas the 1862 Constitution said, "The Prince is Head of State, combines within himself all rights of state authority and exercises them in accordance with the provisions of the present Constitution", that of 1921 says, "The Principality is a constitutional, hereditary monarchy on a democratic and parliamentary basis. The power of the State is inherent in and issues from the Sovereign Prince and the People and shall be exercised by both in accordance with the provisions of the present Constitution" (Article 2).[3] This is the fundamental and much-cited concept of "dualism". It means an active monarchy with strong political powers, together with direct democracy in the form of popular initiatives and referenda.
- All members of Parliament were to be elected by the people. No longer would three out of the fifteen be appointed by the Prince.
- The people gained the right, if they wished, to convene or dissolve the Parliament by popular vote.
- The Head and members of the Government were no longer to be nominated by the Prince but proposed to him by the Parliament. All members of the Government were to be native-born Liechtenstein citizens and (although not members of the Parliament) would have to meet the qualifications for election to the Parliament. There were to be no more Austrian-born Governors.
- The Parliament gained a say in the ratification of international treaties.
- The Parliament gained wider and better means of supervising and controlling the Government and administration, especially in the financial field.
- All courts were to sit in Liechtenstein. The judges were to be elected there instead of being selected, appointed and dismissed by the Prince alone. The courts of second and third instance were no longer to be in Vienna and Innsbruck respectively.
- An Administrative Complaints Court (for grievances against the authorities) and a State Court (to decide on conflicts of jurisdiction and to rule on the constitutionality of laws and regulations) were established.

---

[3] Where possible the author has used the official English translation (from 1998) of the Liechtenstein Constitution. But the reader should be aware that since this translation is not always satisfactory he has sometimes devised his own. Translations of the constitutional amendments of March 2003 are also the author's own, there being as yet no official English version.

– All authorities were to have their seats within the territory of the State and the collegial authorities were to include at least a majority of natives of Liechtenstein

The 1921 Constitution follows the principle of the separation of powers (executive, legislative, judicial). Chapter III, on the functions of the State, defines the State's supreme purpose as being to "promote the general welfare of the people" (Article 14). Since March 2003, Article 1 of the Constitution has contained an additional 'mission statement': "The purpose of the Principality of Liechtenstein is to enable the people living within its borders to live in freedom and peace with each other". This is intended to emphasise that membership of the State is based on free will and that the State is not an end in itself.

No fewer than three articles in Chapter III are devoted to education. Others provide for public health and welfare, the promotion of the economy, sovereignty over waters, hunting, fishing and mining, the regulation of the currency and banking system, an equitable taxation system and the opening up of new sources of revenue. In keeping with Liechtenstein's tradition of "small government", Chapter III lays down only the most general framework for state activity.

Chapter IV, on the general rights and obligations of citizens, provided from the start a comprehensive set of guarantees of basic human and political rights. These include freedom of movement and residence, voting rights, equality before the law, equal access to public office, equal rights between the sexes (since 1992, and also female suffrage since 1984), personal liberty, immunity of the home, inviolability of letters and written matter, freedom from arbitrary arrest and searches, access to justice, liability to lawful penalties only, the right of legal defence, inviolability of private property, freedom of belief and conscience, freedom of communication, association and assembly, the right of petition and complaint, etc. These provisions have been reinforced since 1921 through Liechtenstein's adherence to international agreements such as the European Convention for the Protection of Human Rights and Fundamental Freedoms. Article 33 forbids the institution of special tribunals.[4] Rather curiously for a country that has no army, Article 44 (1) stipulates that "Every man fit to bear arms shall be liable, up to the completion of his 60th year, to serve in the defence of his country in the event of emergency".[5]

The more operational parts of the Constitution contain a complex set of checks and balances. Any one of the main institutions can block the political process if it chooses. This fact puts a premium on consultation, negotiation and compromise. Minority views have to be respected. This means that although

---

[4] In keeping with this clause (and unlike in some other countries after 1945) Liechtenstein's Nazis plotters were tried before ordinary courts in 1946.
[5] However, in 1942 the government instituted one year's compulsory service on the land for 17-year olds as a wartime measure.

direct democracy (a popular vote) usually has the ultimate say, Liechtenstein operates as a consensus democracy as well. There is a high degree of popular and party participation in public and social affairs at every level. Issues are thrashed out at length and in detail. The careful constitutional balance and the pressure for consensus give the system strength, continuity and underlying stability, however heated and partisan the opinions expressed on particular issues at particular times may be. In quiet times the pressure for consensus can inhibit innovation and make it harder to anticipate oncoming problems; the convoy tends to travel at the speed of the slowest ship. But when an emergency is generally recognised and the various elements of the Constitution are in line with each other, the machine can work surprisingly quickly.

HANS-ADAM II:
A REVOLUTIONARY CONSERVATIVE

Hans-Adam and his Family

Hans-Adam II, the thirteenth Sovereign Prince of Liechtenstein and one of the most remarkable members of his dynasty, was the first Sovereign Prince to grow up in Liechtenstein. He was born in 1945. He attended an ordinary primary school in Vaduz before moving to the Schottengymnasium in Vienna and the Lyceum Alpinum in Zuoz (Grisons, Switzerland). After a short spell at a bank in London he studied economics at St Gallen from 1965 to 1969. In 1967 he married Marie Aglaë, Countess Kinsky von Wchinitz und Tettau, who comes from an old Czech noble family. From that marriage, celebrated with a public rejoicing that recalled his father's in 1943, were born the present Hereditary Prince Alois (1968), Maximilian (1969), Constantin (1972) and Tatjana (1973).

Prince Alois attended primary school in Vaduz like his father and then the Liechtenstein Gymnasium (secondary school). After military training at Sandhurst he served as a Coldstream Guards officer in London and Hong Kong. He studied law at Salzburg University from 1988 to 1993 and then worked for three years in London at Arthur Andersen. In 1993 he married HRH Duchess Sophie in Bayern, a member of the Bavarian Royal Family, at Vaduz. They now have three sons and one daughter, the eldest child (Josef Wenzel) having been born in 1995.

All members of the Liechtenstein family pursue their own careers. Most of them live abroad. Of Hans-Adam's two surviving brothers, Prince Philipp (born 1946) is chairman of the LGT Bank in Liechtenstein while Prince Nikolaus (born 1947) has for over thirty years been at the heart of Liechtenstein's foreign policy and is now serving as ambassador to Belgium and the European Union. At present, two other members of the House are serving as ambassadors of Liechtenstein at Berne and Vienna.

Hans-Adam as Prince

Hans-Adam would have preferred to be an archaeologist or scientist; but his first duty was to restore the family finances, which had been badly shaken by the losses incurred during and after the Second World War. In 1970 Franz Josef II established the Prince of Liechtenstein Foundation, to which all the family assets were transferred. Hans-Adam was appointed chairman. In that year also he began his public life with visits to EFTA in Geneva and to Paris for the funeral of General de Gaulle, and made the first of his many controversial speeches (page 149 above). His message about the future of Liechtenstein-Swiss relations (and, consequently, the messenger himself) caused some discomfort. He is unrepentant about causing controversy: he sees it as a way of getting people to look to the wider horizon. It is indeed hard to see how Liechtenstein could have become a member of the United Nations or the European Economic Area when it did without his personal drive.

Very hard working and personally modest, Hans-Adam II has no use for pomp and ceremony; he sees them as a drain of precious time and energy. He is at his best when mixing with people cheerfully and informally in the Castle garden after the National Day ceremonies or walking about at local events. Princess Marie, too, is informal in style and assiduous in attending to her charities, above all the Red Cross.

There is neither a Court nor a large staff at Vaduz. Hans-Adam's first move on becoming his father's representative was to abolish the old Cabinet Chancery ("Kabinettskanzlei"). Since then he has relied on a small office staff and on advisers hired for specific purposes. Aristocratic titles are not conferred on Liechtenstein citizens.[1] Distinguished service is sparingly recognised by the grant of a title such as Princely Councillor ("Fürstlicher Rat") or by the award of one of the classes of the Liechtenstein Order of Merit, founded by Franz I in 1937.

Hans-Adam takes an unsentimental view of his responsibilities: he has said that he works in the morning so that he can be a Prince in the afternoon. Those responsibilities are numerous. In addition to being head of state, he runs both a large business and one of the greatest private art collections in the world, and is head of a large and dispersed family. He also makes time for a variety of intellectual interests. He is quick to point out the disadvantages of his status: "Reigning houses are increasingly becoming the playthings of the mass media. In these circumstances, it is very difficult to lead a normal family life. A normally functioning family is, however, a prerequisite for passing on from generation to generation those values which in the end have been decisive for our family's success. Luckily, until now the smallness of the country and a low-key media policy have to a great extent saved us from becoming fodder for the media with all the associated problems."[2]

---

[1] There are a few rare examples of noble titles being conferred on foreigners, but this has not happened for many decades.
[2] Speech from the Throne, 15 March 1996.

That does not mean that he is detached from his role as monarch. He is proud of his House and deeply conscious of its traditions and possessions, past as well as present. The record shows that from the start he has been passionately concerned about the destinies of the country in which he grew up. But he has repeatedly said that he and his House, although glad to make their contribution to Liechtenstein, will do so only for as long as the people want them and are willing to allow them the necessary political powers. He once wrote of the critics of certain of his constitutional rights, "These are evidently persons who basically would like a republic but who do not dare to say so because this would be extremely unpopular with the people. If the majority of the population wants to turn the Principality of Liechtenstein into a Republic of the Upper Rhine Valley, the Princely House will accept that. The Princely House does not however consider it necessary, and I myself will never accept, that *de facto* the Prince should be no more than a hand-shaking puppet for the Government,[3] which is partly the case in other monarchies."[4]

Hans-Adam as a Thinker and Controversialist

Hans-Adam is an original conceptual and strategic thinker. He has reflected much on history and its revolutions. As a child of the 1960s, he has a questioning and probing mind. He challenges accepted wisdom. He knows that in politics, as in business, time has to be mastered and used if it is not to become an enemy; the initiative must be seized. He is optimistic about the future of small states, provided that they are agile and alert. He is convinced of the benefit that they and their human scale can bring to their populations – and perhaps to the wider world, too.

In forming his convictions, Hans-Adam's method seems to be to go back to first principles. He wrestles with every argument and counter-argument until he is at ease with the result. Once his opinion is settled he is a tenacious negotiator and advocate, all the more formidable for being master of the detail. He has a liking for humour and the unconventional; while still his father's representative he would engage in playful public correspondence with the satirical magazine "Mole" ("Maulwurf"), to the scandal of some. He has no objection to being challenged and seems to have a particular sympathy for young people's doubts and questions. He will take a question head on, whether face-to-face, in a group or in the media. He considers it only honest that his interlocutor should know precisely where he stands. If, however, he is provoked, or considers that his interlocutor is

---

[3] A free translation of "Grüssaugust der Regierung".
[4] Extract from a letter from Prince Hans-Adam II to Professor Arno Waschkuhn dated 3 February 1992, quoted by Waschkuhn, "Politisches System Liechtensteins: Kontinuität und Wandel", LPS Vol. 18, Vaduz, 1994, page 123.

arguing in bad faith or "should know better", the humour is replaced by irony and the irony can become caustic. Wounds can be inflicted without always being intended. The no-nonsense desire for results can become impatience. His public comments can become impetuous. His tactical objectives can suffer.

Self-Determination

Hans-Adam's breadth of vision is reflected in his earlier thinking about military strategy and about a possible constitution for the European Union.[5] More recently, he has been occupied with the concept of self-determination.[6] This began with the thought that great size does not necessarily bring success to either a state or a business. Few communities have been as creative and productive as the city-states of Ancient Greece or Renaissance Italy. In large states, centralisation leads to high taxation and inefficient bureaucracy. Even when large states try to decentralise, the result is usually another layer of local bureaucracy. Global free trade, local discontent and nationalism lead to their collapse, as seen in the dissolution of the Habsburg and Ottoman Empires, the colonial empires, the Soviet Union and Yugoslavia. If anything, free trade favours the smaller countries' economies; but political collapses breed war, international terrorism and economic disaster. That was how Hitler seized his chance to exploit the grievances of German minorities. In Hans-Adam's view, the remedy is not to try to freeze frontiers but to give even the smallest identifiable community the right to decide whether it wants more autonomy (political, fiscal, legislative), or to join another state, or to become independent. The state is intended to serve the people; the ballot box is more humane than the automatic rifle. "States must compete with each other peacefully, to offer their customers service at the lowest price".[7]

Hans-Adam argues that until now the right of self-determination has been exercised in decolonisation (now largely completed), or has been limited to people who have a distinct ethnic, religious or cultural background. All too often, restricting it to the latter has led to ethnic or religious cleansing and the violent destruction of states. If an international convention could establish an agreed concept of self-determination and procedures for its gradual application when required, the poisons of anxiety and violence would be assuaged. Differing levels of autonomy would give states and people time to adjust to the new structures. Politicians who asked for more autonomy or even independence for

---

[5] Waschkuhn, op. cit., pages 100–108.

[6] The details have been elaborated *inter alia* in Hans-Adam's speeches of 26 September 1991 and 25 October 1993 to the UN General Assembly and Third Committee respectively, in "Self-Determination and Self-Administration" (ed. Wolfgang Danspeckgruber and Sir Arthur Watts KCMG QC, pub. Lynne Rienner) and Hans-Adam's lecture at the International Institute for Strategic Studies, London, 25 January 2001.

[7] Lecture at Basel University, reported in the "Liechtensteiner Vaterland", 27 March 2001.

their communities would have to prove in real life that they could deliver what their people wanted. Larger minorities would have to respect smaller minorities. In practice, far from leading to the dissolution of states, self-determination would probably promote their survival: communities within decentralised systems would recognise the need for co-operation and would develop mutual confidence by practising it. The state would learn to manage its minorities better, while minorities would probably come to accept that adequate self-expression was more fruitful than a possibly unrealistic independence.

The concept of self-determination has been proposed at the United Nations (page 359) and included in the Liechtenstein Constitution (pages 263–264). Hans-Adam has endowed a foundation at Princeton University with $12 million to develop the concept and its practical application further.[8] In May 2001, the New York-based Roman Catholic Path to Peace Foundation presented its annual award to him in recognition of his efforts.[9]

The concept has inevitably met opposition at the United Nations, but it is in tune with the times. It fosters diversity. In recent years many states in Europe and elsewhere have tackled intractable internal problems precisely by granting devolution or self-determination, while those that have resorted to force have often come to regret it.[10]

The House Law ("Hausgesetz")

The Princely House's independence, political as well as financial, is an absolute requirement for Hans-Adam II. The Liechtenstein family, having operated for centuries on a European scale, does not wish to be tied down to a smaller stage. Hans-Adam sees this freedom as being anchored in the House Law which, as he never tires of pointing out, existed long before the family provided Sovereign Princes for Liechtenstein.

The House Law is mentioned in Article 3 of the Liechtenstein Constitution to the extent that it determines the succession to the Throne, the coming of age of the Sovereign Prince and any guardianship of the Prince that may be required. It was last amended in the nineteenth century under Johann II. Franz Josef II began, but did not complete, a general revision. In the constitutional debate

---

[8] "Liechtensteiner Vaterland", 15 September 2000.
[9] "Liechtensteiner Vaterland" and "Liechtensteiner Volksblatt", 12 June 2001. Previous recipients include Boutros Boutros-Ghali, Corazon Aquino, Lech Walesa and Kofi Annan.
[10] Some recent examples are the devolution of certain powers to a Scottish Parliament and a Welsh Assembly in the United Kingdom; the peaceful separation of the Czech and Slovak Republics in 1993; and the formation of Canton Jura out of the territory of Canton Berne in Switzerland in 1979. Some delegates to the European Convention have proposed procedures which for the first time would allow an orderly withdrawal from the European Union by a member state that so wished. If accepted, the proposal might reassure those who are disquieted by the perpetual commitment and "ever closer union" envisaged by the Treaty of Rome. It would probably have a stabilising effect rather than the disruptive effect feared by some.

that followed the crisis of 28 October 1992, critics pointed out that although the House Law affected the Constitution nobody in Liechtenstein had ever seen the document as a whole. Hans-Adam II finished the revision, which bears his personal stamp, and secured the family's agreement to it. The new version is dated 26 October 1993. It was countersigned by the then Head of Government, Markus Büchel. This caused controversy since, although Hans-Adam's signature and the document were thus verified as authentic and it was published in the National Law Gazette ("Liechtensteinisches Landesgesetzblatt"), the law itself had not been debated and approved by Parliament and therefore had no constitutional force. (Hans-Adam and the family would not of course have desired such debate and approval.)

The preamble reaffirms the traditions of the family, including the Roman Catholic faith "which shall also serve as a guiding principle in future decisions, whilst respecting the freedom of belief and conscience of the individual". The law defines the family as "an autonomous family community established and organised at the level of the Constitution of the Principality". All male descendants of Johann I (1760–1836), their wives and daughters are members of the House. Membership is not transmitted by female descent, neither is it acquired by adoption or illegitimate descent. All members of the House are Liechtenstein citizens. This citizenship, like membership of the House, can be renounced; membership of the House is based on free will. The Sovereign Prince's consent is required for marriage by its members. This would normally be given subject to a written recognition by the intended spouse of the binding nature of the House Law. Disciplinary measures (reprimand or a temporary deprivation of title or vote) are envisaged for a member whose conduct has adversely affected the reputation, esteem or welfare of the Princely House.

The final body for appeals and decision-making within the family is the assembly of all male members of the family, chaired by the Sovereign Prince and voting by secret ballot.[11] The Prince is to organise a family gathering every five years. Every five years a Family Council, consisting of three members and three substitutes, is to be elected by secret written ballot. The Sovereign Prince is not a member of this body. It is chaired by the elected member who is closest in line of succession to the throne. It acts as a first instance for appeals by members of the family against a decision by the Sovereign Prince.

Article 12 establishes that succession to the Throne is by male primogeniture. Only members who have the right to vote and to stand for election within the meaning of the House Law may succeed to the Throne. The Sovereign Prince is to be Head of State, Ruler of the Princely House and Chairman of the Princely

[11] At present (2003) there are 87 such voting members, most of whom live outside Liechtenstein.

foundations. As Ruler, he is to safeguard the reputation, esteem and welfare of the House with the assistance of its members, and he is to support members who may be in financial difficulties so far as the income from the foundations' assets permits.

Article 14 stipulates that the Family Council is immediately responsible for disciplinary measures against the Sovereign Prince should his conduct adversely affect the reputation, esteem or welfare of the Princely House or of the Principality of Liechtenstein. In that case, the Family Council is to inform the Liechtenstein Head of Government confidentially of the action envisaged, the reasons for it and the Prince's views thereon. The only disciplinary sanctions available are reprimand or removal from the Throne, the latter sanction to be employed only if a reprimand has failed to effect an improvement or the Prince's misconduct has been so grave that a reprimand would be manifestly inadequate. Article 15 provides for action by the Family Council in the event of the Prince's physical or mental incapacity, subject to Liechtenstein law. If the Liechtenstein people have passed a vote of no confidence in the Sovereign Prince, the Family Council is to make a proposal (not further specified in Article 16) to all members of the family with the right to vote, and the Parliament is to be informed of the result. It is open to the family to reject a popular vote of no confidence.[12] Article 17 makes provisions for a regency and guardianship.

The Final Provisions make clear that the House Law cannot be amended or repealed either by the Liechtenstein Constitution or by any international treaty concluded by the Liechtenstein state. A two-thirds majority of all members of the Princely House with the right to vote is needed for any proposal for amendment to the House Law to be adopted.

In answer to media questions, Hans-Adam has said that he proposed that the female members of the family should have voting rights, but that the family and the women themselves had voted against.[13]

Finance

The Liechtenstein monarchy imposes no direct burden on the taxpayer.[14] It lives on its own resources. In 1965 Parliament offered 200,000 francs per year (later increased to 250,000) to Franz Josef II to help towards his official representational expenses. He gave the money to charity. In 1985 Hans-Adam returned this annual

[12] This Article anticipated one of Hans-Adam's constitutional proposals, which were accepted by a popular vote in March 2003.
[13] "Liechtensteiner Vaterland", 3 January 2003.
[14] The Austrian Habsburgs also lived from their own means. The same is true of the British monarchy, although its arrangements are different. Its total expenses are covered at least four times over by the revenues from the Crown Estate (£170.8m. in 2002–2003), which accrue to the British Treasury.

subvention to the State to help towards the expenses of UN membership, expense being one of the main arguments used by opponents of entry to the UN.[15] In 1981 the Sovereign Prince and the Heir Apparent were exempted from all public taxes including those on the Princely Estates and the foundations.

The House of Liechtenstein's finances are a private matter. Nevertheless, some clues are available. Although the family acquired government of the country by purchase in 1699 and 1712, it never owned much property in the Principality. Its assets there in 1914 amounted to the newly restored Castle, one or two other buildings, 178 hectares of forest and 11 hectares of agricultural land. This included the well-known vineyard, to which should be added a restaurant and, from the 1920s, the Bank in Liechtenstein. After the Second World War the family was left with not much more than 10% of its former assets: the bulk of the Princely Collections, some 20,000 hectares of forest and agricultural land (much of it in Soviet-occupied Lower Austria), the old Liechtenstein castle near Vienna and the two great palaces in the city, of which the Town Palace in the Bankgasse had been badly damaged by aerial bombardment in February 1945. The flow of income was insufficient. The financial situation was made worse by some unlucky transactions.

It is not surprising, therefore, that after the war some tracts of land in Austria and some important works from the collection should have been sold, reluctantly and one by one. Eventually, the sale of a Franz Hals portrait to the State of Bavaria for 12 million Deutschmarks in 1969 aroused public and political concern in Liechtenstein.

Hans-Adam tackled his shaky heritage with vigour. Venerable family members were ejected from the board of the Bank in Liechtenstein and other positions, to their audible indignation. New managers were brought in. Some appointments were successful, some not; but before long the graphs were going up. The Austrian estates were revitalised. In the forests of Styria the installations were vertically integrated, from seedbeds to sawmills. The estate and castle at Wilfersdorf (Lower Austria) have been fully restored with the participation of the local authorities.[16] The Town Palace in Vienna has been largely restored after the bomb damage; part is let as offices, part is used by the family, part may yet be devoted to a museum. The portfolio includes Rice Tec, a company specialising in the development and production of high-value types of rice. It is based in Texas but also operates in Arkansas, Puerto Rico, Argentina, Brazil and Uruguay. The LGT Bank in Liechtenstein, which is wholly owned by the Prince of Liechtenstein Foundation, declared in 2001 a dividend of more than 90 million francs (about £37 million).[17]

---

[15] Speech from the Throne, 27 March 1985.
[16] "Liechtensteiner Vaterland", 18 May 2002.
[17] Curiously enough, this figure is quite close to the annual cost of the British Monarchy.

The Swiss economic magazine "Bilanz" estimates Hans-Adam II to be worth between 6 and 7 billion francs (£2.5–2.9 billion).[18] Such guesses need to be treated with caution. The Foundation's assets are not his personal property. The Princely Collections (worth 3–4 billion francs, according to "Bilanz") are scarcely liquid assets, and they need curatorial and other skilled staff to maintain them. The costs of running the Monarchy, the Castle at Vaduz and the Vienna properties must be substantial.

The Princely Collections

The days of sales are now over, except for purposes of tidying up and reorganising the collections. A purchasing programme is in place, not necessarily to recover what has been disposed of in the past but to fill representative gaps in the collection. Thus, a Rubens sketch was bought in 1977, a Rembrandt in 1995 and a Franz Hals in 2003. Hans-Adam prefers modern art, but the historic and financial value of the collections takes priority.

The second Liechtenstein Palace in Vienna (the "Garden" or "Rossau" Palace) has been restored at a cost of 15 million francs. From 28 March 2004 the ground and first floors will be used for the permanent display of the chief glories of the Liechtenstein Collection, including the Rubens Decius Mus cycle and the Golden Coach, to create a "Baroque experience". The collections will continue to be based in the Castle at Vaduz. Of the approximately 1,400 paintings, between 100 and 200 will be on show in Vienna at any one time. There will be smaller rotating exhibitions in Vienna. It is planned to arrange annual rotating exhibitions in Vaduz, instead of every four years, using either the new Art Museum or (still a possibility) a specially built museum under the Castle rock as conceived for the ill-fated Art Museum project of the 1980s. The Vienna project has become possible because the Austrian authorities have *de facto* backed down from their potential claims to the collection under Nazi legislation.[19]

It has fallen to Hans-Adam II to recreate the artistic and financial visions of Hans-Adam I and Johann I. There will be regret in Liechtenstein at the departure of some of the greatest masterpieces of the collection, but they are returning to their original home. It has in any case been impossible for many years for most of the collection, including even its greatest masterpieces, to be displayed, except on rare occasions such as the New York exhibition in 1985. The splendours at Vienna, which is one of the most visited cities of Europe, will re-establish a public Liechtenstein presence there and will contribute to the Principality's international prestige.

---

[18] "Liechtensteiner Vaterland", 26 November 2002.
[19] "Liechtensteiner Vaterland", 14 February 2001, 18 May 2002, 1 October 2002, and 14 February 2003 and the "Liechtensteiner Volksblatt", 2 October 2002.

The Sokolov Dossier and the Liechtenstein Princely Archive

Before the Second World War the archives of the House of Liechtenstein were located in Vienna and Czechoslovakia. The Vienna archive contained, *inter alia,* the family and political records. After 1938 Franz Josef II was able to transfer part of these to Vaduz; the remainder seems to have been lost during or after the war. In 1939 the archive in Czechoslovakia was deposited in Troppau (now Opava) at the demand of the Nazi German authorities, who wanted to create a central Sudeten archive. The Czech archive contained for the most part the myriad documents generated by the management of the Liechtensteins' great estates in Moravia and Bohemia from the fourteenth to the early twentieth centuries. The occupying Soviet Army removed them from Troppau in 1946. All 575 boxes disappeared into the Special Archive in Moscow, the sixth largest archive in the Soviet Union. This secret repository housed documents captured from Germany and elsewhere, including archives originating in non-German countries. After the fall of communism, scholars began to gain access. In 1992 the Liechtenstein archive was discovered by Professor Norman Stone of Oxford University.[20] It was important to the family to recover it as part of their history and, perhaps, as offering proof of ownership of various properties. Hans-Adam II immediately began to take soundings about its return, using various intermediaries. One of these, Andrey Meilunas,[21] drew his attention to the Sokolov dossier as a possible bargaining counter.

During the White Army's brief occupation of Ekaterinburg during the Russian Civil War N. A. Sokolov was appointed Examining Magistrate to investigate the murder of the Russian Imperial Family and their attendants in that town on 16/17 July 1918. Through most of 1919 he worked under difficult conditions to establish what had happened. In large measure, he succeeded. Several copies of his evidence were made; one set was used by Robert Wilton in his book "The Last Days of the Romanovs" (1920). But the original documents seemed to have disappeared, as did a box containing human remains which is believed to be kept at the Russian church at Uccle, a suburb of Brussels.[22] The original Sokolov dossier unexpectedly reappeared at Sotheby's in London in 1990. After the fall of communism, the Russian State wanted to buy it but could not raise the money. It went elsewhere. Between December 1993 and January 1994 Hans-Adam II acquired it from its owner and let it be known to the Russians that it might be available.

---

[20] This account is based on the detailed history of the affair provided by A. I. Stepanov, Russian Ambassador to Switzerland and Liechtenstein from 1992 to 1998, in his book "Neznakomiy Likhtenshteyn" (Mezhdunarodniye Otnosheniya, Moscow, 2002), pages 174–290.

[21] According to Stepanov (op. cit., page 195) Meilunas claims to have been the one to discover the Liechtenstein archive.

[22] Robert Massie, "The Romanovs" (Jonathan Cape, London, 1995), page 126.

The Russians were keen to acquire this unique record of a tragic episode in their history, but the domestic political atmosphere was fraught. There was controversy about the planned interment in St Petersburg of the newly discovered Romanov remains. There was strong political opposition to the return to the West of any wartime trophies, even those of neutral origin. Hans-Adam could not therefore be sure that the Russians would be able to keep their side of any agreement that might be reached.[23] After negotiations which continued up to the very last hours, Hans-Adam II and the Russian Foreign Minister E. M. Primakov signed an agreement at Vaduz on 3 September 1996. The archives themselves were exchanged on 30 July 1997. The 134 items of the Sokolov dossier were not handed over at the Russian Embassy in Berne until the bulk of the 426,933 pages of the Liechtenstein archive had arrived at Vaduz on the same day.

The negotiations shed light on Hans-Adam's personality and style of negotiation. His tenacity and his determination to regain the family property were clear. He was ready to be tactically flexible and he was quick to seize the opportunity offered by the Sokolov dossier. When the negotiations stalled on the Russian side, he made skilful use of the Russian media to whet the public's appetite for the dossier and to underline its importance to Russia. One problem was that the Russian side needed the exchange to take place in the framework of an intergovernmental agreement. Hans-Adam would not hear of the agreement being signed by the Liechtenstein Foreign Minister, as the Russians first proposed. The archive, he pointed out, had no relevance to the history of Liechtenstein; it was his property, not his government's. Underlying this was his concern that involvement by the Liechtenstein Government might create an awkward precedent for the status of other property of the Princely House, both abroad and in Liechtenstein, and might also, perhaps, prejudice his arguments in the constitutional debate about his own prerogatives. He made this clear to the Russian Ambassador from the outset, and showed that he was if necessary prepared to go without both Primakov's visit and the agreement. Hans-Adam eventually signed the agreement in his capacity as Head of State. He seems to have gained most of his points. At one point, the Ambassador felt morally uneasy about the pressure being applied to tiny Liechtenstein.[24] He need not have worried. He later described the Liechtensteiners as energetic and sometimes hard negotiators, standing up for their own interests and counting every franc.[25]

---

[23] In 1994 the return of French archives was interrupted when the Russian Parliament imposed a moratorium on the restitution of items transferred to the USSR as a result of World War II.

[24] Stepanov, op. cit., page 231.

[25] Stepanov, op. cit., page 274. Compare the impressions of the British CSCE negotiators at Helsinki (page 151).

POLITICAL PARTIES AND PRESSURE GROUPS

The origins of the two main parties, the VU and the FBP, have been described in pages 45–46 above. They remain vigorous rivals; but although they can differ sharply on individual issues, to an outsider there is little if any difference in their political and social philosophies. The old geographical distinction between a VU Oberland and a FBP Unterland has long since been blurred. In the 2001 elections, which were an unusually decisive victory for the FBP in terms of votes cast, the Oberland returned seven FBP and seven VU parliamentary members and the Unterland six FBP and four VU. Traditional family political allegiances count for less than they did, although the hard-core party élites remain. There are no class interests at work. In the European political spectrum both parties belong to the Christian Democrat and Conservative European Democratic Union (EDU).

It is hard to judge whether there is wide popular involvement in the bread-and-butter, day-to-day work of the two party machines. The VU claims to have over 3,000 members (about 19% of the electorate). Voter participation in elections is always high (86.8% in 2001) and there are good turnouts at political meetings. As in other countries, the chance of benefiting from political patronage is no doubt an incentive for some to be active in politics.

Since 1984 the State has given financial help to the political parties represented in Parliament (divided in proportion to the number of deputies from each party) and to parties not represented but which have won more than 3% of the votes cast in the last general election. This money is intended for political education, publicity and the formation of public opinion. The total sum is modest: 180,000 francs per year, of which the lion's share goes to the two main parties.[1] The parties' main financial support comes from subscriptions and donations.

The Smaller Parties

From 1962 until 1974 the newly-founded Christian Social Party ("Christlich-soziale Partei" – CSP) tried to set itself up as an alternative to the FBP-VU coalition but won no parliamentary seat. This may have been due to the 18% threshold;

---

[1] Waschkuhn, op. cit., page 272.

but after the latter's abolition and replacement by an 8% threshold the CSP still failed to enter Parliament, perhaps because of its lack of a distinctive programme.

The Free List, sometimes known as "the Whites" ("Freie Liste" – FL) first competed in the parliamentary elections of 1986. It had its origins in the supporters of the Art Museum ("Kunsthaus") initiative (page 196) and the campaign for women's suffrage.[2] It could be described as a radical, ecological, feminist, Third World-conscious party. It made its breakthrough in the February 1993 election in the wake of the 1992 constitutional crisis, when it won two seats, one in each electoral district. It lost a seat in October 1993, regained it in 1997 and fell back again to a single seat in 2001. Despite its small size, internal fractiousness, and occasionally provocative tactics, it has had an enlivening effect on Liechtenstein's internal politics and has exerted some influence. It has sponsored some important constitutional initiatives such as the successful "Double Yes" initiative of 1987, which, in the event of two or more proposals on the same subject in a popular vote, enables a preference voting system to be applied so that a decision can be reached. It also sponsored the State Treaty initiative of 1989 which, though defeated, helped to pave the way for the Liechtenstein Chamber of Commerce and Trade's successful initiative of 1992. The Free List offers an alternative to the two essentially conservative and centrist main parties that represent the mainstream of political opinion. It is likely to remain a minority party.

The Liechtenstein Non-Party List ("Liechtenstein Überparteiliche Liste" – ÜLL) started as a Vaduz local government party. It first competed at the national level in 1989. Like the FL, it has some of its roots in the promoters of the Art Museum initiative and other critics of the system. It, too, sees itself as an alternative to the establishment but tends to campaign on individual issues rather than across the board. Although the ÜLL and the FL may sometimes have common views on specific issues, the two parties tend to see themselves as competitors rather than complementary. It has never won a parliamentary seat and it won no seat in the local government elections of 2003, although one of its members came close to becoming mayor of Mauren.

Apart from special leaflet campaigns, the smaller parties tend to make their views known through readers' letters published in the newspapers that belong to the two big parties (the FBP's "Liechtensteiner Volksblatt" and the VU's "Liechtensteiner Vaterland"). The two newspapers, however, fairly regularly make space available to the FL and the more important pressure groups.

Pressure Groups

For its size, Liechtenstein has a surprisingly large number of economic,

[2] Waschkuhn, op. cit., page 265.

professional, voluntary and social organisations.[3] The government consults these as a matter of course on all relevant issues including future legislation. In turn, they act as pressure and lobbying groups.

Each of the two main parties is a broad church, a coalition of traditions and interests. Consequently they are often divided internally on burning political issues. Moreover, direct democracy weakens their impact as political machines and undermines their ability to present themselves as fully representative of the popular will. As a result, there is in Liechtenstein a long tradition of non-party movements which spring up in response to particular problems.

The Liechtenstein Loyal Union, formed in the threatening days of 1939, is one such example. Sometimes these movements take fanciful names, such as Sleeping Beauty ("Dornröschen") and the Square Heads ("Quadratschädel") poster campaign, both in support of female suffrage in the 1980s.

The later stages of the 1992–2003 constitutional debate provided some good examples of how non-party movements spring up and operate.

The Forum Liechtenstein was founded in 1994. It is led by the industrialist Michael Hilti and includes other senior business people such as Hans Brunhart (a former Head of Government and now Chairman of the "Verwaltungs- und Privat-Bank") and Peter Frick (Chairman of Hoval and Michael Hilti's predecessor as President of the Liechtenstein Chamber of Industry and Trade). Its aim is to work out concepts and projects for tackling the country's existing and potential political, economic, ecological, social and other problems, whether as an initiator, intermediary or catalyst. During the constitutional debate the Forum was anxious that the controversy might harm Liechtenstein's external image and interests. In the summer of 2001 it was active as a confidential intermediary between the Castle, the Government and the leading politicians, in the hope of brokering a compromise that would command general acceptance in Parliament and so avert a referendum campaign which it feared would become a slanging match.

In support of the popular initiative by Hans-Adam II and Prince Alois the "Dual Liechtenstein Citizens' Movement" ("Bürgerbewegung Duales Liechtenstein") was formed on 16 August 2002 as a "citizens' movement" to express, as it put it, the views of the silent majority after 28 citizens had lodged a complaint against the Princes' initiative. With 1,322 members, it claimed to be the biggest grouping. It conducted a vigorous advertising campaign. Another leading cross-party campaign organisation was the "Committee for Prince and People", led by the trustee Herbert Batliner.

The leading non-party organisation opposing the Princes' proposals was the "Democracy Secretariat" ("Demokratie-Sekretariat", or DeSe), which was

---

[3] Some of the main economic organisations are described on pages 280–281 and 285.

established on 18 October 2001. Its founding members were Mario Frick (VU Head of Government 1993–2001), Thomas Nigg (member of the committee of the "Arbeitskreis Demokratie und Monarchie"), Pio Schurti (spokesman of the Wilhelm Beck Group), Peter Sprenger (spokesman of the VU parliamentary party), Paul Vogt (parliamentary member for the Free List) and Sigvard Wohlwend. Other organisations appearing were Well-Constituted Women ("Frauen in guter Verfassung"), the "Verein Trachter", "jung.initiativ.informiert" (a youth grouping) and Subversive Rumours ("Subversive Enten"), whose enigmatic stickers appeared on many a lamp-post. It is hard to say how large the membership of these organisations was (or is). To some extent the memberships overlapped, as was to be the case among the sponsors of the alternative Constitutional Peace Initiative ("Verfassungsfrieden") in October 2002.

The activity of so many groups and people shows that citizens' involvement in public affairs is alive and well in Liechtenstein.

THE CONSTITUTIONAL CONTROVERSY
(1992–2003)

In 1992 some long-standing latent constitutional disagreements broke into the open. The ensuing debate went through several phases until in March 2003 a popular vote approved Prince Hans-Adam's and Hereditary Prince Alois's proposals by a majority of more than 64%.

The debate was never about the existence of the Monarchy as such, but about the extent of its powers and how they should be exercised. The division was not on party political lines. All three parties naturally tried to score points off each other during the debate, but the two main parties always maintained that they supported a strong and politically active monarchy as envisaged by the 1921 Constitution. Although in 2003 the governing FBP recommended in favour of the Princes' proposals and the opposition VU against, both parties were internally divided about them. In 2002 the "Freie Liste" supported with some hesitation the alternative "constitutional peace" proposal because it saw it as a first step towards its goal of a purely representative monarchy; but that proposal gained only 16.5% of the votes.

As always in politics, principles became tangled up with personalities and with extraneous issues. The contenders, as so often in Liechtenstein's modern history, did not hesitate to appeal to the foreign media as a way of influencing the domestic debate. These tactics ultimately extended to the Council of Europe. The foreign media enjoyed the story but were not always well placed to understand the unique local background. The resulting simplifications and distortions did little good for Liechtenstein.[1]

The Origins of the Dispute

The personal standing of Franz Josef II was unassailable after the Second World War. Hans-Adam II has asserted[2] that from the 1960s onwards certain

---

[1] As a mild example: "Its snow-capped peaks have been echoing with furious debate on whether its good people want to live a sleepy life or a truly medieval one. They voted for the medieval option." ("The Times", London, 28 March 2003.)
[2] See, for example, his Speech from the Throne on 6 November 1993.

political circles began to try to exert pressure on the rights of the Monarchy, partly in disregard of the Constitution, in an effort to bring it under their control. He argued that any disregard of the Constitution was a potential threat to the people's rights as well. Since the Monarchy was not openly discussed in Liechtenstein until the 1990s[3] there is little public evidence available from before that date. However, from at least 1968 the Prince's right to appoint officials (Article 11 of the Constitution) was exercised *de facto* by the Government.[4] In his Speech from the Throne on 12 May 1993 Hans-Adam II pointedly expressed the hope that a new procedure would be found to ensure that in future laws would be promulgated only after they had passed through all necessary constitutional stages. (Some had been published without his signature.)

The dynasty's financial problems between 1945 and the early 1970s, at a time when many other people in Liechtenstein were getting richer, may have weakened its standing more subtly and encouraged hopes in some political circles of curtailing its political independence.

Generational and cultural change may have played a part. Liechtenstein has always used experts from the neighbouring countries as a source of advice, and many of its students attend those countries' universities. Switzerland's political culture has been completely republican since 1848.[5] After the Second World War living memories of the monarchical tradition in Austria faded. This environment had its effect on Liechtenstein, although not at the popular level. In the last year of his life Franz Josef II expressed concern that the monarchical-democratic principle of the Constitution was being disregarded by legal and academic specialists who uncritically equated democracy with the republican form of government.[6]

The basic principles of the 1921 Constitution worked well for Liechtenstein. Many details were amended over the years (often after a hard tussle, since in most respects the Constitution had been carefully balanced and any change could be seen as threatening the equilibrium). Inevitably, real life revealed the occasional ambiguity. Some of these were no doubt accidental; others may have been deliberate "constructive" ambiguities at the time. Some problems arose from wording carried over from the 1862 Constitution, a document conceived in a very different era when Liechtenstein was a member of the German Confederation and as such

---

[3] The standing of the Roman Catholic Church was a second taboo. Hans-Adam broke the first taboo by design. The Vatican was to break the second by accident.

[4] From 1993 onwards, the government appointed officials on the basis of annual authorisation by the Prince.

[5] The Bernese patriciate was swept from power in 1831. The last monarchical form of government on Swiss soil (Neuchâtel, whose Prince was the King of Prussia), was formally brought to an end in 1857, having been overthrown by revolution in 1848.

[6] Speech by the President of the Parliament, Karlheinz Ritter, at a parliamentary sitting in memory of Franz Josef II on 21 November 1989. ("Thronfolge", Vaduz, 1990, pages 56–57.)

had certain obligations, which lapsed after 1866. But new questions also began to be aired. At the Act of Homage on 15 August 1990 the President of the Parliament publicly suggested that the rules for the succession to the Throne should be anchored in the Constitution rather than only in the Princely House's laws; this would have meant discussion and approval by the Parliament. A long series of academic publications by the Liechtenstein Institute, the first president of which was Gerard Batliner, analysed many aspects of the Constitution and suggested various interpretations and amendments in the light of modern theory and practice. Some of these suggestions would have reduced the Prince's prerogatives.

Hans-Adam II was not against constitutional change; indeed, he was prepared to be more radical than anyone. But he insisted that any changes must be made openly and by political means, with the consent of the two co-sovereigns. He believed that once he had restored the family fortunes and overseen Liechtenstein's entry into the UN and the EEA he would be free to turn his attention to the Constitution, which he was later to describe as his "last important task".[7] Events moved faster than he had planned.

If Hans-Adam was suspicious of the political establishment, they were wary of him. They knew from his early speeches and his vigorous reform of the family assets that they would have to deal with an unconventional and radical Prince. Before he succeeded his father a foreign observer wrote, "Nobody doubts the extraordinary talents of the future Prince Hans-Adam, but everyone is convinced that under his leadership the monarchy will be different... People worry that he will want to "manage" the state like a business".[8] His intellectual interest in military strategy was seen by some as unsuitable for the Prince of a neutral and unarmed state.[9] His unexpected statements on any matter that sparked his interest, whether in speeches, media interviews or private or open letters sent directly to the person concerned were contrasted with his father's formal reserve. His forceful drive to get Liechtenstein into the UN left bruises. There were, therefore, some who were waiting for the chance to "teach the Prince a lesson". A personal element crept into disagreements about principles.

In the constitutional dispute Hans-Adam II and his opponents each had a strategic problem. If an unelected Prince was to exercise active political power in the late twentieth century he could scarcely do so "by the Grace of God" in an age of secular democracy and religious pluralism. Although the Council of Europe had given the Constitution its blessing as democratic in 1978 (the lack of female suffrage excepted), the Prince himself would always potentially be open to

[7] "Liechtensteiner Vaterland", 17 March 2003.
[8] Alphons Matt, "Unbekannter Nachbar Liechtenstein" (AT Verlag, Aaarau and Stuttgart, 1986), page 41.
[9] Waschkuhn, op. cit., pages 100–104.

the reproach of lacking democratic legitimacy. Hans-Adam decided to solve that problem by submitting his proposals to a democratic vote and by giving the people the last word over their form of government. He must be the first monarch in history to have proposed the means for the legal abolition of the institution that he represents. The dilemma for his opponents was that they had to prove that his proposals would undermine the balance of the 1921 Constitution by producing a decisive shift of power in favour of the Prince. While some of them had their own reservations about the Constitution,[10] they had to present themselves as its defenders if they were not to be accused, in their turn, of undermining "dualism". They were therefore forced into a long defensive action, playing always for time.

The early years of Hans-Adam's reign were punctuated by three episodes, which crystallised some of the fundamental constitutional issues at stake. These were the Art Museum ("Kunsthaus") affair, the political crisis of 28 October 1992 and the end of the Markus Büchel (FBP) government in 1993.

The Art Museum Affair

The so-called Art Museum affair had long-lasting repercussions in Liechtenstein.[11] In 1969, after the occasional sale of paintings from the Princely Collection to foreign purchasers had aroused open disquiet in Liechtenstein, Franz Josef II offered the State a first option for future sales. He also offered a long-term loan of the entire weapons collection and of up to 200 paintings if the State would build a suitable museum for the purpose. In 1979 he added to the offer the Golden Coach, various sculptures and tapestries. The necessary building credits were agreed in a national referendum by only 26 votes. A counter-initiative, inspired by complex motives unrelated to the loan offer but connected with a grassroots feeling that the tax-payers were being taken for granted by the élite, then argued that because a number of changes had been made to the project it should be voted on afresh. The demand for a fresh popular vote was rejected by the commune of Vaduz and the Government; then, on appeal, by the Administrative Complaints Court and the State Court (1984). The State Court's handling of the matter left it open to criticism. Several of its members resigned and in 1987 its president was charged with (and acquitted of) abuse of office. In 1988 he published at his own expense a long report to justify himself and to make some wider observations. The FBP demanded an inquiry into his report and, when the VU majority refused it, withdrew from the Parliament so as to force fresh elections. In 1990 the State Court, with new judges, upheld the complainants' case. By that time the

---

[10] "Certainly it was not the best model of its kind". (From a statement by the Democracy Secretariat ("Demokratie-Sekretariat"), printed in the "Liechtensteiner Vaterland, 30 January 2003.)
[11] The tangled story is told in detail in Waschkuhn, op. cit., pages 217–236.

Art Museum project and the Prince's offer had long since lapsed. Not only was a splendid opportunity lost, but the prestige of the two courts was damaged. The quality of the judges and their method of appointment (election by Parliament) were called into question.

The Crisis of 28 October 1992

When the timing of the referendum on entry to the EEA was being considered there was a natural tendency in Liechtenstein to wait and see how the Swiss people would vote. However, it was clear from the Government's reports that Swiss and Liechtenstein interests were diverging. At the opening of Parliament on 11 March 1992 Hans-Adam II said that the EEA was too important a matter for Liechtenstein's adhesion to depend on Switzerland's decision. The Prince wanted Liechtenstein to vote before Switzerland. The Government and Parliament disagreed. A constitutional crisis developed. The Prince took his stand on his constitutional responsibilities for foreign policy. The Government argued that it was within its own administrative competence to fix the date of a referendum and that the Parliament clearly wished this one to take place after the Swiss referendum. On 27 October the Prince asked the Government either to accept his wish about timing or to resign, failing which he would dissolve Parliament and dismiss the Government. The Government replied that it saw no need to resign.[12]

In the afternoon of 28 October there were negotiations at the Castle with an eight-member non-party committee led by the FBP former Head of Government Gerard Batliner. A compromise was agreed. That evening Hans-Adam II had talks in the Government Building with the Government and Parliament (the latter in extraordinary session) during which the exact wording of the compromise was agreed. A joint statement by Hans-Adam II, the Parliament and the Government contained four points. The Prince accepted the later date for the referendum. The Government and Parliament declared unanimously that entry into the EEA was of "independent importance for Liechtenstein, irrespective of Switzerland's position". The government and a majority of the Parliament also called for a vote in favour. Should the people vote against joining the EEA the "entry variants" (not further specified) would be discussed with Switzerland so that Liechtenstein should not end up in isolation. Finally, the Prince stated that his confidence in the Parliament and the Government had been restored.[13]

Upon his arrival at the Government Building under police protection the Prince was booed by 2,000 organised demonstrators: an unprecedented event which embarrassed observers such as the former Head of Government Alfred

---

[12] "Liechtensteiner Volksblatt", 28 October 1992.
[13] "Liechtensteiner Volksblatt", 29 October 1992.

Hilbe. The Prince later criticised the organisers for imprudence and unfairness in allowing this potentially dangerous manifestation to go ahead without first telling the demonstrators that a compromise had already been achieved.[14]

This episode launched the public constitutional debate. The immediate problem centred round the Prince's constitutional right to dismiss a member of the Government or an entire government and to dissolve Parliament. But it also made Hans-Adam reflect (if he had not already done so) on the power of crowds and the need to provide machinery for an orderly and legal change of regime if that was what the people should ever want. For the organisers of the demonstration it was an occasion to "teach the Prince a lesson" in front of the media. Hans-Adam saw things differently. Ten years later he was to describe the day as "very upsetting" but also as "enormously liberating". In addition to its positive influence on the result of the EEA vote, he was glad that the decades-long festering constitutional conflict had finally come into the open. Furthermore, the shock at last brought the Princely House to adopt the new House Law.[15]

The Fall of the Markus Büchel Government

The 1992 crisis worked in Hans-Adam's favour: not only did his EEA policy succeed, but there was public sympathy for him after the demonstration. Markus Büchel, the FBP candidate for the post of Head of Government, announced in the February 1993 election campaign that if he won he would live in harmony with the Prince. Büchel was successful, and led a FBP-VU coalition; but he did not have an easy relationship with either party. The last straw was his appointment of a member of the VU to a post, apparently on the grounds that he was the best man for the job.

On 14 September 1993 the deputies of his own party, supported by some VU deputies, passed a parliamentary vote of no confidence in him. Hans-Adam saw no reason to dismiss him under Article 80 of the Constitution since Büchel had done nothing to cause the Prince to lose confidence in him. Nor did the Prince think it right that a caucus of politicians should remove a Head of Government who had so recently won the confidence of the electorate. He therefore put the matter to the people by dissolving Parliament. In the October 1993 elections the VU regained their majority. This episode was to some extent October 1992 in reverse, but it showed again that it was necessary to clarify the uncertainties about the constitutional consequences of a loss of confidence in a government by the Prince or the Parliament.

---

[14] Waschkuhn, op. cit., pages 112–113
[15] "Liechtensteiner Vaterland", 28 October 2002.

The Course of the Debate

With hindsight, the ensuing debate may be divided into three overlapping phases. Although some issues had begun to emerge earlier (for example, in 1988 Hans-Adam suggested exchanging his right to appoint state officials for the right to propose judges) the period between 1992 and 1996 was one of elaboration and definition of positions. Between 1996 and 2001 there was an intense debate, primarily between the Prince and the politicians but also more widely, which resulted in some important refinements of detail in the various positions but no major change of principle. Between 2001 and 2003 there was a determined drive for a solution. When the new FBP Government's compromise proposal (supported by the Prince) failed to obtain the necessary three quarters majority in Parliament, the Prince put the question to a popular vote.

1992–1996

Immediately after the 28 October crisis, on 11 November 1992, Parliament resolved that disputed points in the Constitution should in the near future either be changed through precise formulations or be given clear interpretation in agreement with the Prince. On 7 December Hans-Adam had informal talks in the Government Building attended by seven members of each of the two parties then represented in Parliament.[16]

At the opening of the new Parliament[17] on 12 May 1993 Hans-Adam formally set out his position. He said that after 1938 the active political involvement of the Prince had played a crucial part in Liechtenstein's political survival. If he himself had been only a representative monarch, he could not have brought Liechtenstein to join the UN or to become closer to Europe. It would make little sense to confine the Prince to purely representative duties in so small a country as Liechtenstein, where the scope was very limited; the Prince bore his expenses as head of state personally, and he and his successors would in that case soon ask themselves whether they might not be spending their time and money more usefully. "Probably the situation would return to that before 1938, when the Prince lived abroad and concerned himself only marginally with developments in Liechtenstein. Personally I would regret such a development because I grew up in this country and it is my homeland".

After rehearsing his views on the Prince's prime responsibility for foreign policy, the Parliament's secondary role compared with that of the other co-sovereign (the people) whom it represented, the need for a government to enjoy

---

[16] A short but helpful annotated chronology of events between October 1992 and August 2001 is to be found on pages 3–13 of the Government's Report and Proposal to the Landtag on the Alteration of the Constitution No. 87/2001, dated 20 November 2001.

[17] FBP 12 seats, VU 11, Freie Liste (represented for the first time) 2.

the confidence of both Prince and Parliament throughout its term, and the need for new arrangements for the appointment of officials and judges, Hans-Adam turned to the role and future of the Monarchy itself. "The strong position of the Prince in our Constitution is only warranted when it is certain that the ruling Prince has the character and intellect to fulfil these duties." He therefore proposed that the people should have the right to pass a vote of no confidence in a Prince, after which the Princely House would examine the matter and decide what action, if any, to take, including removal of the Prince from office.[18] This would separate the fate of an unpopular individual Prince from that of the Monarchy as an institution. It should not, he said, be assumed that the Princely House would necessarily agree with the people. "It must be taken into account that the majority is not always right and that the duty of the Prince is to protect the rights of minorities and the weak as well as to defend the long-term good of the people and the country."

If, however, matters were to go to extremes, there should be a legal, orderly and democratic procedure for the abolition of the Monarchy. "The Monarchy in Liechtenstein should not give way to pressure from the street or be overthrown because a couple of hotheads think they must start a republic here with a revolution." In keeping with the principle of self-determination, the people should have the final say, irrespective of the wishes of the Prince. If a popular vote for abolition were successful, the Parliament would within a certain time have to propose to the people for their approval a new constitution, republican but still democratic. It would then be for the people to make a final decision whether they wanted the new constitution or the old.

Although many elements of Hans-Adam's thinking were already known, the Speech from the Throne came as a shock. To many people the very idea of votes of no confidence in the Prince and abolition of the Monarchy seemed unnatural and disturbing. On 24 June 1993 Parliament reaffirmed its position as the representative of the people and stated its desire for the continuation of the form of state with two sovereigns, Prince and people. It wanted the Constitution to be made more effective by the removal of obscure and obsolete provisions. It saw no need for a constitutional procedure for the abolition of the Monarchy.

On 6 November 1993, after the fall of the Büchel government and fresh elections, Hans-Adam opened a new Parliament.[19] This Speech from the Throne was partly a lecture in political science, partly a programme declaration. Neither a pure democracy nor a pure monarchy, he said, was a practical possibility in a modern

---

[18] Hans-Adam later clarified that if the Princely House were to depose a Prince, or that Prince were to abdicate, the hereditary successor would take office in his place. ("Liechtensteiner Volksblatt", 29 May 1993.)

[19] Its composition was: VU 13, FBP 11, Freie Liste 1. The new government was a VU-led coalition with the FBP, led by Mario Frick.

constitutional state: people and monarchs both had to delegate decision-making to smaller groups, or oligarchies, which in practice were the strongest element in a state. Oligarchies, however, tended to enlarge their own power at the expense of the common interest, and because of their internal bargaining processes they found it hard to take important but unpopular decisions.[20] Over the longer term, states were politically and economically stable only when the oligarchic element was kept in check by a strongly developed democratic or monarchical element. Among republics, Switzerland was a good example of the democratic element, the USA a good example of a monarchical presidency.

When faced by pressures from the Liechtenstein "oligarchy" (as Hans-Adam saw the situation), the Princely House had two ways of escaping from their control. One was to avoid conflict, to make concessions here and there, and if necessary to move abroad. This course would avoid a potential threat to the country's political and economic stability, liberate resources of time and money to the advantage of the Princely House, enable the Prince and his House to keep out of political controversy, and preserve the outward form of the Monarchy so that it could be reactivated in a serious crisis as it was in 1938. The alternative course was to resist by all constitutional means and so to risk a conflict. He had some years previously decided on the latter course, for several reasons. As long as a majority of the Liechtenstein population wanted the present monarchical form of state, it was the monarch's duty to uphold his constitutional rights. As a citizen of Liechtenstein, a country he loved, he wanted to continue to contribute actively to its welfare. He wanted to extend democratic rights through his constitutional proposals, which might seem revolutionary to some but which the recent political crises had shown to be necessary. If his efforts failed, it would still be possible to fall back on the first course before damage had been done to the country's interests.

"It is the task of the monarch to see that democratic and constitutional institutions are not weakened by the oligarchy, and that state interests are put before party interests. In the long term, the monarch can perform this task only if he knows that the majority of the population supports him. People and Monarchy, as the weaker elements, should be natural allies against the strongest element in the state, the oligarchy." Naturally, he said, the Parliament and everyone else in a direct democracy were free to make their own proposals. But he would consent to no constitutional change that would weaken the monarchy by strengthening the oligarchy. If the people voted for such a change, he would move abroad.

---

[20] "Elites" or "interest groups" might have been a better term than "oligarchies". Among "state oligarchies" Hans-Adam included the courts, parliaments, governments and bureaucracies. Among "private oligarchies" which exercised influence on the state were the political parties, associations, the churches and the media. In his Speech from the Throne on 13 March 1997 he was happy to describe the House of Liechtenstein itself as having been part of the oligarchy in the Holy Roman Empire.

In December 1993, 16 Parliament members from all three parties asked the Government for answers to 19 questions about the recently published House Law. They viewed it with suspicion as a kind of parallel, extraterritorial dynastic constitution which could impinge on the Liechtenstein Constitution without being susceptible to democratic change from within the country. In February 1994 the Government published the results of a consultation, the outcome of which was to oppose the Prince's proposals for the appointment of judges and to find no need for his proposals for a vote of no confidence in the monarch or a procedure for abolishing the Monarchy. In his Speech from the Throne on 9 February 1994, which largely dwelt on EEA membership and relations with Switzerland, Hans-Adam called for an early decision on the constitutional issues. He repeated the advantages of his proposals as a way of handling any possible abuse of power by the Prince. It would be consistent with modern practice for the government, not the Prince, to appoint officials, especially as their number had grown so much since 1921. Moreover, he did not want to interfere in the Government's day-to-day business, which would be the case if he were actively involved in appointing officials. He was, however, anxious to play a part in ensuring that the judges should be removed from any suspicion of party political dependence.

The Herbert Wille Affair

The next Speech from the Throne, on 15 February 1995, was devoted to encouraging a positive popular vote in the second EEA referendum. Hans-Adam had the happy task of congratulating the Government on its success at the negotiating table.

However, constitutional questions were never far away. Herbert Wille (FBP, and Deputy Head of Government from 1986 to 1993) was in 1995 President of the Administrative Complaints Court and research director of the Liechtenstein Institute. In a public lecture on 16 February about the role of the State Court in interpreting differences of opinion between the Government and Parliament on constitutional questions he said that the term "government" included also the Sovereign Prince and the term "Parliament" the people.[21] On 27 February Hans-Adam sent Wille a strongly worded private letter expressing surprise at this view. He went on to allege that during his discussions with the Government in the Castle on 27 October 1992, Wille had said that he did not agree with certain parts of the Constitution and therefore did not consider himself bound by it. The Prince said that since Wille had shown by his lecture that he did not feel himself bound by the Constitution, he would not in future appoint him to a public office should he be proposed to the Prince by the Parliament or any other public forum.

[21] Article 112 of the Constitution. See pages 247–248 below.

Wille sent a copy of the Prince's letter to the President of the Parliament denying that he had ever said that he felt himself not bound by the Constitution or parts thereof.[22] His opinion on the State Court was, he said, a matter of academic conviction. The Prince's letter had put the leadership of the Administrative Complaints Court in question. Wille sent a similar letter to the Prince on 20 March, adding that the statement that he would not be appointed in future to a public office was a violation of freedom of opinion and academic opinion as guaranteed by the Constitution and the European Human Rights Convention. It was also a violation of the independence of the judiciary and of his personal rights.

Rumours about this correspondence soon began to leak out through the "Free List" party. On 1 April the Prince said, in reply to questions from a newspaper, that Wille's term of office had three years to run; nothing would change that. In another letter to Wille, sent on 4 April, the Prince deplored the leaking of private correspondence. He said that his criticism was directed not against the courts and their rulings but against Wille's general attitude to the Constitution. The Prince was free to appoint or not to appoint candidates proposed by Parliament for public office without giving reasons for his decision. But since he and Wille had known each other for many years he had thought it right to justify his decision to him. That decision was no violation of the Constitution or of the European Human Rights Convention. Any citizen was free to work politically for changes to the Constitution or the laws. But mixing up the concepts of people, parliament, prince and government could lead to a dissolution of constitutional order, which it was the Prince's duty to protect.

The correspondence between the Prince and Wille was published on 10 June 1995, after the second EEA referendum was safely over. In August that year, Wille lodged a complaint with the European Human Rights Commission against the State of Liechtenstein for violation of human rights and of freedom of expression. In April 1997 the newly-elected Parliament proposed Wille for reappointment by 13 votes to 12; the Prince refused. In October 1999 the European Court of Human Rights found that the Prince had infringed Wille's right to free speech. It awarded Wille 10,000 francs in compensation and 91,000 francs in costs. The court also criticised the Prince personally.[23]

On 1 September 1995, a petition organised by a non-party group and signed by 2,545 people was handed to the President of the Parliament. It asked the Parliament, the Government and the political parties to clear up the charges made by the Prince against Wille. It also asked them to address the constitutional

---

[22] His denial was supported by Peter Wolff, leader of the VU parliamentary party, in a debate in the Parliament on 14 September 1995.
[23] "The Times" and "Financial Times", 29 October 1999.

problems that had arisen in recent years. A few days later, on 7 September, the Liechtenstein Institute published studies by two German experts (Jochen Frowein, director of the Max Planck Institute for Foreign and Public Law and professor at Heidelberg University and Wolfram Höfling, professor of State and Administrative Law at the Justus Liebig University, Giessen). The two experts agreed that the Prince's letter could not be considered a private document since he was communicating a decision as head of state. They considered that the Prince's action had violated the right of freedom of expression and interfered with the independence of the judiciary. Frowein said that only the State Court could determine whether it had responsibility for a given question and that the Prince could exercise his right to appoint or not to appoint people to public office only through Parliament. Höfling said that since the Prince had appointed Wille to his present office despite knowing his opinion on Article 112 of the Constitution, his refusal to reappoint him was an arbitrary act.

On 14 September the Parliament considered the petition and decided to establish a five-member all-party Constitutional Commission to draw up a list of the open constitutional questions for further consideration by the Prince and the Government. It also asked the State Court to rule on whether the Government and Parliament were entitled to make binding definitions of individual constitutional questions through a simple agreement between them without recourse to the procedures for constitutional amendment under Article 111, and whether the term "government" in Article 112 meant also the Prince or even exclusively the Prince. Parliament was unanimous that the Constitution needed to be changed in certain points which were constantly giving rise to different interpretations. Since the Parliament was unwilling to be the arbiter in such matters, it called for the beginning of constitutional talks.

On 22 September the Prince sent a long letter to the Liechtenstein Institute, which also served as the basis for his Speech from the Throne on 15 March 1996. To the Institute, Hans-Adam II said that the opinions of the two German experts led to the conclusion that he had the duty to appoint any candidate proposed by Parliament. This would undermine the fundamental structure of the Constitution. Until now, it had been the practice in Liechtenstein for a change of parliamentary majority to lead not only to a change of government but also to changes in certain judicial positions. For a judge to be deprived of confidence, it was sufficient that he should originally have been the candidate of the political party that had now lost the election. For the Prince, however, what mattered was not a judge's political affiliation but his character, intellectual qualities and whether he felt committed to the Constitution. The Prince had previously proposed to Wille a compromise by which the Prince would have appointed judges who did not enjoy his confidence provided that they were elected directly by the co-sovereign (the people); but this had been refused. The Prince would not accept that he was subordinate to the State Court. Neither would he accept that the State Court should be used to abolish the House Law, which was, in the end, the only guarantee of the Princely House's independence and neutrality.

To the Parliament, Hans-Adam said that the Prince's formal constitutional responsibilities must be aligned to his real powers, and vice-versa. These must be clearly documented. Otherwise, confusion would set in, the rule of law would be weakened and the Prince could be blamed for mistakes for which he was not responsible. He proposed, as he had to the Liechtenstein Institute, four possible options. One was absolute adherence to the existing Constitution, including the appointment of officials by the Prince. The second was an expansion of democracy along the lines of his own proposals. The third was a symbolic monarchy. This could bring bigger political and economic risks to the country, which might be reduced if the Prince were given reserve constitutional powers to deal with an internal or external emergency. This option was attractive, since it would enable the Prince and his House to withdraw with dignity from political activity at the height of their achievements for the country. The fourth alternative was a collegial republic as in Switzerland or a presidential one as in the USA. This would probably work politically as long as Europe remained reasonably stable, but it might affect foreign investors' confidence in the country's stability. It might end in absorption into Austria or, more probably, into Switzerland as a canton, which would be a pity after the achievements of recent times. In conclusion, "the Prince and the Princely House are happy to provide the Head of State of this country and are ready to undertake this responsibility in future for the benefit of the Liechtenstein population". He favoured the second of his alternatives, "but more important for us is the people's right of self-determination and we shall therefore also respect a different decision".

To this, the Parliament made a unanimous formal reply on 21 March 1996. The Prince's speech, they said, might have given the impression that there was a broad constitutional discussion under way in Liechtenstein about fundamental changes to the State or even the abolition of the Monarchy. This was not correct. The Parliament, the Government and the political parties were not aiming at or discussing abolition of the Monarchy or its reduction to a representative institution. Once the Constitutional Commission had drawn up its list of open questions, work on the necessary texts would start with the involvement of the Prince and the Government. Parliament had no intention of proposing dramatic changes. The Prince's more extreme constitutional variants, and especially his allusion to uniting with one of the neighbouring states, were undesirable. What was intended was a pragmatic and objective revision of certain constitutional provisions, with no fundamental change and with the maintenance of a strong monarchy endowed with substantial political powers. The basic values of the State and its Constitution were not for discussion or disposal.

1996–2001

In October 1996 the Constitutional Commission submitted its report to Parliament, which asked it to start work on textual proposals in consultation with the other state institutions concerned. The February 1997 elections returned another VU majority[24] and, for the first time since 1938, there was a one-party government (led, like its predecessor, by Mario Frick). In his Speech from the Throne on 13 March 1997 the Prince criticised the Commission's report as, in practice, an interim proposal which would logically lead to a symbolic monarchy on the lines desired by the "Free List" party It was therefore unacceptable. However, the discussions had been helpful in that they had eliminated the notions of a republic, of union with a neighbouring state and of staying with an unchanged constitution. He insisted that his far-reaching proposals offered the best guarantee of everyone's democratic rights. If the Parliament would not make a decision, the Prince and the people would have to do so for them. In his reply the President of the Parliament, Peter Wolff, said that the Prince's proposals were not the only way to strengthen democracy. The Parliament and the Commission had indicated other ways, but they were open to discussion.

A new Constitutional Commission resumed work. It met 31 times between April 1997 and November 2000, on nine of those occasions with the Prince. On 1 July 1998 the commission sent textual proposals to the Prince.[25] Agreement was reached on a number of articles, but on 7 June 1999 the Prince told the Commission that on certain questions the Princely House had no more room for manoeuvre. Further attempts at compromise between September and December 1999 failed. The contents of the confidential discussions became public knowledge.

Hans-Adam II now decided to make a direct approach to the citizens, over the heads of the politicians. He revised his proposals and sent them as a finished draft constitutional proposal ("the Red Booklet") to every household in Liechtenstein on 2 February 2000 under cover of a letter from himself and the Hereditary Prince.

The letter singled out as the three main unresolved points: self-determination for the communes; the independence and appointment of the judges; and the provisions for a vote of no confidence in the Prince and possible abolition of the Monarchy. The two Princes invited all citizens who wished to come to the Castle on six different days in March to discuss the issues face-to-face. The Parliament

---

[24] VU 13 seats, FBP 10, Freie Liste 2.
[25] Report signed by Peter Wolff, President of the Parliament, dated 29 March 2000.

and Commission organised two public information events of their own in May 2000, in Mauren and Schaan.

Meanwhile, in November 1999 the Government had sent the Commission's proposals of 1 July 1998 and the Prince's proposals of 7 June 1999 to four constitutional experts for advice. These were Professors Rhinow (Basel), Funk (Vienna), Frowein (Heidelberg) and Breitenmoser (Basel). Their mandate was to state whether and how far the proposals by the Prince and the Constitutional Commission would strengthen the democratic elements and/or strengthen or weaken the monarchical elements in the Liechtenstein Constitution; to assess them in the light of modern constitutional teaching; and to consider their compatibility with Liechtenstein's obligations under international law, especially as defined by the UN, the Council of Europe, the OSCE and the Charter of Paris. Their reports arrived on various dates between April 2000 and January 2001. In the summer of 2000, the Prince commissioned advice from Professors Matscher (Salzburg) and Winkler (Vienna) on the compatibility of his proposals of 2 February 2000 with the Liechtenstein Constitution, European law and international law. The two professors were also given the Constitutional Commission's proposals, the Government's questions to the four experts and the three replies which had so far been received. The Matscher and Winkler reports arrived in December 2000. It is perhaps not surprising that the two groups of experts should have contradicted each other. The Government's experts criticised the Prince's proposals as tending to weaken democratic rights and parliamentary responsibility, although his proposals for the appointment of judges were to some extent regarded more leniently. The Prince's experts found that his proposals conformed to Liechtenstein's international obligations and constitutional practice, and would tend to strengthen popular rights at the expense of the Monarchy.

The Prince's personal relations with his Head of Government, Mario Frick, were by now poor. The political climate was also soured by other problems: the unconnected matter of the creation of the Archdiocese of Vaduz (pages 268–270), the international criticism of Liechtenstein's financial services sector (pages 306–313) and popular fatigue with the constitutional debate. The FBP won the elections of February 2001 by an unexpectedly large majority.[26] This opened the way to a political solution.

The Drive for a Solution

Even before the new one-party FBP government led by Otmar Hasler took office in April, Hans-Adam II and Prince Alois sent a slightly revised version of their proposals to all households in Liechtenstein (the "Green Booklet", dated

---

[26] FBP 13 seats (49.9% of the vote), VU 11 seats (41.3%), FL 1 seat (8.8%).

1 March 2001) and made the reports by Professors Matscher and Winkler publicly available. At a press conference Hans-Adam II called for a solution within the year. He declared himself opposed to another constitutional commission, which would only lead to further delays. Parliament must decide; but whether it decided for or against the proposals, he thought that a popular vote could not be avoided. He was not worried about a split in the population; the people had been divided now for eight or nine years. He himself would withdraw after the matter had been settled, in order not to be a political burden. If the vote went against their proposals he and Prince Alois would move their residence to Austria because the political strife over the existing Constitution, which all the parties had put in question, would continue; the Princes themselves would not wish to continue to be involved in this controversy.[27]

Through the summer of 2001 leading members of Parliament, the Government, the two main political parties and the Forum Liechtenstein conducted intensive confidential negotiations with Hans-Adam II and Prince Alois on the basis of the proposals in the Green Booklet. The negotiations were mediated by the Forum. They focused on the remaining fundamental problems: the right of communes to secede from the State by self-determination; the Prince's right of veto; the Prince's emergency powers; the appointment of judges; the withdrawal of confidence from the Government by the Prince or the Parliament; the power of the State Court to interpret the Constitution (Article 112); a vote of no confidence in the Prince; and a popular initiative to abolish the Monarchy. These questions, which touched on the basic principles of the Constitution, are discussed in more detail in the relevant sections below.

Of the 28 proposals in the Green Booklet, 12 were undisputed. Some of these were of a purely linguistic or technical nature. Others reflected agreement already reached with the Constitutional Commission. For example:

- In order to avoid uncertainty, Article 9 was to make clear that if the Prince had not approved a law within six months it was to be regarded as having been vetoed. (A proposal by the Commission.)
- The antiquated Article 70 ("The Parliament, acting in agreement with the Sovereign Prince, shall have control over the assets of the State Treasury") was replaced by "The Government administers the country's finances according to policies which it is to agree with the Parliament. It reports to the Parliament along with its Annual Report". (A proposal by the Commission.)
- Holders of certain high public offices must, as before, be Liechtenstein citizens but it was no longer necessary for them to have been born in Liechtenstein. (A proposal by the VU members of the Parliament in 1992.)

---

[27] "Liechtensteiner Volksblatt", 14 March 2001.

– Provision was made in several articles for international treaty obligations to be taken into account.

By mid-July 2001, after the negotiators had exchanged and discussed many working papers, there had been enough progress on the fundamental points for a feeling to develop that it might be possible to find an agreed basis for a constitutional proposal to be made by the Government. At the National Day ceremonies on 15 August, euphoria spread when Hans-Adam announced that he could accept the compromise. He thanked all who had worked for it, especially the Forum Liechtenstein, while the President of the Parliament, Klaus Wanger, praised it as the way out of a disastrous confrontation.

The problem was that, except for the parties to the negotiations, no-one knew what the compromise actually proposed.[28] Over the next few weeks, as the details began to sink in, the incipient mood of unity dissolved. The momentum slipped. For some, the compromise offered the way forward; for others, it marked no change. Otmar Hasler announced on 5 September that his government would submit a constitutional proposal to Parliament, based on the Forum Liechtenstein's text. The question now was, whether a popular vote (which all agreed to be inevitable) would be on a constitutional proposal agreed by Parliament or on a non-agreed initiative submitted by the Prince. The answer was quick to come. At the next session of the Parliament, on 13 September, the spokesman of the opposition VU parliamentary party, Peter Sprenger, bitterly attacked the Government and Wanger for allegedly betraying democracy. The FBP party leadership was divided over the government's tactical handling. Strains soon showed in the VU as well.

On 20 November the Government submitted its constitutional proposal to Parliament. Its accompanying report said that the eight major new formulations had been studied and had been found to conform to Liechtenstein's international human and political rights obligations.[29] At the Parliament's first reading of the bill on 20 and 22 December neither the FBP nor the VU made a party statement. Four members of the VU, including Sprenger, voted with the "Free List" against taking the bill further; the FBP and the rest of the VU voted in favour. The Parliament appointed a five-member commission led by its President and including the Vice-President to consult Hans-Adam II about the points raised in the debate. This commission worked out a new confidential discussion paper, which it presented to the Princes on 3 May 2002. The Princes accepted some suggestions and came back with further proposals on 15 May. These exchanges of papers continued into June.

---

[28] To the annoyance of the Forum Liechtenstein, the Free List, which was not a participant in the negotiations, published a leaked version of the text (but without the accompanying explanatory material) on its website, "in the interest of transparency" ("Liechtensteiner Vaterland", 9 August 2001).

[29] Government Report and Proposal Nr. 87/2001, pages 22–31.

In parallel, during the first half of 2002 the three political parties and other interested organisations arranged a large number of well-attended discussion meetings throughout the country, as part of the traditional opinion-forming process. The correspondence columns of the newspapers overflowed. The VU official line tended increasingly to advocate a negative vote on the grounds that this would leave the 1921 Constitution in place and unchanged. Peter Wolff (Vice-President of the Parliament) dismissed the Princes' stated intention to leave the country if the vote went against them. He argued that if that happened, life would continue as normal and that in due course Hans-Adam, or at least Prince Alois, would make his way back.[30] In the Speech from the Throne on 7 February 2002 Hans-Adam II listed the political powers that he would be sacrificing under the Government's (and his own) proposals. In pressing for an early decision he described the coming popular vote as a vote of confidence in the Monarchy; the Parliament, he said, should in so decisive a question beware of voting differently from the people that it was elected to represent. Meanwhile the opponents of his proposals opened a new front. In May, a group of 32 private persons asked the Council of Europe Parliamentary Assembly's Monitoring Committee to consider the implications for Liechtenstein's human rights obligations of the House Law, including its disciplinary measures, sanctions against children born out of wedlock and lack of female suffrage, in view of the House Law's place in the Constitution.[31]

On 24 June the two Princes and the Constitutional Commission hammered out a new draft constitutional proposal (dated 27 June) for discussion by the parliamentary parties.

The Princes said that they would be willing to discuss it personally with the parliamentary parties. For Hans-Adam II, this text was to be the test of whether a three-quarters majority in Parliament (19 votes) was likely to be obtained. Failing that, he would use it as the basis for his own popular initiative. Wolff reserved his position on whether the changes went far enough.[32] His caution was justified. On 2 August, after consulting their party colleagues, the Commission reported to the Princes that of its five participants the three FBP members could agree to the draft but the two VU members could not. Hans-Adam II declared his intention to call for a popular vote on the draft. The Government withdrew its own proposal of 20 November 2001, since it had been overtaken by the changes negotiated during the summer.

---

[30] "Liechtensteiner Vaterland", 26 February 2002.
[31] "Committee on the Honouring of Obligations and Commitments by Member States of the Council of Europe". This complaint ranged beyond the scope of the provisions of Article 3 of the Constitution.
[32] "Liechtensteiner Volksblatt", 25 June 2002.

Two Complaints

These decisions unleashed a storm of political activity, which lasted for seven months. The basic issues had been thrashed out so thoroughly over the past ten years that there was little new to say. The debate was increasingly marked by tactical manoeuvrings, emotion and questions of personal trust.

The first move was made by 28 citizens who, on 5 August, complained to the government that Hans-Adam's threat to leave Liechtenstein if his initiative were defeated infringed their right to express their opinion on his initiative freely and independently. They further argued that he had in any case no right to launch an initiative: this was reserved to the people, whereas under Article 64 (1) of the Constitution the Prince had only the right to introduce legislation in the form of Government bills. On 17 September the Government rejected the complaint on the grounds that the two Princes enjoyed the same civil rights as all other Liechtenstein citizens, and that the threat to leave Liechtenstein did not form part of their written constitutional proposals. It was, furthermore, premature to complain about the procedures and results of a vote which had not yet taken place. The complainants appealed to the Administrative Complaints Court on the grounds that the Government had not taken due account of their arguments. The court ruled against them on 12 November, pointing out that the extensive public discussion gave plenty of opportunity for the free formation of opinion and that the secret ballot would give the opportunity for its free expression. The State Court upheld this judgment on 3 February 2003, and so removed the last potential legal obstacle to a popular vote. The judgment was of wider constitutional significance in that it established that a popular vote was not to be preempted, or thwarted, by a procedural complaint.

In September a second complaint was made, this time to the Parliamentary Assembly of the Council of Europe. 53 citizens expressed "great concern about democracy, constitutional order and basic rights in Liechtenstein" and asked that the Princes' constitutional proposals should be examined for their conformity with the Council of Europe's democratic and constitutional rules and principles. The letter was based on a memorandum prepared the previous month by Gerard Batliner, Herbert Wille and Professor Andreas Kley (Berne). The Democracy Secretariat ("Demokratie-Sekretariat") urged that these questions should be clarified before any popular vote took place.[33] This move touched a very raw nerve in Liechtenstein. The country was still smarting from hostile international publicity about its financial services sector (pages 306–313 below). Many people resented the deliberate dragging of the country before yet another international forum. "Nest foulers" was among the more printable terms used. The atmosphere had been

---

[33] "Liechtensteiner Volksblatt", 11 September 2002.

deteriorating for some time and anonymous threatening letters were already being received by persons in both camps. Mario Frick, the VU former Head of Government and a leading member of the Democracy Secretariat, now found parts of dead pigs and cats in his mail and at his office entrance.[34]

The "Peace" Initiative

Under the Liechtenstein Constitution, the Government and the Parliament have to decide whether an initiative for a popular vote is legally and technically admissible before its initiators can start to collect the necessary 1,500 signatures in support. On 1 October 2002 the Government formally reported to the Parliament[35] that Hans-Adam II and Prince Alois were constitutionally entitled as Liechtenstein citizens to propose an initiative, and that examination had shown that the proposals in it were consistent with Liechtenstein's international treaty obligations.

On 21 October, two days before Parliament was due to consider the Government's report, a group of citizens launched an alternative proposal, the "Constitutional Peace" initiative ("Verfassungsfrieden"). They were a cross-party group which included a former FBP Party secretary, a former VU member of Parliament, the deputy to the single serving "Free List" member of Parliament and a member of the "Subversive Rumours" group. They presented themselves as offering a loyal and conciliatory third way between the 1921 Constitution and the Princes' proposals.

Unlike the Princes' comprehensive proposals, the "peace" initiative concerned only four articles (the veto, emergency powers, appointment of judges and the competences of the State Court). It thus left untouched the other problems of the 1921 Constitution, and also the points on which agreement for change had already been reached. It would, *inter alia,* have allowed the Prince's veto of a law to be overridden by a referendum commissioned by Parliament. Hans-Adam immediately denounced it as a spoiling tactic, designed either to delay the vote or to confuse the voters: "a Punch and Judy show", a "labelling trick" and a "stillbirth" which he would never sanction. The Government acted swiftly to avoid any delay. It declared the "peace" initiative admissible in record time.[36] On 24 October the Parliament, after an emotional debate that lasted more than five hours, declared both initiatives admissible in the sense of being compatible with Liechtenstein's international obligations: the "peace" initiative by a unanimous vote and the Princes' initiative by 20 votes to 5 (the five opponents being Peter Sprenger, three other VU members and the "Free List" member Paul Vogt).

[34] "Liechtensteiner Vaterland", 24 October 2002.
[35] Report and Proposal No. 88/2002.
[36] Government Report and Proposal to parliament No. 104/2002, dated 22 October 2002.

Preparations for the Vote

The way was now clear for signatures to be collected. The two Princes sent a copy of their proposal, dated 2 August 2002 and bound in the national colours of blue and red, to every household.

By 13 December, when the statutory period of six weeks elapsed, 6,240 persons (37.2% of the electorate) had subscribed to the Princes' initiative and 2,199 (13.1%) to the "peace" initiative. The previous record number of signatures was 2,548, collected in late 1991 for the 1992 vote on the international treaty initiative. The Princes ran an efficient campaign; every subscriber to their initiative received a personal letter of thanks.

Both initiatives were discussed for many hours in Parliament on 18 and 19 December: not with a view to amending them, but to see whether either could win the 19 votes necessary for acceptance at parliamentary level. The 13 FBP members voted for the Princes' initiative; 5 VU and the single "Free List" member voted for the "peace" initiative; and 6 VU members voted against both initiatives (i.e., in favour of the maintenance of the 1921 Constitution unchanged). There was now no alternative to going to a popular vote, the time of which was fixed for 14 and 16 March 2003.

The Council of Europe

Meanwhile, the Bureau of the Parliamentary Assembly of the Council of Europe had referred the request of the 53 citizens to the Venice Commission, an advisory body of constitutional experts set up in 1990 to advise the newly emerging European democracies such as Albania and Azerbaidjan on best practice. Three professors (from Belgium, Denmark and the Netherlands) prepared an opinion, which the Commission considered at its meetings on 13/14 December. The Commission described the Princes' proposals as a step backwards that was likely to isolate Liechtenstein in Europe and could cause problems for its membership of the Council of Europe.

For its part, the Liechtenstein Government described the Commission's report as one-sided and hastily compiled, arguing that it relied too uncritically on outdated material and on the "Democracy Secretariat's" memorandum. Furthermore, the Government (which after all represented a sovereign member state of the Council of Europe) had been given no proper opportunity to tell its side of the story.

An attempt to hold an emergency debate in the Parliamentary Assembly on 30 January 2003 failed when its Social Democrat and Liberal proponents found themselves, to their chagrin, out-lobbied. They could not muster the necessary two-thirds majority against the Conservatives and Christian Democrats, who argued that it was for the Liechtenstein people to make the decision by using their rights of direct democracy.[37] The Bureau decided to await the result of the popular vote.

The Decision

It was now for the Liechtenstein political parties to make up their minds. On 9 January 2003, 76% of the FBP National Committee voted to support the Princes' initiative, 14% for the "peace" initiative and 7% for a double negative (to keep the Constitution unchanged). On 10 February 87% of the VU National Committee voted for a double negative and 13% for the Princes' initiative. The "Free List" came out for the "peace" initiative. These decisions were later confirmed at national party meetings. But Peter Marxer (honorary president of the FBP) and other senior members of the governing party came out for a double negative. Attendance at the VU party meeting was rather low. Some VU grandees who had called for a free vote by the party abstained from the meeting when this was refused. They then campaigned for the Princes' initiative.

The divisive and wearing campaign continued up to the very days of the vote. The issues were explained and repeatedly debated in public meetings and in the media; no-one could have complained of lack of information. When the arguments had been exhausted, it became a question of personal confidence. The press published appeals by members of the Princely Family and advertisements by their supporters. "We can be proud of this family: we support it in the vote" and "This family" (with photographs) "deserves our support and gratitude". There was scare-mongering by both sides. What would become of Liechtenstein if the Princely House left the country? On the other hand, might not the Prince abuse his new powers? Might not his proposals isolate Liechtenstein from Europe and subject it to another wave of international criticism? One of his opponents described the Princes' proposals as "political pornography".

In his Speech from the Throne on 13 February 2003 Hans-Adam II criticised those who had tried to turn Liechtenstein into a "protectorate of the Council of Europe". In no other European state did the people have so many rights as in Liechtenstein, where the monarch himself exercised his rights only for as long as a majority of the people wished. As so often in the past, he painted the opponents of his proposals as the enemies of the Monarchy itself. He was confident that there would be a majority for his proposals. "As happened a good 50 years ago, we shall again succeed in healing the internal political divisions and reintegrating the domestic opponents of the Principality politically and socially". This allusion

---

[37] In contrast, a member of the "Democracy Secretariat" regretted that "Liechtenstein had missed the chance to call in the Council of Europe as a mediator before the popular vote in March ("Liechtensteiner Vaterland", 28 January 2003).

to the events of 1945 outraged the VU, whose parliamentary party described it as "intolerable". They formally stated that their vote against the Princes' proposals in December 2002 "was never a withdrawal of confidence from the Princely House, let alone from the Principality; we were complying with our obligation to vote 'solely' according to our conviction, as required by Article 57 of our Constitution." As for the Prince's assertion that opponents of his proposals were enemies of the country, "we reject these condemnations, which ultimately extend to a large part of the population."[38]

In this sombre mood, the vote took place on 14 and 16 March in raw and snowy weather. The turn-out was 87.7%. The verdict was clear, to an extent that took even some Liechtensteiners by surprise. 9,412 (64.3%) voted for the Princes' initiative and 2,394 (16.5%) for the "peace" initiative. There was very little preference voting, which suggests that people were clear in their minds as to which option they wanted. Only 3,012 voters (20.2%) followed the VU's recommendation to vote against both initiatives and so preserve unchanged the 1921 Constitution (as amended up to 1998). These results mean that 84.6% of the voters opted for the continuation of a strong and politically active Monarchy, whether under the Princes' proposals or according to the unamended 1921 Constitution.

Implementation of the Decision

Since the Princes' initiative took the form of a fully drafted constitutional amendment, it can be incorporated into the current version of the 1921 Constitution once it has been countersigned by the Sovereign Prince and formally promulgated. Some new legislation will also be needed, in particular to provide for changes in the judicial system.

The Secretary-General of the Council of Europe, Walter Schwimmer, said on 16 March, "The sovereign will of the people, which has been expressed in a free and democratic way, must be respected". He continued, "The Council of Europe will observe constitutional practice closely and I hope that the new constitutional provisions will be used to strengthen democratic institutions and safeguard the independence of the courts."[39] The Liechtenstein Government invited representatives of the Monitoring Committee to visit the Principality. Two (Michael Hancock, a British Liberal Democrat, and Erik Jurgens, a Dutch Social Democrat) did so on 3–4 July 2003. Unlike the procedure envisaged in January 2003, they were able to form their impressions at first hand, with the benefit of access to all concerned.[40]

---

[38] "Liechtensteiner Vaterland", 15 February 2003.
[39] Quoted in the "Liechtensteiner Vaterland", 17 March 2003.
[40] Their report is till awaited at the time of writing.

THE POWERS AND CONSTITUTIONAL ROLE OF THE PRINCE

A Constitutional Monarch

The Prince enjoys far-reaching direct and indirect powers in his capacity as co-sovereign with the people. They are not mere formalities, but neither may they be exercised arbitrarily. In addition to Article 2 of the Constitution ("dualism"), Article 7 (1) binds the Prince by saying, "The Prince is the Head of State and exercises his sovereign authority in conformity with the provisions of the present Constitution and of the other laws". Upon his accession the Prince must declare in writing that "he will govern the Principality of Liechtenstein in conformity with the Constitution and the other laws, that he will maintain its integrity, and will observe his rights as sovereign indivisibly and equally" (Article 13 (1).)[1] Only then does he receive Parliament's oath of allegiance (Article 51).

As a result of the constitutional changes agreed in March 2003 a Sovereign Prince may now be subjected to a popular vote of no confidence. The people also have the right to vote for the abolition of the monarchy. These new constraints on the Monarchy are covered in the section on Direct Democracy (pages 238–242).

The House of Liechtenstein and the Succession

Under Article 3, succession to the throne is hereditary in the Princely House of Liechtenstein. The rules of succession, the coming-of-age of the Sovereign Prince and the Heir Apparent and any guardianship that may be required are to be determined by the Princely House through a House Law ("Hausgesetz" since March 2003 but previously referred to in the plural as "the House Laws").

The House Law and its provisions are not otherwise mentioned in the Constitution. It is a law *sui generis*. Amendments to it cannot change the Constitution, and *vice versa*. Its rules on such matters as adoption, marriage and membership of the Princely House could affect the succession. The members of the House are unlikely to intervene so dramatically in Liechtenstein's affairs as to take, without

---

[1] The author's translation of "…und die landesfürstlichen Rechte unzertrennlich und in gleicher Weise beobachten wird".

the most pressing and obvious reason, a unilateral decision to depose a Sovereign Prince. There is however a less extreme precedent from 1923, when the family agreed among themselves to change the order of succession.

In 1998 the Constitutional Commission proposed that an expanded version of those aspects of the House Law that directly concerned the State should be put to Parliament for a positive or negative vote without the possibility of amendment. For the Prince this was non-negotiable. His slight revision of Article 3 was put to the people as part of his set of proposals and was approved by them.

Delegation by the Prince

The Prince may entrust the Heir Apparent who has attained majority with the exercise of his sovereign powers as his representative "should he be temporarily prevented or in preparation for the succession". (Article 13 (1).)

This was done by Franz I in 1938 and Franz Josef II in 1984. Both remained formally Head of State until their deaths. On 15 August 2003 Hans-Adam II declared his intention to delegate his powers to Hereditary Prince Alois in one year's time.

Legal Immunity

Until March 2003 the Prince's person was described as "sacred and inviolable". (Article 7 (2).) This clause provided the personal immunity normally enjoyed by a head of state, whether monarchical or republican. It has now been modernised to read, "The Prince's person is not subject to judicial proceedings and is legally not responsible. The same applies to a member of the Princely House who exercises the function of Head of State for the Prince". This immunity applies to their persons but not to their official acts, which may be contested. Officials of the Princely Estates, like revenue officers, appear before the ordinary courts as plaintiffs and defendants (Article 100, now re-numbered 99).

Foreign Affairs

The Prince represents the state in all its relations with foreign powers, "without prejudice to the necessary participation of the responsible government" (Article 8 (1)). However, treaties that cede national territory, alienate national property, dispose of rights of sovereignty or state prerogatives or impose any new burden on the Principality or its citizens or any obligation to the detriment of the people's rights are not valid unless they receive the consent of Parliament. (Article 8 (2).) Since 1992 treaties which have been approved by the Parliament may also be subjected to a popular referendum (Article 66 bis).

In foreign affairs the Prince plays an active part which goes well beyond a purely formal or representational role. This has been particularly the case with

Hans-Adam II; but it was also true of Franz Josef II, especially in the earlier part of his reign. One striking precedent was Franz Josef's re-establishment of the legation in Berne in 1944 at his own expense, in the teeth of opposition from the Government and Parliament (page 111). Since 1952 the establishment and financing of permanent official missions to foreign Governments has been regulated by a law requiring the involvement of the Government and Parliament. But it follows from Article 8 (1) that if the Prince is to contribute to promoting Liechtenstein's foreign policy, he must be involved in the Government's planning, preparation and conduct of it.[2]

The Veto

Under the 1921 Constitution no law is valid without the Prince's sanction (Article 9). He therefore has the right of veto, even over the results of a popular vote. Two changes were introduced in March 2003. First, the Prince would, logically enough, have no right to veto a successful popular initiative to abolish the monarchy (new Article 113). Secondly, an addition to Article 65 provides that if the Prince does not approve a law within six months it is to be regarded as having been refused his sanction.[3]

Because of the confidentiality of discussions between the Prince and his Head of Government it is impossible to know how many times government policy may have been influenced by the possibility of a veto. Franz Josef II described his methods in the following terms:

"If the Government introduces a law into Parliament it discusses it with me beforehand. It is the same with changes proposed by the Parliament or if an individual Member of Parliament takes an initiative for a law. If I have doubts on constitutional grounds, I make them known. It never comes to a veto because we agree on matters first."[4]

The only exception was Franz Josef's veto of a popular vote on a minor matter (a hunting law) in 1961, because the change proposed would have contradicted the remaining parts of the law. Knowing that the result of the popular vote was

---

[2] Peter Wolff, "Die Vertretung des Staates nach aussen", in "Die liechtensteinische Verfassung 1921", LPS Vol. 21, 1994, page 283.

[3] The Prince vetoes a law either in writing or simply by withholding his signature. The problem with a formal written refusal is that the Head of Government has to countersign every official act by the Prince. The Head of Government would then be obliged either to countersign a document with which he disagreed (thereby getting into conflict with the rest of the government and Parliament) or to withhold his signature from a document which the Prince had every constitutional right to issue. The "silent" procedure is therefore easier for both parties, particularly if the Prince otherwise has a good understanding with his Head of Government. (See Gerard Batliner in "Einführung in das liechtensteinische Verfassungsrecht" (LPS Vol. 21, pages 91–92) and Hilmar Hoch, "Verfassung- und Gesetzgebung", in LPS Vol. 21, pages 223–225.) The new time limit adds clarity by putting a term to any possible period of uncertainty about a "silent" refusal.

[4] Alphons Matt, "Unbekannter Nachbar Liechtenstein" (AT Verlag Aarau Stuttgart, 1986), pages 27–30.

unwelcome to the Parliament, the Government and both parties, he used his prerogative under Article 64 to instruct his government to reach agreement with the Parliament on a revised bill, the principles of which he set out in writing.[5] This resulted in an improved and more generally acceptable law.

Hans-Adam II is known to have used or threatened a veto on several occasions. In 1992 he vetoed a revised law on the State Court. He also hinted at a possible veto of the Free List's initiative for referenda on state treaties in 1989 because he thought that it did not go far enough.[6] He once indicated that he would veto a law which he favoured in principle (on the appointment of officials), because he was not going to receive the desired *quid pro quo* on the appointment of judges.

The Constitutional Commission proposed in 1998 that if the Prince refused his sanction to a law passed by Parliament or failed to give it within six months, a majority in Parliament should have the right to put the law to a popular vote. If the vote succeeded, the Prince's veto would be overridden. This amendment would have applied to the legislative process but not to certain specified provisions of the Constitution which entrench the Prince's position in the State. The Commission thought it unlikely that the Parliament would embark on a referendum unless it were convinced that a large majority of the population supported the proposed law. The Free List party programme of 1993 and the constitutional "peace" initiative of 2002 also envisaged the overriding of the veto by referendum, but without the reserved rights proposed by the Commission.

Hans-Adam II made it clear that such a change to the 1921 Constitution would not be acceptable to him: the erosion of the veto would weaken the Prince's power to have his views taken into account and so would undermine the principles of dualism and of co-operation between the various constitutional organs. That was also the position of the FBP Government in the vote of March 2003.

Executive and Emergency Powers

Under Article 10 of the 1921 Constitution the Prince takes, through the Government and independently of Parliament, the steps required for the execution and administration of the laws (since March 2003: "implementation and enforcement") and any action required in pursuance of the powers of administration and supervision, and issues the requisite ordinances. The last sentence of Article 10 (now re-numbered 10 (1)) covers emergency powers in a vague and general way. It simply says, "In urgent cases he shall take the necessary measures for the security and welfare of the State".

Emergency decrees under Article 10 have been used only three times. In 1943

---

[5] Franz Josef II's letter of 2 January 1962. Photograph in "125 Jahre Landtag" (Paul Vogt), page 244.
[6] The Government and the two main parties, on the other hand, thought that it went too far.

Franz Josef II extended the term of Parliament in order to avoid an election in wartime. This was in accordance with the known wish of the Government, the two main parties, the Parliament and most of the population. In 1982 he brought in emergency anti-drug-trafficking legislation by decree, again by general agreement. On 10 August 1990 Hans-Adam II imposed sanctions on Iraq by decree, again with the Government's support, because on that day Liechtenstein was submitting its application to join the United Nations.

However, the latent possibility of rule by emergency decree can be a potent weapon, as Franz Josef II showed in 1953. The Parliament was paralysed because the two parties could not agree on the division between them of jobs on the board of the Old Age Pensions and Social Security scheme. After a second general election in that year Franz Josef declared, "I hope that I, as Sovereign Prince, will not have to make use of it, but I am obliged to say that in my view a state of emergency will have arisen if the Parliament assembled here today is not able to function, and I will not hesitate, if that happens, to put emergency powers into effect. As Sovereign Prince I cannot allow the country to suffer as a result of differences of opinion between the political parties and a consequent inability to deal with state business. I will only very unwillingly invoke Article 10, but I would be obliged to do so."[7] The threat worked.

The new Article 10 (2) proposed by Hans-Adam II for the first time restricts the potential impact of emergency decrees by specifically safeguarding the Constitution and basic human rights and by imposing a time limit on their validity:

"Emergency decrees may not abrogate the Constitution as a whole or any of its individual provisions, but only limit the applicability of individual provisions of the Constitution. Emergency decrees cannot infringe any person's right to life, the prohibition of torture and inhuman treatment, the prohibition of slavery and forced labour nor the rule of 'no punishment without a law' ". They cannot affect the provisions of Article 3, the House Law, nor the articles that provide for a vote of no confidence in the Prince or for the abolition of the Monarchy. "Emergency decrees lose their force at the latest six months after their enactment".

Under pre-existing constitutional provisions, which remain unchanged, emergency decrees must be formally promulgated as before and must bear the counter-signature of the Head of Government or his legal substitute. Only if no member of the Government is available may the Prince in urgent circumstances act on his own authority.

The 1998 recommendations of the Constitutional Commission would have set

---

[7] Quoted by Waschkuhn, op. cit., page 87. As he points out, the "forgotten" speech of 9 July 1953 does not, for some reason, appear in the government's printed collection of Franz Josef's Speeches from the Throne published in 1986.

a time limit of four weeks within which Parliament or the National Committee would have had to vote on them. The constitutional "peace" initiative of 2002 would have set a limit of two weeks.

In reality, the debate about Article 10 was not so much about Hans-Adam II's proposed changes (which imposed new limitations on his emergency powers) as about the theoretical risk of abuse of emergency powers by a Sovereign Prince, either as a blank cheque for imposing arbitrary rule or as a means of pre-empting or influencing decisions by the Government or Parliament. Memories of October 1992 were invoked.

In fact, most democratic governments hold sweeping powers in reserve. In commenting on the objections to Hans-Adam's proposals, the former Head of Government Walter Kieber pointed out that it was impossible to predict in advance what form an emergency might take. Whatever it was, it would need to be tackled quickly. Parliament would move too slowly and might even cause obstruction by stalemate if the political situation were inflamed; but Parliament was not ultimately excluded since the Head of Government was answerable to it.[8] To this, it might be added that there are several other safeguards against abuse of emergency powers, including the people's right to convene Parliament independently of the Prince, the judicial procedures for complaints, Hans-Adam's own proposals for popular sanctions against an erring monarch and the Prince's lack of an armed force.

Appointments

The Prince has surrendered to the government his power under Article 11 to appoint state officials. He has gained the power to appoint judges, subject to Article 96 of the Constitution. (See "The Courts", pages 245–246 below).

The Prerogative of Mercy

The Prince may remit, mitigate or commute legally pronounced sentences and may quash prosecutions that have been initiated. However, only at the instigation of the Parliament may he exercise these prerogatives in favour of a member of the Government who has been sentenced on account of his official acts (Article 12).

The Prince and the Parliament

Subject to the reserved rights of the people and the communes (page 238 below), the Prince has the right to convene Parliament, to close it, and, for important reasons, which must on each occasion be communicated to the assembled Parliament, to prorogue it for three months or to dissolve it. The prorogation, closing

---

[8] "Liechtensteiner Volksblatt", 16 January 2003.

or dissolution of Parliament must be proclaimed in the presence of the assembled Parliament (Article 48). Following a dissolution, a four-year mandate of the new Parliament begins after the ensuing elections. Article 54 prescribes that Parliament shall be opened with due solemnity by the Prince, in person or by proxy. Article 64 gives the Prince the right to introduce legislation in the form of government bills. (The Parliament, the people and the communes also have the right of legislative initiative.)

These provisions of the 1921 Constitution remain unchanged by the amendments of March 2003. However, the precedent has now been clearly established that in addition to Article 64 the Sovereign Prince has the same right as any other Liechtenstein citizen to introduce legislation through direct democracy in the form of a popular initiative.

The Prince's power to dissolve prematurely or to retain the Parliament is generally exercised as a means of unblocking a party political stalemate. For example, appeals for co-operation between the parties were a recurrent theme in Franz Josef II's speeches. On 12 November 1957 he made it clear that he was unwilling to contemplate a premature dissolution of Parliament because that would be useless before the parties had settled their intractable differences over electoral legislation. "It cannot be the sense of a constitution that calls itself democratic that the Prince is called on to intervene because the representatives of the people in the Parliament do not want to work together owing to party political differences."[9]

In December 1989, on the other hand, Hans-Adam II made it clear that he would dissolve Parliament if a vote on admission to the UN were postponed. Thanks to skilful handling by the President of the Parliament and the Head of Government, the Parliament (whose members were at that point unaware of the Prince's intention) produced a unanimous favourable vote in time.[10] Hans-Adam was less successful when he tried publicly to dissolve Parliament and dismiss his Government in the October 1992 crisis, but he did dissolve a new Parliament a year later in order to seek a fresh popular mandate for the Government.

The Prince and the Government

The Prince appoints the members of the Government with the concurrence of Parliament and on its proposal (Article 79 (2)). The Prince swears in the new Head of Government (Article 87). (This takes place in the Castle chapel.) He receives reports from the Head of Government on matters within the Prince's competence and signs the texts of decisions adopted by himself on the Head of Government's proposal. The latter are countersigned by the Head of Government

[9] "Die Thronreden", page 60.
[10] Waschkuhn, op. cit., page 94.

(Article 86), whose signature is a crucial part of the Liechtenstein system of checks and balances.

The constitutional changes of March 2003 resolved a long-standing ambiguity: whether the Prince had the right to dismiss a member of the Government who had lost his confidence, or even the whole Government. The old Article 80 implied, but did not state in terms, that he had the power to retain or dismiss a government. It empowered Parliament to request the Prince to remove from office a member of the Government who had lost Parliament's confidence, but it did not oblige the Prince to grant the request; indeed, Hans-Adam II refused such a request in 1993. The actions of Johann II in 1928 and Franz Josef II in 1945 suggest that the Prince has always had the power to enforce the resignation of a government that has lost his confidence. In 1965, in order to clear up this obscurity in the 1921 Constitution, the Government, the Parliament and Franz Josef II arrived at an agreed interpretation according to which the Government would always need to enjoy the confidence of both the Prince and the Parliament. If one or the other side were to lose confidence in the Government or one of its members, the persons or person concerned were to be dismissed.[11] This interpretation is set out in the official Liechtenstein handbooks of the time.[12]

The new Article 80 (1) says, "If the Government loses the confidence of the Prince or of Parliament, then its authority to exercise its office expires". Until a new government takes office, the Prince appoints an interim government, which may include members of the old government. The interim government must receive a vote of confidence from Parliament within four months unless the Prince has previously appointed a new government in agreement with Parliament on the latter's proposal. Under the new Article 80 (2), if an individual member of the Government loses the confidence of the Prince or of the Parliament, the Prince and the Parliament jointly decide on his or her dismissal. Until the appointment of a successor, the substantive colleague who normally acts for him in his absence (not his personal deputy) takes over his or her portfolios. Incidentally, this provision appears to protect the Head of Government himself from arbitrary dismissal should he fall into disfavour with the Prince.[13]

Critics have represented this expanded Article 80 as an enlargement of the Prince's powers. They have argued that the Prince could at his pleasure dismiss

---

[11] Article by former head of government Walter Kieber, in "Liechtensteiner Volksblatt", 28 November 2002. See also a letter by former head of government Alfred Hilbe in "Liechtensteiner Vaterland", 21 September 2002.

[12] Article by Walter Kieber in "The Principality of Liechtenstein" (ed. Walter Kranz), 1973, page 41; also page 56 of the 1982 German edition.

[13] The Constitutional Commission's 1998 proposals confined themselves to stating more clearly than before that the Prince and Parliament would have to agree on the dismissal of an individual member of the government, but did not touch on the wider implications of the 1965 interpretation.

the Government and appoint another, and that during its existence any government would continuously be looking over its shoulder to assure itself that it still enjoyed the Prince's confidence. In theory, this has always been so. In practice, the Prince and his Government, whose members are proposed by Parliament, have always had to work together. It is most unlikely that dismissal would come out of the blue. If friction were to become insupportable, it is likely that before the Prince took any action his soundings would have given him a good idea of what sort of government would be acceptable to Parliament as a successor. Parliament has its own weapon against arbitrary action in its power to vote money. Parliament itself now has, for the first time, its own clear right to overturn a government. If the Prince and the Parliament could not agree in this area, the differences would have to be solved by fresh elections.

The Prince's Political Role

Taken together, the Prince's prerogatives go beyond Bagehot's classical trinity of "the right to be consulted, the right to encourage, the right to warn".[14] Many of them are similar to those of the British Monarchy, but in the British case they are exercised on the advice of the Sovereign's ministers and the royal veto has not been used since the reign of Queen Anne (1702–1714). The right to encourage and to warn (indeed, to admonish) is often exercised in the Speech from the Throne at the annual opening of Parliament and in the speech at the National Day ceremony on 15 August. The Prince delivers these speeches on his personal authority. Much more than his father, Hans-Adam II also makes his views known though less formal channels such as lectures, media interviews, conversations and correspondence. They have their own political impact.

In Liechtenstein, the two main parties and most public opinion favour a strong and politically active monarchy. Among the reasons for this are:
 – It is part of the national identity;[15]
 – It represents continuity;
 – There are strong memories of the economic and political benefits conferred by the Princely House, including its unifying role during the Second World War;
 – The Princes have never abused their power. Nor could they, since they have no armed force at their disposal. Their influence depends on the Constitution and the laws, on their experience and on their own personal, moral and intellectual impact;

---

[14] Walter Bagehot (1826–1877), "The English Constitution", 1867.
[15] "This form of state gives us identity and political stability". (Otmar Hasler, Head of Government, speaking in Parliament, quoted in the "Liechtensteiner Volksblatt", 21 December 2001.)

– The Princely House's international background, contacts and insights make an important contribution to the country's policies and standing, particularly in foreign affairs;

– In a country where a small population, entrenched party allegiances and vested interests can make for parish-pump politics, an independent monarch can intervene to break up blockages in the political system and so cause the constitutional processes to start working again.

Since 1920 the Prince of the time has often intervened in politics as *deus ex arce* to act as a mediator and arbiter. More controversial are the occasions when the present Prince has descended from the Castle to become himself an actor in the political arena. Hans-Adam II has sometimes been described as a party in his own right. Gerard Batliner has pleaded eloquently for the head of state to hold himself in reserve as an integrating, representative force in normal times and as an impartial arbiter in time of need.[16] Hans-Adam II, while regretting the necessity to embroil himself in the seemingly endless constitutional controversy up to 2003, sees the monarch as constitutionally empowered to be an independent and active force in the government and life of the country until such time as the people may decide otherwise. In the words of another activist prince:

"Why are princes alone to be denied the credit of having political opinions, based upon an anxiety for the national interests, their country's honour, and the welfare of mankind? Are they not more independently placed than any other politician in the State? Are their interests not most intimately bound up with those of their country? Is the Sovereign not the natural guardian of the honour of his country? Is he not necessarily a politician?"[17]

---

[16] Gerard Batliner, op. cit., pages 92–96.
[17] From a private memorandum by HRH Prince Albert of Saxe-Coburg-Gotha (1819–1861), Prince Consort of Queen Victoria, quoted by Sir Charles Petrie in "The Modern British Monarchy" (Eyre and Spottiswoode, London, 1961), pages 59–60.

THE POWERS AND CONSTITUTIONAL ROLE OF PARLIAMENT (LANDTAG)

The importance of the Parliament as the representation of the people is symbolised by the fact that its President (Speaker) is the chief commoner. In terms of protocol, he takes precedence over the Head of Government.[1] It is he who addresses the Prince at the National Day ceremony.

The Constitutional Position

Under the 1921 Constitution, "The Parliament is the legal organ representing all the citizens of the Principality and as such has the duty of safeguarding and vindicating the rights and interests of the People in relation to the Government in conformity with the provisions of the present Constitution and also of promoting as far as possible the welfare of the Princely House and of the country while faithfully adhering to the principles laid down in this Constitution" (Article 45 (1)).

The Parliament has 25 members elected by universal, equal, secret and direct suffrage on the basis of proportional representation. The Oberland is represented by 15 members, the Unterland by 10, each as a distinct electoral district. In each of these electoral districts one substitute member may be elected for every three representatives of a party; but if a party has only one representative, it may have at least one substitute. The number of substitutes may therefore vary slightly from time to time. To be awarded seats a party must obtain at least 8% of the valid votes cast in the country as a whole. Members of the Government and the courts may not simultaneously be members of the Parliament (Article 46).

Unless prematurely dissolved, the Parliament's mandate is for four years, counting from each new general election. Regular elections are held in February or March every fourth year (Article 47). New elections must be held within six weeks of a dissolution (Article 50). At the beginning of each parliamentary year the Parliament elects a President and Vice-President (Article 52). (By agreement between the two main parties, the President is customarily from the majority

---

[1] Similarly, in Switzerland the President of the House of Parliament that represents the people (the National Council, or "Nationalrat") outranks the Federal President.

party and the Vice-President from the largest minority party.) Members enjoy the usual legal immunity from arrest (Article 56). They must vote solely according to their oath and their convictions. They cannot be made to answer for their votes. They are responsible to the Parliament alone for their utterances in parliamentary and committee sittings and they cannot be sued before a court of law in respect thereof (Article 57).

For a decision of the Parliament to be valid, at least two thirds of the members must be present and it must be adopted by an absolute majority of those present. The president has the casting vote (Article 58).

Under Article 62, the Parliament has particular competence for:

(a) participation in the work of legislation in accordance with the Constitution;

(b) participation in the conclusion of treaties (Article 8);

(c) the establishment of the annual budget and the authorisation of taxes and other public dues;

(d) resolutions on credits, pledges and loans chargeable to the state, and the purchase and sale of state property;

(e) the resolution on the annual report ("Rechenschaftsbericht") by the Government on the whole of the state administration;

(f) the submission of suggestions and complaints about the state administration as a whole and its various branches;

(g) the impeachment of members of the Government before the State Court for breaches of the Constitution or of other laws.

The constitutional amendments of March 2003 added two new elements to Article 62. Sub-paragraph (f) has been enlarged to recognise explicitly the Parliament's competence for supervising the state administration. A new sub-paragraph (h) includes among its competences the Parliament's new power under Article 80 to withdraw its confidence from the Government or one of its members.

Article 63 gives the Parliament the right to supervise the whole of the state administration, including the administration of justice, through an audit committee; to bring any defects or abuses directly to the Prince's notice through memorials or complaints; to be informed of the outcome of the resulting inquiries and of the action taken; and to put questions to members of the Government. It has the right to appoint investigatory committees and a finance commission. The changes of March 2003 made it clear that the supervisory means at the Parliament's disposal are not limited to the audit committee They also made it clear, in the interests of the separation of powers, that neither the courts' judicial functions nor the Prince's constitutional functions are subject to parliamentary supervision. They modernised procedures by empowering Parliament to bring complaints to the attention of the Government as an alternative to that of the Prince.

The Parliament may initiate legislation (Article 64). Without the Parliament's participation, no law may be issued, amended or declared to be in force. For a law to become valid it must in every case receive the assent of the Parliament, the sanction of the Prince and the counter-signature of the Head of Government or his deputy and be promulgated in the National Law Gazette ("Landesgesetzblatt") (Article 65). If the Parliament declares a law or financial resolution to be urgent, it is not liable to a popular referendum (Article 66 (1)).[2] (In practice, the annual budget is always declared urgent.) Without the Parliament's approval no direct or indirect taxes or any other public dues or general levies, under any designation whatsoever, may be imposed or collected. Tax demands must expressly state that parliamentary approval has been given. The system by which all public taxes and dues are to be apportioned, their effect on persons and objects and the manner of their collection must be approved by Parliament. The Parliament authorises taxes and dues for a year at a time (Article 68). The Government submits for approval preliminary estimates of all expenditure and revenue for the coming year, together with its proposals for taxation, and it accounts to the Parliament for expenditure in the previous year. If the estimates have been exceeded, the Parliament's approval for the extra expenditure must be sought (Article 69).

New permanent official posts (old Article 11 and new Article 106 (1)) and new permanent judicial posts (new Article 106 (2)) may be created only with the Parliament's approval.

The National Committee

When the Parliament is not sitting (including after a dissolution) its business may be carried out on a provisional basis by the National Committee ("Landesausschuss"). This body, *inter alia,* acts as a parliamentary constitutional watchdog between the Parliament's sittings. It consists of the Parliament President and four other members (two from each electoral district) who are elected by Parliament (Articles 71–77). In practice, the National Committee has lost much of its former significance now that the Parliament meets several times through the year.

The Composition of the Parliament

The 1862 Constitution gave eight elected representatives to the Oberland and four to the Unterland. These figures were adjusted to seven and five respectively in 1878 after the unrest caused by the gold currency crisis, when the Unterland deputies twice boycotted Parliament. It was also in 1878 that the country was formally divided into the two electoral districts in response to the Unterland's sensitivities. Until 1921 the Prince had the right to nominate three representatives

---

[2] See also the sections on direct democracy and local government, below.

of his own. The 1921 Constitution changed the ratio of representatives to nine (Oberland) and six (Unterland), with as many as fourteen substitutes. Repeated attempts to raise the number of representatives from fifteen were defeated in referenda in 1919, 1945, 1972 and 1985, largely because of suspicions about the division of seats between the two electoral districts. The electorate accepted the current arrangements in 1988. By that time an increase had become imperative owing to the growth of population, female suffrage, the burden of parliamentary work and increasing international obligations.

Voters' participation in parliamentary elections is high (86.93% in 1997, 86.8% in 2001). In 1997 they elected seven members from the legal and trusts world, five from industry and engineering, five teachers, two from the banking sector, two doctors, one mayor, one dentist, one insurance expert and one professional archivist. (These figures include two members who doubled as mayors, so that altogether there were three mayors.) The pattern in 2001 was broadly similar, but this time it included a master joiner. There is only a single woman member at present. Since 1989 no farmer has served in Parliament.

The Parliament at Work

From 1868 to 1905 the Parliament occupied a purpose-built building.[3] It then moved into a spacious hall in the new Government Building. At present (2003) a new parliament building is being built, an earlier proposal for a much larger project having been rejected by popular referendum in 1993.

As in Switzerland, the members of the Liechtenstein Parliament function part-time. It is very much a working parliament rather than a stage for political drama, though the latter can occur. It meets about eight or ten times a year, for two or three days at a time. Its members are therefore free to exercise their own trades and professions; they are not divorced from day-to-day life. Members receive an annual lump sum of 10,000 francs and a daily rate of 200 francs (140 for half a day). They are similarly remunerated for each day of meeting for preparatory work.[4]

Sittings are usually open and are audio-broadcast in full. Closed sittings are normally reserved for occasions when the Government wishes to present confidential information or when there are internal parliamentary or personnel matters to be discussed.

Bills are initially considered in a preliminary debate, when the Parliament decides whether it will deal with a bill at all. Thereafter, in the first reading

---

[3] This later became a school. It was demolished in 1970 to make way for the abortive art museum project. (Paul Vogt, "Brücken zur Vergangenheit", Vaduz, 1990, page 179)

[4] "The Parliament" (Landtagssekretariat, Vaduz, 1998), page 5.

the Parliament makes suggestions for consideration by the Government, which the Government then examines in detail. In the second reading, each article is debated and voted on separately. The Parliament then votes on the bill as a whole. The Parliament cannot amend a treaty signed by the Government, but only accept or reject it as a whole. The Parliament may amend any item in the Budget. For projects spreading over several years the Government must ask the Parliament to pledge a credit.

In practice draft legislation tends to stem from the Government and its experts, but the Parliament and its members are free to make their own legislative proposals and requests for action. Oral and written questions are frequently put to the Government. The Government's legislative reports and proposals to Parliament are an important source of information for members. No research assistance is available for members as parliamentarians.

In addition to electing the Government, which must enjoy its confidence during its whole term of office, the Parliament also elects the boards of directors and supervisory boards of state institutions such as the social security, electricity and gas authorities, some directors of the Liechtensteinische Landesbank, members of various committees and foundations, the board of the State Art Collection and holders of a range of other appointments. These posts are allocated according to elaborate ratios agreed between the parties. Until the amendments of March 2003 the Parliament used to be solely responsible for electing judges. The new arrangements are described below in the section on the courts.

The workload and paper-load are considerable. Apart from formal sessions, a good deal of parliamentary work is done in committee. There are three standing committees: Audit, Finance and Foreign Affairs, each consisting of five members. Special committees, with finite mandates, may be set up to deal with specific problems. Since 1989 it has been possible to set up a parliamentary investigation committee at the request of seven members.

In practice, much of the real parliamentary business, including the thrashing out of issues, formulation of party positions and questioning of their own party's ministers, is done behind closed doors at meetings of the parliamentary parties ("Fraktionen").

After this process the parliamentary party spokesmen or spokeswomen ("Fraktionssprecher") take the lead in the Parliament's plenary sessions.

The main function of the substitute members, who are unique to Liechtenstein, is to ensure that if a substantive member is prevented from attending a plenary sitting the voting ratio will not be upset. Substitutes may not be appointed to a committee, but they may be elected to parliamentary delegations to international organisations such as the Council of Europe, the EEA, EFTA and the OSCE. This reduces the burden on the substantive members.

The 8% Threshold

A threshold of 18% was introduced by law in 1939 as one of the measures to keep Nazi supporters out of office and Parliament. The law was repealed after the State Court ruled it in 1962 to be unconstitutional. The present 8% threshold was introduced by referendum in 1973. It survived by a healthy majority a popular initiative by the Free List minority party to abolish it in 1992. The new but lower threshold keeps out smaller parties who might otherwise proliferate under the proportional representation system. However, in February 1993 the Free List was able to surmount it and so broke for the first time the parliamentary monopoly of the two main parties.

Parliamentary Boycotts

The Parliament is far from absolute: Prince, people and Government all have considerable decision-making powers of their own. Political life in Liechtenstein therefore demands a large measure of consensus even when there is a one-party government. Building a new consensus after an election entails hammering out a hard-fought accord within the Parliament and between Parliament and the Government. When the two main parties are fairly evenly balanced, which has been the case up to now, the weaker of the two has an ultimate weapon if it has a grievance which it feels is being wilfully ignored by the stronger: it can use (or misuse) the two-thirds quorum rule (Article 58) by withdrawing from the Parliament and so making it incapable of functioning. This is colloquially known as "blowing up" ("sprengen") Parliament. This tactic has been used in 1877, 1878, 1926, 1953 and 1988, and a threat to use it brought results in 1974. When carried to the limit, it results in paralysis of the system, a dissolution of Parliament and fresh elections. These do not necessarily benefit the party that provoked them; the Liechtensteiners as a rule dislike polarisation. The FBP's withdrawal from Parliament in December 1988 did not win them an election victory in March 1989. It was however followed by a referendum victory, which established in the Constitution the right to set up parliamentary investigatory committees (Article 63 bis).[5]

---

[5] This was one of the many consequences of the so-called Art Museum affair (page 196 above).

THE POWERS AND CONSTITUTIONAL ROLE OF THE GOVERNMENT

In keeping with the "dualism" of the Liechtenstein Constitution, the Government is placed as a link between the Prince and the Parliament. Without detracting from the prerogatives of either, it enjoys considerable executive powers in its own right.

As in most continental European countries, members of the Government are not members of Parliament.

The Constitutional Position

Under Article 78, the collegial government is responsible to the Prince and the Parliament. It conducts the whole of the national administration according to the letter and the spirit of the Constitution and the other laws. It may delegate specific functions to particular officials, government offices, or special commissions, subject to recourse to the government. It may set up special commissions by law to deal with complaints. Special corporations, institutions and public law foundations ("Körperschaften, Anstalten und Stiftungen des öffentlichen Rechts") may be established by law to fulfil economic, social and cultural obligations under the supervision of the Government.

The Government consists of the Head of Government (Regierungschef) and four Government Councillors (Regierungsräte). They are increasingly being described, particularly for external purposes, as Prime Minister and Ministers respectively. They are appointed by the Prince with the concurrence of the Parliament and on the proposal of the latter.

On the proposal of the Parliament the Prince appoints one of them as Deputy Head of Government. Each of them has a substitute, appointed in the same manner, to represent the relevant member of the Government if the latter is prevented from attending meetings of the Government.

All must be citizens of Liechtenstein, but since March 2003 there is no longer a requirement for them to be native-born Liechtensteiners. At least two members of the Government (and their two substitutes) must be chosen from each of the two electoral districts, to ensure that neither the Oberland nor the Unterland is under-represented.[1] The Government holds office for four years and after an election carries on the business of the State until a new government has been appointed (Article 79), unless there is to be an interim government under Article 80 as it was amended in March 2003.

Both the Prince and the Parliament, as we have seen, are equally empowered to dismiss a government or one of its members (Article 80 (1) and (2), as amended in March 2003).[2]

For a decision of the collegial Government to be valid, at least four members must be present. The chairman of the meeting has the casting vote (Article 81). The Head of Government presides at meetings of the government, deals with business directly entrusted to him by the Prince and countersigns the laws, decrees and ordinances issued by the Prince or a Regent (Article 85). He reports to the Prince orally or in writing on matters placed under the Prince's authority. The texts of decisions adopted by the Prince on the Head of Government's proposal are signed personally by the Prince and countersigned by the Head of Government (Article 86). Having been sworn in by the Prince, the Head of Government himself swears in the other members of the Government and state officials (Article 87).

All important business, and in particular the settlement of administrative disputes, is discussed and decided by the Government collectively. Certain less important matters may be assigned by law to be dealt with independently by the relevant individual members of the Government. The Head of Government is responsible for executing the collegial Government's decisions. He may delay action only if he considers that a decision is contrary to existing laws or regulations, in which case he must immediately notify the Administrative Court. The latter, without prejudice to the right of appeal of a party involved, determines whether or not the decision may be implemented (Article 90). The Government agrees on the distribution of business among its members at the beginning of each term of office and arranges for a system of mutual deputising in case of non-availability (Article 91). The Government is responsible for the execution of all laws and of all such tasks as may be lawfully entrusted to it by the Prince and the Parliament.

To give effect to the laws it issues the necessary decrees, which must, however, remain within the limits of those laws (Article 92 (1)). "All organs of the national administration may act only within the limits of the Constitution and the other laws. Even in matters where the law allows the administrative authorities freedom of judgment, the limits imposed by the law must be scrupulously observed" (Article 92 (2)). In Article 92 the amendments of March 2003 have added to the Government's constitutional and legal obligations those imposed by international

---

[1] Another example of an entrenched safeguard for the Unterland minority.
[2] See the section on the Prince's powers, page…above.

treaties to which Liechtenstein is party. Article 93 defines the Government's particular sphere of action as including in particular the supervision of all sub-ordinate officials and authorities placed under the government and the exercise of disciplinary powers over officials; allocation of the necessary staff; supervision of the prisons and of the treatment of their inmates; the administration of state buildings; the supervision of the despatch of court business to ensure that it is carried on lawfully and uninterruptedly and the notification of the High Court of Appeal of any irregularities observed; the preparation of the annual report on its official activities to the Parliament; the preparation of government bills for submission to the Parliament and the expression of its opinion on proposals submitted to it for that purpose by Parliament; and ordering urgent expenditure not provided for in the estimates.

The Evolution of the Government

Between 1862 and 1921 the Government consisted of the Governor ("Landes-verweser"), who up to 1918 was an official of Austrian origin appointed autono-mously by his employer, the Prince; two National Councillors ("Landräte") who were appointed by the Prince from among the Liechtenstein citizens eligible for election to the Parliament; and a Secretary (also an employee of the Prince). The National Councillors served for six years. After 1921 the Head and Deputy Head of Government were proposed by the Parliament to the Prince for a period of six years, but the Parliament elected two additional Government Councillors ("Regierungsräte") and their substitutes for a period of four years. The Govern-ment was deliberately given a strong position in the 1921 Constitution, not least because the FBP distrusted a fully parliamentary system. That also explains the decoupling of the terms of office of the Head and Deputy Head of Government from that of the Parliament. At that time, the Head of Government was the only full-time member of the Government. Traditionally he kept all the main threads in his hands, while the Deputy Head of Government stood ready to help if needed. In 1934 Josef Hoop and Fr Frommelt (both FBP) divided the portfolios more evenly between them. The other two Government Councillors, one of whom belonged to the opposition VU, were assigned nothing. Although Deputy Head of Gov-ernment, Fr Frommelt nevertheless managed to be President of the Parliament and Education Commissioner as well;[3] an accumulation of offices that would be constitutionally impossible today. In 1938 the Constitution was changed to make the post of Deputy Head formally a full-time office. In that year, and as a result of the coalition agreement, the post was given to the VU minority. This created the curious situation that if the Head of Government happened to be absent, the

---

[3] Geiger, "Krisenzeit", Vol. 1, page 324.

minority party would have a majority in the four-member Government. In the 1965 reforms a fifth (part-time) member was added and the Government's term of office was reduced to four years, to coincide with that of the Parliament. In this way the nominations for a new government in its entirety came for the first time to depend on the majority in a newly-elected Parliament.[4]

Pressure of business over the years has eroded the part-time character of the Government Councillors (Ministers). In the Hasler administration, appointed in 2001, they all work full-time except for Ernst Walch, who officially devotes 50% of his time to the Government. His predecessor as Foreign Minister held several other portfolios concurrently, including Culture and Sport, but it is a sign of the times that Walch deals exclusively with foreign affairs.

Article 78 of the Constitution describes the Government as "collegial". A departmental system has gradually evolved over the years in response to the pressures of business, but it is not as strongly developed as in most other European countries. The distribution of responsibilities between ministers can vary considerably from one administration to another. Until 1993 the Head of Government was usually also Foreign Minister. Since then, the burdens of that portfolio have required that another Government Councillor should shoulder them. As an illustration, the current distribution of portfolios is:

Otmar Hasler (Head of Government): Presidency, Finance, Construction, Family and Equality.

Rita Kieber-Beck (Deputy Head of Government): Education, Transport and Communications, Justice.

Ernst Walch: Foreign Affairs.

Alois Ospelt: Internal Affairs, Culture, Sport, Environment, Planning, Agriculture and Forestry.

Hansjörg Frick: Health, Social Affairs, Economy.

The substitute members of the Government stand in for their principals (when absent) at meetings of the cabinet, represent their views and vote in their place. During a coalition government, a substitute would prevent the majority party from being outvoted at a cabinet meeting if a substantive minister were absent. Substitutes are not able to initiate business at cabinet meetings. In the absence of the Head of Government it is not his substitute but the Deputy Head of Government who presides over the meeting. At meetings of the Parliament an absent minister is represented by one of his substantive colleagues, not by his personal substitute. Despite these limitations the substitutes play an important part in supporting their principals in their official and representational work. Without the substitutes, the Government would not be able to function under modern pressures.

---

[4] Vogt, "125 Jahre Landtag", page 135.

The Role of the Head of Government

Notwithstanding the officially collegial nature of the Government, the Head of Government occupies a particularly strong position. He is personally responsible for the implementation of government policy. As holder of the presidency, he is at the heart of the administrative machine.[5] As Minister of Finance, he controls the public purse. In addition to his responsibility for public policy and administration, the Constitution gives him a close official relationship with the Prince and a unique balancing, intermediary and negotiating role in the relationship between the Prince and the Parliament, to each of whom he is equally responsible.

Since the Head of Government emerges from the party machine without necessarily having a parliamentary background, he can at the outset be relatively unknown to the wider public. He is sometimes surprisingly young. Recent examples of young Heads of Government include Hans Brunhart (VU, 1978–1993, aged 33 at the time of his appointment), Markus Büchel, (FBP, 1993, aged 33) and Mario Frick (VU, 1993–2001), who at 28 was the youngest Prime Minister in Europe. From earlier generations, Alexander Frick (FBP, 1945–1962) and Gerard Batliner (FBP, 1962–1970), were 35 and 33 respectively when appointed.[6] Both later entered Parliament and became Presidents of the Parliament.

The Government and Legislation

Although the Parliament also has the right to initiate legislation, it is usually in practice the Government that launches draft bills. This is because the Government, unlike the members of Parliament, has at its disposal the expert advice of the civil service and is better placed to seek expert advice from abroad. (It is quite common for foreign legislation, especially Swiss and Austrian, to be adopted in Liechtenstein.) The Government usually proceeds with great caution. It consults all those in Liechtenstein who may have an interest (but not, usually, the political parties themselves in any formal manner). When it presents a proposal to Parliament there is an accompanying report, which is painstakingly and objectively drafted. The report sets out the pre-history of the matter, the main reasons for the proposal, the legal and constitutional implications, the result of the consultative process and the financial and staffing consequences. The Government usually tries to find a broadly based consensus. This is a necessary precaution since the people will have the last word should a referendum be called. Even so, the result

---

[5] The "Administration" (government, civil service, courts and parliament secretariat) comprised 639 persons at 31 December 2000, of whom 136 worked part-time. (Government Report ("Rechenschaftsbericht") for 2000, page 231.) By 2003 it stood at 708 persons.

[6] The National Archives and the National Library seem to be a seedbed of politicians. Hans Brunhart and Alois Ospelt were both National Archivist/National Librarian, and Paul Vogt, leader of the Free List, is currently Head of the National Archives.

of a referendum cannot be taken for granted. The voters have a long record of refusing to accept the official wisdom, even if it is unanimously endorsed by the Parliament and both the main political parties.[7]

Coalition Governments

The two-party coalition formed in 1938 lasted until 1997. It was, perhaps, the last relic of the Second World War. In 1946 the party leaders continued the coalition at the request of Franz Josef II. Until 1970, by which time the Homeland Service generation had left the scene, the FBP led the coalition. In that year the VU unexpectedly took over the leadership, to be replaced in 1974 by the FBP. The VU took the lead again in 1978. After the short-lived FBP-led coalition in 1993 the VU resumed the lead. In 1997 it formed a one-party government, in which role it was replaced by the FBP in 2001.

Under the coalition system the post of Head of Government was held by the majority party and that of Deputy Head by the minority; the majority party took three places in the Government and the minority party two. A number of important official, judicial and non-governmental posts were shared out according to carefully (and sometimes toughly) negotiated inter-party agreements. There was no coalition programme as such, but only a broad understanding between the parties. This arrangement has been described as "co-opposition". The only area which was clearly understood to be bipartisan was foreign affairs.

The minority coalition party gained by being able to press for its policies at the centre of government and, in particular, from access to official information, which it might otherwise have been denied. However, during the 15 years of VU dominance after 1978 the FBP began to feel itself stifled and taken for granted. After its electoral defeat in 1997 the FBP decided that it needed to refresh itself and to put a public distance between itself and the VU. It therefore went into formal opposition. Since then Liechtenstein politics have resembled the alternating, single-party government system characteristic of the Anglo-Saxon countries rather than the coalition system that prevails in Switzerland, Austria and many other continental countries. This does not mean that consensus has been abandoned. It is forced upon the government of the day by the Constitution's checks and balances and by the mentality of the people who, even though ready to plunge into polemics on individual issues, at heart dislike extremes. Respect for the minority continues to be shown in the allocation of public and official posts.

---

[7] Examples of such negative popular votes include those on raising civil servants' and teachers' salaries (1927), introducing unemployment insurance (1931), raising the number of Parliament members (1945 and 1972), introducing compulsory vocational qualifications (1949), new gun regulations (1950), civil defence (1962), votes for women (1971 and 1973), the Art Museum credit (1980) and a planning law (2002). Except for those on female suffrage, most of these votes against united parliamentary and party recommendations were motivated by a suspicion of increased state interference and higher taxes.

DIRECT DEMOCRACY

Liechtenstein followed Swiss practice by introducing the rights of popular referendum and initiative in 1921. Both political parties supported this radical change.

In Switzerland, the formation of the Confederation in 1848 resulted in some *de facto* (albeit not *de jure*) loss of power by the cantons to the centre. To help redress the balance, reform movements introduced referenda and initiatives in the second half of the nineteenth century. These reflected the older tradition of the direct democratic assemblies in the alpine cantons and the general councils in the city cantons.

Direct democracy in Liechtenstein reflects the tradition of communal self-government, which was never forgotten even during the absolutism of the eighteenth and early nineteenth centuries. The Liechtenstein Constitution enables members of the public to launch their own initiatives for legislation and for constitutional change. The right of referendum (a braking and stabilising force) enables the people to strike down legislation of which they disapprove. As in Switzerland, a popular vote against a government proposal is not regarded as a vote of no confidence. The Government is not expected to resign; that would be seen as politically ill-mannered. However, the Government is expected to adjust its programme accordingly.

The Constitutional Position

Direct democracy is embedded in several parts of the 1921 Constitution.

Parliament must be convened in response to a valid written request by at least 1,000 citizens with voting rights or by resolutions adopted by the communal assemblies of at least three communes (Article 48 (2)). If at least 1,500 citizens or four communal assemblies request it, there must be a popular referendum on dissolving Parliament (Article 48 (3)).[1] These rights have never yet been exercised, but they are a powerful weapon in reserve against any possible misuse of author

---

[1] The thresholds for signatories were raised in 1984 from 600 and 900 to 1,000 and 1,500 respectively. In 2003 the electorate stood at 16, 932 persons.

ity either by the Prince (should he, for example, fail to convene Parliament) or by Parliament itself.

If at least 1,000 citizens submit a written proposal or at least three communes pass resolutions requesting the enactment, amendment or revocation of a law, the request must be debated at the next parliamentary session. If it would involve new expenditure, Parliament may discuss it only if it is accompanied by proposals for providing the necessary funds (Article 64 (2) and (3)).

At least 1,500 citizens or four communes may make a proposal affecting the Constitution under the right of initiative (Article 64 (4)).

Every law or any financial resolution passed by Parliament, but not declared urgent, involving new non-recurrent expenditure of not less than 300,000 francs or a new annual expenditure of 150,000 francs,[2] is to be submitted to a referendum if Parliament so decides, or if at least 1,000 citizens or at least three communes so request within thirty days of its official publication. If the matter affects the Constitution in whole or in part, the demand for a referendum requires support by a minimum of 1,500 citizens or four communes. Parliament may call for a referendum on the individual principles which are to be embodied in a proposed law. (Article 66 (1), (2) and (3))

If Parliament rejects a bill which has been drawn up in due form, accompanied if appropriate by proposals for the necessary funding, and which has been submitted to it by the procedure for a popular initiative, the bill must be submitted to a popular vote. If it succeeds, it has the same force as a parliamentary resolution (Article 66 (6)).

Any resolution of the Parliament concerning assent to a treaty under Article 8 must be submitted to a popular referendum if the Parliament so decides or if at least 1,500 citizens or at least four communes request a referendum within thirty days of the official publication of the Parliament's resolution (Article 66 bis).

The amendments of March 2003 enlarged direct democratic rights in some fundamental ways.

A new Article 13 ter (in the Constitution's chapter on the Sovereign Prince) provides that at least 1,500 voters may propose, with reasons, a vote of no confidence in the Sovereign Prince. At its next sitting Parliament must make a recommendation on the proposal and arrange a popular vote. If the people vote for the proposal, it is communicated to the Prince to be handled according to the House Law. The decision made by the Princely House under the House Law is to be made known to Parliament by the Prince within six months.

In the chapter on the maintenance of the Constitution, a new Article 113

---

[2] The financial thresholds were raised in 1996 from 50,000 and 20,000 to 300,000 and 150,000 francs respectively.

provides that at least 1,500 voters may propose an initiative for the abolition of the Monarchy. If it succeeds, Parliament is to work out a new, republican constitution and submit it to a popular vote between one and two years later. The Prince has the right to propose his own new constitution for the same vote. In the event of two rival new versions being proposed, the voters would still have the option of choosing to keep the old constitution. Under the new Article 112 (2), a successful initiative for the abolition of the Monarchy would not be subject to the Prince's veto.

In the same chapter, Article 111 formerly stipulated that any changes to, or interpretations of, the Constitution that might be proposed either by the Government or the Parliament or a popular initiative must have the Parliament's approval, either by a unanimous vote of the members present or by a majority of three-quarters of the members present at two successive sittings. The sense of this Article has been retained in the newly numbered Article 112 (2), but has been tightened up in two important aspects. It is now only "generally binding interpretations" that, in addition to proposed amendments, are to be subject to the procedures for constitutional change outlined in the article. On the other hand, it is now explicit that in each and every case such interpretations are to be subject to a popular vote and to sanction by the Prince.

In case of disagreement about the appointment of a judge, the people will in future have the last word. (See the section on the courts, pages 245–246 below.)

Some General Rules

There are no routinely obligatory referenda in Liechtenstein (unlike Switzerland), with a single exception that is not mentioned in the Constitution. Under the Tax Law, a referendum is compulsory in the case of a proposal to raise tax rates by more than one and a half times the rates prevailing in the previous financial year.[3]

Popular votes are held commune by commune, but acceptance or rejection of a proposal is decided by an absolute majority of the valid votes recorded in the whole of the country. Laws that are subject to a referendum are not submitted to the Prince for signature until the referendum has been held or until the statutory period of thirty days within which a request for a referendum may be submitted has expired.

If an initiative is rejected by the voters, it may not be proposed again until at least two years have elapsed. An initiative may take the form of either a simple proposal or (as in the 2003 constitutional vote) a detailed draft. Once the Government has examined an initiative and declared it valid, it goes to the next session

---

[3] Waschkuhn, op. cit., page 325.

of Parliament for consideration. If Parliament rejects it, a popular vote must be held within three months. The schedule is therefore quite brisk. But the process of gathering 1,500 signatures and the public debate before even that stage is reached ensure that the voters are thoroughly familiar with an issue long before the proposal reaches the ballot box.

Exemptions from Referenda

Although "urgent" legislation is not subject to referendum, the checks and balances built into the system provide enough ultimate safeguards against abuse of this exemption.

Many Swiss decrees and regulations are in force in Liechtenstein but are not subject to referenda because they have been issued under the Customs Treaty, which takes precedence as an international agreement. Since 1995 numerous EEA and EU regulations have also taken effect in Liechtenstein. Article 67 of the Constitution provides for a simplified form of publication of these measures and also (since 1996) of obligations arising from other international treaties. Although such obligations are not subject to referenda they enjoy the democratic legitimacy conferred by the people's right, since 1992, to accept or reject treaties negotiated by the government.

Direct Democracy and the Monarchy

Hans-Adam II consistently argued the case for the new Articles 13 ter and 113 along the lines of his Speech from the Throne on 12 May 1993 (pages 199–200 above). The content of these articles was always controversial. Both supporters and opponents of the Princes' initiative disliked them. Nobody, on either side, wanted to abolish the Monarchy[4], but opponents of the initiative considered the proposals deceptive and dangerous. They argued that a vote of no confidence in the Prince, so far from putting the democratic will into effect, would be no more than a proposal to the unaccountable and largely unknown members of the Princely House, who would have the last word. It would always, they said, have been open to the people to vote for a new republican constitution if they so wished; but the new article on abolition of the Monarchy could help a Sovereign Prince to enforce his will in some future matter of lesser importance by staking everything on an all-or-nothing popular vote on the existence of the Monarchy. Furthermore, the Prince's right to make a constitutional counter-proposal would only complicate matters if the people had already voted for a republic.[5]

---

[4] "Liechtensteiner Volksblatt", 9 December 2002.
[5] Arguments by Peter Sprenger, Peter Wolff, Paul Vogt and Professor René Rhinow, quoted in "Liechtensteiner Vaterland", 19 October 2002. Fuller argumentation on these points by Prof. Rhinow is to be found on pages 82–100 of his advisory opinion of 18 April 2000.

At the heart of this part of the debate lay the question of whether the new articles would confer additional democratic legitimacy and, therefore, more political influence, on an already powerful Prince; and, if so, how he would use that influence. This can only be tested in practice. From the formal point of view, there seems little doubt that the balance of the Constitution has been tipped in favour of popular rights

The Power of Direct Democracy

Since popular initiatives and referenda are not particularly frequent in Liechtenstein, there is little sign of "voter fatigue". The lowest ever turnout was 36.5% in June 1992, on a proposal to lower the voting age; but in December of the same year the turnout to vote on the EEA Agreement was as high as 87%. In the 82 years between October 1921 and March 2003 there have been 76 popular votes and one consultative referendum on female suffrage. This makes an average of rather less than one per year, although the frequency has increased in recent years: 16 in the 1980s, 11 in the 1990s and 7 since February 2000.

Direct democracy in Liechtenstein is a living force, whether in the form of the initiative (an engine of change)[6] or of the referendum (the people's veto). It works indirectly as well as directly: the Government and Parliament, when weighing possible legislation, need always to take into account the possibility that a referendum may be called.

Direct democracy fosters a sense of involvement and ownership. As practised in Liechtenstein and Switzerland it is far from being a crude plebiscite or a seedbed of demagogy, as foreign critics of direct democracy sometimes allege. The long public debate before the vote is more than an educational and informative process. Its main role is to help the voters to form their opinion[7] and to refine the proposals under discussion, whether the subject be the Constitution, an international treaty, town planning or a tax. The Liechtenstein voter enjoys political rights which would be the envy of many other countries and could be a model for some.

---

[6] Waschkuhn (op. cit. page 328) calculated that by 1993 about one in every two initiatives had been successful.

[7] One of the objections to the constitutional "peace" initiative launched at a late stage in October 2002 was that it had not been previously discussed with the two Princes and had not gone through the long mill of parliamentary, academic and public debate, unlike the other ideas on the table.

THE COURTS

The 1921 Constitution's chapter on the judicial system has been substantially re-ordered. Few of these changes were more hotly disputed than those concerning the appointment of judges and the constitutional functions of the State Court.

Historical Background

Before 1921 the judges of the courts of first and second instance were appointed and dismissed by the Prince alone. Only the court of first instance, the Princely Court ("Landgericht"), sat at Vaduz. The Court of Appeal sat as a judicial function of the Prince's Court Chancery ("Hofkanzlei") at Vienna. The supreme court for civil and criminal cases was the High Court ("Oberlandesgericht") at Innsbruck, whose judges were of course appointed by the Austrian Emperor. This arrangement guaranteed judicial independence at the third instance. The international background explains why Liechtenstein's civil and criminal law is, even today, a mixture of Austrian, Swiss and native elements.

The Ordinary Courts since 1921

Jurisdiction is exercised in the first instance by the Princely Court ("Fürstliches Landgericht"), in the second instance by the High Court of Appeal ("Fürstliches Obergericht") and in the third instance by the Supreme Court ("Fürstlicher Oberster Gerichtshof"), all at Vaduz.[1]

The Princely Court ("Landgericht") judges ("Landrichter") have permanent appointments until retirement age. Judges of foreign nationality (usually Swiss or Austrian) are a feature of the Liechtenstein judicial system, partly because of a shortage of local applicants, partly because of the need for impartiality in a small country.[2] These are appointed either permanently or on fixed but renewable

---

[1] Waschkuhn, op. cit., page 137. For this account of the Liechtenstein judicial system as it was before the constitutional referendum of March 2003 I have, in addition to the Constitution, drawn on Waschkuhn (op. cit., pages 191–207), Gerard Batliner, "Einführung in das liechtensteinische Verfassungsrecht" (in Liechtenstein Politische Schriften, Vol. 21, Vaduz, 1994) pages 53 and 80–87 and Hanspeter Jehle in "The Principality of Liechtenstein", ed. Walter Kranz, Vaduz, pages 49–51.

[2] Because of the close family, personal and professional relationships in Liechtenstein the individual's right to reject a judge in a particular case is quite often exercised.

contracts.[3] The Princely Court judges work full-time. The rules of evidence and procedure are based on Austrian models. Misdemeanours are tried before the Magistrates Court ("Schöffengericht"), a bench consisting of one Princely Court judge and two lay assessors. Felonies go before the Princely Court in the capacity of a Criminal Court (a bench of five). Juvenile cases are handled by the Princely Court in the capacity of a Juvenile Court (a bench of three, chaired by a Princely Court judge).

The purpose of the part-time lay assessors is to keep the administration of justice close to the people and, in passing, to help ensure that the terminology used is readily understandable by them.

The High Court of Appeal and the Supreme Court are collegiate judicial bodies. The High Court until recently had two Senates (benches) with five judges each. It now has three benches, to cope with the increased volume of work arising from the financial services sector. By tradition, its president is a Swiss citizen and his deputy an Austrian. The president is the only member to work full-time. The President of the Supreme Court is traditionally an Austrian and his assistant Swiss. All the judges in this court work part-time. Most of the judges in the collegiate courts are laymen. In theory, they are chosen so as to be as representative as possible of the Oberland and Unterland and of the main trades and professions.

The Administrative Court and the State Court

The Administrative Complaints Court ("Verwaltungsbeschwerdeinstanz") and the State Court ("Staatsgerichthof") were among the most important innovations of the 1921 Constitution. Each is distinct from the ordinary judicial system and has its own place in the Constitution.

Under Article 97, slightly expanded by the new Article 102 (5), all decisions or dispositions of the Government and of complaints commissions established by the Government are subject to appeal before the Administrative Complaints Court (now renamed the Administrative Court, or "Verwaltungsgerichtshof"). This court plays a particularly important part in Liechtenstein public life.

The function of the State Court is to protect rights accorded by the Constitution, to decide in conflicts of jurisdiction between the law courts and the administrative authorities and to act as a disciplinary court for members of the Government. The court has jurisdiction to determine whether laws conform to the Constitution and whether government regulations are in conformity with the

---

[3] In 1993 there were eight Princely Court judges, of whom three were Austrian citizens. Waschkuhn (op. cit., page 193) points out that this large number of judges would have sufficed for a Swiss town of 100,000 inhabitants. It was needed in Liechtenstein because of the burden of work generated by all the entities registered under the Persons and Companies Act 1926. Even so, it proved to be insufficient, as events were to show (page 309 below).

laws. If not, it can annul them. It also acts as an electoral tribunal (Article 104). Until March 2003 it also acted as an administrative complaints court. It has now lost this role in order to eliminate duplication with the Administrative Court, but it has gained the role of ruling on the conformity of state treaties with the Constitution.

The Appointment of Judges

In 1921 "Liechtenstein for the Liechtensteiners" meant also the appointment of judges by Liechtensteiners, as a break with the past. Partly because of the varied origins of the legal system, the methods of appointment varied in detail. However, a common feature was election by the Parliament, by a majority secret vote.

After 1921 the judges for the ordinary courts of all three instances were appointed by the Prince on the proposal of the Parliament and in agreement with it. The President of the Administrative Complaints Court and his deputy were appointed by the Prince on the proposal of the Parliament; the four other judges and their substitutes were elected directly by Parliament. Article 97 stipulated that the term of office of the judges of this court should coincide with that of Parliament, to the extent that it was cut short if Parliament were dissolved prematurely. The President of the State Court was elected by Parliament, subject to confirmation by the Prince; the other four members were elected directly by Parliament. The State Court judges held office for five years. The Prince could always refuse a judge proposed by Parliament, but he could not nominate a candidate of his own.

This system was open to the appearance, justified or not, of political influence in the selection of judges. The dependence of the term of office of the Administrative Complaints Court judges on that of the Parliament was particularly striking. The prestige of the State Court had already suffered in the Art Museum affair.[4] As a separate problem, the speed and efficiency of the ordinary courts came to be criticised in the late 1990s when the financial services sector was under international fire. One former head of government has written bluntly about the selection process: "In reality judges have been chosen now for decades by the political party functionaries, and the parties in Parliament have felt bound by their proposals. Because of these party-political connections some isolated wrong choices have been made with serious consequences."[5] Hans-Adam II set out his proposed remedy as early as 1989 and again in the Speech from the Throne in May 1993. In its 1998 proposals, the Constitutional Commission was unwilling

---

[4] "In wide sections of our population the opinion prevails, rightly or wrongly, that the State Court and the Administrative Complaints Court are political bodies which in the first instance reflect the prevailing majority in the Parliament." (Hans-Adam II, Speech from the Throne, 12 May 1993)
[5] Walter Kieber, "Liechtensteiner Volksblatt", 28 November 2002.

to give up the election of judges by the Parliament, which it saw as an important achievement of 1921. It recognised the problem of the link with elections to the Parliament, however, and was willing to lengthen the mandates of judges of the Administrative and State Courts to twelve years. The judges were to be elected in groups of three every four years. Their mandates would not be renewable.

Hans-Adam's solution was to change the procedure for the selection and appointment of judges and to make it identical in all cases. His proposal (now Article 96 of the Constitution) was that the Prince and the Parliament should have a joint confidential selection panel, to be chaired by himself. He has the casting vote, if necessary. The Parliament sends one representative from each of the political parties there represented, the Government sends the minister responsible for justice, and the Prince appoints a number of members equal to those sent by Parliament. The panel may nominate a candidate (or candidates) to Parliament only with the Prince's agreement. Thus the Prince's veto is retained but exercised, if at all, at an earlier and less public stage than used to be the case. If the Parliament accepts the candidate, the Prince appoints him or her. If Parliament rejects the candidate and no agreement on a substitute can be reached within four weeks, the Parliament is free to propose its own candidate and the matter is settled by a popular vote. In that case members of the public, too, may propose their own candidates under the rules for a popular initiative.

The judges of the Administrative and State Courts expressed dislike for Hans-Adam's proposals when the Government consulted them in 2002. They feared that the procedures would give the Prince too much behind-the-scenes power over the selection process, and that the dignity and perceived impartiality of a candidate would be damaged if he were to be subjected to a public contest in a political tug-of-war between the Prince and the Parliament.[6] Prince Alois has argued that the participation of experienced and expert jurists appointed by the Prince, the creation of shortlists and the holding of interviews will result in a better selection process and a good probability of finding a generally acceptable candidate.[7]

As with other important constitutional changes agreed in March 2003, much will depend on practice, and above all on the tone set by the handling of the first few cases.

In future the Administrative and State Courts will each have five judges and five substitute judges, each serving for five years. Each year one judge and one substitute will retire, on the basis that it is easier to find a couple of good candidates per year than to replace a whole bench at one time.

---

[6] "Liechtensteiner Vaterland", 7 March 2003.
[7] "Liechtensteiner Volksblatt", 5 March 2003.

Independence of the Judiciary

Justice, formerly administered in the Prince's name, will in future be administered "in the name of the Prince and the People".

The Constitution formerly guaranteed the Administrative Complaints Court and members of the State Court judicial independence, while the ordinary courts were guaranteed independence of "any influence on the part of the Government". Since March 2003 there has been a uniform guarantee of independence for all judges at all levels. The reference to the Government has been deleted so as to make it clear that influence from any quarter (Government, Parliament or Prince) is to be excluded.

The State Court and the Interpretation of the Constitution

Until the amendments of March 2003, Article 112 of the Constitution read, "Should any doubts arise with regard to the interpretation of particular clauses of the Constitution which cannot be removed by agreement between the Government and the Parliament, the State Court shall decide in respect thereof". This clause was imported from the 1862 Constitution. At that time, Liechtenstein was a member of the German Confederation, where there was a federal court of arbitration to settle disagreements between the governments and parliaments of the member states.[8] In practice, after 1921 amendments to and interpretations of the Constitution were handled under the procedures set out in Article 111 (2) for a parliamentary or popular vote[9] and Article 112 was never invoked.

Although the 1921 Constitution in most cases clearly distinguishes between the Prince and the Government, a school of thought grew up which argued that in the particular case of Article 112 the term "Government" included the Prince.[10] To Hans-Adam II, this was not only a wilful misreading of the text but an attempt to subject the Monarchy to the arbitration of a court which, as he saw it, might not be politically neutral owing to the way in which its members were appointed. In his view, constitutional questions could only be settled politically: in the last resort, by the people and the Prince. Otherwise, Liechtenstein would become a state ruled by judges. His solution was to delete the old Article 112 and to re-confirm the existing parliamentary and direct democratic procedures for constitutional change and interpretation.

Like so much else, this debate was fed by the clash between Hans-Adam II, the Government and the Parliament in October 1992 and the mutual suspicions that it had inflamed. The VU government's four advisory experts (2000/2001) did not

---

[8] Hans-Adam II and Hereditary Prince Alois, "Liechtensteiner Vaterland", 7 September 2002.

[9] Page 240

[10] See, for example, Gerard Batliner in LPS Vol. 21 (1994), pages 98–100. It was this interpretation of Article 112 that lay at the heart of the Herbert Wille affair of 1995 (pages 202–203).

pronounce on whether the term "Government" included the Prince. Although recognising that practice varies from country to country (Switzerland, for example, does not have a constitutional court because the people are sovereign), they concluded that it would generally not be advisable to abolish a possibility for constitutional arbitration that had existed for many years.[11] The Constitutional Commission in 1998 recognised the potential problem of principle that Article 112 might enable the Government and Parliament to bypass the Prince and the people by agreeing a constitutional interpretation between themselves. Its solution was to propose that in case of doubt the Prince, the Parliament, the Government or a court might call on the State Court to decide the matter. The opponents of Hans-Adam's proposals argued that in a dual constitution it was essential to have an independent court whose rulings would guard against arbitrary actions or offer a way out of a constitutional impasse.[12]

The FBP government, in its report of 20 November 2001 to the Parliament, sided with Hans-Adam II in recommending the deletion of Article 112 on the grounds that, compared with the elected Parliament, the State Court had no immediate democratic mandate for offering an authentic interpretation of the Constitution. It was this view that prevailed in the popular vote of March 2003.

---

[11] "It belongs to the great development of constitutional order in Europe that a broad competence for constitutional courts contributes substantially to the restraining of political power and the rationalisation of the political process" (Professor Frowein's opinion of 2 February 2000, page 25).

[12] "Liechtensteiner Vaterland", 5 October 2002.

LOCAL GOVERNMENT

Outsiders often overlook the importance of local government in Liechtenstein.[1] The autonomy of the communes ("Gemeinden")[2] is not merely a matter of administrative machinery. It is deeply rooted in history and is part of the national identity. It is guaranteed in the Constitution. Although centralising tendencies exist, the communes have powerful entrenched rights at national level which would have a formidable effect if used. They may also complain to the Administrative Court or the State Court if they consider that the state has ignored or harmed their interests. In the last resort, they may secede from the state.

The Communes and their History

There are eleven communes. The Oberland (the "Upper Country", or the old County of Vaduz) comprises six: Vaduz (population 4,949), Balzers (4,299), Planken (357), Schaan (5,556), Triesen (4,509) and Triesenberg (2,596). In the Unterland (the "Lower Country", or the old Lordship of Schellenberg) there are five: Eschen (3,863), Gamprin (1,207), Mauren (3,457), Ruggell (1,754) and Schellenberg (978)[3]. Triesenberg, Planken and Schellenberg are in mountainous or hilly territory.

The communes began as agrarian village communities with common use of certain lands and water. By 1699 they were responsible for poor relief and had the right to elect their leaders, make regulations, levy fines and accept or reject strangers (who, if accepted, would enjoy the right to use common land). All these features persist today. Some communes continue to own land, for example alpine pastures, within the administrative boundaries of other communes, but most of

---

[1] Most of this section, except for the changes of March 2003 and the right of secession, is based on the 1921 Constitution (as of 1 January 1998), the new Communes Act ("Gemeindegesetz") of 20 March 1996, "Die politischen Gemeinden im Fürstentum Liechtenstein" by Job von Nell (LPS Vol. 12, Vaduz, 1987) and "Dezentralisierter Einheitstaat" (pages 343–366 of "Politisches System Liechtensteins: Kontinuität und Wandel" by Arno Waschkuhn, LPS Vol. 18, Vaduz, 1994).

[2] "Gemeinde" is usually translated as "commune". Because they are essentially rural communities the word "municipality" does not apply. In the United Kingdom "parish" would be applicable, or in the USA "township".

[3] Population figures for 2001. (Statistisches Jahrbuch 2002, page 21)

the complex pattern of common land holdings was arbitrarily simplified in the eighteenth and early nineteenth centuries.

In 1808 the communes lost their autonomy and were given only an administrative role. Some progress was represented in 1810 by a law on freedom of movement, which obliged communes to accept a Liechtenstein subject from another commune if he was able to support himself. The 1862 Constitution and subsequent legislation restored autonomy to the communes, and the 1921 Constitution guaranteed it.

The Powers and Constitutional Role of the Communes

Article 1 of the Constitution stated until March 2003 that the Principality of Liechtenstein "...constitutes, by the union of both its regions, Vaduz and Schellenberg, an indivisible and inalienable whole". This sentence now reads, "...is a State union of two districts and eleven communes". It proceeds, as in 1921, to list the communes by name and the regions to which they belong. A controversial new Article 4(2), which is explained in more detail below, says: "Individual communes have the right to withdraw from the State union. A majority of the citizens resident there and eligible to vote decides on initiating the procedure for withdrawal. The modalities of the withdrawal are settled by a law or if appropriate by an international treaty. In the case of a treaty a second vote must be held in the commune after the conclusion of the treaty negotiations."

The vote of March 2003 left the other 1921 constitutional provisions concerning local government unchanged.

Article 110 (2) sets out the basic rights and duties of local government:
(a) free election of the mayor and of the other officials of the commune by the communal assembly;
(b) autonomous management of the communal property and administration of the local police under the supervision of the government;
(c) maintenance of a well-ordered poor-relief system under the supervision of the government;
(d) the right of the commune to grant citizenship and the freedom of citizens of the Principality to reside in any commune.

The section on direct democracy (pages 238–239) has already outlined the rights of a minimum number of communes jointly able to launch procedures for the convening or dissolution of Parliament, for the enactment, amendment or revocation of a law, for a change to the Constitution, for a popular referendum on certain laws or financial resolutions passed by Parliament or for a popular referendum on an international treaty. In each of these cases, the will of the commune is to be expressed by a resolution passed by its assembly (i.e. its citizens).

According to Article 4 of the Communes Act ("Gemeindegesetz") the communes order and administer their affairs in their own sphere of activity independently, under the supervision of the State. The communes' sphere of activity comprises everything affecting their interests and which they are able to run themselves. In particular, it includes the election of the commune authorities, the organisation of the commune, the conferment of commune citizenship, the administration of communal property and the erection of public buildings and installations, the levying of taxes, the promotion of social, cultural and religious life, the erection and maintenance of kindergartens and primary schools, the maintenance of calm, security and order, town and country planning, water supply, sewerage and refuse removal.[4] Article 25 of the Constitution makes them responsible for administering public poor relief, in conformity with specific laws and under supervision of the State and if necessary with financial help from the State. The communes also carry out tasks delegated by the state according to laws. The means for these tasks are supplied by the state and the laws must specify whether a particular activity is within the communes' own sphere or has been delegated.[5] There is therefore a clear formal distinction between State and commune. In practice, the needs of a small and highly industrialised country and the mobility of the citizens demand and receive a great deal of day-to-day co-operation between the communes themselves and between the communes and the State.

Organisation and Elections

The supreme organ of the commune is the communal assembly. This consists of all commune citizens with voting rights, citizens of other communes resident in the commune and honorary citizens of the commune who are living in it. Because of population growth and, in particular, the increase in the electorate caused by female suffrage, the assemblies no longer meet; they have become too large. At the same time, the communes are not large enough to make communal "parliaments" worthwhile. These would in any case be suspect as a derogation from direct democracy. Since 1974, therefore, the assemblies have been entitled to transact their business by secret ballot. Some people have regretted this change as a loss of the political education that comes from the give and take of open debate. Elections, however, continue to be keenly fought. The turnout of voters is respectable (between 74% and 88% in the February 2003 local elections). Between elections specific local issues, including important financial decisions, are often the subject of long and thorough consultation and heated public discussion before they are put to the vote. At any time, one-sixth of a commune's voters may propose their own initiative or subject a Commune Council decision to a

---

[4] Article 12 of the Communes Act.
[5] Article 13 of the Communes Act.

referendum. These might include decisions on expenditure above the delegated level (between 100,000 and 300,000 francs), local taxes, building permits, the sale and exchange of land by the commune, etc.[6]

Since 1861 the Mayor of Vaduz has been styled "Bürgermeister" in recognition of his commune's status as the capital of the country. The other mayors are called "Vorsteher". A mayor occupies a strong personal position as the leader, chief executive and formal representative of his commune. At present, the mayors of Vaduz, Schaan, Triesenberg, Balzers and Mauren serve full-time, the mayor of Eschen half-time and the rest part-time. The mayor may personally authorise expenditure of up to 5,000 francs, but the communes may decide to allow the ceiling to rise to 30,000 francs.

Elections for mayors and councillors are held every four years. The mayors are elected by an absolute majority. The councillors ("Gemeinderäte") are elected by proportional voting. This means that a popular and successful mayor can be, and sometimes is, a member of a minority party within a commune. A commune with a population of up to 1,500 elects six or eight councillors in addition to the mayor; up to 3,000, eight or ten; and more than 3,000, ten or twelve. Auditors and other office-holders are also elected. In order to prevent domination of a commune by cosy family clans, the law forbids the election of relations of an existing council member, whether in the direct line or down to the third degree of a collateral line, or of married partners or relations by marriage down to the second degree. Members of the Government, senior judges and commune employees are also not eligible for election.[7]

In a few communes the members of the council divide sectoral responsibilities between them. That, however, is not usually the case; there are fears that a portfolio system could lead to specialist exclusiveness on the part of individual members and to a weakening of their collective supervision of the mayor.[8]

Co-operation between the Communes

Since 1968 a Mayors' Conference, chaired by the Mayor of Vaduz, has met five or six times a year to consult informally about common concerns. The Government is represented during at least part of the session. The communes also enter into binding agreements with each other for common objectives, e.g. water supply, the management of abattoirs, social-psychiatric help and old people's homes. For refuse disposal all the communes are united with the adjoining Swiss districts of Sargans and Werdenberg in an organisation that has its seat at Buchs, across

[6] Article 41 of the Communes Act.
[7] Article 47 of the Communes Act.
[8] Waschkuhn, op. cit., page 355.

17. The first official visit by a British Minister, 6 October 1994. Left to right: David Davis MP (Minister of State for Foreign and Commonwealth Affairs), Andrea Willi (Liechtenstein Foreign Minister), Bryan Jeeves (Honorary British Consul).

18. Some of the leading Liechtenstein banks.

19. The Hilti Corporation's headquarters and factory, Schaan.

20. The Ospelt Group's headquarters and factory, Bendern.

21. Hilcona AG's headquarters and factory, Schaan.

22. Ivoclar Vivadent AG's headquarters and factory, Schaan.

23. The Liechtenstein University of Applied Sciences (Fachhochschule), Vaduz. The photograph shows the modern additions to the nineteenth-century Jenny Spoerry spinning mill.

24. Triesenberg, looking south up the Rhine valley. The low hill in the background, centre left, is the Ellhorn, ceded to Switzerland in 1948.

25. Visit by the British Foreign Secretary, 2 February 1997. Left to right: Prince Nikolaus, Bryan Jeeves (Honorary British Consul), Andrea Willi (Liechtenstein Foreign Minister), The Rt. Hon. Malcolm Rifkind MP, Mrs Rifkind, David Beattie (British Ambassador).

26. Landscape design by Günther Vogt and Dieter Kienast for Tate Modern, London.

27. The Government Building, Vaduz.

28. The Art Museum, Vaduz.

29. The Opening of Parliament, 13 February 2003. Left to right: Ernst Walch (Foreign Minister), Alois Ospelt (Minister of the Interior), Otmar Hasler (Prime Minister), Hans-Adam II.

the Rhine in Switzerland. Such arrangements reinforce the autonomy of the communes in settling matters among themselves without state intervention. They also relieve the State of a considerable administrative burden.

There are areas where more cooperation would be desirable, for example in planning: a conurbation is creeping along the Rhine valley from Triesen to Schaan and may now be unstoppable. Nevertheless, in 2002 a proposed national planning law was heavily defeated in a referendum. Private interests contributed to this defeat, but also fears of a dilution of the communes' autonomy.

State Supervision

The autonomy of the communes is not absolute. They are subject to the Constitution and the national laws. Their budgets, accounts and financial administration are subject to regulation by government decree.[9] However, within their own competences state supervision is limited to scrutinising the legality of the communal authorities' decisions and activities; outside those competences, it is the "appropriateness" of their decisions and activities that is scrutinised.[10] When the State gives a commune a subvention for a designated purpose its oversight is particularly strict. There is a grey area of cooperation, consultation and information in the wide range of areas for which the Government also has responsibility, such as building, public works, education, welfare, the environment and finances. Here, there is always a danger of creeping centralisation. In the last resort, the Government could compulsorily take over the administration of a failed commune, but this has never happened. In reality, the communes' high level of responsibility is well entrenched. This helps to explain the strong participation of voters in local elections, which would be the envy of politicians in most other European countries.

Taxation, Finances and Assets

The communes levy modest taxes on households, theatre and other tickets and dogs. More significant is their percentage surcharge on the national taxes on wealth and earnings, which varies from commune to commune. (Vaduz was able to reduce its surcharge from 200% to 190% in 1999 and to 160% in 2003.) All the communes are in a healthy financial state and most have substantial investments of their own, with obligations and contingencies amply covered. In 1999 Vaduz's interest earnings amounted to 43.24 million francs, compared with total tax receipts of 45.25 million.[11]

---

[9] Article 94 of the Gemeindegesetz.
[10] Article 116 of the Gemeindegesetz.
[11] Vaduz Jahresbericht 1999, pages 76 and 77.

The receipts from most national taxes are divided between State and communes in varying ratios. For example, in 2001 the wealth and earnings tax brought 39.17 million francs to the State and 74.47 million to the communes, the larger sum resulting from the communes' surcharge. The land sale profits tax was divided by one third and two thirds, so that the State received 6.32 million francs and the communes 12.64. Inheritance and gift taxes brought 3.37 million francs to the State and 0.59 to the communes. The capital and profits tax brought 100.33 and 87.50 million francs respectively; the special company tax, 83.49 million and 9.23 million; and VAT, 151.47 and 26.73 million.[12] These receipts are shared between the communes according to an extremely complicated formula which is designed to compensate the less populous and economically weaker communes for their natural disadvantages. This process, known as the "fiscal equalisation" ("Finanzausgleich") resulted in 2001 in 528.8 million francs going to the State and 235.1 million to the communes.[13]

The communes own a good deal of property in addition to their investments: 91% of Liechtenstein's forests belong to the communes and to eight alpine co-operatives.

Citizenship

Under Article 14 of the Communes Act every Liechtenstein citizen must be a citizen of a commune except for members of the Princely House, most of whom live abroad. Nobody may be a citizen of more than one commune and nobody may be a citizen of a commune without also holding Liechtenstein citizenship.

This means that normally a foreign-born applicant for naturalisation will have to be accepted by a general vote in a commune before his or her application can be considered by the government. This is sometimes criticised as a potentially humiliating "popularity contest" for an applicant. It does however ensure that foreign applicants take trouble to integrate themselves in advance into the local community and to learn the local customs and language.

As a relic of the mediaeval past, Liechtensteiners who are living in a commune other than their own enjoy full political rights there but may not vote on questions concerning the commune's property or on the election of new citizens (Liechtenstein- or foreign-born) to that commune. They must live in their adopted commune for five years before they are eligible to ask the Commune Council to admit them to citizenship. Once admitted, they cease to be citizens of their former commune.

Since 1996 it has been legally possible for a commune to establish a Citizens' Cooperative ("Bürgergenossenschaft"). This is an attempt to simplify the ancient

---

[12] Statistisches Jahrbuch 2002, pages 279–283.
[13] "Liechtenstein in Figures 2002", page 45.

tangle of duties and common property rights. By "Gemeinde" is understood the political local authority in which all Liechtenstein residents, whether citizens of the commune or not, have a stake. A cooperative, if established, administers the long-held property of the commune on behalf of the actual citizens of the commune. Some communes have adopted this system, others not. Where a cooperative has been introduced by popular vote, the political commune's assets are divided between the two organisations. This can be a difficult negotiation. Another innovation is that citizens no longer acquire membership of a cooperative automatically, for example by birth: they must apply for it. This ensures that only resident Liechtenstein citizens may become members, and then only if they show a genuine interest by applying and are not members of another cooperative. Otherwise, local membership could gradually become diluted and a kind of absentee property right be created, for example by descent to Liechtenstein citizens, former citizens and their descendants living permanently abroad.

The Right of Secession

Hans-Adam II's proposal for the communes' right of secession is based on his concept of self-determination and free will. It was never popular and was modified several times over the years. It began as a proposal to enable individuals, the communes and even the two districts to withdraw from the Principality. In the case of the communes and districts this would have happened through a local majority decision, to be put into effect by a law or a treaty. The Constitutional Commission said in 1998 that this proposal went too far: the Constitution should first testify to the solidarity and cohesion of the eleven communes and the two districts, as in the 1921 version. Secession by a commune, which would entail a change in the territory of the State, should only be approved at the level of constitutional legislation. In any case, individuals were already free to leave the country without this right having to be enshrined in the Constitution. Professor Rhinow later pointed out in April 2000 that if one of the two districts were to secede it was not clear which of them would then represent the State of Liechtenstein.[14]

The Red Book of February 2000 dropped the references to individuals and the districts. A decision would be taken by majority vote in the commune concerned, after which the Prince could within thirty days call for a second vote after six months. (This would allow a pause for reflection.) An eventual withdrawal would be effected under a law or treaty.

The explanatory notes to Hans-Adam's final proposal of August 2002, with which the FBP Government broadly agreed in its own proposals of 20 November 2001, make it clear that any law or treaty governing the departure of a commune

---

[14] Rhinow, op. cit., pages 37–41.

would be subject to the consent of the Prince, Parliament and the people. (This makes it clearer than before that the common interest of the whole land would not be ignored.) This proposal no longer gave the Prince personal discretion to call a second vote in the commune concerned.

In the light of history, these discussions seem to have turned by 180 degrees. In the eighteenth and early nineteenth centuries the Sovereign Princes worked for a completely unitary state; it was the people who insisted on the preservation of the two distinct districts and the autonomy of the communes. By 1921 there was a strong popular sense of the need for a unitary but still decentralised state, an instinct which proved its worth in the 1930s and 1940s. By the late 1990s, it was the Prince who could envisage secession by a district or a commune.

Critics of Hans-Adam's proposals described them at best as fanciful and impracticable, at worst as tinkering with the country's unity and threatening the very existence of a tiny state. The communes, they argued, could not be described as "distinct communities" in the sense of Liechtenstein's draft UN Convention on Self-determination.[15] The secession of Vaduz, for example, complete with Castle and Government Building, would leave a large and fatal hole in the middle of the Principality.

Hans-Adam II's view was that the proposal had no internal relevance.[16] It was already the case (an opinion supported by the Head of Government, Otmar Hasler[17]) that a commune could leave the State under existing constitutional provisions for the alteration of the state frontiers, subject to legislation endorsed by the people and the Prince. But he maintained that the proposal was no mere theoretical exercise. Apart from the international example to be set by the proposal, there could be practical advantages. For example, Liechtenstein might one day for political or economic reasons follow Switzerland if it joined the EU. However, the EU acknowledged no right of withdrawal for its members. In such circumstances, a commune which did not wish to belong to the EU might need a guaranteed exit. He argued that the history of the Holy Roman Empire and Germany showed how quickly states could vanish from the map without their peoples being consulted. Liechtenstein had saved its independence with great skill and good luck, but in the 21st century it needed new strategies to guarantee its sovereignty and its people's right of self-determination in the longer term. In short, Hans-Adam II appears to see it as another way of keeping the country's options open and preserving the people's power of decision.

---

[15] See, for example the arguments of Peter Wolff, Peter Sprenger and Paul Vogt as reported in the "Liechtensteiner Vaterland of 9 November 2002 and 25 February 2003 and the "Liechtensteiner Volksblatt" of 19 November 2002.

[16] Interview in the "Liechtensteiner Vaterland", 15 December 2001.

[17] Quoted in the "Liechtensteiner Volksblatt", 19 November 2002.

STATE AND CHURCH

Liechtenstein has always been a Roman Catholic country. About 80% of the total population of Liechtenstein (including foreigners) and about 95% of the native Liechtensteiners profess to be Roman Catholics. No doubt the proportion of those who practice their faith is lower, but for modern Europe this remains a very high percentage.

Nevertheless, the 97.3% Roman Catholic monolithic dominance recorded in 1930 has long since been eroded, not least by the economy's demand for foreign labour. Some 7% of the population now belongs to two Evangelical church congregations. The 1990 census recorded 9 Muslims among the native population and 680 among the resident foreigners.[1] Although himself a devout Roman Catholic, Franz Josef II drew attention to the need to cater for this growing pluralism as long ago as 1959. In 1970 he called for the institution of civil marriage and divorce, which came into effect in 1974. Nevertheless, the old allegiances and social traditions remain strong.

The Constitutional Position

At present the Church's position is governed by the following provisions of the 1921 Constitution:

Article 37

1) Freedom of belief and conscience are guaranteed for all persons.

2) The Roman Catholic Church is the National Church ("Landeskirche") and as such enjoys the full protection of the State; other confessions shall be entitled to practise their creeds and to hold religious services to the extent consistent with morality and public order.

Article 38

The right of ownership and all other proprietary rights of ecclesiastical communities and religious associations in respect of their institutions, foundations and other possessions devoted to worship, education and charity are guaranteed. The administration of Church property in the parishes shall be regulated by a

[1] Statistisches Jahrbuch 2001, page 35

265

special law; the assent of the Church authorities shall be sought before the said law is promulgated.

Article 15

The state shall devote particular attention to education and schooling. This must be so ordered and administered that, from the cooperation of the family, the school and the Church, the younger generation may be imbued with religious and moral principles and patriotic sentiments and may be fitted for their future occupations.

Article 16

1) The whole field of education and schooling shall be under the supervision of the state, without prejudice to the inviolability of the doctrine of the Church.

4) Religious education shall be given by the Church authorities.

The "full protection" afforded by the state under Article 37 is a unilateral commitment by the state; its exact nature was not negotiated or agreed with the Church authorities in 1921 (page 48). Over the years, the administration and even the ownership of certain church revenues and properties, including some parish churches and clergy houses, have come to be assumed by the communes. The state (after the First World War) and then the communes (since the 1970s) have employed and paid the clergy. In practice, the civil authorities have a large say in who is to give religious instruction in schools.

Increasingly the communes have come to support the parish budgets, so that church expenses are largely met indirectly by ordinary taxpayers irrespective of their wishes. Unlike many Western European countries, Liechtenstein has no church tax. In 1987 the State decided to give the Church 0.5 million francs per year for church activities on the national level, such as religious education in state schools, the pastoral care of foreigners, cultural and youth work, publications and administration. By 1997 this contribution had risen to 1.2 million francs: half for church purposes and half for educational and youth work. The communes were giving as much as 6.9 million francs. This close and intertwined relationship between State, local authorities and Church worked well in less questioning times. In modern times, when the purpose and authority of both State and Church are increasingly debated, the Church itself, partly by accident and partly by design, has caused the relationship to be scrutinised afresh.

Liechtenstein and Chur

Historically, Liechtenstein was from the beginning under the jurisdiction of the Diocese of Chur. That diocese lost its territories in Vorarlberg and South Tyrol after the Congress of Vienna but received some compensation within Switzerland. It became a purely Swiss diocese, except for Liechtenstein. It is large and varied: its parishes range from the conservative alpine and rural areas of the inner-Swiss cantons to the large cosmopolitan city of Zurich. Within this diocese Liechtenstein, with its ten ecclesiastical parishes and two convents, was an episcopal vicariate ("bischöfliches Landesvikariat") until 1971. A Priests' Chapter ("Priesterkapitel") was formed in 1850. In 1971 the chapter became a deanery ("Dekanat") within the diocese and replaced the vicariate. At the time, the Liechtenstein clergy protested to the Bishop of Chur about this change. They argued that Liechtenstein's status as a sovereign state should be recognised, and said that the diocesan authorities at Chur had little knowledge or understanding of conditions in Liechtenstein. In 1982 and 1983 the Government asked the bishop to abolish the deanery and reinstate the vicariate. There was some local talk of having an auxiliary bishop for Liechtenstein within the Diocese of Chur.[2] In 1982 the former Landesvikar, Canon Johannes Tschuor, argued in the church magazine "In Christo" for an independent Bishop of Liechtenstein on pastoral grounds at a time when the country's identity and Christian values were increasingly under threat. It could, he said, be a model diocese.[3]

Mgr Wolfgang Haas

On 14 August 1978 Dr Johannes Vonderach, Bishop of Chur, appointed Fr Wolfgang Haas as Chancellor of the Diocese. This was the first time that a native Liechtenstein priest had held that office, and the appointment was taken as a compliment in the Principality. On 7 April 1988 Pope John Paul II appointed Mgr Haas Bishop Coadjutor with the right of succession. This decision caused a storm of controversy in Switzerland. Some Swiss maintained that there were local rights of election which had been infringed by the manner of his appointment. More generally, the "liberals" disliked his personal style and his "conservative" views. At his consecration there were demonstrations both of opposition (with people lying down on the path to block his entry into Chur Cathedral) and of support.[4] On 23 May 1990 Mgr Haas succeeded Mgr Vonderach as diocesan bishop upon the latter's resignation. His Swiss opponents prevented him from using his diocesan offices. The work of the diocese was disrupted. Mgr Haas became a special target for the media and "liberal" church circles in Switzerland and beyond.[5] For his part, he asserted his authority vigorously wherever he could, and he was not without support.

---

[2] For fuller accounts of the historical and political background see "Staat und Kirche", Verlag der Liechtensteinischen Akademischen Gesellschaft, Vaduz, 1999, "Das Dekanat Liechtenstein 1970 bis 1997", Klaus Biedermann, Schalun Verlag, Vaduz, 2000 and "Die Errichtung des Erzbistums Vaduz", Mgr Markus Walser (offprint), passim.

[3] "In Christo" 46 (1982) No. 21, 2 October 1982. Text reproduced in the Archbishopric's website www.erzbistum-vaduz.li

[4] The Liechtenstein press estimated the numbers at 150 opponents, 400 supporters. ("Liechtenstein 1978–1988")

[5] Some of these critics used virulent personal abuse. He did not reply in kind.

From at least 1991 the Vatican pondered possible solutions to this deadlock. One idea, which seems to have originated in Zurich, was the possible creation of a bishopric in Liechtenstein for Mgr Haas. Archbishop Karl-Josef Rauber, who served as a special envoy concerning the problem in 1991 and as Apostolic Nuncio in Berne from 1993 to April 1997, sounded the main personalities concerned, including Prince Hans-Adam II, the Head of Government Mario Frick and the Dean. Hans-Adam II was consistently against the idea but said that ultimately the Church's autonomy would have to be respected, a view which he repeated when sounded later by Mgr Rauber's successor as Nuncio, Archbishop Oriano Quilici.

The Archbishopric of Vaduz

Despite this discouragement, Mgr Quilici informed the Prince and the Foreign Minister Andrea Willi in confidence on 28 November 1997 that the Deanery of Liechtenstein was to be separated from the Diocese of Chur and converted into an Archdiocese of Vaduz with Mgr Haas as incumbent. The "Osservatore Romano" announced the decision on 2 December. The Nunciature in Berne explained that it was intended as an honour to a zealous population who had surmounted many problems without losing their religious faith. The news caught Liechtenstein completely by surprise. This time there had been no consultation, not even with the Deanery, which was itself divided on the matter. The new Archbishop opposed the decision to the last moment but accepted it out of obedience.

A popular petition with the unprecedented number of 8,492 signatures was presented to Parliament on 17 December 1997. It expressed opposition to severance from Chur after a union that had lasted more than 1,600 years. It argued that the decision had been sudden and that there was no clear concept behind it. The people and the local Church had been ignored. There was no infrastructure in Liechtenstein to support an archbishopric. The expense would be excessive.

The Parliament accepted the petition and asked the Government to protest to the Vatican. They argued that in view of the National Church's place in the Constitution the State should have been consulted and that Liechtenstein's sovereignty had been slighted.[6] The Holy See's action, they said, had endangered religious and social peace in the country.

A delegation led by Andrea Willi met Archbishop Jean-Louis Tauran (the Vatican's Foreign Secretary) in Rome on 18 December. The Minister expressed the government's "astonishment and disappointment". The Vatican replied that the creation of a new diocese was a matter within the Church's own competence and

---

[6] Unlike the Swiss Constitution (from 1874 to 2001) the Liechtenstein Constitution has never contained an article forbidding the creation of a new diocese on its territory without the previous consent of the Government.

that the status of the National Church and the other constitutional provisions did not create a reciprocal commitment binding on the Holy See.

On 21 December 1997 Archbishop Haas was installed in the parish church of Vaduz. About 1,200 people expressed varying degrees of opposition in a demonstration outside the nearby Government Building. The members of Parliament boycotted the ceremony.

The Consequences

In Rome, the decision may have seemed an elegant solution to the problems of Chur. In Liechtenstein, it put everyone concerned in a position of unsought difficulty. The political context was unfortunate, since the decision instantly became tangled up with the emotions that had been unleashed by the constitutional dispute. Perhaps too much of the debate revolved around the person of the new Archbishop; the controversy about his style and views was one more symptom of the differences within the wider Church in the German-speaking and Anglo-Saxon countries.[7]

Opinions were polarised. Many felt that Liechtenstein had been "used". Practical details such as church property, church finances, religious education and local government autonomy had not been thought through or agreed in advance. For example, the Holy See unilaterally declared St Florin's Church in Vaduz to be a cathedral, whereas the building belongs to the commune of Vaduz and the commune was not keen to prejudice any future settlement by adopting the new style.[8]

Archbishop Haas dissolved the Deanery as superfluous in the new dispensation. Its Administrative Council finally came to an end in 2000. Its magazine "In Christo" was replaced by a new one called "Vobiscum". The Archbishop took various other steps to reinforce the directing role of the clergy and to reduce secular influences. Meanwhile, a group of adherents of the old Deanery set up a Society for an Open Church ("Verein für eine offene Kirche") in February 1998. It took over the Deanery's adult educational work and started a successor to "In Christo". In 2001 it set up an alternative Lent offerings scheme, arguing that under the Archbishop the existing scheme started in Liechtenstein in 1962 had become insufficiently ecumenical and was directed too much towards exclusively Roman Catholic missionary and aid projects around the world. The State's

---

[7] The "Liechtensteiner Vaterland" for 2 December 2002, in commenting on the fifth anniversary of the Archdiocese, said, "In the Diocese of Chur the former Bishop Wolfgang Haas was always considered to be the cause of the internal church tensions. However, after some time the Grisons media have concluded with disappointment that Wolfgang Haas's transfer to Liechtenstein has had no effect whatever in the sense expected by those who had seen him as the cause of the disputes."

[8] The problem, such as it is, is provisionally being handled in a pragmatic way. When the Archbishop is officiating there, it is the cathedral. When he is not, it is the parish church.

financial contribution to the church work of the Archbishopric was halved to 300,000 francs per year and frozen for three years.

The Way Forward?

In principle, there is nothing exceptional in Liechtenstein's being an independent diocese. Since the Congress of Vienna the Roman Catholic Church has generally proceeded on the basis that dioceses should not extend across international boundaries, and this was also the view of the Second Vatican Council. Thus, Luxembourg became an independent diocese in 1870, as did the Principality of Monaco (a state much smaller than Liechtenstein) in 1886. However, there is as yet no uniform practice: Andorra belongs to the larger Spanish diocese of Urgel (whose bishop is one of its two co-sovereigns) and San Marino is part of the Italian diocese of Montefeltro. One advantage of the new dispensation is that the Archdiocese will give the Liechtenstein National Church its own voice in the wider Church, for example at episcopal synods.

In his Speeches from the Throne in 1998 and 1999 Prince Hans-Adam II argued for a clear separation of Church and state on grounds of personal freedom and fiscal transparency. He did not think that the wish expressed in Parliament for a concordat with the Holy See was realistic. First, the Holy See would not agree to give the State a say in matters of church personnel, organisation and faith; second, since there was no unanimity in the country a Liechtenstein delegation would lack a unified negotiating position. In March 1999 he surrendered to the Archdiocese his right to present priests to the livings of Triesenberg, Eschen, Vaduz and Ruggell. The patrons of the other livings continue to be the local communes.

In June 1999 the Government set up a "State and Church" working group to consider the implications of the new situation for the Constitution, religious education, church property, church personnel, pastoral care, the legal recognition of religious communities, state financial contributions and taxes. This work is expected to end in a constitutional amendment and a new law on religious affairs. It has wisely been kept separate from the wider constitutional debate. It is intended that the affairs of State and Church should be disentangled, but also that the two should work together in mutual confidence.[9] The present Head of Government, Otmar Hasler, was surely right when he told Parliament that a relationship that had grown over centuries and had been fundamentally changed by the events of December 1997 could not simply be replaced by a new settlement at short notice; the new settlement must be based on a broad consensus, which would take time.[10]

---

[9] Rechenschaftsbericht 2001, page 25.
[10] "Liechtensteiner Volksblatt", 20 October 2001

A SUMMING UP

Why the Majority for the Princes' Proposals?

The first and most obvious reason for the decisive 64.3% vote in favour of the Princes' initiative was traditional loyalty to the dynasty and willingness to follow Hans-Adam's lead. Weariness with the constitutional controversy also have played a part. More than ten years of debilitating argument, often conducted at either theoretical or polemical levels, had lowered the national spirit and distracted attention from other urgent problems; there was a great wish to bring it to an end. Some voters would have preferred to leave the 1921 Constitution without further change, but it was clear that this, like the "peace initiative", would only have prolonged the dispute indefinitely.

Others, whether out of personal loyalty or a fear for the country's identity and economic interests, were worried by the possibility of the Prince's moving his place of residence from Vaduz to Vienna.

The opposition VU's "Liechtensteiner Vaterland" commented on 17 March 2003, "The people have decided for the safe economic haven, where it is expected that the Prince will ensure political stability and economic well-being". As other comments put it, the Princes' initiative offered a more calculable future than the other options.

In that sense, the result was a vote of confidence in its authors.

The opponents of the Princes' initiative, and with them some of the foreign media, have argued that the Princes' victory was due to the exploitation of fears and emotions. This argument implies that the result was not quite legitimate.

In fact both camps used psychological tactics, as is usual in any political campaign. The supporters of the Princes' initiative, with active help from the family members, exploited the family's personal, historical and sentimental appeal to the full. Hans-Adam II's stated intention to move to Vienna in the event of defeat was described by his opponents as a threat which unfairly influenced the voters. It was certainly an important factor, and it was intended as such. Hans-Adam II has always maintained that on this, as on the other issues, the voters needed to know all the facts beforehand; if he had been defeated and had then left the country without previous warning, the shock, indignation and damage to the country's interests would have been all the greater.[1] The Princes' opponents, on their side, made full use of dire warnings about the loss of the gains of 1921, the risk of princely despotism, a return to neo-absolutism and isolation from the rest of Europe if the initiative were accepted.

It is hard to say how far the psychological tactics of either side actually influenced the voting. It is probable that most voters had quietly made up their minds well before polling day. They had had a good ten years to mull over the main issues, including Hans-Adam's possible move to Vienna. It is reasonable to conclude that most votes were not cast in haste and had been fully considered.

Who Won?

Clearly, Hans-Adam II was the victor, in the sense that the result vindicated the constitutional thinking that he had been single-mindedly articulating since at least 1986 and especially since 1993. That does not mean that there has been a massive shift of power towards the Sovereign Prince. If anything, the shift is towards the people, at least in formal terms. It was the people he appealed to in the end; and the people supported him.

Hans-Adam's achievement has been to put a stop to any gradual and piecemeal erosion of his constitutional powers (or evolution, depending on one's point of view). He has done this by a rigid dialectic. "Dualism" in his view meant a strong and active monarchy according to the letter and spirit of the 1921 Constitution. Anyone who proposed a weakening of the Monarchy's competences as set out in that document was described as being objectively an opponent of the Constitution and the Monarchy, however much they might protest their loyalty.

This dialectic caused some pain, since most Liechtensteiners are naturally and instinctively loyal to the Monarchy. Those who in good faith took a different view from the Prince felt insulted. Claudia Heeb-Fleck (a member of the minority Free List party and a proponent of the "peace" initiative) complained that it was to be either a monarchy in the form defined by the Prince or no monarchy.[2] The fact remains that the overwhelming majority voted for a strong monarchy and only 16.5% voted for a weaker one.

How Radical Were the Changes?

The Prince's veto and emergency powers have been preserved, although the latter have been more tightly defined to reduce any theoretical possibility of misuse. His power to dismiss a government, always implicit and fully acknowledged in 1965, has now been clearly set out. So has the Parliament's own right to overturn

---

[1] See, for example, his extensive interview with the "Neue Zürcher Zeitung", 7 February 2003.
[2] "Liechtensteiner Vaterland", 6 September 2001.

a government, which was newly accepted in principle in 1965. Any ambiguity about the people's right to have the last word in important constitutional decisions has been removed.

One important innovation is that the Prince is now actively involved in the selection and appointment of all judges by the new independent panel, instead of possessing only the negative power to veto the appointment of some. This arrangement means a loss of power and patronage for Parliament. But Parliament will continue to be involved in the process, and in case of a dispute the last word will remain with the people.

The most intriguing innovations are the people's newly acquired rights to pass a vote of no confidence in a Sovereign Prince or to vote for the abolition of the Monarchy. From the formal point of view, this is a decisive shift from the concept of monarchy as part of a natural or "eternal" order of things. Hans-Adam II argues that the people's new rights will give democratic legitimacy to a strong and active monarchy unless and until the people change their minds about the value of the institution and its powers. Should they ever vote it out, the dynasty would withdraw from the scene and a new constitution would be introduced in an orderly and legitimate manner. The vote of censure offers an alternative solution to one of the theoretical objections to hereditary monarchy: how to solve the problem of an unsatisfactory or incapable ruler without demolishing the whole institution? The usual solution is a regency, as in Britain under George III or Bavaria under King Otto (reigned 1886–1913, died 1916).

The opponents of the Princes' initiative argued that these new rights were a sleight of hand. They would not confer on the Prince the same democratic legitimacy as regular and repeated elections to office. A popular vote of no confidence would be considered only by an unelected and unaccountable body, the Princely House, who would hand down their verdict to Parliament via the Prince. The opponents argued that it was unlikely, if only for practical reasons, that the voters would ever want to go to the extreme of abolishing the Monarchy. This meant that in a crisis the Prince of the time might use a "take it or leave it" approach to give himself a free hand.

These arguments are understandable, but they under-estimate the political realities. Removal to Vienna is not a card that can be played often. In real life, a Sovereign Prince who received a vote of no confidence from the citizens would be politically dead whatever the other members of the Princely House might say. Hans-Adam II's proposals will serve to keep the dynasty's management skills well sharpened. He has always shown himself an astute judge of public opinion. If the citizen shareholders now have the power to pass a vote of censure on the chairman of the board or to dismiss the entire board, corporate dialogue and communication will more than ever be at a premium.

Critics of the initiative also argued that the Prince's powers of veto, emergency rule and dismissal could enable him to enforce his will through the possibility or the threat of his using them. But that has always been the case; and, in the last resort, he has no physical means of enforcing his will. The Prince is not alone in having formidable powers; other elements of the Constitution, too, have powerful means of getting their way, blocking progress or threatening to do so. Parliament can refuse to approve the budget or to vote credits, can dismiss the government and can impeach a minister. The Head of Government can refuse the Prince his counter-signature. A large minority party can make Parliament inquorate. Hanging over them all is the Damoclean sword of the popular initiative and referendum.

The Future

Liechtensteiners sometimes hark back to a golden age of bipartisan co-operation and general harmony. That is a myth. Since 1862, and decidedly since 1918, Liechtenstein's domestic politics have been as partisan as those of any other European country.

The vote of March 2003 was unusual. It was the first time that a Sovereign Prince, after exhausting all other methods, had gone directly to the people. It was also the first time that the citizens of Liechtenstein had voted on the basic principles of their Constitution as distinct from individual amendments to it. Most of the big changes are designed to cope with circumstances that are out of the ordinary; only the new procedures for appointing judges are part of everyday constitutional life. The tone set when those procedures are used for the first few times will have an important influence, for better or for worse, on the constitutional atmospherics.

In general, the main political actors will, as before, have to stay in constant dialogue with each other in the perennial search for the consensus that Liechtenstein's small size and vulnerability need. It is the dialogue and the consensus that give Liechtenstein its inner stability, with the Prince ready to intervene should the normal political process falter and with the people empowered to make the ultimate decisions. Feelings ran deep during the constitutional dispute. Liechtenstein's history has many examples of previous deep divisions which, despite long memories, have been bridged in practice. There is no reason why this should not be achieved again, given prudence and generosity on all sides.

PART III
THE ECONOMY

A SURVEY OF THE ECONOMY

Liechtenstein's sovereign rating is AAA. There is no national debt. There has been no budget deficit for many years. The budget surplus, which in recent years has been unusually (and probably temporarily) high, is mostly reinvested so that the proceeds can contribute to the public finances. This is a prudent policy in view of the country's dependence on changeable foreign markets. The windfall of 600 million francs (£250 million) from the partial privatisation of the Liechtenstein Landesbank is to be devoted to a Future Fund which will be used to finance long term development projects should they at any time be beyond the reach of normal budgets.

In general, a virtuous circle is in operation. A strong currency like the Swiss franc is a disadvantage for a country, which like Liechtenstein lives entirely from its exports and services. However, as a partial compensation the strong franc reduces the cost of industrial and energy imports into a country with virtually no natural resources. The disadvantage is further offset by the State's policy of moderate taxation, which helps firms to invest in research and development and to offer good salaries for the highly qualified staff needed for high technology manufacturing and financial services.

The Constitution requires the State to "promote the general welfare of the people" (Article 14) and to "promote and assist agriculture, alpine farming, trade and industry" (Article 20). The State interprets this as an obligation to create the most favourable framework possible for the economy but not as a compulsion to intervene aggressively in its workings. After the Second World War there was a national consensus, which included the workforce, that industry, the small and medium enterprises and the liberal professions should be given time to build up capital so that the country's economy might be consolidated and the uncertainties of the 1930s not repeated.[1] The private sector's responsible use of the opportunities given by moderate taxation brought it success and has, in turn, profited the State. The State's demands are kept in bounds by the small size of its territory

---

[1] Alois Vogt, in "The Principality of Liechtenstein – a Documentary Handbook" (1973), page 79. Liechtenstein did not, of course, benefit from Marshall Aid after the war.

and administration and by the traditional, sometimes excessive, vigilance of the voters, who have a strong prejudice against "big government".

By its own means, or by cooperation through international agreements, or by sub-contracting, Liechtenstein supplies its population with almost everything that is expected of a modern European state: justice, internal security, health care, social security, education, transport, foreign representation, etc. The chief omission is armed defence, where Liechtenstein, itself militarily indefensible and sandwiched between two neutral but armed states, could be said to be a free rider. But it is doubtful whether the lack of standing armed forces alone gives Liechtenstein much of a competitive advantage, since the defence expenditure of most other west European countries is not high enough to distort their budgets significantly.[2]

The National Budget, 1950–2001 (in millions of Swiss francs)[3]

		1960	1970	1980	1990	2000	2001
Income	5.3	15.8	75.3	202.5	361.1	825.4	788.8
Expenditure	4.2	9.7	49.7	139.8	294.3	594.5	638.5
Surplus	1.1	6.1	25.6	62.7	66.8	230.9	150.3

Income in 2001 was composed of revenue from taxes and duties (CHF 690.2 million, or 87.5%); charges and fees (CHF 40.3 million, or 5.1%); repayments from local authorities (CHF 15 million, or 1.9%) and investment proceeds (CHF 43.3 million, or 5.5%). Since 2000–2001 the world-wide economic downturn has, as in other countries, begun to affect the income from taxes and the State's investment assets. In a spirit of caution the Government has always tended to under-estimate its likely income, which in practice usually exceeds the forecasts. For the immediate future it expects its income to remain broadly level. For 2003 the Government forecasts a current account surplus of only CHF 12.3 million, as against the 34.5 million budgeted for the previous year.[4] Nevertheless, the State's commitments are covered to the extent of 481%.[5] As the industrialist Michael Hilti has said about the economy in general, if people in Liechtenstein are complaining, "then we are complaining at a very high level".[6]

---

[2] In 2001 Luxembourg, the nearest comparable state, devoted 0.8% of its GDP to military expenditure. The neighbouring countries Switzerland and Austria spent 1.2% and 0.8% respectively. Germany spent 1.5%. ("The Military Balance 2002–2003", IISS, London)

[3] "Liechtenstein in Figures", 2002, page 43. The figure for income in 2000 omits the windfall profit of 290.5m. francs from the sale of Landesbank shares.

[4] "Liechtensteiner Volksblatt", 26 October 2002.

[5] The Head of Government, Otmar Hasler, quoted in the "Liechtensteiner Volksblatt", 5 September 2002.

[6] "Liechtensteiner Vaterland", 14 November 2002.

Tax Revenue

The Liechtenstein tax system is relatively straightforward and transparent. It makes no distinction between Liechtensteiners and resident foreigners. There are no state aids to industry, no inward investment incentives, no free-trade zones, no tax-free investment concessions to the citizens and no special tax deals with wealthy resident foreigners.[7] The tax law is, however, comprehensive rather than detailed, so that tax administrators have considerable scope for decisions at their own discretion within the law.[8] Tax rates are confirmed annually by Parliament.[9]

Taxation of persons currently includes a progressive tax on earnings ("Erwerb-steuer") from 3.24% to 17.01% and a separate wealth or assets tax ("Vermögens-steuer") from 1.62‰ to 8.50‰. These figures include both national and local taxes. This system means that certain items, which in the United Kingdom would be lumped together as subject to income tax, are taxed separately in Liechtenstein. Families are treated as a single unit. There are tax thresholds and various legal tax deductions. In addition, there are taxes on capital gains from the sale of real estate (3.2% to 34.02%), death duties (1% to 5%), an inheritance and gift tax (0.5% to 27%) and minor local taxes.

A small tax is payable upon the formation of a company or an increase in its capital. Otherwise, corporate tax levels depend on whether or not a company is doing business within Liechtenstein. Companies trading in the Principality are subject to a capital tax ("Kapitalsteuer") of 2‰ and profit tax ("Ertragsteuer") of 7.5% to 20%. Holding, domiciliary and investment companies based in Liechten-stein but not operating in its territory do not pay tax on profits. They are subject to a special company tax ("Besondere Gesellschaftssteuer") of 1‰ of paid-in capital and reserves, but in no case less than CHF 1,000 per year. The rate is reduced for foundations where the assets involved are more than 2 million francs. Foreign insurance companies do not pay capital or earnings tax; instead, they pay 1% on premium receipts from life and old age insurance and 2% on all other premium receipts. Captive insurance companies pay 1‰ tax on equity capital. A coupon tax ("Couponsteuer") of 4% is payable on dividend distributions and stamp duty of 1% on domestic equities (after the first CHF 250,000) and 1.5‰ or 3‰ on transfers of securities.

Until 1 January 1995, Switzerland collected turnover tax in Liechtenstein and returned the Principality's share pro rata. When, after a referendum, Switzerland

---

7 There used to be special tax deals for foreigners who came to live in Liechtenstein as retired (non-working) persons. The practice has stopped, but many foreigners still benefit from it.

8 "Doing Business in Liechtenstein" Information Guide, Price Waterhouse, 1991, page 54.

9 The following summary is by necessity very compressed and general. It is based, *inter alia*, on the Price Waterhouse Information Guide, "Principality of Liechtenstein" (Press and Information Office, Vaduz, 2000) and "Liechtenstein in Figures 2002" (Office of the National Economy, Vaduz).

adopted value added tax ("Mehrwertsteuer") at a rate of 7.5%, Liechtenstein followed suit but decided to administer the tax itself. The current basic rate is 7.6%, with some rates at 3.6% or 2.4%. The VAT threshold is CHF 75,000 (£31,250). The motor vehicle tax is from CHF 50 to CHF 2,200. There are also customs duties.

The following table shows the fluctuations in importance to the Liechtenstein economy of the main sources of income over the last two decades. The figures are in thousands of Swiss francs, rounded up or down.[10]

	1980	1990	2000
Total revenue	202,527	361,101	825,546
"Income" taxes	37,676 (19%)	62,173 (17%)	106,230 (13%)
Death and Gift taxes	39,066 (19%)	50,178 (14%)	66,348 (8%)
Capital and Profit taxes	14,317 (7%)	37,300 (10%)	131,123 (16%)
Special Company tax	48,587 (24%)	68,947 (19%)	92,921 (11%)
Coupon tax	8,049 (4%)	20,242 (6%)	56,779 (7%)
Turnover tax/VAT	15,924 (8%)	38,762 (11%)	161,611 (20%)
Investment income	8,957 (4%)	22,412 (6%)	101,736 (12%)

Although all sources of income have produced absolute increases, the rise in the volume and importance of VAT revenue (since 1995) is particularly striking. Revenue from companies manufacturing and trading within Liechtenstein has risen almost tenfold. On the other hand, revenue from the special company tax has not even doubled and this tax's contribution to the State's income has fallen from 24% to 11%.

This pattern continued into the financially more turbulent year of 2001. The special company tax receipts declined slightly to CHF 92.723 million but their proportion of the tax revenue in that year rose to 11.75%. However, capital and profit tax receipts rose to CHF 187.830 million (23.8%) and VAT receipts to CHF 178.200 million (22.5%)[11]. It is an important indicator of Liechtenstein's manufacturing role that the tax revenue from trade and industry now far exceeds that from the holding and domiciliary companies.

Public Expenditure

Expenditure in 2001 was divided on the following lines (in millions of Swiss francs):[12]

---

[10] Figures taken from the "Statistisches Jahrbuch" 2001, pages 283 and 285–289.
[11] Statistisches Jahrbuch 2002, pages 281–283.
[12] "Liechtenstein in Figures" 2002 and Statistisches Jahrbuch 2002..

General administration (salaries, office expenses, etc)	76.6 (10.4%)
Public safety (including courts, police and the FSA)	41.4 (5.7%)
Education	105.6 (14.4%)
Culture, leisure, youth	23.2 (3.2%)
Health	14.7 (2.0%)
Social welfare (includes asylum seekers and some foreign aid)	146.3 (20.0%)
Transport	35.8 (4.9%)
Environment and planning	4.8 (0.6%)
Economy	22.5 (3.1%)
Finance (most of it tax allocations to the communes)	261.6 (35.7%)

National Economic Statistics

The growth in income from gainful activity since 1960 has been[13]:

Year	Swiss Francs (millions)
1960	56.7
1970	194.4
1980	549.5
1990	1,092.7
1999	1,832.4
2000	1,867.1
2001	1,988.6

It is not possible to calculate the Gross Domestic Product per capita because so much work is done in Liechtenstein by commuters from neighbouring countries. However, the 1999 GDP total was CHF 4 billion. This compares with Switzerland (CHF 388.6 billion), Austria (CHF 315.5 billion) and Germany (CHF 3,165.8 billion).[14] The Gross National Income in 1999 was CHF 4.002 billion (CHF 121,000 per capita).[15]

In 1999 industry and goods production contributed 40% gross value added to the national economy, financial services 30%, general services 24% and households, agriculture, etc. 6%.

[13] "Liechtenstein in Figures" 2002, page 17. Figures calculated to include the active resident population, minus outward trans-frontier commuters, plus inward trans-frontier commuters and those not gainfully employed with voluntary old age and survivors insurance.
[14] Ibid., page 18.
[15] Statistisches Jahrbuch 2002, page 115.

Comparative employment percentages for 2000 are:[16]

	Agriculture and forestry	Industry and skilled trades	Trade and services
Liechtenstein	1.3%	44.9%	53.8%
Switzerland	4.7%	24.8%	70.5%
Austria	6.1%	30.0%	63.0%
Germany	2.6%	33.5%	63.9%

Of the totals for 2000, manufacturing industry employed 7,971 people (5.9% more than in 1999) in 31 enterprises. The 16 banks then existing employed 1,758 (6.6% more than in 1999).[17]

These figures, again, show what a strong manufacturing base Liechtenstein has, contrary to the common belief that it is solely a financial centre. Statistically it is one of the most industrialised countries in the world: more so, even, than Germany. The economy is very diverse for so small a country. It covers 15 of the 16 internationally classified sectors.[18] The emphasis on high quality and innovation is shown by the fact that in 2000 the firms belonging to the Liechtenstein Chamber of Industry and Trade spent CHF 232.9 billion (about 5% of their export turnover) on research and development and employed more than 11% of their personnel in that area.[19] With good reason, the Upper Rhine is sometimes called "Precision Valley".

Industry and financial services are examined in greater detail in the following chapters. If rather more space is devoted to financial services, it is simply because in recent years they have attracted more international attention than industry.

The Liechtenstein Chamber of Industry and Trade

The Liechtenstein Chamber of Industry and Trade ("Liechtensteinische Industrie- und Handelskammer" – LIHK) was founded in 1947. It counts among its members 33 industrial concerns (in 2002; 31 in 2001) and the three largest banks. It therefore represents corporate Liechtenstein, with one or two exceptions such as the Ospelt Group (food manufacturers). Since Michael Hilti took over as president in 2001 it has begun to be more dynamic in foreign relations in addition to its traditional role in internal affairs. It has, for example, helped to organise visits by US Congressmen to Liechtenstein, to help them to get a balanced picture of the Principality.

---

[16] "Liechtenstein in Figures" 2002, page 24.
[17] Annual Reports for 2000 of the Liechtensteinische Industrie- und Handelskammer (LIHK) and the Liechtenstein Bankers Association.
[18] Only the fishing industry is missing, as might be expected.
[19] LIHK Annual Report 2000.

Small and Medium Enterprises

In addition to its large, internationally known companies Liechtenstein has numerous and very diverse small and medium enterprises (SMEs), which together number some 3,600 businesses employing 8,500 people. These businesses add flexibility and stability to the economy in general and to employment. They are represented by the Liechtenstein Chamber of Commerce and Trade ("Gewerbe- und Wirtschaftskammer – GWK, founded in 1936), membership of which is compulsory. While many SMEs are active in the traditional areas of shops, building and decorating, transport, etc., others serve as suppliers to the larger companies. The Government is setting up a Competence Centre to support SMEs looking for know-how at the start-up phase, to help them to negotiate partnerships and to promote the transfer of technology and knowledge. The SMEs and the GWK play an important part in vocational training, the high quality of which is one of the main reasons for the success of Liechtenstein's industry and skilled trades (page 340). For over 70 years craftsmen (builders, decorators, tailors, dressmakers, cooks, butchers, etc.) have been allowed to exercise their craft independently only if they have undergone an apprenticeship or equivalent vocational course, followed by three years of practical experience. Compulsory training for the hotel and catering trade was introduced in 1969.

Agriculture

Liechtenstein's surface area may be divided into agricultural land (38.9km² or 24.3%), alpine meadows (25.1km² or 15.7%), woodland (55.6km² or 34.8%) and unproductive or built-up land (40.4km² or 25.2%).

About two thirds of the agricultural land is used for grazing; the rest for arable farming, market gardening, fruit culture and vine growing. The variety of agricultural operations is represented by no fewer than three organisations: the Farmers' Association ("Bauernverband"), which dates from the end of the nineteenth century, the Brown Cattle Breeders' Association and the Dairy Association (a cooperative organisation).

The farms have always been small family businesses. The pressures on agriculture are reflected in their numerical decline from 1,366 in 1955 to 401 in 1995. The total agricultural work force was then 231, of whom only 136 were running a farm on a full-time basis. Financial pressures have not been the only problem. Split holdings, leasehold tenure and the spread of built-up areas have all contributed. Nevertheless, the State is determined to keep agriculture in being as a productive industry; there is no intention that the remaining farmers should become mere alpine park-keepers.

Although many branches of farming have declined in recent decades, the cow population, immortalised by the novelist Paul Gallico, has remained remarkably static at around 2,600 for well over 70 years, during which time milk production has risen from 3.33 million kilos in 1950 to 13.53 million kilos in 2001.[20]

Tourism

Liechtenstein's small size tends to work against it in respect of extended-stay tourism tourism. Although there is much to enjoy (alpine scenery, monuments, the new Art Museum, other sights and restaurants) the average tourist bus stops briefly in Vaduz on its way to other destinations. The high point to date was reached in 1985, when nearly 86,000 visitors spent nearly 168,000 nights in 65 hotels. In 2000 nearly 63,000 visitors (over 23,000 of them Germans) spent more than 133,000 nights in 49 hotels. Many of these will have been business visitors, except in the mountain areas. For attracting tourist visitors, the future may lie in cooperating more closely with neighbouring resorts in Switzerland and Austria. The tourist industry has begun to promote Liechtenstein as a centre for corporate conferences and seminars, exploiting the country's small and intimate scale.

Postage Stamps

Since 1912 Liechtenstein has prided itself on the design of its postage stamps, which at one time contributed an important part of the country's revenue. Their financial importance has declined, but their quality remains high and they are taken seriously as ambassadors for the country. They are printed in Austria and Switzerland. They retain an international following: more than 53,000 subscribers in 2000 (the great majority Germans, followed by Swiss and Austrians), and another 10,000 purchasers without subscriptions.[21]

Transport

Liechtenstein has a higher proportion of private cars than most countries: 894 per thousand inhabitants in 1999. Nevertheless, there is an excellent and much used public bus service, which covers all the communes and is integrated into the timetables of the adjacent Swiss bus and rail services. In recent years, the Government and public opinion have become concerned about the growing numbers of heavy goods vehicles passing through the country between Austria and Switzerland. Regional co-operation on road and tunnel building plans has proved to be difficult.

Employment

At the end of 2001 Liechtenstein had 33,525 inhabitants (22,030 citizens and

---

[20] Sources: Statistisches Jahrbuch 2002, "Principality of Liechtenstein" 2000 and 1973.
[21] Rechenschaftsbericht 2000, page 139.

11,495 foreigners); yet it gave employment to 28,783 people, almost the same number as the entire population.[22] A year later, the population had risen to 34,000 and the number of employed to more than 30,000. Like Luxembourg, Liechtenstein is an important source of employment for the surrounding region. This is the opposite of the situation in the 1920s and 1930s. It has been said that Liechtenstein may be part of Greater Switzerland, but that the neighbouring Swiss cantons have increasingly become part of Greater Liechtenstein.[23] The same could be said of Vorarlberg.

At the end of 2001, 9,797 Liechtenstein citizens and 6,078 resident foreigners were gainfully employed in Liechtenstein. The gap of 12,908 workers was filled by commuters from abroad, mainly Swiss (5,434), Austrians (6,924) and Germans (357). Of the total 28,783 jobs, 18,728 (65.1%) were filled by foreigners. Since 1998 the number of commuters has grown by over 30% and the number of foreign employees by over 23%. In 1970 the number of commuters from Switzerland and Austria was only 2,601; but even then, foreigners occupied almost 54% of the jobs.[24]

Of the three sectors of the economy, agriculture currently employs 359 persons, industry and skilled trades 13,032 and trades and services 15,392. However, a closer look at the figures shows that in the secondary sector the processing industries employ 10, 434 persons while in the tertiary sector banking, insurance, legal consultancy and trust management together employ only 3,799. Public administration employs 1,375, education 843, and health and social services 1,308. Manufacturing, broadly defined, is therefore the largest single employer.[25]

It is noticeable that a far higher proportion of foreigners than Liechtensteiners (9,833 as against 3,199) work in the industry and skilled trades sector. In the trade and services sector the disparity is less marked (8,758 foreigners as against 6,634 Liechtensteiners). In the financial services, consultancy and fiduciary sector the numbers are close to being balanced (2,021 foreigners as against 1,778 Liechtensteiners).[26]

Unemployment is low by international standards. In 1980 it was 0.0%, with only 3 people completely unemployed, 26 other job-seekers and 40 vacancies. This happy state of affairs continued for a decade until unemployment began to rise gently. It reached a peak of 2% as a percentage of employed (482 unemployed, 75 other jobseekers and 28 vacancies) in 1998. In 2001 it was 1.2% (354

[22] Statistisches Jahrbuch 2002 page 91.
[23] "Liechtenstein in the New European and Global Order" by Peter Ludlow (CEPS, Brussels, 2000), page 7.
[24] Statistisches Jahrbuch 2002, pages 91, 24, 105–107, 98, 90. In 2001 1,136 Liechtenstein citizens and resident foreigners commuted across the frontier to work in neighbouring countries.
[25] "Liechtenstein in Figures 2002", page 23.
[26] Statistisches Jahrbuch 2002, page 104.

unemployed, 56 other jobseekers and 66 vacancies). It is likely that the percentage figures for 2002 will increase despite a rise of 1,500 in the number of jobs.[27]

The Labour Climate

The entrepreneurial and innovative spirit of most of the company managements is backed by a hard-working and well-qualified workforce. Vocational training and apprenticeships are the norm. The relative paucity, until recently, of higher educational institutions in the country means that most managers have studied abroad, acquiring in the process international experience and a good command of foreign languages. Not only is the native workforce well educated and well trained, but the nature of the economy and the strict rules governing the employment of foreigners mean that the foreign employees tend also to be highly qualified, except for those from southern Europe and Turkey who do the lower classified industrial jobs. Liechtenstein knows that the world does not owe it a living. The population works perceptibly longer hours than is now usual in Europe: about 40 hours per week in the metal-working industry and up to 42½ hours in other branches.[28]

There has been no strike or other form of serious economic friction since the 1930s (and only the threat of a strike in 1941). There are various reasons for this. They include awareness of the country's vulnerability, its dynamic and continuing growth since the war, a good quality of life combined with a high standard of living, high salaries and the general lack of a hierarchical atmosphere in the workplace and society. May Day is a public holiday, but is an occasion for relaxing rather than demonstrating.

In 1998 the national average pay of a full-time employee was around CHF 72,000 (£30,000) per year. The average pay in industry and the manufacturing SMEs was CHF 74,000, in general services CHF 62,000 and in financial services CHF 95,000. The differentials between the different branches were less marked in Liechtenstein than in Switzerland. If overall the average pay in Liechtenstein was 12% higher than in Switzerland, that of bank and insurance staff was 12% lower.[29]

Trade Unions

The main trade-union organisation is the Liechtenstein Employees' Association ("Liechtensteiner Arbeitnehmerverband" – LANV). It was founded in 1920 and at present has around 1,400 members. Most of them are Liechtensteiners;

[27] Statistisches Jahrbuch 2002, pages 111 and 110.
[28] "Neue Zürcher Zeitung Folio", August 1996, page 42.
[29] The Office for the Economy, quoted in the "Liechtensteiner Vaterland" of 3 March 2001.

the LANV has yet to catch on with trans-frontier commuters. Its attractiveness to workers has fallen since it became legally possible for all workers (and not only LANV members) to profit from collective workplace agreements. In the bigger industrial concerns wage negotiations take place between the management and the elected workers' representatives, the latter being an institution with a long tradition. The LANV keeps in touch with these representatives and organises courses in negotiation and the interpretation of business data. It also negotiates for the raising of minimum wages and the improvement of collective agreements. The LANV sees itself as having a more direct role to play in the small and medium enterprises, where workers' elected representation is rarer. Under the 1997 Co-operation Act, enterprises with more than 50 employees are supposed to arrange for the election by secret ballot of employees to represent the staff to the management and to serve as a link to the advantage of both sides. (This is not to be confused with co-determination). In medium-sized enterprises, this has not happened as quickly as the LANV would like. The LANV's target is a legal minimum wage of CHF 3,000 (£1,250) per month, which lies considerably below the subsistence minimum.[30] In most industrial enterprises and for most workers the wages are higher (see the preceding paragraph), but the LANV would like a legal floor to be fixed in case of harder times to come. In the event of disagreement with a company the LANV, by local tradition, prefers to intervene discreetly with the enterprise rather than to pillory it publicly. It usually finds this style more effective. In the case of infraction of the labour laws it would, as a second step, invoke the help of the Office for the Economy.

In general, "Trade union work has no tradition in Liechtenstein. Many people don't even know that a trade union exists in Liechtenstein and mistake us for a free service or as part of the administration."[31] Since membership subscriptions are not enough to keep the organisation going, the LANV receives an annual subsidy from the State (CHF 125,000 in 2000), a contribution from the LIHK and contributions negotiated as part of certain collective agreements.

---

[30] The average subsistence minimum was CHF 4,171 in 2000. (Rechenschaftsbericht 2000, page 196).
[31] Sigi Langenbahn, President of the LANV. Most of the material in this and the preceding paragraph is taken from his interview published in the "Liechtensteiner Vaterland" for 7 December 2002.

INDUSTRY

The customs union with Switzerland, which in effect provides the domestic market for most Liechtenstein companies, complicates the task of establishing precise import and export figures for Liechtenstein. The available figures indicate, however, a substantial and continuing worldwide foreign trade surplus.

For imports (chiefly machinery, vehicles, metal goods, building materials, foodstuffs, energy and raw and half-finished metals) the trade partners are largely European. Switzerland not included, they are led by Germany and Austria (35.6% and 33.0% respectively).

For industrial exports, the official statistics rely on figures supplied by the firms belonging to the Liechtenstein Chamber of Commerce and Industry (LIHK). The true export figures are therefore slightly higher.

Industrial exports since 1950 (in millions of Swiss francs)[1]

1950	15
1960	83
1970	333
1980	887
1990	2,213
2000	4,622
2001	4,422

Exports by groups of countries in 2001

Country or group	Value (millions of francs)	Percentage
Switzerland	580	13.1%
European Economic Area	1,916	43.3%
Other countries	1,927	43.6%

[1] "Liechtenstein in Figures 2002" page 30.

286

The top ten export partners (in thousands of Swiss francs) are:[2]

2000		2001	
1. USA	876,874	1. USA	741,017
2. Germany	748,029	2. Germany	665,665
3. Switzerland	586,765	3. Switzerland	579,654
4. France	268,728	4. France	345,473
5. Italy	232,033	5. Italy	257,010
6. Taiwan	178,260	6. Taiwan	212,520
7. Japan	156,652	7. Hong Kong	174,863
8. Austria	136,274	8. Austria	163,986
9. UK	133,740	9. Japan	161,504
10. Hong Kong	133,568	10. UK	159,780

Activities Abroad

It is a striking fact that Liechtenstein industry employs almost as many people abroad as does the entire economy within the Principality. In December 2001 the total was 24,217, divided as follows:[3]

	Branches Abroad	Number of Persons Employed			
		Admin/Sales	Production	R & D	TOTAL
Europe	108	7,578	8,539	701	16,818
America	27	3,027	1,469	71	4,567
Asia	29	1,439	1,023	3	2,465
Australia	4	233	38	—	271
Africa	1	76	20	—	96
TOTAL	169	12,353	11,089	775	24,217

The total number of people employed abroad shows an increase of more than 68% compared with December 1994 (14,384)[4]. The increase is a sign of Liechtenstein industry's outgrowing its domestic constraints (territorial limits and tight labour market) rather than of a massive shift of employment abroad, since employment within the country has grown by over 36% during the same period. The most dynamic growth areas abroad since December 1994 have been in Europe (from 88 establishments, 2,635 production staff and 235 R & D staff), America (from 15 establishments, 196 production staff and 15 R & D staff) and Asia (from 15 establishments and 374 production staff).

---

[2] LIHK Annual Reports for 2000 and 2001
[3] Ibid., page 31. These figures exclude the Unaxis AG works at Trübbach, directly across the Rhine in Switzerland.
[4] "Statistisches Jahrbuch 1999", page 174.

Industrial Diversity

The diversity of export markets and industrial operations abroad is in keeping with the diversity of Liechtenstein's industry itself, which comprises:

Metals, engineering, equipment
- Securing systems (direct and drill assembly for the construction industry, shipbuilding and steelworks)
- Vacuum engineering (fine, high and ultra-high vacuum engineering) equipment for optic and electronic thin-film products
- Electrical and electronic control systems
- Electronic systems, measuring equipment, testing and sorting equipment
- Measurement and sorting equipment
- Precision tools and machinery
- Heating and hot water equipment, heat recovery, waste processing equipment
- Cold extrusion elements, powder metallurgy parts
- Commercial vehicles (hydraulic and mobile excavators, specialised street-cleaning vehicles)
- Electrical equipment, electrical components
- Electro-acoustic and audio equipment
- Equipment for the chemicals and heating engineering industries, tank and container construction, steel services
- Heat screening shields for the motor industry
- Smoke extraction ducts and exhaust piping

Ceramics, chemicals, pharmaceuticals
- False teeth (ceramic and plastic)
- Equipment for dental prophylaxis, prosthetics and dentistry
- Varnish, paints, plastic coatings
- Pharmaceutical preparations
- Household and decorative ceramics, oven tiles

Other
- Foodstuffs industry (deep-frozen products, prepared meals, convenience foods and preserves)
- Form etching materials, profile projector screens
- Professional lighting equipment
- Duvets and feather pillows
- Embroidery and homespun fabrics
- Magnetised punch sheet plate

– Lead crystal and glass giftware
– Non-explosive demolition material, specialised plaster and casting materials
– Philately supplies[5]

The Leading Companies

This diversity is illustrated by the following profiles of ten companies (both Liechtenstein- and foreign owned). These have been selected on the basis of being among the biggest industrial employers in the Principality.[6]

Hilcona

Food products (refrigerated, deep-frozen, convenience foods and preserves). 920 employees in total, of whom 650 work at the parent factory in Schaan. CHF 272 million turnover. Production in Liechtenstein, Switzerland, Germany and France. Its market is Switzerland and the European Economic Area.

The company was founded in 1935 at Schaan by the 22-year-old Toni Hilti as Scana Konservenfabrik. He and his brother Martin (see Hilti, below) belonged to a family of eleven children. Their parents, who ran a butcher's shop in Schaan, left the family orphaned at a young age but ensured that their children had received a good education. In 1971 the company broke away from the other Scana companies in Switzerland and in 1973 was renamed Hilcona AG. From 1980 the company branched out into high-quality deep-frozen and refrigerated products, rebuilt its parent factory and extended its retail and wholesale activities throughout western Europe. It is now organised into three independent process-orientated business areas.

Hilti

A world leader in fixing, drilling, building and demolition technology. Over 14,000 employees worldwide, of whom around 1,500 work in Liechtenstein. CHF 3,123 million turnover. Production in Liechtenstein, Austria, Germany, Hungary, the USA, Mexico and China. Its own direct marketing organisation handles the sale of products, service and consulting in over 100 countries. It has more than 100 subsidiaries throughout the world and is active in 120 countries.

The company was founded in a garage workshop in Schaan in 1941 by Martin Hilti and five employees. It started with wartime German orders for automotive components. It also supplied parts to a Swiss textile machinery firm and worked

---

[5] "Liechtenstein in Figures 2002", page 32.
[6] Information derived from Annual Reports of the LIHK, company websites and other publications, "The Principality of Liechtenstein" (Government Press and Information Office, Vaduz, 2000), the "Financial Times" Survey of Liechtenstein of 23 June 1997 and "Unbekannter Nachbar Liechtenstein" (Alphons Matt, AT Verlag, Aarau, 1986).

on its own designs for minor household products. Business fell off sharply at the end of the war and prospects were shaky for a time, but at the end of the 1940s Martin Hilti bought existing patents for high-velocity fastening tools (then a technologically under-developed and physically dangerous item) and began to design and produce his own models. By the end of the 1950s his engineers had devised a piston-driven tool which was more efficient and much safer than previous variants. As the post-war reconstruction boom drew to an end, the company diversified into drilling and electric tools. Direct marketing became the rule, to ensure consistency. Soon the Hilti red boxes and livery became a familiar sight around the world. An employee committee was founded as early as 1955 to keep the workforce and management in touch. Good salaries and social benefits, combined with careful selection and training, ensured a high-quality workforce.

The management of rapid international growth and the safeguarding of continuity were problems for Hilti, as for any successful company. In consultation with the University of St Gallen, management structures were kept under constant review and evolution from the early 1970s. Structural change to keep the company in continuous touch with its customers and to promote technological innovation was, and still is, constant. Production in Austria began in 1970, in the USA[7] and Germany in 1971 and in China (transferred from the United Kingdom) in 1995. In the 1980s the company diversified further, into construction chemicals. One of its most successful innovations in the 1990s was a drill with an integrated dust remover.

Hilti has been involved in all the recent big international construction projects such as the Channel Tunnel, Hong Kong airport and the Storebaelt bridge and tunnel link between Sweden and Denmark. Its latest innovative venture is a partnership in laser distance-measuring instruments with the East German company Jenoptic.[8]

In an arrangement to guarantee the company's future and to protect the family's interests, Martin Hilti's family handed over all their voting shares (88% of the total) to the newly-created Martin Hilti Trust in 1980. The remaining 12% followed in 2000. In 1994 the executive board ceased to be chaired by a member of the Hilti family. The family has not withdrawn from the company (Michael Hilti, Martin's son, is chairman of the board of directors); but family members are scrutinised carefully to determine their suitability for service on the board.[9]

---

[7] On 11 September 2001 the Hilti plant at Tulsa was quick to despatch machinery to the scene of the terrorist attacks in New York and Washington. ("Liechtensteiner Volksblatt", 14 September 2001)

[8] "Liechtensteiner Vaterland", 23 May 2002.

[9] An account of the company's history and philosophy is to be found in "Martin Hilti", published to mark his 80th birthday in 1995.

Hoval

Conventional energy (oil, gas, solid fuels), solar and alternative energy heating systems. Steam and hot-water boilers. Environmentally friendly refuse incinerators and systems for heat recovery from waste. Industrial ventilation equipment and plate-type heat exchangers for heat recovery in ventilation and air conditioning systems. Hovalwerk is the world's largest manufacturer of aluminium plate-type heat exchangers. 1,000 employees worldwide, of whom 350 work in Liechtenstein. CHF 220 million turnover. Production in Liechtenstein, Austria, the United Kingdom and Italy. Represented in 50 countries.

"Hoval" is the acronym of Heizapparate Ospelt Vaduz Liechtenstein. It was founded in 1932 by the 26-year-old Gustav Ospelt who, because of his father's illness, had to break off his studies and take over his father's business as a mechanic. In that year he built his first central heating device, from which he went on to develop and apply a range of innovative concepts based on economy, conservation and efficiency. Hoval was the first large company in the branch to introduce fuel value techniques in oil heating.

Inficon

Vacuum technology, including pressure gauges, mass spectrometers, leak testing equipment and plasma purifying systems for the analysis, supervision, measuring and control of manufacturing processes. Its products are used in the production of semiconductors, flat screens, computer hard drives and other drives and electronic storage media such as CDs, DVDs and diskettes. 691 employees worldwide, of whom 245 work in Liechtenstein (at Balzers). CHF 270 million turnover. Production in Liechtenstein, Finland, Germany and USA. Active in more than 20 countries.

Ivoclar Vivadent

An international leader in dental medicine, dental technology and dental prosthetics. 2,100 employees worldwide, of whom 700 work in Liechtenstein. CHF 500 million turnover. Production in Liechtenstein, Austria, Italy and the Philippines. 19 subsidiary companies. Represented in more than 100 countries.

The company was founded in 1933 at Schaan under the name of Ramco. At that time it concentrated on the manufacture of porcelain dentures. It was renamed Ivoclar in 1951 by a new owner and was joined by Vivadent in 1956. It acquired the Williams Dental Division in Buffalo, New York, in 1986. The whole group was joined together and given its present name in 2001. Modern dental technology is fast-moving and competitive. It requires an advanced command not only of dental and other medical sciences but also of physics, chemistry and even aesthetics. It is therefore not surprising that Ivoclar Vivadent should maintain a formidable research complement at Schaan, comprising the majority of the staff there, and an ultra-modern training centre which was inaugurated in June 2000. It aims to bring together within itself all the diverse and fragmented branches of the dental trade, and to be close to its customers through its subsidiaries. It is also strong in prophylactic advice for the prevention of dental illness.

Krupp Presta

Automotive components, in particular steering columns, camshafts and security parts. 2,100 employees worldwide, of whom about 1,100 work in the parent factory at Eschen and 100 in the tool factory nearby at Oberegg (Switzerland). About CHF 700 million turnover. Production in Liechtenstein, Brazil, China, Germany, France, Mexico and USA.

Founded in 1941 to produce ammunition components. From 1946 it manufactured standard screws. From the mid-1960s it developed into an important innovative supplier of extruded and forged parts to the automotive industry. The manufacture of steering joints began in 1982. The German-owned company supplies Ford (USA), VW/Audi (worldwide), Renault/Nissan, Daimler Chrysler (USA) and Fiat. In 1999 the company invested about CHF 50 million in research and development and CHF 30 million in machines, systems and buildings. Although much of the production is now carried on abroad owing to limited space and labour resources, the heart of the Krupp Presta Group remains in Liechtenstein, where much high-quality development work is undertaken.

Neutrik

Connectors for the audio industry. 500 employees, of whom 200 work at the company's headquarters in Liechtenstein. CHF 65 million turnover. Active worldwide.

Founded in 1975. Represented by subsidiaries in the USA, UK, Germany, Switzerland, Japan, China and Hong Kong and by agents elsewhere. The company produces more than one million connectors per week in Liechtenstein.

The Ospelt Group

Meat and other food products, convenience meals, pet-food. 1,400 employees. CHF 500 million turnover. Production in Liechtenstein (Bendern), Switzerland (Sargans, Weite and Landquart), Austria (Frastanz) and Germany (Apolda). Sales throughout Europe. The group does not belong to the Liechtenstein Chamber of Industry and Trade.

The firm was founded by Herbert Ospelt (generally known in Liechtenstein as "Uncle Herbert") when he took over a butcher's shop in Vaduz in 1958. In 1960 he built a factory in Vaduz for producing sausage specialities and in 1967 a much larger, and steadily enlarged, modern factory in Bendern. In 1973 he established the trademark "Malbuner", which now covers 80% of the group's meat products. The acquisition or building of factories in Sargans (1982), Frastanz (1991) and Apolda (1999) was accompanied by the acquisition and integration of fish smokeries (1990 and 2000) and a fully automated logistics centre (1996). The Apolda factory has a capacity of more than 100 million pizzas per year. A completely separate factory for pet-food was built in 1987 (it is now third in the Swiss market, after Nestlé and Mars). This business accounts for a third of the group's turnover.[10]

Swarovski

Cut glass and natural stones for jewellery, giftware, decoration, architecture and chandeliers. Also optical precision instruments and cutting and grinding tools. 13,000 employees worldwide, of whom 540 work in Liechtenstein. More than CHF 2 billion turnover, of which 1 billion is in Liechtenstein. Production in Liechtenstein, Austria, the UK, USA, Brazil, Thailand and India. Active worldwide. Its central storage logistics, international sales and service headquarters are also located in Liechtenstein.

Unaxis Balzers

An international leader in vacuum and thin-layer technology. Its products include appliances for vacuum measurement, gas analysis and leak detection; coating plants, materials and process technology for the production of storage media, electronic components and displays; thin-film components and coating service for the optical and electro-optical industry; and wear-resistant coatings for tools and precision parts. Some of these products find application in the space industry. 7,700 employees worldwide, of whom 1,700 work in Balzers and on the opposite bank of the Rhine in Trübbach (Switzerland). CHF 3,285 million turnover. Active in Europe, America and the Asia/Pacific region, with more than 90 sales and service centres.

Gerätebauanstalt Balzers was founded in 1946 by Professor Max Auwärter (a German physicist whose vacuum-technology factory had been destroyed in the war), Prince Franz Josef II (who wished to attract industry to Liechtenstein) and Emil Bührle (a Swiss financier). Production and marketing facilities began to be established in other countries from 1953. Since 1976 the Balzers Group has been exclusively owned by Oerlikon-Bührle, Zurich. It merged with the Leybold Group in 1995.

---

[10] "Liechtensteiner Vaterland", 27 July 2002.

FINANCIAL SERVICES

Liechtenstein is not a financial centre in its own right. The financial services sector's influence and attraction extend well beyond Liechtenstein's frontiers by virtue of the country's political stability, membership of the European Economic Area, close association with Switzerland, use of the strong and stable Swiss franc, liberal company and taxation law and niche products. However, its total volume of business is small compared with other centres. There is no stock exchange. It is chiefly to be seen as an adjunct of the Swiss financial centre.

The Banks

The banking sector makes an important contribution to the Liechtenstein economy, but its total balance sheet assets (CHF 34,788 billion in 2001)[1] amount to only 1.56% of those of the Swiss banks (CHF 2,227.4 billion). They are, for example, dwarfed by the UBS alone (CHF 1,016.48 billion). The assets which Liechtenstein manages offshore are less than 1% of the world total and about 2.75% of the CHF 3,240 billion ascribed to Switzerland.[2]

The sector's post-war development has nevertheless been dynamic, from an insignificant start:[3]

	Staff Employed	Balance Sheet Total (millions of Swiss francs)	Total Assets under Management (millions of Swiss francs)
1940	21	20.6	
1950	24	67.7	
1960	96	244.4	
1970	272	1,478.8	
1980	485	4,364.0	
1990	1,144	17, 347.9	
1995	1,353	24,281.7	56,124.4
2000	1,758	36,963.5	112,679.8
2001	1,769	34,788.0	105,655.6[4]

Until 1992 there were only three banks. When the sector was opened to competition, two new banks were quickly founded by Liechtenstein citizens (the Neue Bank and the Centrum Bank). Foreign banks, mostly Swiss and Austrian, began to establish wholly-owned subsidiaries from 1997. By 2002 there were 17 banks in Liechtenstein, with over 200,000 customer relationships. Inevitably, the largest market shares are still held by the three oldest banks: the Liechtensteinische Landesbank (LLB), the LGT Bank in Liechtenstein and the Verwaltungs-und Privat-Bank (VPB).[5] (The figures in the columns marked * in the following table indicate millions.)

	*Balance sheet total	*Net profits	*Capital funds	*Client assets managed	Staff employed	Market share
LLB	11,481.6	141.4	1,628.5	33,775.4	493	33%
LGT BiL	11,697.2	159.1	1,160.5	42,481.0	481	33%
VPB	8,272.5	107.5	750.3	29,586.0	451	24%

The LLB celebrated its 140th anniversary in 2001. It has long outgrown its original modest role as Liechtenstein's local savings and loans bank, but it retains a state guarantee on savings deposits and medium term notes. It was privatised in 1993. The bank intends to reduce the State's equity participation to below 50%, but wishes the State to remain a major shareholder. It operates as a universal bank in the Principality, with four branches. In addition to its mortgage and savings business it now offers asset management, advisory and trust services. It has a wholly owned subsidiary in Zurich, a fund management office in the Cayman Islands and significant stakes in two Swiss private banking firms and an insurance company.

The LGT Bank in Liechtenstein is now wholly owned by the Princely Family through the Prince of Liechtenstein Foundation. The chairman of the board is Prince Philipp, a younger brother of Hans-Adam II. It is one of the few private banks to be assigned an official rating by Standard and Poor's and Moody's (AA-and Aa3 respectively, among the highest ratings available). It specialises in asset

---

[1] Liechtenstein Bankers Association, Annual Report for 2001
[2] Quoted from a Gemini Consulting study published in "Finanz und Wirtschaft" of 4 August 1999, page 17. ("30 Jahre Liechtensteinischer Bankenverband 1969–1999", page 6.)
[3] Statistisches Jahrbuch 2002, page 225.
[4] For comparison, in September 2002 Bank Julius Baer, Switzerland's largest family-controlled bank, had assets of CHF 107,000 million under management. (British-Swiss Chamber of Commerce News Digest, No. 49/02.)
[5] Liechtenstein Bankers Association, Annual Report for 2001. These figures are of course only a snapshot for one particular year, to give a rough idea of the respective sizes of the three banks concerned. The LGT BiL staff figure would have been higher but for the transfer of certain staff to LGT Financial Services AG.

and wealth management. It was the first Liechtenstein bank to venture outside the Principality (to London, in 1982). In 1989 the Bank in Liechtenstein acquired GT Management, one of the leading UK fund management groups, for £91.5 million. The two wings of the business are now fully integrated. LGT BiL is well established in Switzerland, Germany, Dublin, the Cayman Islands, Hong Kong, Singapore and Tokyo.

The VPB's founder was Guido Feger, founder also of one of the oldest trust companies, the Allgemeine Treuhandunternehmen (ATU). The Guido Feger Foundation continues to hold 48% of the equity. The current chairman of the board is Hans Brunhart (Head of Government from 1978 to 1993). True to its origins, the VPB specialises in international business and private trust banking. It has subsidiaries in Zurich, Luxembourg and the British Virgin Islands (the latter with ATU), and representative offices in Munich and Montevideo.

All of these banks pay great attention to the professional training required to keep them nimble and ahead in their specialised niche markets. The LGT runs its own corporate university, the LGT Academy. The Liechtenstein banks are active in art sponsorship and social and charitable activities. The VPB publishes a valuable series of economic studies.

Trusts, Foundations and Companies

This sector of the economy dates back to the Persons and Company Act of 1926 and the Trust Enterprises Law of 1928 (page above). There are at present 276 corporate and 79 independent trustees in Liechtenstein, together with 87 lawyers who are entitled to carry out financial transactions on behalf of their clients.[6] Like other professionals, they are subject to strict state licensing qualifications. They are also subject to the provisions of both civil and criminal law. These include identification of customers and beneficiaries, due diligence and the protection of client confidentiality.

There are five main forms of entity, all of which must keep accounts.[7]

Company limited by shares ("Aktiengesellschaft"). This corresponds to limited companies as known elsewhere in continental Europe.

Foundation ("Stiftung"). This may be formed by persons, legal entities or firms for a specific purpose. It is used for defined ecclesiastical, family or non-

---

[6] IMF Assessment of the Supervision and Regulation of the Financial Sector, Principality of Liechtenstein (August 2003), Vol. I, paragraph 12 and Table 2 on page 13.

[7] A good overview, now somewhat dated, is provided in "Companies and Taxes in Liechtenstein" by Marxer, Goop and Kieber. (Liechtenstein Verlag, Vaduz, 1982). See also "Doing Business in Liechtenstein" (Price Waterhouse 1991 and Supplement 1995). For legislation up to 1999, see "Liechtenstein Company Law" by Bryan Jeeves, (second edition), Liechtenstein Verlag, Vaduz, 1999.

profit making purposes. These purposes are restricted by law, but commercial activities may be undertaken in certain circumstances. The foundation deeds and statutes are in principle unalterable. They are not open to public scrutiny, but must be deposited with the Register Office to ensure that the proposed foundation conforms with the law and cannot be misused. Its objects must be specific, possible and reasonable; they may not be illegal or immoral. Beneficiaries' and other third parties' interests are normally regulated in a separate document which is private and not lodged with the authorities.

Establishment ("Anstalt"). This is unique to Liechtenstein and is a very flexible form of incorporation It is a company for private business or investment-holding purposes with an independent legal personality and trading name. It must have a minimum capital of 30,000 Swiss francs. It may be formed and operated by an individual, a firm, a community or other legal entity. Authority is vested in the bearer of the founder's rights or his/her legal successor. The board of directors is responsible for management as specified in the articles. If the establishment has commercial objectives (i.e. any purpose other than administering its own assets), it must have an audit authority. The founder may at any time amend the articles and objects. An establishment must be registered.

Trust Settlement ("Treuhänderschaft"). This is based on Anglo-Saxon common law and, as such, is unique in continental Europe. It is not a legal entity but a contractual relationship permitting objectives to be pursued, similar to a foundation. The trustor transfers the assets to the trustee and instructs him to manage them on his behalf in accordance with the trust deed. Unlike a foundation, there are no restrictions (subject to legal requirements) on its objects or activities. It may be entered in the Public Register or the trust deed may be deposited at the Registry depending on the trustor's wishes.

Trust Enterprise ("Treuunternehmen"). This can best be understood as a business trust to which the trustor transfers the assets, specifying the purpose to which they are to be applied. Supreme authority lies with the owner of the trustor's rights. The company may be either commercial or, for example, designed to protect a family's assets. It must be entered in the Commercial Register.

The use of foundations, trusts and similar entities for personal and private purposes dates back to the Crusades, when crusaders needed to ensure that their assets would be safeguarded during their absence. Increasingly in the modern world, such entities are being used for legal and legitimate tax planning and asset protection. They offer continuity and provision for the future of a family, a friend or a business in a way that a testament cannot always guarantee. Their use for the crude objective of illegal tax evasion is declining in the modern world for several reasons, including the need to make more productive use of assets and, perhaps, modern governments' enhanced means of prevention and detection. The responsibility for any such evasion lies with the individual. The prudent citizen will always make his peace with his own national tax authorities, if only to ensure that his funds can be retrieved and used when needed. (For example, the change to the euro caught many people in continental Europe by surprise. The German authorities posted guards on their frontiers to question their citizens who were found to have more than DM 30,000 in their possession when returning to the Federal Republic.)

In the commercial field, the variety of forms of incorporation enables companies active in a number of countries, and therefore potentially liable to different or conflicting taxation regimes, to concentrate their assets while deciding where their profits are to be taxed.

It is also a useful strategic tool for such companies. Courtaulds, in the 1930s, was a case in point (page 73 above). Holding companies (Holdinggesellschaften) are businesses whose object consists exclusively or largely in the management of other concerns and/or their assets, inside and/or outside Liechtenstein. Domiciled companies (Sitzunternehmen) merely have their domicile in Liechtenstein while carrying out their business activities wholly in other countries. Companies which are classified as commercially active (i.e. which engage in trading activities) must produce audited accounts.

There are at present some 85,000[8] trusts, foundations, establishments and other types of corporate structures in Liechtenstein. These include about 31,000 registered incorporated entities, about 51,000 foundations (of which about 2,900 have commercial objectives) and about 1,500 family trusts.

Fund Management and Investment Companies ("Investment-Unternehmen")

These were permitted by legislation in 1996. As an onshore development, they represent a new and lively form of diversification in the Liechtenstein financial sector. By June 2002 there were 16 licensed fund-management companies and 5 licensed investment companies, managing a total of 81 authorised funds with CHF 5.2 billion in client funds under management.[9] The funds are of three types, investing either only in securities traded on the stock exchange or another regulated market, or in real estate, or in "other assets" (which may be of higher risk than the securities handled by the first type). The companies enjoy non-discriminatory access to the whole of the EEA.

---

[8] IMF report, August 2003, Vol. I, Table 2 on page 13. The Council of Europe report, February 2000, paragraph 87, indicated about 90,000 entities. The "Neue Zürcher Zeitung" Folio for August 1996 (page 32) said that of the 75,500 entities then listed in the Commercial Register, 1,800 were commercially active in Liechtenstein. Of the remainder, 9,000 were companies limited by shares, 21,700 were establishments, 37,000 were foundations, 3,000 were trusts and another 3,000 trust settlements.

[9] IMF report, August 2003, Vol. I, paragraph 11 and Table 2 on page 13.

Insurance

The versatility of the Liechtenstein onshore financial services sector is also shown by the remarkable growth of the insurance industry in recent years. Until 1995 international insurance was weakly developed in the Principality because of its small size and relative isolation. The situation then changed, first as a result of entry into the EEA and then by the conclusion in 1997 of a treaty with Switzerland which enabled insurance companies of each country to establish themselves and offer services in the other.

Liechtenstein's legislation obliges the insurance companies and their operators to be professionally well qualified, well organised and financially stable. They must also comply fully with the strict new due diligence and other anti-money laundering measures. They benefit from the country's liberal company legislation, political and fiscal stability and the ready accessibility of banking and other professional services. Less tangibly, they benefit from starting with a clean slate. They are not, like insurance companies in some other countries, overcoming the legacies of past deregulation, restructuring and staff reductions.

As a result, there were (in July 2002) 21 insurance companies in Liechtenstein (12 life, 4 non-life and 5 reinsurance), and the number is growing. They have a premium volume of CHF 500 billion and assets totalling CHF 1.8 billion.[10] Their operations include financial services (annuities, capital growth policies, etc.), indemnity insurance and reinsurance. Liechtenstein is becoming a centre for so-called "captive" insurance companies, which insure the risks of their parent companies or the risks of members of an association or a group of companies. Some important insurance companies from Switzerland, Italy, Austria, Germany, Sweden, France and the US are now represented in Liechtenstein. The Swiss Federal Railways, Swisscom and the Schindler group have established reinsurance captives there.

---

[10] IMF report, August 2003, Vol. I, paragraph 13. In addition, 34 Swiss and 1 EEA insurance provider operate in Liechtenstein with an agency, and more than 100 Swiss and EEA providers have notified their intention to operate there by the way of freedom to provide services.

FINANCIAL SERVICES:
SUPERVISION AND REGULATION

Alexander Frick (Head of Government from 1945 to 1962) once said, "Before a great power has found it has a problem, we have already half solved it".[1] That has not always been the case in the fast changing climate of financial services regulation, where Liechtenstein's small size has sometimes proved a disadvantage rather than a help.

Liechtenstein neither wants, nor can afford, to harbour criminal money. As a small country, it does not wish to make itself vulnerable to the sinister political and social pressures that such money brings. Its financial services tend to cater for conservative-minded clients averse to risk, who are concerned for safety and predictability. Furthermore, a poor reputation in financial services could, by association, harm the prestige of its manufacturing sector. A small country cannot shrug off as easily as a large one the damage done to its reputation by a financial scandal.

In the past the authorities were not always quick to spot impending problems and their possible ramifications in advance; and, having passed the necessary laws, they did not always supply the resources needed to put them into full effect. Between 1999 and 2001 Liechtenstein became the target for an extraordinary crossfire of international criticisms. Some were justified. Others were not. In some cases Liechtenstein was, accidentally or by design, dragged into the international policies or domestic politics of other countries. The country's small size made it an easy target. The media headlines were damaging.

The Government and the financial services sector took quick and strenuous action to deal with those criticisms that were justified. A recent report by the International Monetary Fund (IMF) has praised Liechtenstein's high level of compliance with current international standards. Indeed, Liechtenstein now claims to have regulatory legislation and institutions that in some respects surpass them.

---

[1] Quoted by Hereditary Prince Hans-Adam in his Speech from the Throne, 27 March 1984.

Criminal Money

Until the late 1980s international attention was chiefly focussed on criminal money derived from drugs trafficking. At that point globalisation, the internet, the European Single Market and the fall of communism suddenly gave enormous new scope for the laundering of criminal money, which was now being generated by an even wider range of activities including fraud and corruption. Technology and human ingenuity gave wings to crime.

Money laundering has been neatly defined as "rendering the proceeds of crime unrecognisable as such".[2] By its very nature it is hard to determine the true size of the black economy, but the IMF estimates that the aggregate volume of money-laundering in the world could be somewhere between 2% and 5% of the world's Gross Domestic Product. The Financial Action Task Force (FATF) calculates that, using 1996 statistics, these figures could range between US$ 590 billion and 1.5 trillion, the lower figure being roughly equivalent to the value of the total output of an economy the size of Spain's.[3] Stuart Eizenstat (former US Deputy Secretary of the Treasury) told a Senate committee on 26 September 2001 that "at least a third of that amount, up to half a trillion dollars annually, is thought to pass through US financial institutions at least once on its clandestine journey".[4]

The "Financial Times" for 20 October 2000 reported that the United Kingdom accounted for half of the late Nigerian General Abacha's $208 million that flowed into Switzerland through the international banking system and for $219 million of the $514 million that flowed out.[5]

The British Financial Services Authority concluded in March 2001 that 23 unnamed London banks had handled $1.3 billion (£890 million) for the Abacha family and their friends. Fifteen of these banks (which had handled 98% of the money) had had "significant control weaknesses", including weaknesses in the verification of identity of beneficial owners of companies and in reporting suspicious transactions to the authorities.[6] These examples show that money laundering is a problem experienced by every financial centre, not excluding the larger ones. It is a problem without frontiers. The international cash flows that finance terrorist organisations and activities have added a separate but related dimension.

---

[2] Stephen Gleeson, quoted in Butterworths Financial Services Law Guide, second edition, 2002, page 175.
[3] FATF Website: http://www.oecd.org/fatf/
[4] US Senate Committee on Banking, Housing and Urban Affairs
[5] In an editorial comment on this report the "Financial Times" said, "The lack of urgency in London is in disturbing contrast with the actions taken in Switzerland, Luxembourg, Liechtenstein and Jersey, traditional havens of banking secrecy".
[6] FSA press release, 8 March 2001. The banks concerned are unlikely to be prosecuted, according to the "Financial Times" for 24 September 2002.

The Evolution of Regulation and Supervision in Liechtenstein

Before the company and trust legislation of 1926 and 1928, commerce in Liechtenstein (long before there was a financial services industry) was regulated by Austrian and German company law dating from 1811 and 1861 respectively. Although the main purpose of the Persons and Company Act of 1926 was to attract foreign capital to Liechtenstein, the act was also inspired by the egalitarian thought that it should be open to anyone to found a company. It was held unfair that the economically strong (for example, limited companies) should be liable only for their capital, while the economically weaker natural persons should be exposed to unlimited liability.[7]

In Liechtenstein banking supervision, probably because of the small size of the country and its banking industry, has historically been the direct responsibility of the Government (though this is about to change). The Government is advised by the Banking Commission (founded in 1961), whose role has evolved over the years and has been supplemented significantly by new organisations since 1993. The commission is elected by Parliament for a period of four years. At present it consists of five independent experts, three of them Liechtenstein citizens, two of them Swiss. This arrangement is different from that in Switzerland, where it is the Federal Banking Commission, an independent body appointed by the Federal Council (Government), that is responsible for bank supervision.

In 1977, shortly after the Chiasso affair (page 144 above), the independent Swiss National Bank and the Swiss commercial banks concluded an agreement on due diligence in accepting funds and the use of banking secrecy. The Liechtenstein Government and the Liechtenstein Bankers Association concluded a similar agreement independently, on 27 June 1977. The aim was to ensure the reliable identification of clients of the three banks then licensed and to prevent the misuse of banking secrecy for purposes that were criminal or extraditable under Liechtenstein law. There was one important difference between the two agreements which attracted repeated Swiss criticism: a Liechtenstein bank did not need to verify the beneficial owner of an account or other facility if the owner was represented by a qualified Liechtenstein person such as a lawyer, trustee or auditor who could certify that he had always been aware of the identity of the beneficial owner and that there was nothing to indicate abuse of banking secrecy. The agreement was modified on 5 October 1989, but this exemption remained.

The company law reform of 1980 required entities that conducted commercial business to keep proper accounts and to present formal balance sheets. The qualified Liechtenstein citizens who by law sat on the boards of such companies were supposed to be given a detailed insight into their companies' activities, and

---

[7] Edmund Frick, in "Wandel im Finanzdienstleistungssektor", Physica-Verlag, Heidelberg, 2001, page 32.

could be held responsible for breaches of the law. The Government established obligatory checks for most of the companies. These measures, however, tended to be treated as formalities.

The more unpleasant aspects of modern society were slow to appear in daily life in Liechtenstein. The crime rate was, and remains, low.[8] This very fact may have helped to make the authorities complacent about the possibility of the country being exploited for handling the proceeds of crimes committed elsewhere. When a drugs dealer was arrested and tried in 1982, there was outrage when he had to be acquitted because there was no legislation under which he could be convicted. Such legislation had not previously been thought necessary. Acting in agreement with his Government, Franz Josef II used his emergency powers under Article 10 of the Constitution to take over Swiss narcotics legislation. The following year (20 April 1983) Parliament replaced it with its own legislation. Article 20 (2) (b) and (c) of the new Narcotics Act made organised drug trafficking punishable by imprisonment for up to twenty years. Liechtenstein therefore had no difficulty, when it entered the EEA in 1995, in taking over the EC Council's Directive of 10 June 1991 on prevention of the use of the financial system for the purpose of money laundering. This directive built on the 1988 UN Convention Against Illicit Traffic in Narcotic Drugs and Psychotropic Substances, but made it clear that the EC's concerns ranged beyond drug trafficking to organised crime and terrorism.[9]

In 1990, when the Swiss banks adopted a new due diligence code, the Swiss Federal Banking Commission criticised the quality of the state supervision of the Liechtenstein banks. The Liechtenstein Government set up a study group to examine the Swiss regulations and the implications of entry into the EEA, including the likely opening up of the banking sector. This resulted in the Banking Act of 21 October 1992 (amended in 1996), which reorganised and tightened up banking supervision and turned the former Secretariat of the Banking Commission into a Bank Supervisory Office ("Dienststelle für Bankenaufsicht"). Article 36 built on Liechtenstein's existing international commitments by authorising the Government or the Bank Supervisory Office to supply information to foreign banking supervisory authorities, subject to the latter providing a guarantee of reciprocity and to undertaking that the information would be used only for supervisory purposes and that their staff concerned would be bound by official and/or professional secrecy. Money laundering as such became a criminal offence on 21 March 1996 (Article 165 of the Criminal Code).

The next step was the Due Diligence Act of 22 May 1996 and the accompany-

---

[8] Until recent years, a car could safely be left unlocked in the street.
[9] Official Journal of the European Communities, 28 June 1991, No. L 166/77 to 82.

ing Executive Order of 18 February 1997. These superseded the 1989 agreement between the Government and the banks. They reached out beyond the banks and finance companies to include lawyers, trustees and trust companies, investment undertakings and insurance companies. (In 1998 the new legislation was extended to branches of foreign banks and companies in Liechtenstein.) The law obliged them to verify the identities of new clients not already known to them, but still with an exemption in the case of beneficial owners whose qualified representatives in Liechtenstein were prepared to vouch for them. Article 9 obliged them to check transactions about which there was "strong suspicion" and to freeze the relevant assets. They were to report "strong" suspicions of money laundering to the authorities without informing anyone else that they had done so or that investigations were in hand, unless officially authorised to do so or until eight working days had elapsed. Documentation was to be kept for ten years after a business relationship had ended, for random checks by the authorities.

In keeping with the enlarged scope of the 1996 supervisory legislation the Bank Supervisory Office became, on 1 May 1999, the Financial Services Authority ("Amt für Finanzdienstleistungen" – FSA). It was made responsible for supervising the legal compliance not only of banks, banking corporations and investment companies but also of trustees, lawyers, patent lawyers, accountants and auditing companies, as well as for protecting the interests of investors. It was empowered to demand all necessary information, to commission extraordinary audits and to pass information about suspicious transactions to the Public Prosecution Service. It was to follow international and local legal developments. It was given the right to participate in, and if necessary to lead, national and international working groups and negotiating delegations.

The Maxwell Affair

When the scale of Robert Maxwell's criminal activity came to light after his death at sea on 5 November 1991, his foundations in Liechtenstein featured prominently in the media. In them was vested the ownership of both the majority of the shares in his public company, Maxwell Communication Corporation (MCC), and also of Headington Investments, which controlled the family's shares in other private companies. A confusing network of some 400 other private companies also existed. Contrary to Liechtenstein law, the foundations (or at least, their names) were used in part for the channelling of funds from one company to another, mostly between London and New York, in order to prop up MCC's share price. Maxwell boasted of the existence of the foundations in order to impress bankers and politicians in Britain and elsewhere with the supposed size of his private fortune. In the end the foundations were worthless, since their assets had all been pledged. Any private cash that might have remained had been hidden in other countries, not in Liechtenstein. Maxwell broke Liechtenstein law as much as British law; but his association with Liechtenstein inevitably helped to darken the background when international criticism of that country's financial services sector grew later in the decade.

The Council of Europe Report, 1999–2000

In December 1997 Liechtenstein voluntarily agreed to participate in the first round of evaluations by examiners appointed by a Council of Europe Select Committee of Experts on the Evaluation of Anti-Money Laundering Measures, of which Liechtenstein was a founding member. The Council of Europe team visited the Principality in September 1999. It was accompanied by two examiners from the FATF (pages 311–313 below). Liechtenstein was the eleventh country to be so evaluated. The team's report noted that the Liechtenstein authorities had recognised their country's vulnerability to money laundering and had made "considerable efforts" over the past few years to reduce the threat. Liechtenstein's legislation was "of a generally satisfactory standard containing most of the ingredients that one would expect to see in a legislation of this kind." …. "Many building blocks of a sound anti-laundering regime are in place…."[10]

There were, however, some important warnings. The examiners considered that Liechtenstein's geographical location, highly developed financial services industry and off-shore business sector, combined with strict professional secrecy rules, made it an attractive target for money laundering operations, e.g. by international organised crime. The advantages offered by offshore centres to legitimate users (favourable tax treatment of non-residents, bank secrecy, customer confidentiality and attractive trust legislation) might operate as a magnet for others of less agreeable background. To counter that risk, "stringent anti-money laundering measures, resolute enforcement and unrelenting vigilance are required. The examiners note with concern that not all these elements are instantly present in Liechtenstein's current anti-laundering policy."[11]

The examiners' main criticism was that the Liechtenstein system was too passive, too formal and too reliant on outside initiatives; they considered that it should be more active in tackling the problem. In particular, it was under-staffed. For example, the FSA had a team of only five persons, none of whom was specialised in the prevention or repression of money laundering, and the police had only two staff dealing with economic crime including money laundering. The FSA was thought to be over-burdened by its regulatory and supervisory functions

---

[10] First Evaluation Report on the Principality of Liechtenstein PC-R-EV (99) rev. dated 11 February 2000, paragraphs 70, 72 and 130.
[11] First Evaluation Report, paragraphs 19 and 88.

at the expense of operational work. The examiners considered that the role of the police should be enhanced. They welcomed the Government's intention to set up a special police unit to deal with economic crime in general and money laundering in particular, but thought that inter-departmental cooperation should be improved. The number of reports of suspicious transactions in 1997 and 1998 (47) was thought to be rather low. Moreover, 80% of them stemmed from abroad or from the press, while none referred to transactions carried out by the more than 70,000 Liechtenstein off-shore companies.

The report recommended, *inter alia*, that the adequacy of the "strong suspicion" provision, the absence of a penalty for "tipping off" a client that he was under suspicion and the desirability of granting immunity from liability under client confidentiality legislation for disclosures made to the authorities in good faith should be reviewed urgently.

Bureaux de change should be regulated. Attempts at suspicious transactions (and not merely the actual transactions) should be reportable. Article 165 of the Criminal Code should be brought into line with the stiffer provisions of the 1983 Narcotics Act by criminalising the laundering in Liechtenstein of the proceeds of crimes committed elsewhere. The threshold of 150,000 francs for the confiscation of criminal assets should be removed. International cooperation should be stepped up, including in matters of tax evasion and tax fraud. Financial institutions should systematically appoint qualified compliance officers. The audit process should be made more frequent and comprehensive. Compliance training of the staff in financial institutions should be improved. Customer identification and record keeping procedures should be tightened.

Follow-up to the Report

Experience of the 1996 legislation had already shown that it had some gaps. A further law (of 22 October 1998) introduced measures for the freezing and seizing of assets in the event of suspicion of criminal activity. The Council of Europe report and, to some extent, the discussions in Brussels that were to result in European Commission proposals (14 July 1999) to update and extend the 1991 Money-Laundering Directive caused the Liechtenstein Government to commission a review of due diligence measures in September 1999.

The "Spiegel" Article

While these reforms were getting under way the German magazine "Der Spiegel" published, on 8 November 1999, an article about a secret report of the German Intelligence Service ("Bundesnachtrichtendienst" – BND) dated 8 April 1999.

It said that the report relied for much of its information on electronic communications intercepted by a listening station in the Black Forest.[12] The article described Liechtenstein as "an entire country, in the middle of Europe, in the service of criminals all over the world." According to the BND report, there was allegedly "a network of relationships between high-ranking officials, judges, politicians, bank managers and investment advisers who assist each other with illegal financial transactions on behalf of international criminals". The latter were said to include the Russian underworld chiefs, Italian Mafia bosses and Latin American drugs barons. The article hinted at the identities of certain highly-placed Liechtensteiners. The Liechtenstein Government and some individuals started legal action in the German courts for defamation. These cases seem not to have reached substantive hearings, on procedural grounds.

As "Der Spiegel" made clear, the German authorities had long had their sights on Liechtenstein as a haven for German citizens' assets. They had been further irritated by delays in Mutual Legal Assistance. The article's publication coincided with a political furore in Germany about secret funds from German and French sources for the benefit of the CDU, which had reportedly been handled by the former Chancellor Helmut Kohl. Some of this money had allegedly passed through Liechtenstein trusts and bank accounts. It is not known who leaked the BND report, but it was no doubt a lucky political bonus for those attacking the CDU that Liechtenstein should have been painted as black as possible. As Prince Hans-Adam pointed out, Liechtenstein had no evidence of criminal activity on its own territory in this connection.

External Consequences: Relations with Germany

The Liechtenstein Government immediately demanded clarification from the German Embassy in Berne. After some delay the German Embassy, on 15 December 1999, confirmed that a BND report existed but took up no position on press comment about it.[13] Throughout January 2000 the Liechtenstein Government seems to have had difficulty in finding an interlocutor in Germany: the Ministry of Justice said that not it, but the Chancellor's Office, was responsible for the BND, while the federal states ("Länder") were responsible for matters concerning Mutal Legal Assistance. During a visit to Berlin the Liechtenstein Minister of Justice, Heinz Frommelt, said that he found Germany's behaviour "astonishing".[14] The tone rose. Prince Hans-Adam said to an Austrian magazine, "We have survived three German Reichs and hopefully we shall survive the fourth".[15] In

---

[12] "Der Spiegel" had previously published in December 1997 some personal details about German citizens, based on a disk sent to it by an employee of a Liechtenstein trust company.
[13] "Liechtensteiner Volksblatt", 18 December 1999
[14] "Liechtensteiner Vaterland", 26 January 2000
[15] "Profil"; quoted in the "Liechtensteiner Vaterland", 3 February 2000

Brussels on 28 February the German Finance Minister, Hans Eichel, complained about money laundering, unfair taxation practices and lack of cooperation in pursuing financial offences and said that a low-tax country could not sit in the middle of Europe like a "maggot in the bacon". ("Made im Speck").[16] Eichel proposed that the European Commission should investigate these matters; an idea which, as the Liechtenstein Head of Government Mario Frick observed, was not particularly helpful when Liechtenstein had not been vouchsafed a word of consultation about it beforehand.[17]

Some sort of dialogue seems nevertheless to have developed. The Chancellor's Office said that Germany would help Liechtenstein to clarify matters "within the limits of its legal possibilities". The BND denied that it had used listening stations against Liechtenstein.[18]

Internal Consequences: the Spitzer Report

On 23 December 1999 the Liechtenstein Government appointed an Austrian judge, Kurt Spitzer, Chief Prosecutor at Innsbruck, as Special Prosecutor. After three months of investigations his initial report (6 April 2000) confirmed that there was no criminal network between the Government, judiciary, civil service and the private economy as "Der Spiegel" had alleged. The allegations against a former Head of Government and a former chief of police were completely unfounded. His concluding report (31 August 2000) showed that the BND's report, far from having been compiled by "cyber-spies", was in fact largely based on the fabrications and mistakes of a German citizen who had meanwhile (on 8 June 2000) been sentenced by a German court to five years imprisonment on quite separate charges of investment fraud and attempted blackmail.[19] This man had previously circulated in Liechtenstein two anonymous papers dated 23 February 1997 (posted from Frankfurt) and 10 February 1998 (posted from Cologne). They were so full of obvious errors that the Liechtenstein Prosecutor's Office had not taken them seriously at the time.

Nevertheless, while Spitzer easily demolished the more sensational allegations in the "Spiegel" report which had pilloried the whole country, his conclusions about the weaknesses of the system were very much in line with those of the Council of Europe experts. He agreed with the BND's criticisms of the delays in

---

[16] "Neue Zürcher Zeitung", 29 February 2000. According to this report, it was not banking secrecy that worried Eichel so much as low taxation, which in his view would make it impossible for European countries to fulfil their obligations. On this, see page 276.

[17] "Liechtensteiner Vaterland", 1 March 2000. The resulting report, being an internal and theoretically confidential ommission document, played no part in the Liechtenstein reform process.

[18] "Liechtensteiner Vaterland", 4 February and 4 March 2000

[19] According to the "Liechtensteiner Vaterland" for 1 March 2000, Spitzer got the information he needed from Germany "through the appropriate channels".

granting legal assistance to foreign states; the courts and legal services had indeed been acting too slowly. Moreover, he said, some domestic criminal proceedings had remained unprocessed for years in the offices of various judges, while applications by the Prosecutor's Office for the initiation of judicial investigations, for pre-trial custody or for building searches had not been processed, so that even in serious cases the possibility of prosecution had become barred owing to lapse of time. The Government, Spitzer said, had been aware for some time of the need to create additional established posts for judges. Not only were the courts and the police understaffed, but the courts imposed so much red tape that the Prosecutor's Office was unable to do its job properly. Spitzer called on the courts to be more rigorous with trustees and lawyers, and on the banks to be more thorough in due diligence procedures. That said, he found white-collar crime in Liechtenstein to be no different from that in other European countries. He concluded, "I have noticed that most assets coming into the Principality for the purpose of money laundering have already undergone a pre-wash in other countries. This ought also to serve as a reminder to those countries which are now pointing the finger at the Principality".

As a result of Spitzer's investigations, inquiries were started against two judges on suspicion of negligence. They were not in the end indicted: the conclusion was that they had simply been over-burdened. One continued in office, the other retired. There were house searches and arrests for investigation purposes, among them, on 15 May 2000, the arrests of five men including a member of Parliament and a brother of the Minister for the Economy. Wider investigations unearthed a number of far-reaching cases. Some serious prison sentences and fines have already been imposed, but the facts disclosed at the trials have fallen far short of the more sensational allegations against the Principality. The package of legislative work already in progress was speeded up. A new head of the Prosecution Service, the Austrian Robert Wallner, was recruited from the Innsbruck Prosecutor's Office. Under him, more than a hundred building searches were carried out between August 2000 and August 2001.[20] Staffing in several critical sectors was increased.

Inevitably, there were political repercussions. It was only when the "Spiegel" story broke that Prince Hans-Adam became aware of the 1997 anonymous paper, which the Government had not shown to him because apparently they believed that he had already seen it. (The Prince did not see the 1998 paper until 22 December 1999.) The Prince publicly called on the Government to mount a thoroughgoing investigation.[21] In successive press interviews he expressed his

---

[20] See Wallner's extensive interview in "Liechtensteiner Vaterland", 11 August 2001.
[21] Press statement, 20 December 1999

dissatisfaction with what he described as years of inactivity. This added to the tension with the Government that already existed over constitutional questions. In time, a party political element crept in. The unexpected storm of which the "Spiegel" article was the first squall contributed to the VU's defeat in the parliamentary elections of February 2001.

The Montebourg Report

In April 2000 another report, this time by a French parliamentary delegation consisting of two Socialist deputies, Vincent Peillon (chairman) and Arnaud Montebourg (*rapporteur*), was published in Paris. It attracted much attention from the press. It denounced the Principality as the most dangerous tax haven in Europe, living and flourishing on terrorism, corruption, international Mafia money and company and political slush funds.[22] The deputies' visit to Vaduz (escorted by television cameras and a team of journalists)[23] took place on 14 January 2000 at such short notice from their side that the Liechtenstein side was unable to organise an extensive programme for them. Nevertheless, the President of the Parliament, the Minister of Justice and some senior officials were able to meet them for a frank but civil exchange of views which concentrated on the identification of beneficial owners of trusts in criminal cases and on delays in providing international legal assistance. The Liechtenstein side did not at that stage know that the previous day, even before the talks in Vaduz, Montebourg had already announced his conclusions to journalists in Vienna, to the effect that "Liechtenstein is a criminal state".[24]

The RPR and DL members of the commission[25] (seven in all) dissented from the Montebourg report, arguing in some detail that the *rapporteur* had not proved his allegations of criminal connivance and that Liechtenstein had shown its practical readiness to co-operate in international efforts against money laundering. In a protest to the French Embassy in Berne after the publication of the report, the Liechtenstein Government pointed out that Montebourg had not analysed the recent and current reforms and that he had repeated passages from the BND report "whose accusations have been invalidated to a great extent". The Liechtenstein Minister of Justice said that the report's conclusions lacked information; before the end of the year, Liechtenstein would have in place a simplified and reinforced arsenal of laws and regulations against financial crime which would be one of the best in Europe.[26]

---

[22] The full text (30 March 2000) can be found at www.assemblee-nationale.fr. These deputies were part of a 20-member all-party information commission set up by the French National Assembly to inquire into the obstacles to the supervision and repression of financial crime and money laundering in Europe.
[23] "Le Monde", 16 January 2000
[24] "Der Standard", Vienna, 15/16 January 2000
[25] Five deputies of the Rassemblement pour la République (Gaullists) and two of the Démocratie libérale.

The FATF Blacklist

Much more serious in substance than sensational media reports was the decision by the Financial Action Task Force on Money Laundering (FATF) to place Liechtenstein on its list of non-co-operative states. It was this black-listing and the dialogue with the FATF that really galvanised the reform process in Liechtenstein.

The FATF, an inter-governmental body, was set up in 1989 by the Group of Seven Leading Industrial Countries (G7)[27] Its purpose is to develop and promote policies at both national and international levels to combat money laundering and, to that end, to work to generate the necessary political will to bring about national legislative and regulatory reforms. Its secretariat is based at the Organisation for Economic Co-operation and Development (OECD) in Paris, but it is not part of that organisation. It monitors its own members' progress by a process of peer review and peer pressure, and promotes the adoption and implementation of anti-money laundering measures globally. To this end it co-operates with other organisations active in the same field, such as the Council of Europe. The original Task Force comprised representatives of the G7 member states, the European Commission and eight other countries. Its membership currently comprises 29 states, the European Commission and the Gulf Co-operation Council. It has completed two rounds of mutual evaluations of its member countries and jurisdictions. It bases its work on the Forty Recommendations which it adopted in 1990 and has since updated. Since October 2001 it has expanded its mission with eight new recommendations which focus on the financing of terrorism.

In 1999–2000 the FATF conducted a review to identify jurisdictions with "serious deficiencies in their anti-money laundering regimes". Its report of 14 February 2000 set out 25 criteria for jurisdictions which were "non-co-operative in the international fight against money laundering". On 22 June 2000 it included Liechtenstein in a list of 15 "non-co-operative" countries or territories; Switzerland voted for inclusion. The report said that "although the situation has recently improved significantly" Liechtenstein fell foul of several of the 25 criteria

---

[26] This commission, the longest in the parliamentary history of the French Fifth Republic (June 1999–April 2002), also examined Monaco, Switzerland, the United Kingdom, Luxembourg and France. It caused controversy in several countries. In February 2001 it accused Switzerland of lacking political will in the battle against money laundering. A Swiss official spokesman described the report as "arrogant and tendentious" and said that the Swiss Government was considering an official protest. ("Liechtensteiner Vaterland", 23 February 2001.) In October 2001 another report condemned the City of London and the UK's offshore centres for their "feeble" efforts against money laundering and alleged failure to co-operate with European countries. *Inter alia,* it criticised the basic constitutional right of *habeas corpus* as an obstruction to investigations. A spokesman for No. 10 Downing Street said that the report "was inaccurate before September 11 [2001] and it is even more inaccurate now". A British Treasury spokesman described Montebourg as "a maverick MP who has been writing these reports for years to raise his own profile". ("Financial Times" and "Times" for 11 October 2001.)

[27] Canada, France, Germany, Italy, Japan, the United Kingdom, the United States of America.

either wholly or in part. "The system for reporting suspicious transactions is still inadequate, there are not proper laws in place for exchanging information about money laundering investigations and co-operating with foreign authorities in prosecuting cases, and the resources devoted to tackling money laundering are inadequate." The review acknowledged the measures under way in Liechtenstein, which it strongly supported: "They are intended to rectify most of the shortcomings which have been identified". The review advised Liechtenstein to consider whether additional measures were needed to require banks to obtain more information on customers introduced by lawyers and fiduciaries, and to encourage banks to report suspicious transactions.[28]

The inclusion in the black list caused indignation in Liechtenstein.[29] The Government considered that the dialogue with the FATF beforehand had been inadequate. It argued in particular that it was strange to brand Liechtenstein as "non-co-operative" when only recently it had willingly undergone a review by the Council of Europe (based on the Forty Recommendations) in which two FATF examiners had participated. Liechtenstein, it pointed out, was already putting in place the reforms suggested by that review; these reforms had indeed been started before the FATF process began at the end of January 2000. Liechtenstein expected the FATF's expression of support to take the form of a constructive dialogue. It also expected other countries to take account of the FATF's positive assessment of recent developments. The Foreign Minister said that "the tendency of international working groups such as the FATF to draw up reports on other states – excluding those states from the process of investigation – and subsequently to draw up lists or even take sanctions is definitely questionable from the point of view of international law and … can by no means replace a fruitful dialogue and transparent cooperation on both a bilateral and multilateral basis".[30]

Since Liechtenstein and the FATF nevertheless had the same objectives, a constructive dialogue now began. It continued through the year. The legislative programme already planned rolled ahead at impressive speed; much of it was in place by September. (Perhaps, in this case, Liechtenstein's small size was helpful.) The dialogue with the FATF resulted in certain improvements concerning "suspicion" and the criminalisation of the laundering of "own proceeds" of crime. The recruitment of staff, many of them from Austria and Switzerland, went ahead

---

[28] FATF Review to Identify Non-Co-operative Countries or Territories, 22 July 2000, paragraphs 35–37.

[29] Individual national agendas may possibly have influenced the inclusion or exclusion of particular countries. The "Financial Times" for 23 June 2000 commented, "Unfortunately there is still the suspicion of political horse trading by FATF members in the countries on the list".

[30] Statements by Mario Frick (Head of Government), Heinz Frommelt (Minister of Justice) and Andrea Willi (Foreign Minister), 23 June 2000. "Soft law" may indeed be ripe for closer study. See "Lawmaking Through the Back Door" by Professors Richard Rose and Edward Page, European Policy Forum, London, April 2001.

briskly. The new Due Diligence Act of 14 September 2000 removed a long-standing and serious bone of contention with Switzerland (and with the FATF) by requiring the banks to verify the identity of all new clients from 1 January 2001 including those introduced by intermediaries such as trustees. ("Know Your Customer", or "KYC".) It also required the banks to verify all existing account holders by 31 December 2002. The Liechtenstein Bankers Association had already decided unilaterally to verify new clients and to bring forward the date for verifying existing clients to 31 December 2001; any accounts where identity could not be established by that date would be closed. The Government and Parliament, under pressure from the FATF, changed the Due Diligence Law on 16 November 2001 to make the earlier deadline mandatory. Intermediaries who already knew their clients had no fundamental problem with this change. It was much harder to trace the beneficial owners of, say, companies and trusts which had been inactive for decades or which had complex ramifications abroad. Nevertheless, by 31 December 2001, after strenuous efforts, the owners of 98% of all Liechtenstein bank accounts were known and customer profiles had been established for 97.2% of them.[31]

In June 2001 the FATF listed and welcomed Liechtenstein's achievements and removed it from the list of non-co-operative countries. One year later it reported that "Liechtenstein has addressed all previously identified deficiencies and therefore will no longer require monitoring by the FATF".[32]

Modern Standards

The legislation adopted in 2000 brought amendments to many existing laws. The leading elements are to be found in the Mutual Legal Assistance Act (15 September 2000), Amendment of the Narcotics Act (25 October), amendments to the Criminal Code (25 October) and the Due Diligence Act and Due Diligence Order (6 November and 5 December respectively). They were, therefore, in place by the time that the amended Money Laundering Directive of the European Parliament and of the Council of 4 December 2001 came into force.[33]

Mutual Legal Assistance

Few subjects cause so much international irritation as Mutual Legal Assistance (an official request by one state to another for help in criminal investigations, including if necessary the extradition of persons accused). Differences between national legal systems, philosophies and procedures, and the need to have a

---

[31] "Liechtensteiner Vaterland", 4 February 2002
[32] FATF Reviews to Identify Non-Co-operative Countries or Territories of 22 June 2001 (paragraphs 27–30) and of 21 June 2002 (paragraphs 93–95).
[33] Official Journal of the European Communities, 28 December 2001, L344/76 to 81.

request precisely formulated in terms that will enable the receiving state to act on it, all too often provoke complaints and accusations of bad faith between otherwise friendly countries.[34] In the case of Liechtenstein, however, there were good grounds for dissatisfaction. This was probably the single most important reason why the FATF member states took so strong a line against Liechtenstein.

The Liechtenstein Government maintains that even under the old system some 90% of cases were handled promptly and efficiently. It was certainly ready to help in the high-profile cases of Norgren (insider trading, 1989) and Maxwell (1992). Some cases, however, dragged on for years and were never completed satisfactorily. This was because there were three separate formal procedures to be gone through (sixteen steps in all), with twelve possibilities for appealing at different stages. The new law, based on Austrian legislation, allows for only three main stages (evaluation of admissibility by the Ministry of Justice, substantive examination by the court and execution by the court with the possibility of appeal). These can be taken quite quickly. Procedures for the enforcement of foreign confiscation orders and the transfer of objects and documents have been reformed and simplified.

Money Laundering Offences

The tightening of criminal provisions for money laundering entailed a series of changes to the Criminal Code, the Narcotics Act and other related criminal legislation. The laundering of "own funds" became an offence. The element of "knowledge" (always difficult to prove) was removed; "intent" alone became sufficient grounds for conviction. The list of predicate offences (i.e. prior offences by which money had been illegally generated) was extended from crimes to misdemeanours in relation to corruption offences. The offence of active bribery was extended to include bribery of foreign officials and office holders. The seizure, forfeit and confiscation of the proceeds of crime were introduced in line with the 1996 amendments to the Austrian Criminal Code. These sanctions now apply also to assets of members of criminal organisations as newly defined, and to assets resulting from criminal acts committed in foreign countries. (A very necessary provision, in view of Liechtenstein's small area.) Punishment for founding or belonging to a criminal organisation has been increased. The threshold of the value of criminal assets attracting prison sentences of from six months to five years was reduced from 150,000 to 75,000 francs (about £32,000).

---

[34] The Lord Mayor of London, Alderman Michael Oliver, was alarmed to be told in South Africa during a recent visit that requests for British assistance were allegedly taking "many months and, in at least one case, two years". ("Financial Times", 9 August 2002.)

Due Diligence

The Due Diligence Act 2000 now extends to everyone who, on a professional basis, accepts or keeps in custody other people's assets or helps to invest or transfer them, ranging from banks and fiduciaries to bureaux de change. Together with the provisions of the Due Diligence Order, it eliminated certain potential loopholes in previous legislation. It strengthened the obligation to be clear about a client's financial background, the purpose of transactions and the origin of assets. It is no longer a matter simply of knowing one's client; a full and continuing profile must be built up. For example, activities on behalf of a company would require due diligence on that company to be carried out. Proceeds from the sale of a house would need to be accompanied by full and satisfactory documentation. Assets from a foundation would have to be accompanied by the registration details of the foundation, the names of the directors and a satisfactory account of the source of the funds. In the case of a commercial company, substantiation of each transaction would be needed.

A "strong" suspicion of money laundering is no longer the threshold for making a report to the authorities; suspicion alone makes a report compulsory. A report may be made before a business relationship has started. There is immunity from legal liability for breach of confidentiality, provided the service provider who makes the report to the authorities has not acted in a grossly negligent or intentionally harmful manner. A service provider may not inform his contractual partner or third parties that he has reported them or that investigations are in train until he has been authorised by the FSA or until ten working days have elapsed. If necessary, the authorities may extend this period by another twenty working days. The act regulates co-operation by authorities within the country and also by Liechtenstein authorities with foreign powers. The Due Diligence Executive Order, *inter alia,* provides for checks by independent auditors and requires firms to maintain records, appoint compliance officers, train staff and draw up clear guidelines.

Personnel and Accommodation

Lack of qualified personnel has always been a problem in Liechtenstein. It contributed to the deficiencies indicated by the Council of Europe and the FATF. The appointment of four new judges for the Princely Court ("Landgericht") and two supporting staff was approved in October 2000. Three of these judges are Austrian citizens and one is Swiss, as is common in Liechtenstein. A third bench was created in the High Court of Appeal ("Obergericht") to lighten the workload. The number of public prosecutors was raised from three to seven. As noted above, a Head of the Prosecution Service (Robert Wallner) was appointed and his office was reorganised. Extra support staff were found for his office.

The strength of the National Police was raised from 74 to 89; it is planned to rise to 130 by 2007. A special police unit (EWOK, consisting of eight persons) was established to combat economic and organised crime. A special Unit for the Enforcement of Due Diligence (DDU, four persons) was approved in October 2001. A separate Financial Intelligence Unit (FIU, six persons) was approved in February 2001 to receive and investigate intelligence about economic crime. This unit is responsible for sharing intelligence with foreign FIUs. It is a member of the Egmont Group (an informal international gathering of FIUs). When Germany, slightly later than Liechtenstein, established its own FIU, it was the Liechtenstein FIU that introduced its new German colleagues to the Group. The creation of these new units has enabled the FSA (now eight persons) to concentrate on its supervisory duties.

The Prosecutor's Office, the FIU, the DDU and the FSA are housed together in a state-of-the-art modern building in the centre of Vaduz, a co-location that would be the envy of many supervisory authorities.

The Consequences of Change

Liechtenstein's reputation suffered greatly between 1999 and 2001, but the detailed and demanding nature of the new legislation is beginning to be appreciated abroad. This legislation is the more easily enforced because Liechtenstein is a small country. The Liechtenstein Government considers that the standard of the new anti-money laundering legislation is superior to that of the Wolfsberg Principles (adopted by twelve leading international banks in October 2000).[35] In the opinion of the Liechtenstein Bankers Association, the legislation meets the requirements of the 1991 and 2001 EC Money Laundering Directives and in some respects exceeds them.[36] The new FIU is already playing an active international role. For example, it was host at a meeting of Council of Europe money laundering and terrorist financing typology experts in Vaduz on 9–11 April 2002.

So far as the author has been able to ascertain, Mutual Legal Assistance is now working smoothly in the case of the United Kingdom, which made six requests in 2000. (It had become a serious irritant in UK-Liechtenstein relations.) A new Treaty on Mutual Legal Assistance with the USA was signed in July 2002. In 2000 Vaduz received a total of 301 requests for assistance from foreign states, of which 134 came from Switzerland, 54 from Germany, 30 from Austria and 12 from Italy. Liechtenstein made 188 requests. In 2001 Liechtenstein received 385 requests and made 300. In 2002 it received 304 and made 472. There have been numerous convictions abroad and a number of foreigners have chosen to leave Liechtenstein.

[35] Liechtenstein Government briefing of foreign ambassadors, 5 June 2002
[36] "The EC Money Laundering Directive and its Implementation in the Principality of Liechtenstein", by Michael Breuer, published by the LBA, Vaduz, 2002

The new measures have not brought the financial services industry into crisis, which would have been the case if Liechtenstein really had been a "criminal state". The repercussions seem perfectly manageable, insofar as they can be distinguished from the effects of the current difficult market conditions. For example, in 2001 assets under LGT BiL's management fell by 5.1 billion francs (10.7%). Of this, some 3.4 billion francs (about £1.4 billion, or 7% of the total under management) represented asset outflows, the larger part of which, in the bank's opinion, was related to the new "Know Your Client" principles and involved funds which had previously arrived via intermediaries.[37] In October 2002 only 423 accounts throughout the entire Liechtenstein banking system were still blocked on KYC grounds.

For the first time, more fiduciaries have deregistered than registered. The casualties have mostly been among smaller operators who have been unable to cope with the extra paperwork required or to recruit additional qualified staff. According to the Minister for the Economy, Hansjörg Frick,[38] in the first eleven months of 2002 3,758 new domiciliary and holding companies were entered in the Public Register against 4,545 for the whole of 2001. In the same period 6,684 companies were liquidated against 6,309 for the whole of 2001. These figures represent a net decrease of 4,690 in 23 months (about 6%). Some of the decrease will have been due to market conditions. Where clients have left because of KYC, it shows that the system is working.

The Liechtenstein Government has set up a working group to consider a repositioning of financial services as part of the economy of the whole country, and a commission to review the law on foundations. Among other measures, it intends to establish a single integrated supervisory authority which will exercise the functions at present divided between the Government, the FSA, the Office for the Public Economy the DDU and the Insurance Supervisory Authority. The new authority will be completely independent.

Liechtenstein's efforts to combat the financing of terrorism have been publicly praised by Jimmy Gurulé, Under Secretary of the US Treasury for Enforcement: "Liechtenstein and the US have fought side by side to expose, isolate and incapacitate the financial holding of terrorist financiers.

To suggest that Liechtenstein is anything but a key ally in the financial war against terrorism is simply wrong".[39]

---

[37] LGT BiL Annual Report 2001 and the "Liechtensteiner Volksblatt", 6 March 2002. Prince Hans-Adam told the "Liechtensteiner Vaterland" for 11 December 2001, "We have noticed that considerable sums have been withdrawn. Interestingly, so far as we could ascertain most of this money has flowed back into OECD countries which are not as strict as Liechtenstein".
[38] "Liechtensteiner Volksblatt", 23 December 2002
[39] Letter published in the London "Observer", 17 November 2002.

For the time being, the last word rests with the International Monetary Fund which, from 28 October to 8 November 2002, made a thorough and objective examination of Liechtenstein's supervision and regulation of its financial services at the Liechtenstein Government's invitation. For the Liechtenstein side, this process included three months of preparation, drafting answers to about 650 detailed questions and holding 27 meetings in Liechtenstein with a team of eight highly qualified IMF experts. The IMF's findings were published in September 2003. The report commended Liechtenstein's high quality modern legislation and "high level of compliance with international standards for anti-money laundering and combating the financing of terrorism". It welcomed and supported the Government's intention to set up an independent and integrated financial supervisory authority. This, the IMF thought, would add strength and flexibility to the system and would help with the problem of staff resources. The report noted that the legal authority to share information with foreign supervisory authorities was in line with EU requirements.

It also noted the "very dedicated and professional staff in each of the agencies carrying out their tasks diligently"[40] and that "the Bankers Association, the Funds Association and the Trustees Association appear to be very professional and quite proactive in their approach to regulation."[41] So far as Mutual Legal Assistance (MLA) to foreign governments was concerned, the IMF found that the situation had "changed dramatically for the better" The backlog of older requests had been largely cleared.

The length of time in providing MLA had fallen sharply. It was not Liechtenstein's practice to refuse requests on the grounds that there were no bilateral or multilateral treaties or agreements with the requesting state.[42]

The IMF's main criticism was that bank and investment company supervision and, to some extent, the supervision of insurance companies continued to be under-staffed.

To this, the Government replied that to begin with it had necessarily had to give priority to fighting money laundering and the financing of terrorism. It was however already (in June 2003) in the process of filling two new posts in the area of bank supervision, and further measures would follow. The Government said that many of the IMF's detailed recommendations for new legislation and administrative procedures were already being implemented; others would be given serious study (for example, the creation of a special licence for asset managers). The Government's general reaction was one of pleasure that its efforts had

---

[40] IMF report, Vol I, Preface, page 5.
[41] IMF report, Vol. II, page 30, paragraph 39.
[42] IMF report, Vol. II, pages 89–90.

been noted and had borne fruit, and determination not to rest on its laurels in a rapidly changing world.[43]

No regulatory and supervisory system can guarantee total protection against criminal abuse. However, the recent reforms have put Liechtenstein in a much stronger position to combat such abuse, to vindicate its reputation and to promote its financial services sector internationally.

---

[43] Press statements by Prime Minister Hasler and Dr Stephan Ochsner (Director, Due Diligence Unit), 27 June, 2003.

BANK SECRECY AND TAX COMPETITION

Bank secrecy or confidentiality exists in every country that has a financial services sector. The German term Bankkundengeheimnis (literally, "bank client secrecy") makes the important point that it is above all a duty owed by the bank to the client, not a privilege arrogated by the bank; although a strong legal reinforcement of that duty can certainly be a commercial asset to a bank. In common law countries, the legal framework tends to be based on the notion of contract between bank and client or of the legal professional privilege which exists between lawyer and client. In some continental European countries the banker is bound by a civil duty of confidentiality, violation of which can make him liable under civil, but not criminal, law. In Germany the matter is largely governed by the concept of contract. In Luxembourg, a banker's duty of secrecy is reinforced by Article 458 of the Criminal Code, which provides for penalties of imprisonment from eight days to six months and fines of from 10,000 to 50,000 former Luxembourg francs. In Austria, bank secrecy has constitutional force except in certain defined circumstances including criminal proceedings.

In Switzerland, bank secrecy is governed by contractual, civil and administrative law. Property administrators and lawyers are not subject to bank secrecy legislation but are bound by professional confidentiality. In addition, Article 47 of the 1934 Federal Banking Law provides for penalties of up to six months imprisonment or a fine of up to 50,000 francs for a deliberate breach of bank secrecy, or up 30,000 francs in the case of negligence. This law was enacted after Nazi German legislation obliged all German citizens, under threat of the death penalty, to inform the authorities of all funds held abroad. The motives for the Swiss law are still a matter for debate. There is no doubt that it helped to protect foreign clients, even if the prime motive at the time may have been the deterrence of all foreign espionage and the defence of the country's economy.[1]

---

[1] For a brief comparison of certain countries' legislation, see "Money Laundering" by Guy Stessens (Cambridge University Press, 2000), pages 312–318 and "Das Bankkundengeheimniss in Europa" by Heinz Klaus (BHW Trust Reg, Vaduz, 2001), passim. On the origins of the Swiss legislation of 1934, see Stessens, op. cit., page 317 and "Geschichte des Bankwesens in Liechtenstein (1945–1980)" by Alexander Meili (Verlag Huber, Frauenfeld, Stuttgart, Vienna), page 66.

In Liechtenstein, bank secrecy was first made a formal legal obligation by the Banking Act of 1960. But the concept clearly dates back to legislation in 1923, and personal privacy has always been taken for granted as part of the country's culture. Personal privacy is indeed explicitly protected by the Constitution. In the close-knit community of a small village, knowledge is power. Today's librarian, tax official, village councillor or teacher might be tomorrow's Head of Government. All the more reason, therefore, why bank officials should be legally obliged to keep a citizen's private affairs confidential from all comers, including the authorities. The tax officials, too, are bound to silence vis-à-vis the other Liechtenstein authorities.[2]

The 1960 Act provided for imprisonment for up to six months or a fine of up to 20,000 francs for deliberate breach of bank secrecy (it is possible to combine the sentences) or a fine of up to 10,000 francs for negligence. The fines have since been made more flexible to take account of inflation and personal circumstances. There is no time limit to the obligation of secrecy. As in Switzerland, lawyers, trustees and other intermediaries are subject to their own legally binding rules of secrecy.[3]

The Limits of Bank Secrecy

In Liechtenstein, as in other countries including Switzerland, bank secrecy is not absolute. In civil cases a bank may refuse to give evidence. In criminal cases, the obligation of secrecy and the right of silence do not apply. The bank must produce documents if required and, if it fails to do so, the examining magistrate has the power to order a search. Anonymous accounts such as the Austrian "Sparbuch" are unknown in Liechtenstein. A client may use a number or pseudonym if he wishes, but his identity and personal details are always known to the bank and there is no protection in case of criminal activity.

Bank secrecy may be lifted whenever knowledge of a person's private financial data is essential to the conduct of domestic or, subject to Liechtenstein's multilateral and bilateral commitments, foreign criminal proceedings. It is therefore no obstacle to the detection and repression of money laundering and terrorism. After the terrorist attacks in the United States on 11 September 2001 Liechtenstein was quick to commit itself to UN Resolution 1373 on terrorist financing, to report

---

[2] Meili (page 65) quotes an amusing anecdote from the early days of the Bank in Liechtenstein when the manager once rebuked an employee for breaking banking secrecy because he had told colleagues that the chairman's child was suffering from measles.

[3] Under Article 121 of the Liechtenstein Criminal Code they are subject to the same penalties as bank staff. So are doctors, dentists, pharmacists, youth, marriage and family counsellors, social workers, hospital staff, etc. Personal privacy is therefore underpinned by the law in many areas of daily life. The prison sentences for breaches of industrial or commercial confidentiality or for economic espionage are potentially even more severe (up to three or five years respectively).

to the UN Counter-Terrorism Committee in December 2001, to implement UN measures against the Taliban and to set up a national task force co-ordinated by the Liechtenstein FIU with the aim of tracking suspected persons and entities on the basis of the new Due Diligence legislation. The accounts of suspected persons were blocked. There was, and continues to be, close co-operation and exchange of information with foreign law enforcement agencies under the Mutual Legal Assistance legislation.

Banking Secrecy and Fiscal Offences

The Legal Assistance Law of 15 September 2000 imposes certain limitations on the granting of foreign requests for legal assistance. One, which is not uncommon in legislation of this kind, states that the request must not "violate public order or other essential interests" of the Principality (Article 2). For a foreign request to be accepted, it must be guaranteed that the state making the request would comply with an identical request made by Liechtenstein. A Liechtenstein authority may not, save in exceptional circumstances, make a request in a matter where Liechtenstein itself could not guarantee reciprocity. However, the absence of an international agreement is no bar to Liechtenstein's making a request if the law would permit Liechtenstein to comply with an identical request (Article 3 (1), (2) and (4), somewhat compressed). Extradition and legal assistance are not permissible for political offences[4] (Article 14), for military offences or for offences connected with taxes, monopolies, customs or foreign currencies or the controlled movement of goods or foreign trade (Article 15), or where human rights are unlikely to be observed in the other country concerned (Article 19).

Legal assistance may not be granted if the alleged offence would not be legally punishable or extraditable under Liechtenstein law (Article 51 (1) (1)). In Liechtenstein, tax evasion is a civil, not a criminal, offence. This approach is based on the concept that the citizen is to be regarded as a trustworthy and informed person rather than an administered unit. Together with the stringent bank secrecy legislation, this means that Liechtenstein will not help other countries in fiscal cases. This position is consistent with the European Convention on Mutual Assistance in Criminal Matters, which Liechtenstein signed as long ago as 1970, but it attracts strong criticism from many European governments. The Liechtenstein philosophy is that a breach of the financial, economic and administrative regulations of one state need not necessarily be considered by another state as a punishable offence. (The case of Nazi Germany in and after 1933 offers an extreme example. So does the Soviet Union until its collapse. It is possible to think of comparable examples in the modern world.) Liechtenstein considers that

---

[4] However, terrorism is to be made a criminal offence in order to close a potential legal loophole.

there is no moral obligation, and no obligation under international law, to help other states in collecting taxes.

There is no great incentive for tax evasion in Liechtenstein. Tax rates are moderate. The taxes are accepted as being intended to meet the needs of the State rather than to serve a partisan or ideological purpose. Tax policy is long-term, stable and predictable. The intention is to leave as much freedom as possible to the citizens to decide on the best use for their own money. Tax decisions are taken close to the citizens, and sometimes by them. Central and local government expenditure is transparent and closely monitored. The administration is not plagued by fraud. There are no large and wasteful bureaucracies and no speculative grand projects whose budgetary outcome is uncertain.

Since Liechtenstein is a small place, the tax authorities are likely to have a shrewd idea of what people are earning despite the legislation on privacy. In the case of suspected tax evasion (e. g. false or incomplete completion of a tax return) banks and other financial services are, as in Switzerland, not allowed to divulge information to the tax authorities. The authorities are, however, entitled to demand information from the taxpayer himself and to examine business records and accounts as much as is necessary for tax purposes. If matters cannot be settled amicably, they will be resolved by a civil court decision which may involve a financial penalty.

Tax fraud (falsification of accounts or documents) is, as in Switzerland, a criminal matter. As such it is handled in a magistrate's court ("Schöffengericht") and bank secrecy does not apply. However, for the time being at least Liechtenstein will not allow bank secrecy to be lifted in response to foreign requests for help in tax fraud matters. The only exceptions are Switzerland (in the case of VAT fraud, because of the customs union)[5] and the USA (page 333 below). The IMF has recommended that Liechtenstein should review its interpretation of what constitutes a fiscal offence.[6]

The refusal to help other countries in fiscal matters does not mean that the Liechtenstein authorities will deny assistance in a money laundering case or a terrorist financing case where fiscal matters are involved. In such cases assistance (including the lifting of bank secrecy) will certainly be granted, subject to a proviso that the information given may not be used to prosecute a fiscal matter.

The OECD Initiative on Harmful Tax Competition

Decolonisation gave political freedom to a number of small territories that were left economically dependent on their former colonial masters, on the vagaries

---

[5] Klaus, op. cit., pages 46–47.
[6] IMF report, Vol. II, page 91.

of tourism or on single crops such as bananas. In many cases their response was to create financial centres and tax havens, often with the help of the former colonial powers, in order to accumulate capital and to develop and diversify their economies. As in other areas of economic life, globalisation and information technology speeded the process and contributed customers. The demise of the Soviet Union brought new potential financial centres onto the scene. Liechtenstein, with its highly developed industry and long established financial services, was not comparable with the new arrivals in the Caribbean and South Pacific; but, inevitably, it was swept up into the growing concern of larger countries who began to be worried about losing control of their national tax bases.

In 1996 the ministers of the member states of the OECD called on that organisation to "develop measures to counter the distorting effects of harmful tax competition on investment and financing decisions and the consequences for national tax bases". The heads of government of the G7 countries endorsed this project. In 1998 the OECD's Committee on Fiscal Affairs produced a report entitled, "Harmful Tax Competition: An Emerging Global Issue". The report paid tribute to the beneficial effects of globalisation and liberalisation on economic growth and living standards. But it argued (paragraph 23) that globalisation had also had "the negative effect of opening up new ways by which companies and individuals can minimise and avoid taxes and in which countries can exploit these new opportunities by developing tax policies aimed primarily at diverting financial and other geographically mobile capital. These actions induce potential distortions in the patterns of trade and investment and reduce global welfare... These schemes can erode national tax bases of other countries, may alter the structure of taxation... ...and may hamper the application of progressive tax rates and the achievement of redistributive goals." The report recognised (paragraph 26) that there were no particular reasons why any two countries should have the same level and structure of taxation. "Countries should remain free to design their own tax systems as long as they abide by internationally accepted standards in doing so."

The report set out to define tax-haven jurisdictions and harmful preferential tax régimes in non-haven jurisdictions. It suggested four factors in identifying a tax haven:
- No or only nominal taxation on relevant income
- Lack of effective international exchange of information on taxpayers benefiting from the low tax jurisdiction
- Lack of transparency in the operation of legislative, legal or administrative provisions
- Absence of a requirement that activity be substantial.[7]

---

[7] Summarised from paragraphs 52–56.

The report recognised (paragraph 89) that in the absence of co-ordinated international action there was little incentive for a country, whether or not it was a member of OECD, to eliminate the activities described as harmful since those activities would simply move elsewhere. It called for "severe counter-measures" against countries with extreme types of harmful tax competition. It set out a list of recommendations for member and non-member countries, which included the promotion of dialogue with non-members and the compilation of a list of tax haven jurisdictions.

Luxembourg and Switzerland (both founding members of OECD) abstained from approving the report and its recommendations. Luxembourg considered the report one-sided in confining itself to financial activities and excluding industrial and commercial activities. It did not share the report's "implicit belief that bank secrecy is necessarily a source of harmful tax competition". Limitations on the exchange of information that were based on international and national laws should not be considered a criterion for identifying a harmful preferential tax regime and a tax haven.[8] Luxembourg supported international co-operation against the abuse of bank secrecy in criminal matters and the criminal violation of tax law, but administrative assistance in tax matters should be subject to certain conditions and precise limits. The report, it said, ignored the validity of the "coexistence model", in which withholding taxes constituted an alternative to exchange of information. Luxembourg was concerned that the report "lends credence to the so-called criterion of reputation – a criterion without any objective basis".

Switzerland considered that a certain degree of competition in tax matters was positive. "In particular, it discourages governments from adopting confiscatory regimes, which hamper entrepreneurial spirit and hurt the economy, and it avoids alignment of tax burdens at the highest level." Switzerland found the report "partial and unbalanced"; it had failed to take non-tax factors in economic competitiveness into account. The report gave "unacceptable protection" to "countries with high levels of taxation which is, moreover, contrary to the economic philosophy of the OECD". The report ignored the structural diversity of existing tax regimes, such as the withholding tax, which had advantages compared with the exchange of information. Switzerland considered it legitimate and necessary to protect the confidentiality of personal data, in keeping with its legal system. It described the report's approach to territories that made tax attraction a pillar of their economies as "selective and repressive" and a discouragement to their co-operation.[9]

---

[8] This sentence represents the author's interpretation of some rather convoluted English.
[9] Annex II, pages 73–78.

Luxembourg and Switzerland have maintained their abstentions on subsequent reports and recommendations.

The Committee on Fiscal Affairs' next report, "Towards Global Tax Co-operation" (16 June 2000), responded to criticism that the 1998 report had been drafted largely with the interests of revenue authorities in mind by saying, "…the project is not primarily about collecting taxes and is not intended to promote the harmonisation of income taxes or tax structures generally within or outside the OECD, nor is it about dictating to any country what should be the appropriate level of tax rates. Rather, the project is about ensuring that the burden of taxation is fairly shared and that tax should not be the dominant factor in making capital allocation decisions." By promoting international co-operation, it would "support the effective fiscal sovereignty of countries over the design of their tax systems".[10]

The committee said that dialogue with a number of jurisdictions had begun. Reporting on individual jurisdictions was not intended to be "condemnatory or final"; the process "aims to move forward co-operatively so long as a co-operative approach bears fruit".[11] Having listed 47 preferential tax regimes in OECD member states that it deemed to be potentially harmful, the report named 35 jurisdictions, including Liechtenstein, as meeting the tax haven criteria of the 1998 report.[12] These jurisdictions were invited to commit themselves to an agreed schedule of progressive changes to eliminate their harmful tax practices by 31 December 2005, to agree not to enhance existing regimes or introduce new ones meanwhile and to undertake an annual progress review with the OECD's Forum on Harmful Tax Practices. Failing that, they would be placed on a List of Uncooperative Tax Havens. The Committee on Fiscal Affairs would work out a list of possible coordinated "defensive measures" against them, both fiscal and non-tax in nature.[13] Such measures would be for consideration by the individual member states.

The 2001 Progress Report (on which Belgium and Portugal abstained as well as Luxembourg and Switzerland) said that the OECD project sought to encourage an environment in which free and fair tax competition could take place. After regional and bilateral dialogue with numerous jurisdictions the committee had decided to drop the criterion of "no substantial activity" and to seek commitments only to transparency and effective exchange of information.[14] Such commitments were, *inter alia*, to ensure that information could be supplied to another country's tax authority "relevant to a specific tax inquiry". However, in

---

[10] Executive Summary, page 5, second paragraph.
[11] ibid., page 6, second paragraph.
[12] Paragraph 17.
[13] Paragraphs 35–36.
[14] Paragraphs 27–28. Press reports suggest that these discussions were not easy, and that at one point the Commonwealth Secretariat acted as mediator. ("Financial Times", 17 January 2001)

the case of a criminal tax matter, the requested jurisdiction was to provide information without a requirement that the conduct being investigated would constitute a crime in its own territory (i.e. without regard to "double criminality"); and in the case of a civil tax matter the requested jurisdiction should provide information regardless of whether it had an interest in obtaining the information for its own domestic tax purposes.[15] These were commitments that conflicted with Liechtenstein's long-standing legislation and practice. 31 jurisdictions made the required commitments. Liechtenstein's further dialogue with the OECD was not successful. On 18 April 2002 Liechtenstein was listed as an Uncooperative Tax Haven along with Andorra, Liberia, Monaco, The Marshall Islands, Nauru and Vanuatu.

The European Union: Withholding Tax or Exchange of Information?

The right to set taxes and taxation levels goes to the heart of sovereignty and democracy. In the European Union many national leaders, the Commission and many members of the European Parliament advocate the harmonisation of taxes and the abolition of the national veto on tax matters. The areas envisaged range from VAT (where harmonisation is already quite far advanced) and corporate taxation to, in the minds of some, personal taxation. Advocates argue variously that harmonisation would help to complete the Single Market, support the Single Currency and promote European political unification. Opponents argue that it would be uncompetitive, and destructive of the sort of innovation and prosperity that have, for example, been created in Ireland. It is likely to become an increasingly difficult issue.[16]

In 1999 the Commission revived a proposal, previously opposed by Mrs Thatcher, for a directive on a common system of withholding tax on interest income paid to non-resident savers. The German Government in particular was worried about the number of German citizens who were illegally failing to declare interest on their savings banked in Luxembourg. However, such a tax would have damaged the $3.5 trillion (£1,864 billion) London eurobond market, which had grown up in the City precisely as a result of the US Government's having imposed a withholding tax in its own territory. At the European Council meeting in Feira (Portugal) on 20 June 2000 the British Government secured an agreement which appeared to avert the threat of a withholding tax. The solution was based on the principle that within the EU, member states would supply the

---

[15] Paragraphs 37–38.

[16] In his speech at Cardiff on 28 November 2002 the British Prime Minister said, "All Member States in practice have their red lines on Qualified Majority Voting, some of which must remain – for Britain on national control of taxes for example". The Liechtenstein Government would no doubt agree with the underlying principle.

tax authorities of the saver's own country with information about the interest paid. For a transitional period of seven years Austria, Belgium and Luxembourg would impose a withholding tax on interest paid to non-residents at 15% for the first three years and 20% thereafter. They would transfer 75% of the revenue generated to the saver's country of residence.[17]

However, for obvious reasons the EU also agreed that the introduction of the legislation should be conditional on agreement on "equivalent measures" being reached with certain third countries. The EU was to decide by the end of 2002, on the basis of unanimity, on the implementation of the Feira agreement. Among the key third countries to be approached were Switzerland and the USA. Liechtenstein, Monaco, Andorra, San Marino and dependencies of member states such as Jersey and Guernsey were also to be tackled. In the case of Switzerland (and Liechtenstein) the "equivalent measure" required was the effective abolition of bank secrecy through the exchange of information about clients belonging to EU member states. The European Commission concentrated on Switzerland first, as the largest of the European non-EU financial centres.

Switzerland repeatedly made the point that an agreement with only the six third-party countries mentioned in the Feira conclusions would carry the risk that savings investments by nationals of EU member countries would flow out of Europe to financial centres in Asia. It remains to be seen how effectively the Asian financial centres can be associated with the EU project.

The EU-Swiss Negotiations

Although there are similarities between Liechtenstein and Switzerland on this question, there are different dimensions to the two countries' relationships to the EU. Liechtenstein is closer to the EU, in that it is a member of the EEA (although the EEA agreement does not cover fiscal matters). After the Swiss people's refusal to join the EEA in 1992, Switzerland and the EU opened negotiations on seven separate subjects, or sectors, ranging from market access for agricultural products to the free movement of persons, in order to fill certain important gaps in the relationship which the refusal had left open. The Commission was wary of Swiss "cherry-picking". It therefore insisted that no single agreement should come into force until the whole package had been agreed. It termed this "appropriate parallelism". The negotiations lasted from 1993 to 1998. The Swiss people approved the package by referendum in May 2000. Switzerland and the EU then agreed to enter negotiations about a further ten subjects: some new, others left over from the earlier negotiations. These subjects included the taxation of interest on

---

[17] See also "European Tax Harmonisation", Theresa Villiers MEP (Centre for Policy Studies, 2001), pages 45–48.

savings and the prevention of fraud (at the EU's wish) and Swiss participation in the Schengen and Dublin system[18] (at Switzerland's wish). This time it was Switzerland, wary of cherry-picking by the EU, that insisted on the package approach. It wanted the negotiations to reach a "swift and balanced conclusion" in "a parallel and co-ordinated manner". Formal negotiations on four of the subjects, including fraud prevention, began in July 2001. Negotiations on the others, including taxation of interest and Schengen, began in June 2002 as soon as the Commission had agreed its own negotiating mandate.

In 1999 the Commission had discussed with Switzerland a "coexistence model" which would have offered a choice between levying a withholding tax and providing information. However, the Feira decision narrowed the Commission's options. The stakes within the EU were high. Having put itself under time pressure by its own decision, the EU pressed Switzerland for agreement so vigorously that in October 2002 it took the highly unusual step of openly discussing sanctions against a friendly state. The public rhetoric became strong. "I cannot stand Switzerland cheating on tax", wrote Commissioner Bolkestein, adding that the EU was not asking Switzerland to change its laws, practices or traditions concerning its own citizens.[19] For their part, Swiss and Liechtenstein bankers speculated that London and other EU financial centres would not be averse to picking up such business as might flow their way as a result of any weakening of their own centres.

The Swiss Government maintained that it had no interest in profiting from tax evasion in the EU. It argued that its withholding tax of 35% on savings income (deducted by its banks at source) was steep enough to make tax evasion unprofitable. Subject to the EU's negotiating similar arrangements with the main financial centres outside the EU and (where applicable) with the dependencies of the EU member states themselves, Switzerland proposed an arrangement by which it would continue to tax the interest on foreign capital of EU residents at 35% but would transfer 75% of the tax deducted directly to EU member states. This, it argued, would be simpler, and more profitable to the other countries concerned, than exchanging masses of information. It was willing to give EU residents a free choice between paying the tax and having their details reported to their home countries. Furthermore, it was willing to offer legal assistance in cases of tax fraud (though not evasion) by companies as well as by individuals. These proposals, it said, went beyond the Feira requirements.[20] Switzerland would not, however, dismantle or adapt its bank secrecy legislation: any such measure was likely to be

---

[18] For co-operation and the exchange of information on European internal security matters, e.g. police, justice, asylum and migration.
[19] "Financial Times", 7 October 2002.
[20] The Swiss position is set out in www.europa.admin.ch (CH-EU Bilateral Negotiations)

opposed by a popular vote, which could be launched by 50,000 signatures. In short, such a proposal was not negotiable.

Although the limelight was on Switzerland, it was not clear where the United States stood. There were signs of American reluctance to become involved, out of concern for their own financial services industry and perhaps also because of the extra-territorial implications of the EU's proposal (extra-territoriality being a perennially thorny problem on either side of the Atlantic). There were also divisions within the EU. A meeting of the Economic and Finance Ministers' Council (ECOFIN) on 9 December 2002 failed to reach agreement, and the negotiations within the EU over-ran the deadline.

On 21 January 2003 ECOFIN eventually reached a hard-fought political compromise. The text, which bears signs of complex negotiation,[21] repeated the EU's ultimate objective of securing the exchange of information on as wide a base as possible. ECOFIN decided that it had received satisfactory assurances from the USA about "equivalent measures" (apparently, on the strength of the USA's network of bilateral treaties). It asked the Commission to negotiate agreements with Switzerland, Liechtenstein, Monaco, Andorra and San Marino on the basis of a steadily increasing rate of withholding tax, rising to 35% as of 1 January 2010. The agreements were to contain a review clause for consultations at least every three years about the functioning of the agreements. Switzerland was to grant exchange of information on request "for all criminal or civil cases of fraud or similar misbehaviour on the part of taxpayers." Austria, Belgium and Luxembourg were to move to the automatic exchange of information if and when the Commission entered into agreement (by unanimity in ECOFIN) with Switzerland, Liechtenstein, San Marino, Monaco and Andorra on the exchange of information upon request as defined in the OECD Agreement on Exchange of Information on Tax Matters, and if and when ECOFIN unanimously agreed that the USA had similarly committed itself to the exchange of information on request. The Commission was to continue to press for exchange of information and to report back to ECOFIN before 2007.

The Swiss authorities took cautious but positive note of these proposals. Switzerland and the EU have since reached agreement in principle on a treaty (approved by EU finance ministers on 3 June 2003) which will ensure that the EU's directive on the taxation of savings income cannot be circumvented via Switzerland but which will uphold Swiss law and bank confidentiality. Switzerland is ready to sign the treaty once agreement has been reached on the other subjects under negotiation.

Among those subjects, EU-Swiss negotiations on fraud (e.g. cigarette

---

[21] 5566/03, FISC 8, dated 22 January 2003.

smuggling) have been in progress since 2001. Switzerland has offered to extend its help beyond customs duty fraud to consumption taxes such as VAT, if an offence that is also criminal in Switzerland would attract there a sentence of at least six months imprisonment. Switzerland would allow EU officials to be present at investigations. But Switzerland has been unable to accept the EU's demand that the full *acquis communautaire* should apply in such matters. In this, as in other current or pending negotiations such as Schengen/Dublin and the liberalisation of cross-border services, issues concerning mutual legal assistance in fiscal matters and the application of the *acquis communautaire* will have their own potential linkages to the savings tax question.

Liechtenstein's Position

The OECD and EU initiatives once again embroiled Liechtenstein in global and European politics.

Prince Hans-Adam's comments on the OECD's tax project were characteristically direct. In his Speech from the Throne on 29 March 2001 he described the OECD as aiming at a world-wide tax cartel. A comprehensive and world-wide exchange of information would leave citizens completely transparent before the state in all their financial affairs,[22] obliged permanently (unlike the common criminal) to prove their innocence to the authorities. The intentions might be good; but the logical consequence would be a world government called the OECD, responsible to nobody except perhaps a few politicians pulling the strings in the background. Threats of sanctions against non-members were, he said, a clear breach of international law. If the OECD had proposals, there were fora where they could be openly discussed and where the interests of the taxpayers would not be forgotten.

In the following months the Liechtenstein Government said that it was ready to co-operate with the OECD, in the confidence that its own tax system was transparent. It had a strong preference for co-operation based on bilateral treaties negotiated between sovereign states.[23] In its letter of 14 February 2002 to the OECD, the Government pointed out that taxation was a core area of state sovereignty. It would be prepared to co-operate with the OECD on tax matters

---

[22] The Prince's comments about the "glass man" may seem far-fetched, but in 2002 even the United Kingdom provided two examples of attempted invasions of privacy. These were defeated. The House of Lords ruled against the Inland Revenue's practice of forcing companies and wealthy individuals to disclose confidential legal advice. Lord Hoffman referred to the human right to legal professional privilege. ("Financial Times", 17 May 2002.) Under parliamentary and public pressure, the British Government withdrew for further consultation proposals which would have allowed seven Government departments, all local authorities, a number of agencies such as the Financial Services Authority, the Office of Fair Trading and the Food Standards Agency and also the Royal Mail to eavesdrop on telephone calls, e-mails and post. ("Financial Times", 18 and 19 June 2002.)

[23] Statement by the Head of Government, Otmar Hasler. ("Liechtensteiner Volksblatt", 28 February 2002)

subject to four conditions: Liechtenstein must receive equal treatment with OECD members and non-members; procedures must be fair, transparent and equally applied; as a sovereign state, its constitutional and legal principles must be respected; and Liechtenstein must be deleted from the list of unco-operative tax havens. The OECD found this answer insufficient and wanted further assurances. After more contacts a Liechtenstein delegation led by the Foreign Minister visited Paris on 7 March 2002. It set out Liechtenstein's standard positions concerning "double criminality" and the requirement for all OECD countries and other important financial centres to be prepared to divulge private bank information if Liechtenstein were to discuss the matter. Both sides came close to an agreement. However, the OECD changed its position after the visit and sent a late negotiating text that would have entailed commitments going considerably beyond what had previously been negotiated. In its reply of 9 April 2002 Liechtenstein said that these demands could not be met, but offered to continue the dialogue on the basis of transparency and equal treatment.[24] Its inclusion in the OECD's new list followed. Liechtenstein has declared itself willing to continue talking. It has also said that it would welcome the development of appropriate standards for fiscal co-operation, in the context of international economic relationships, by international organisations whose membership is more representative than that of the OECD.

Liechtenstein has had several discussions with the European Commission about the EU initiative. These are still in progress. Since Liechtenstein and Switzerland have different starting points, different issues to negotiate and different requirements, the resulting agreements are unlikely to be identical. In practice, Liechtenstein will no doubt aim for an agreement that leaves the competitiveness of its financial services sector broadly in line with that of Switzerland, however that may be worked out in detail.

The results of the EU-Swiss negotiations on fraud will probably be valid for Liechtenstein too, in view of the Swiss-Liechtenstein common customs area.

Schengen is of less practical interest to Liechtenstein than to Switzerland, since the country has neither an airport nor a railway station and the problem of asylum seekers and refugees is much less dramatic. (Switzerland has – or had – the highest proportion of refugees from Former Yugoslavia in Europe). In view of the open frontier with Switzerland, Liechtenstein would probably go along with any agreement reached with the EU provided of course that the exchange of information required by the Schengen Information System was, as negotiated by Switzerland, consistent with Liechtenstein laws and practice. Schengen is a "dynamic" process (i.e. potentially open-ended), and bank information

---

[24] "Liechtensteiner Vaterland", 11 April 2002.

is certainly part of the EU's agenda. Negotiations with the Commission are expected to begin in 2003.

The Liechtenstein-USA treaty of 8 July 2002

Liechtenstein has no bilateral double taxation treaties except with Austria (to cover cross-frontier workers) and Switzerland (of limited scope). Its Treaty and accompanying exchange of notes with the United States of America on Mutual Legal Assistance in Criminal Matters, signed at Vaduz on 8 July 2002 by Otmar Hasler (Head of Government) and Mercer Reynolds (the US Ambassador), was a landmark in Liechtenstein's international co-operation and an important achievement of the current Government. For the first time, Liechtenstein has agreed to provide help to a foreign country in cases of tax fraud (among other criminal matters).

For some years the USA's declared intention has been to conclude mutual legal aid agreements with all important jurisdictions, especially those which are of financial and economic significance. By mid-2002 the USA had agreements with 47 states and jurisdictions. Until the new treaty, Liechtenstein-US mutual legal assistance was conducted on a voluntary or *ad hoc* basis. (The US is not, of course, a party to the 1959 European Convention on Mutual Assistance in Criminal matters.) This situation became increasingly unsatisfactory for both countries: for the USA because of Liechtenstein's slow and cumbersome procedures and for Liechtenstein because, as a result of the legislation of 1999–2000, requests for legal assistance to the USA on serious drugs and fraud matters were beginning to run at a noticeably higher rate than requests by the USA to Liechtenstein. The Americans proposed negotiations in September 2000. The first round took place in April 2001. By the time of the second round, in February 2002, the whole scene had been changed by the terrorist attacks of 11 September.

After those attacks the counter-terrorist Patriot Act of 2001 gave the US Administration far-reaching powers against jurisdictions deemed uncooperative, to the point of forbidding American financial institutions to do business with them. However, there had already been important developments for Liechtenstein banks operating in America.

Since January 2001 the US Inland Revenue Service has applied a world-wide 31% withholding tax to interest and dividends from American securities. The US has concluded agreements with a number of countries and banks to the effect that the names of persons liable to US tax must be disclosed to the US authorities; otherwise, capital gains or other income from all the funds that the banks invest in the USA will be taxed at source. Foreign banks which agree to these arrangements and which are awarded Qualified Intermediary Status (QIS) deduct the 31% withholding tax at source and transfer it to the US tax authorities, but are allowed to pay untaxed interest and dividends to non-US tax-payers. In this way banking confidentiality is preserved (at least to some extent) while the banks in practice become agents of the US Inland Revenue Service.

It was clear that without a bilateral Mutual Legal Assistance Treaty the Liechtenstein banks' QIS would not be extended and that the resulting lack of confidence in Liechtenstein might come to affect other areas of economic relations. Conversely, a treaty could only improve Liechtenstein's standing in the USA and strengthen its international position generally.

The treaty[25] is on the same general lines as those between the USA and, for example, Austria and Luxembourg. It contains the usual reservations about military and political offences and the security or similar essential interests of the requested state (Article 3). Article 1(3) breaks new ground for Liechtenstein in that it commits each state to give assistance whether or not the alleged offence would be an offence in its own territory; but the requested state may decline if the request "would require a court order for search and seizure or other coercive measures." Article 1(4), again for the first time, requires Liechtenstein to help a foreign state in matters of tax fraud, "defined as tax evasion committed by means of the intentional use of false, falsified, or incorrect business records or other documents, provided the tax due….is substantial." This definition is very close to the existing definition of tax fraud in Liechtenstein law. Examples of the activities that would constitute a presumption of tax fraud were set out in the accompanying exchange of notes. The Americans had begun by demanding a very comprehensive exchange of information in all tax matters. After some hard negotiating the Liechtenstein side found the resulting treaty an acceptable compromise: it took account of the very different legal and taxation systems of the two countries, and the main Liechtenstein banks kept their Qualified Intermediary Status.

[25] Report and Proposal of the Liechtenstein Government to the Landtag No. 82/2002, dated 24 September 2002.

PART IV
MODERN LIECHTENSTEIN

LIFE IN LIECHTENSTEIN

The Population

In 2001 the resident population stood at 33,525. Of these, 22,030 were Liechtenstein citizens and 11,495 (34.3%) were foreigners. The proportion of resident foreigners has fallen from the high point of 37.6% recorded in 1990. This may be due in part to the easier naturalisation procedures introduced in 2000.

Resident foreigners are defined as those settled in Liechtenstein, those with annual or short-stay residence permits who live there for more than twelve months, Swiss customs officials and their dependants, and foreigners who are temporarily accepted and who live for more than twelve months in Liechtenstein. Seasonal workers, foreigners with short-stay permits who live for less than twelve months in Liechtenstein, asylum seekers and others in need of humanitarian protection are not included in the definition.

The concept of "foreigner" is somewhat relative. In 2001, 3,750 of the foreign population (11.2% of the total resident population) were Swiss citizens, 1,997 (5.9%) were Austrians and 1,143 (3.4%) were Germans. 60% of the "foreigners", therefore, share Liechtenstein's regional language, background and culture. A further 1,109 foreigners (3.3% of the total population) are citizens of Italy, a close neighbour which also has a Roman Catholic culture. Of the remaining foreigners, the largest contingents come from the states of Former Yugoslavia (1,027, or 3%), Turkey (876, or 2.6%), Portugal (476, or 1.4%) and Spain (432, or 1.3%).

Liechtenstein's economic dependence on foreign workers, whether residents or commuters, has already been noted (pages 146 and 283); but this dependence extends beyond the economy. If one third of banking staff are Swiss and one tenth are Austrian[1], one fifth of the schoolteachers are also from outside Liechtenstein. In December 2000, 51 teachers commuted from Switzerland, 88 from Austria and one from Germany.[2]

The traffic naturally goes in both directions. In 2001, 2,529 Liechtenstein citizens were recorded as living abroad. Of these, the great majority (2,284) were

---

[1] "Liechtensteiner Vaterland", 4 May 2001
[2] "Liechtensteiner Vaterland", 4 April 2002.

in Europe, of whom 1,611 were living in Switzerland, 373 in Austria and 136 in Germany. It is striking that the number of Liechtenstein citizens living abroad, or at least registering as such, has fallen. It stood at 2,935 in 1950 and between 1970 and 1983 it exceeded 3,000. Presumably the recent decline reflects the labour shortage in Liechtenstein.

As elsewhere in Europe, the population of Liechtenstein is ageing. The number of live births, the overwhelming majority of which are within marriage, stays reasonably steady at around 400 per year in an increasing population. The number of deaths per year has risen steadily from 123 in 1960 to 382 in 1998. The annual surplus of births over deaths has declined from 257 in 1960 to 174 in 1998.

The change in the structure of the population between 1961 and 2001 can be seen in the following table:

	Age 0–14 years		Age 15–64 years		Age 65+	
	Total	Percentage of resident population	Total	Percentage of resident population	Total	Percentage of resident population
1961	4,844	28.28%	10,901	63.66%	1,380	8.06%
2001	6,189	18.46%	23,826	71.07%	3,510	10.47%

The relatively slow growth of that part of the population aged 65 and above is surprising in view of wider European trends.

After the age of 60 the proportion of foreigners in the population begins to fall quite sharply. This suggests that at that stage of life many foreigners return to their home countries. If so, rising health service and pension provision costs may make less of an economic impact on Liechtenstein than on other countries in western Europe.

The institution of marriage has so far remained more stable than in many other European countries. In 2001 43.9% of the population was single, 46.1% was married, 4.5% was widowed and 5.5% was divorced or separated. The figure for marriages conceals an important fact originating in the smallness of the country and in modern mobility. Of the marriages concluded in 1998, only 21.3% were between Liechtenstein men and Liechtenstein women. 30.3% were between Liechtenstein men and women from other countries, 29.8% were between Liechtenstein women and foreign men and 18.6% were between foreign men and foreign women.[3]

---

[3] Except where stated, all the figures in the foregoing paragraphs are derived from the Statistisches Jahrbuch 2002 and "Liechtenstein in Figures 2002".

Foreigners and Citizenship

The feeling or fear of being swamped by foreigners ("Überfremdung") has been a preoccupation of the Liechtensteiners for decades and is likely to remain so. It is a feeling that stems from the small size of the country, the historic sense of vulnerability and the tightly-knit nature of village communities. The dilemma is that the economy cannot prosper without the foreigners. However, unlike other western European countries, where the feeling has developed more recently and has taken more aggressive forms, there is little outward sign of tension. The majority of the foreigners are from the same regional background as the Liechtensteiners and are well-qualified and well-educated people. One perceptive observer has suggested that it is precisely because these foreigners are so like the Liechtensteiners that the latter sometimes worry about losing some of their identity through their presence.[4] Foreigners who come from further afield (notably the states of Former Yugoslavia and Turkey) to work in the less skilled sectors of industry seem to find a niche in the country. Their ethnic associations are accepted. Their position is safeguarded by the legal guarantees of human rights, the social control that exists in small communities and the general sense of order and propriety. Any manifestation of "right-wing radicalism" receives prompt attention from the authorities. Whether any foreigner can ever feel fully accepted, or be able to master completely the intricacies of the village dialects and genealogies, is another matter.[5]

The marriage statistics suggest that in real life there is a constant osmosis between the native Liechtenstein population and foreigners from inside or outside the Principality. This process is being helped, or accompanied, by the gradual amendments to citizenship legislation in recent years. Until 1974 a Liechtenstein woman lost her Liechtenstein citizenship upon marriage to a foreign man, but a foreign woman who married a Liechtenstein man acquired his nationality automatically. After 1974 Liechtenstein women who had lost their citizenship by marriage were entitled to reclaim it. 445 did so, most of whom were married to Swiss, Austrian, German and Italian citizens. In 1984, by contrast, new legislation made it harder for foreign women to acquire Liechtenstein citizenship by marriage. It was at that point made necessary for them to have lived in Liechtenstein for twelve years, to have been married for three years, and to be willing to renounce their former nationality. This change was made because of the pattern of foreign marriages by Liechtenstein men.[6]

[4] Alphons Matt, "Unbekannter Nachbar Liechtenstein", 1986, page 62.
[5] In some communities the descendants of those who denounced victims to the witch-hunters in the seventeenth century are still known. The false informers are sometimes referred to as "Tobelhocker". A Tobel is a dark, cold mountain cleft in which their souls were believed to have been damned to linger for ever. (Barbara Greene, "Liechtenstein, Valley of Peace", page 67.
[6] Alphons Matt (op. cit., page 64) says that between 1970 and 1984 no less than 57% of foreign brides were resident in Liechtenstein before marriage.

In 1986 a popular vote made it easier for the foreign children of Liechtenstein women to acquire citizenship.[7] This brought 1,853 new citizens between 1987 and 1997. It also made it easier for foreign wives to acquire citizenship. By 2001, 202 had done so. As a result of new legislation in 1995, 246 foreign husbands of Liechtenstein women had become Liechtenstein citizens by 2001. A judgment by the State Court in 1997 on equality of the sexes enabled 739 more persons to acquire citizenship by 2001. The qualifying period for foreign spouses of all Liechtenstein citizens, both men and women, is now identical

The next step was the popular vote of June 2000, which was even more closely fought than that of 1986.[8] This allowed long-standing foreign residents in Liechtenstein to apply for citizenship. The initial rush brought a total of 345 successful applications in 2000 and 2001. In 2002 the number fell to 135, of whom 65% already possessed Swiss and Austrian citizenship. Since 1997, 4,196 persons of Liechtenstein descent living abroad have claimed and acquired Liechtenstein nationality.

The normal procedure for naturalisation continues to be for foreign candidates to submit their applications to the communes where they live. The citizens of the commune decide on each application by ballot. Subject to approval by Parliament, the Sovereign Prince then grants the rights of citizenship. Liechtenstein's laws and procedures for naturalisation have often been criticised for their exclusiveness. The legislative changes during the last few years have in fact enabled the naturalisation of a large number of new citizens in proportion to the native population. Between 1970 and 2001 there were 5,313 naturalisations. No doubt many of these reflected a catching up with what would be regarded in other countries as normal practice; but the number is equivalent to almost a quarter of Liechtenstein citizens currently living within the Principality.

Health and Welfare

Little needs to be said here except that health and welfare are amply provided for. In 2001 there was one practising doctor for every 540 inhabitants: a high ratio which has contributed to the ever-rising costs of the compulsory semi-private health insurance schemes. The Liechtenstein National Hospital at Vaduz is managed by a foundation and is committed to provide services formally agreed with the Government. Three members of its board are appointed by the Government, one by the commune of Vaduz and one by the doctors' association. The Government's financial contribution amounted to more than 3.75 million francs in 2000. Other hospital services are provided, through formal agreements, by hospitals in

---

[7] It was a close result: 4,874 for, 4,492 against, with a turnout of 78.6%.

[8] 3,858 votes for and 3,843 against, but with an unusually low turnout of 48.6%.

the neighbouring Swiss cantons of St Gallen and Grisons and in Vorarlberg (Feldkirch). These cost the Government more than 5.8 million francs in 2000.

There is a very full range of social and welfare pension and compensation schemes. These began as long ago as 1910 with the first sickness and maternity and occupational accident insurance schemes. The latest (so far) is the company pension scheme of 1989. As examples of state expenditure in this domain, in 2000 the Government spent over 21.4 million francs on old age and survivors insurance, over 15 million on disability insurance and over 47 million on sickness insurance (including 1.65 million francs on premium reductions for the less well off).[9]

Schools

In keeping with Chapter III of the Constitution, Liechtenstein devotes great attention to education. The system is made as flexible as possible and is constantly evolving. It is orientated towards the Swiss system, but with some specific Liechtenstein characteristics. The country's small scale enables it to aim for the highest standards.

Schooling is compulsory and free of charge for nine years (from 7 to 15) with the option of a tenth year. Kindergarten education (from 5 to 6) is free of charge and voluntary, except that children whose native language is not German must attend for the second year in order to receive German language teaching. To help such children integrate into the system, tuition in German is available up to and including lower secondary school level (from 12 to 15).

In parallel with the general system, schooling for children with special needs runs from 5 to 15 years, one aim being to reintegrate such children into the general system whenever possible. The Special School at Schaan takes pupils from Canton St Gallen, which adds to variety in the classes as well as to numbers.

All children attend primary school ("Primarschule"), normally from 7 to 11 years. Thereafter they begin to branch out. The lower secondary school ("Oberschule"), from 12 to 15, provides a general education for working life or for transfer to an intermediate secondary school ("Realschule"), which is also from 12 to 15 years. The latter provides a wider ranging education in greater depth, for example in preparation for a demanding vocational apprenticeship. The voluntary tenth year (for 16-year olds) is a school in its own right, with a bias towards vocational education. It emphasises training in languages and information technology and tries in all ways, for example through workplace experience, to foster personal development and self-reliance. Pupils who are more academically inclined transfer from the primary school to the grammar school ("Gymnasium"), from 12 to the completion of 18 years, graduating in practice at 19. At senior level (from 15

---

[9] Rechenschaftsbericht 2000.

to 18/19) the grammar school offers five different options: Language (including Latin); Modern Languages; Art, Music and Pedagogy; Business and Law; and Mathematics and Natural Sciences. Pupils can transfer from one form of school to another at almost any stage up to and including the age of 15. The grammar school's matriculation certificate ("Matura") entitles pupils to examination-free admission to Swiss and Austrian universities.

There are at present two private, fee-paying schools: the Formatio, which follows the Liechtenstein curricula but is bilingual in German and English, and the Waldorf, which follows the theories of Dr Rudolf Steiner. Both cover years 1 to 9 of schooling.

In 1996 English replaced French as the first foreign language to be taught in Liechtenstein schools. Pupils now start English in their third year (at primary school) and French in their seventh year (at secondary school). The change was prepared in advance by training a number of Liechtenstein teachers at a language school in Cambridge under a contract organised by the British Council.

In the school year 2001–2002 the Liechtenstein state educational system presented the following picture:

	Type of school	Pupils
58	Kindergarten departments	862
14	Primary Schools ("Primarschulen")	2,122
3	Lower secondary schools ("Oberschulen")	430
5	Intermediate secondary schools ("Realschulen")	686
1	Voluntary tenth year at school	51
1	Grammar school ("Gymnasium")	684
1	Advanced-level vocational training school (4 terms)	87
	Total	4,922

This system employed 370 full-time and 216 part-time teachers.

Vocational Education

Vocational training at all levels is one of the outstanding features of the Liechtenstein educational system. Although in recent times there has been a trend towards the grammar school type of education, about 70% of the 350–400 pupils who leave school each year start vocational apprenticeships lasting three or four years with the help of about 700 firms. These apprenticeships cover about 100 occupations in most walks of life. When completed they are now recognised as the start of life-long learning, not (as in the old days) the end of training. Apprentices can advance to higher qualifications such as master. In 2001 there were in all 1,089 apprentices: 669 men and 420 women, of whom 612 were Liechtensteiners, 278 Swiss and 27 Austrian. Higher level continuation courses can be taken in Switzerland and Austria. In 1968 Liechtenstein joined the Worldskills organisation, which is devoted to vocational training and has some forty member-countries from all over the world. For the last twenty years at least, Liechtenstein has never failed to win medals at its "Olympics", an important global competition.

Tertiary Education

Most Liechtenstein students obtain their university education abroad. In 2000/01 there were 351 Liechtenstein students in Switzerland, 98 in Austria and 13 in Germany. However, in recent years some important new opportunities have opened up in Liechtenstein itself. The most important of these is the Liechtenstein University of Applied Sciences ("Fachhochschule", or FHL), which started life in 1961 as a humble evening technical college in shared premises in Vaduz. It later became the Liechtenstein Engineering School and acquired its present title in 1997. The closure of the Jenny Spoerry spinning mill in Vaduz in 1992 offered the possibility of housing the establishment under one roof for the first time. After a skilful architectural transformation, the new university building was opened on 19 April 2002 in the presence of Prince Hans-Adam II. From 38 students and eight part-time staff in 1961 it grew to 493 students and 219 part-time staff in 2001. Many of the students come from Switzerland, Austria and Germany. Having exported its own students for centuries, Liechtenstein now attracts foreign students as an important regional centre of tertiary education in its own right.

In coordination with St Gallen, Grisons and Vorarlberg the FHL decided in 1998 to run down its machine-building and construction engineering courses and to expand its courses in architecture and business sciences. It now offers internationally recognised bachelor and master degrees in architecture, financial services and business informatics (with strong vocational emphasis) as well as postgraduate courses. It has some 30 partnerships with universities around the world and takes part in various EU training and research programmes. It has established a Business Forum as a regional centre for information and networking between managers and political decision-makers. With support from the State, the Chamber of Commerce and Trade (GWK), individual companies and private persons the FHL is to house the new Competence Centre for Small and Medium Enterprises. This may develop further into a regional economic think-tank and a centre for economic analysis and forecasting.[10]

---

[10] See, for example, the interview with the rector, Klaus Näscher, in "Liechtensteiner Vaterland", 26 April 2003.

Liechtenstein is co-sponsor, along with Cantons St Gallen and Grisons, of the Interstate University of Applied Science at Buchs, just across the Rhine in Switzerland. This specialises in advanced and high technology engineering, with a strong practical orientation and an emphasis on technology transfer with industry.

The University for Human Sciences ("Universität für Humanwissenschaften") was given initial recognition by the Liechtenstein Government in February 2003. It offers a four-term postgraduate course in psychology and neurosciences and was awarded a 350,000-euro research project by the European Commission in 2002. It is housed in the former Jenny Spoerry weaving mill at Triesen, which closed in 1982.

The International Academy of Philosophy is a private university whose degrees are recognised by Germany and Austria. It was founded in Dallas in 1980 and moved to Liechtenstein in 1986.

The Liechtenstein Institute, which opened at Bendern in 1987, occupies a special place as a centre for Liechtenstein-related research and teaching in jurisprudence, political science, economic and social sciences and history. It does not offer courses or provide degrees. It receives an annual grant of 750,000 francs from the State. The institute has its origins in the Liechtenstein Academic Society ("Liechtensteinische Akademische Gesellschaft") which Gerard Batliner, Georg Malin, Rudolf Wenaweser and Felix Marxer founded in 1951 in order to subject the Principality and its affairs to critical analysis. The Institute's library is an important resource, as are its lectures, conferences and the Society's publications in the series "Liechtenstein Politische Schriften" and "Kleine Schriften" which began in 1972 and 1974 respectively. The Institute's critical approach has not been blunted by time. Where constitutional questions are concerned, some of its members' academic conclusions and political actions have been controversial.

Other Education

Adult Education was formerly run by the Deanery of the Roman Catholic Church. After the Deanery's dissolution in 1997 its Adult Education Office was converted into the autonomous Stein-Egerta Adult Education Institute and the Government set up its own foundation to coordinate adult education.

The Liechtenstein Music School, founded in 1963, is supported by the State, the communes and pupils' fees. It is administered from the house in Vaduz where Rheinberger was born. It has a large centre at Eschen and new buildings in Vaduz and Triesen. In 2002 it had 93 staff and almost 2,500 pupils of all ages, equivalent to almost 8% of the population. The Liechtenstein Art School was opened in 1993 to foster creativity and self-confidence in students of all ages.[11]

---

[11] Much of the material on the Liechtenstein education system is derived from a documentary account published by the Liechtenstein Government Press and Information Office in May 2002. I am also indebted to the Head of the Education Office for background information about the teaching of English.

Societies

For a small population, the number of voluntary political, charitable, cultural, sporting, service, social and ethnic organisations, each with its officers and committee, is astonishing. In Vaduz alone there are fifty societies, in consultation with which the commune has built common accommodation on the Jenny Spoerry site complete with six meeting rooms, storage rooms, a kitchen and a crèche.

Two societies deserve special mention. The Liechtenstein History Society ("Historischer Verein für das Fürstentum Liechtenstein") was founded in 1901 by a group of men who were to play leading parts in the country's history after the First World War. It now has 840 members. From the start, it enjoyed financial support from the Princely House, the Government (nearly 490,000 francs in 2000) and the communes. Its well-produced Yearbook is an indispensable source for any student of Liechtenstein's history and archaeology. The society sponsors individual historical works and reference material, its collections have contributed to the National Museum and it plays an active part in the designation and protection of ancient monuments.

The Liechtenstein Red Cross was founded on 30 April 1945, at a time of humanitarian crisis, by Princess Gina. She remained an extremely active president until 1985, when she handed over to Princess Marie, the consort of Hans-Adam II. Princess Gina's services were recognised by the International Red Cross in 1987 with its highest award, the Henri Dunant Medal. Princess Marie has continued the tradition of energetic leadership and personal involvement in the work of the organisation, including visits to the war-torn areas of Yugoslavia.[12] She takes a particular interest in children, including those with special needs.

The Liechtenstein Red Cross has 1,398 members (as of 2001). Within Liechtenstein it runs the ambulance service, a children's home which has given holidays to several thousand refugee children over the years, an advisory service for mothers and fathers, a blood donation service, the Samaritans organisation and a Christmas presents scheme for handicapped old people and hospital patients. Outside Liechtenstein, it serves as a channel for aid from its own members, the Government and other organisations to victims of conflict, poverty and natural disasters throughout the world (almost 1.7 million francs in 2001). It attracts substantial support not only from its individual members but also from industry and the financial services sector.

Among other activities, music and sport of all kinds are particularly prominent. The music societies include those for classical and folk music, two operetta societies, the Liechtenstein Musical Company in Balzers, two symphony

[12] Speech by Dr Heinz Batliner, reported in the "Liechtensteiner Volksblatt", 18 May 2002.

orchestras, 36 choirs, ten village brass bands which compete annually, and jazz, blues and rock. The Tangente, in Eschen, has won an international reputation for experimental jazz.

In the absence of military service, and for wider social reasons, the Government is a generous patron of sport. In 2001 it contributed over 2.9 million francs to sporting organisations. These are more than forty in number, representing more than 100 clubs. Their umbrella organisation is the Liechtenstein Olympic Sport Association ("Liechtensteinischer Olympischer Sportverband", or LOSV). The most popular sporting and leisure organisations are the Alpine Association ("Alpenverein" for climbing and walking, 2,005 members, founded in 1909); the Scouts and Guides (752 members, founded in 1931); the Football Association (1,900 members, founded in 1934); the Skiing Association (2,398 members, founded in 1936); the Gymnastic and Light Athletics Association (1,384 members, founded in 1936); and the Tennis Association (1,964 members, founded in 1969).[13] Liechtenstein skiers such as Hanni Wenzel have scored notable international successes, including at Olympic level; they have probably been Liechtenstein's finest ambassadors abroad.

Museums, Theatres and Libraries

The National Museum ("Landesmuseum") was founded in 1894 at the initiative of the then Governor, Friedrich Stellwag von Carion, with financial support from Prince Johann II. Over the years it led a nomadic existence, from the Castle to the Government Building, back to the Castle, to the Vaduz Town Hall, to the Liechtensteinische Landesbank and finally (1972–1992) to the former residence of the Governor. Excavations for the new Landesbank building across the road then threatened it with collapse and it had to be evacuated. After the reinforcement and complete re-modelling of the Governor's residence, the museum, when it re-opens in November 2003, will offer a modern and vividly-presented picture of Liechtenstein's history and culture.

The Postal Museum, founded in 1930 and now housed in the renovated "English Building" ("Engländerbau") in the centre of Vaduz, is an obvious attraction to philatelists from all over the world.

The flagship of the Liechtenstein museums is the new Art Museum ("Kunstmuseum"). In order to fill the gap left by the collapse of the Art Museum ("Kunsthaus") project in the 1980s a group of private patrons set up a private foundation in 1996. They acted so quickly that in 2000 they were able to present the new museum as a gift to the State, which supports it to the tune of about 2.8 million francs per year. This distinctive polished black angular building houses

---

[13] Membership figures for 2001.

344

the Liechtenstein State Art Collection, rotating exhibitions from the Princely Collection and occasional exhibitions by artists-in-residence and others, and provides space for lectures and concerts. It has already made its mark in the region and in the wider German-speaking world. The Arts Space ("Kunstraum") in the Engländerbau offers an important platform for Liechtenstein artists.

The principal theatre in Liechtenstein, the Theater am Kirchplatz (TaK) in Schaan, was founded in 1970. It originated with a group of young people who in 1964 started the Kaktus Cabaret in a Vaduz hotel. It now enjoys a region-wide reputation for its speech, music and dance productions as well as its film club, children's theatre and many other activities. Its state subsidy amounted to nearly 2.3 million francs in 2000. It is also supported by the communes of Schaan and Vaduz. In addition to the TaK, there are many amateur companies and productions throughout the Principality.

The National Library ("Landesbibliothek") was founded in 1961 as the result of private initiative. It serves a triple purpose as a national collection, a research library and a popular lending library. The collection includes newspapers, graphics, tapes, records, CDs, microfilms and micro-fiches. It is linked to the major German-Swiss libraries.[14]

The Media

There are two main newspapers, which now appear six days a week. The Liechtenstein People's Paper ("Liechtensteiner Volksblatt") appeared in 1878 as a non-political newspaper for official and social announcements and articles of general interest. Since 1918 it has been the official mouthpiece of the FBP. The Liechtenstein Fatherland ("Liechtensteiner Vaterland") is the organ of the VU. Wilhelm Beck founded it in 1914 as the Upper Rhine News ("Oberrheinische Nachrichten"), which became the Liechtenstein News ("Liechtensteinische Nachrichten") in 1924. It took its present title in 1936 after merging with the Liechtenstein Homeland Service's newspaper. Both newspapers provide thorough national coverage, a selection of regional news (particularly economic reporting) and the main topical world news stories. They are fiercely partisan on national party political issues: it is advisable to read both newspapers in order not to come away with the impression of irredeemable incompetence in one party and sustained heroic virtue in the other. Both depend quite heavily on government advertising, but this does not affect their freedom of expression. Both follow the local culture of respect for personal privacy.

The "Neue Liewo" (formerly the "Liechtensteiner Woche", or "Liechtenstein

---

[14] The preceding paragraphs are based in part on "Kultur und Sport", published by the Liechtenstein Government's Press and Information Office, 2001.

Week") is a free newspaper delivered to households once a week on Sundays. The rival church publications "Vobiscum" (published by the Archbishopric) and "In Christo" (published by the "Verein für eine Offene Kirche") appear regularly, as does the Protestant community's magazine "Forum". There are also numerous specialist publications. The satirical magazine Mole ("Maulwurf") appeared from 1985 to 1989, to be followed briefly by the Dandelion ("Löwenzahn") from 1990 to 1992.

Television viewers are connected by cable to a wealth of services from neighbouring countries and beyond. Since 1992 there has existed a national television channel (the "Landeskanal"), which is run by the Government's Press and Information Office. It broadcasts still pictures, teletext announcements and sometimes important official statements or debates in Parliament. A private television service, XML, began in 1998. William Kenmore's vision of a Liechtenstein radio was finally realised in 1995 when the private "Radio L" broadcast for the first time. Radio Ri is based across the Rhine in Buchs.

Since January 2003 "e-government" has been available to the population through the administration's electronic portal www.llv.li

Social Problems

Liechtenstein has a high quality of life and a high standard of living. There is no absolute poverty. There are however pockets of relative poverty and other problems, which have been carefully analysed in recent years. The main clients of the Office of Social Services are those aged up to 20 (25% of its clients in 2000) and those between 31 and 40 (24%). The elderly (only 6% of clients in 2000) seem in general to be well provided for. The increase in the number of clients from 745 in 1993 to 1,036 in 2000 could have several causes, including modern pressures on family structures and values, economic fluctuations, better knowledge of the help available from the State and less reluctance to use it. 48% of the clients in 2000 were Liechtenstein citizens, 22% were from EU countries, 10% from Switzerland and 20% from other countries. This means that foreigners (34.4% of the population) were making use of 52% of the social services help available.

Of these clients, 443 (45%) needed financial help, which cost the State 3.5 million francs. In 46 cases the State took over payment of their health insurance premiums. Of the remainder, 272 needed regular help for more than six months, 98 needed short-term or sporadic help for less than six months and 27 needed one-off help. Single-parent families were the biggest category of those needing help (31%), followed by the unemployed (23%). A lot of attention has recently been devoted to the problems of the "working poor", defined as persons who, despite being at least 90% employed, are unable fully to support themselves and their families in a country where the subsistence minimum is 4,171 francs per month.

39 such cases were identified in 2000. These were mostly foreign couples aged between 20 and 40, married with several children, possessing few or no professional qualifications and working as often as not in the cleaning industry.

State help is given on the basis of a reciprocal commitment from those who are able to make it. An unemployed recipient is obliged to seek work actively. An individual help-plan defining the rights and duties of each side is drawn up in the form of a written agreement between the Social Services Office and the client, to enhance the client's sense of personal responsibility and to wean him or her away from any dependence on a benefits culture. In October 2000 the State and the communes agreed between them to create 30 places for the long-term unemployed for up to six months each. The aim of these jobs is to improve the skills of the unemployed, to give them a better chance in the labour market and in the process to enhance their self-esteem.[15]

The remaining 593 (55%) of the Social Services Office's clients in 2000 had a variety of social, family and personal problems. The largest element (280 persons, or 17%) consisted of those with psychological disorders, whether clinical or induced by alcohol (55 cases) or drugs (22 cases). In handling such cases the Office makes much use of qualified voluntary helpers and counsellors.

Since 2000 the total number of clients has risen: in 2001 it was 1,146, of whom 474 needed financial help. The Government's policies seem to have succeeded in reducing the number of long-term unemployed and of single-parent families needing help. On the other hand, the number of young people needing help (running away from home, truancy, violent behaviour) seems to be rising. Physical abuse and violence within the family seem to be low (12 known cases in 2001). A women's refuge was opened in 1991. Since then, legislation has made it possible to expel a violent partner from the home.

In the field of drugs, alcohol and nicotine abuse Liechtenstein's philosophy is to give support to everyone in their personal responsibility for looking after their own health, rather than to prosecute them for behaviour that endangers it. The logical consequence of this approach will ultimately be to decriminalise drug consumption: a complex and long-term policy which Liechtenstein is pursuing with the greatest care and caution in order not to compromise its neighbours' interests, send out wrong signals to the rest of the world or provoke an uncontrollable expansion of dealing and consumption. At the international level Liechtenstein works with the United Nations and the Council of Europe. At the regional level (the Lake Constance region, or Euregio Bodensee) Liechtenstein's Drugs Commission exchanges information and experience with a new coordinating body set up in March 2000 at the proposal of Vorarlberg. Since 1992 the Commission has

---

[15] Rechenschaftsbericht 2000, pages 189–190 and 195–198.

been working on data collection and evaluation and educational programmes with institutions in Vorarlberg, St Gallen and Grisons. The eventual success of any decriminalisation of drugs consumption will greatly depend on educational, preventative, diversionary and youth protection measures. These are in train.

In the absence of reliable data it is hard to assess how serious the drugs problem may be. There is little outward sign of one. A youth survey in 1999 suggested that 14% of 15–16 year-olds in Liechtenstein had tried cannabis, compared with 5% in Portugal, 7% in Sweden, 10% in Greece, 19% in Italy and 24% in Denmark. Criminal statistics in any country depend very much on the scale of activity of the police in any given year. With that proviso, in 1998 there were 98 charges in connection with cannabis, 92 in connection with cocaine (an untypically high figure), 22 in connection with heroin, 35 in connection with synthetic drugs and 4 in connection with others.[16] In 2002 146 persons were charged under narcotics legislation, of whom one third were young people.

Asylum-Seekers

Liechtenstein is not an obvious goal for asylum-seekers since it has no airport or railway station. Strangers are soon noticed. Those who have entered illegally can be returned to the country at which they first arrived. Nevertheless, Liechtenstein has a long tradition of accepting people in need, from Smyslovsky's Russian troops in 1945 to Hungarians in 1956, Czechoslovaks in 1968 and boat people from Indochina in the 1970s and 1980s. The country is bound by international agreements to give protection to refugees and asylum-seekers.

In recent years most of the asylum-seekers have come from former Yugoslavia. In 1992, for example, 566 persons arrived illegally in Liechtenstein, of whom about 450 were refugees from former Yugoslavia. There were 157 such arrivals in 1993, 175 in 1994 and 140 in 1995. Except for those from Former Yugoslavia, most of them were sent back either to the countries in which they had first arrived or to their homelands, according to international agreements. At the end of 1995 Liechtenstein sheltered around 330 refugees (more than 1% of the then population), most of whom were housed in private accommodation or by friends and relations. Asylum-seekers are now accommodated in a newly constructed building next to the police station. The annual cost to the State rose from around 80,000 francs in 1993 to over 2 million francs in 1997, to which should be added 1.9 million francs for the reception centre.[17]

In all, more than 700 persons came to Liechtenstein from Kosovo alone. As the situation in that area was stabilised it became possible for most of them to

---

[16] Rechenschaftsbericht 2000, page 224.
[17] Liechtenstein Government's Foreign Policy Report, 1997, pages 60–61.

return. 220 of them claimed asylum when their protected status was withdrawn. They pursued the matter to the Administrative Complaints Court, which in most cases upheld the Government's decision. By the end of 2000, 127 refugees remained in the country, most of whom were due to leave in the following spring. During their stay in Liechtenstein four school classes were established so that their children could be taught in their own language. Since 2000 the number of new arrivals and applicants has continued to fall.

Unlike many other countries, Liechtenstein allows and encourages refugees and asylum-seekers to work. This promotes their self-respect and work ethic and reduces the burden on the public purse. In order to limit Liechtenstein's attractiveness to economic refugees, their employers hand over their pay to the State. The refugees receive three francs for each hour worked in addition to social security payments and medical care. When they return home, or are finally allowed to stay in Liechtenstein, they receive the balance of the sum earned as a nest egg to start them in their new lives.[18]

Crime

Liechtenstein is one of the safest countries in Europe. No case of murder was reported in 2001 or 2002. On the other hand, some of the old innocence has been lost. Petty vandalism and graffiti, which are mainly juvenile crimes that would have been unthinkable a few years ago, have increased from 150 cases in 2001 to 195 in 2002. Crimes of violence against the person rose from 60 to 79 in the same period; cases of white-collar crime fell from 218 to 197. Overall, reported crime rose from 971 cases in 2001 to 1,049 in 2002. The detection rate was 21%.[19] The Swiss frontier guards' successes in seizing drugs being smuggled into Liechtenstein and stolen property being taken out suggest that a good deal of the more serious crime originates abroad.

The prison population is quite small. The original gaol consisted of a few cells in the basement of the Government Building. The new police station complex, opened in 1991, contains a National Prison with 19 cells, of which 16 are for men and three for women. The occupancy rate in 2000 was 69.89% for men and 10.47% for women. The prison is intended for people who are on remand or serving short sentences. People sentenced to more than two years serve their time in Austrian prisons. There were 22 such prisoners in 2000.

Police and Security

When it was founded in 1933 the Liechtenstein police force consisted of seven

---

[18] Rechenschaftsbericht 2000, page 44. "Liechtensteiner Vaterland", 28 March 2001.
[19] "Liechtensteiner Volksblatt", 9 July 2003. In the United Kingdom the detection rate in 2002 was 23.5%.

men. By 1991 numbers had risen to 55. The state-of-the-art police station opened at that time was designed for a staff of 75. It allowed room for expansion to 105, but even those margins are about to be exceeded. 30 million francs have been allocated for additional building works. At the end of 2001 there were 73 police officers, 18 civilian staff and 24 auxiliary police. The number of police is to rise to 130 by 2007.

These increases are not due to any great increase in lawlessness in Liechtenstein, but to the Principality's need to meet the obligations of a modern state. This includes the deterrence of crime as much as its detection. A parliamentary investigation committee reported in August 2001 that perceived deficiencies in the police were due to chronic under-staffing in the 1990s and a lack of strategy for further training and higher qualification. These are now being corrected. The need to deal with white-collar crime (page 316) and growing international obligations have also contributed to the increase. The Unit for Combating Economic and Organised Crime (EWOK) was established in 2000. Its founding staff comprised three Austrians, one German, two Liechtenstein citizens from the financial services sector and one Liechtenstein police officer. The law has been changed to make it easier to employ foreign citizens in the police, not simply because of economic crime but also because of the growing demands of Interpol (to which Liechtenstein has belonged since 1960), the threat of terrorism and the need to protect the State.

Normal police training is carried out in Switzerland. The Liechtenstein anti-terrorist intervention squad and the riot police conduct regular exercises in the Principality. Their facilities include a shooting range in the police station.

Liechtenstein makes an active contribution to regional police activities. A treaty between Liechtenstein, Switzerland and Austria concluded in 2000 allows joint police patrols in the frontier areas of the three countries, and other forms of co-operation. Liechtenstein police officers help to protect the World Economic Forum meetings at Davos each January. In turn, police officers from St Gallen and Vorarlberg were deployed to help the Liechtenstein police during the Liechtenstein-England football match in Vaduz in March 2003.

Civil defence is another important contributor to Liechtenstein's sense of security. Each of the eleven communes and eight of the biggest manufacturing companies has its own volunteer fire brigade, backed up by regular training and a support point in Vaduz. These 19 brigades comprise some 650 people (with double counting of those who belong to both a commune and a factory brigade). The mountain rescue team has nearly 30 members.

Since 1963 the Government has had an emergency command post. A more modern version is to be installed beneath the new Parliament building and the Castle rock. Each commune has its own civil emergency rooms, which could in total accommodate up to 45% of the population. Many companies and private persons have their own secure accommodation. There is a nation-wide alarm system.

Through its own efforts and its arrangements with the neighbouring countries, Liechtenstein seems as well prepared as it could be to meet any foreseeable emergency.

FOREIGN POLICY:
OBJECTIVES AND RESOURCES

Liechtenstein's foreign policy objectives are the same as those of most other countries: to protect the country's sovereignty, independence and security and to advance its political and economic interests. Liechtenstein works for these objectives at the bilateral level and the multilateral European and global level.

It is sometimes argued that "sovereignty" is meaningless in an age of globalisation and supranational organisations. Such arguments confuse sovereignty with autarky (self-sufficiency). Not even Stalin in the 1930s or Mao Tse-tung in the 1960s quite succeeded in making their countries self-sufficient, although in the attempt they did great harm to them. Individual persons have to take account of their families, their employers, the laws and the prevailing political and economic environment; nevertheless, they still have free will. Sovereign states, too, have to take account of circumstances, but in the end they are free to choose how to try to influence them or to steer their way through them. Without that freedom democracy itself becomes meaningless.

A large and powerful state may choose to pool (that is to say, give up) some of its sovereignty in a supranational organisation in the calculation that its negotiating weight in that organisation will enable it to win equivalent benefits. That choice is likely to be less rewarding to a very small state. From the time of the Holy Roman Empire, Liechtenstein has been accustomed to working with other states and with international organisations.[1] It exercises and safeguards its sovereignty through economic and political involvement with others. Liechtenstein prefers to operate with a wide range of partners in carefully defined treaty relationships, so that its own rights and identity will be respected and its room for manoeuvre assured. It resists as strongly as it can decisions from others in which it has not participated.

Not having an army, Liechtenstein is in practice an "unarmed neutral". Switzerland's neutrality (which is an armed neutrality) was guaranteed by the Congress of Vienna (1815). Austria's neutrality is defined by its State Treaty (1955). Liechtenstein's neutrality has not been acknowledged by any such international

---

[1] It was the only member to vote against the dissolution of the German Confederation in 1866.

act. However, the Principality considers itself "*de facto* permanently neutral", as in both World Wars. It aligns itself in this respect closely to its two neighbours, especially Switzerland.

Liechtenstein has little political and no military weight. Consequently it has, even more than most European countries, a strong interest in the preservation of peace, the rule of international law and the observance of treaties. It knows that sovereignty has constantly to be asserted if the big, bustling states and supranational organisations are not to brush aside their smaller partners, who have equal legitimacy and who are equally (perhaps more) democratic. Liechtenstein also knows that it is not enough to assert sovereignty in arid legalistic terms. It must act in a practical and realistic way, knowing its limits and showing itself a sensible, constructive and reliable partner. "The preservation and cultivation of the Liechtenstein identity needs special attention. However this should mean not a cutting off, but rather an openness at the international, European and regional levels."[2]

After a long struggle lasting into the 1990s Liechtenstein has been accepted internationally as a sovereign and independent state. It can now pay more attention to the questions of how it is to live in the international community and what special contribution it can make through its own national expertise, for example in human rights, the drafting and application of the Statute of the International Criminal Court or financial sector matters. As a practical contribution, it has offered its financial expertise to the UN Counter-Terrorism Committee. It has to be selective. As an obvious example, in environmental matters it will contribute to debate on the Alps, about which it has something useful to say, rather than the Antarctic or the Sahara.

Practical Cooperation with Neighbouring States and Governments

There is a long history of interaction between the territories that now comprise Liechtenstein, the neighbouring Swiss cantons and Vorarlberg in Austria. In modern times, co-operation at the most basic level may take the form of agreements between the Liechtenstein communes and the adjacent territories about such routine necessities as refuse and sewage disposal. At a higher level, it may include formal agreements between the Principality's Government and the central, Swiss cantonal or Austrian federal Land authorities as appropriate for the delegation of functions or the outsourcing of Liechtenstein's requirements. Such agreements enable the Principality to meet its obligations to its citizens as a state. They also denote its sovereign status, since agreements freely concluded may be freely denounced.

---

[2] "Zielsetzungen und Prioritäten der liechtensteinsichen Aussenpolitik" (Liechtenstein Government, Vaduz, 1997), page 78.

Bilateral Relations

This book has already described Liechtenstein's historical, political, economic, cultural, diplomatic and consular relationship with Switzerland. Little needs to be added here. It is a special relationship which remains the most important strand in Liechtenstein's foreign policy. It is strengthened by public affection and positive historical memories, including Switzerland's helpfulness during the negotiations for Liechtenstein's entry into the EEA in 1995. Historically, the relationship has not always been free of friction, for example at times in the 1930s and 1940s; but such periods have been brief and both countries have taken great care to keep the relationship in good repair.[3] In 2000 Switzerland appointed a Foreign Ministry official as its first, non-resident, ambassador to Liechtenstein. The two countries have always worked closely together in international organisations, where Liechtenstein has benefited from exchanges of information with Switzerland. Since Switzerland joined the United Nations as a full member in 2002 there has been scope for even closer cooperation in that organisation.

Relations with Liechtenstein's other neutral neighbour, Austria, also have deep historical foundations. They have intensified since Austria joined the EU and Liechtenstein became its partner in the EEA. There is a regular political dialogue between the two countries. There is a large number of agreements covering almost every aspect of day-to-day life including education, social services, legal affairs and also consular protection in those foreign countries where Austria but not Switzerland is represented. Since 1983 the Principality has awarded an annual prize for research at Innsbruck University as a token of gratitude for the university's contribution to higher education in Liechtenstein over the years.

Relations with the Federal Republic of Germany, the fourth and largest member of the German-speaking world, have been more chequered. Liechtenstein helped Germany in the CSCE talks; Germany helped Liechtenstein in its negotiations to join the Council of Europe, the UN and the EEA. However, the dislike felt by a high-taxing government for low-tax policies has found expression in critical comments by certain German politicians including Chancellor Schröder (during the August 2002 election campaign) and Finance Minister Eichel. In 1999 someone in Germany launched what was seen by many people in Liechtenstein as a deliberate disinformation campaign. On its side, Liechtenstein has started proceedings against Germany at the International Court of Justice for violating its sovereignty (pages 362–364). However, both countries have taken pains to ensure that these differences should not impinge on normal relations, as Prince Hans-Adam II and the German Federal President Rau made clear during the latter's

---

[3] In this spirit, rare incidents such as the forest fire caused by the accidental bombardment of Liechtenstein territory by Swiss troops during an exercise in 1985 have been quickly smoothed over.

official visit to Vaduz on 27 August 2002. The German Ambassador Reinhard Hilger said on his retirement in June 2003 that Liechtenstein's efforts to open up financial transactions were recognised by the German Government and Chancellor Schröder, and that German criminal experts had told him that they had no complaints about Liechtenstein's readiness to co-operate.[4] Liechtenstein opened a non-resident embassy in Berlin in 2000. Since 2003 Josef Wolf has been resident ambassador there, with the aim of making better direct contacts and ensuring a more objective assessment of Liechtenstein by German politicians, officials and media. There is already a solid Liechtenstein economic presence in Germany in the form of industrial investment (especially in eastern Germany) and financial services.

Relations with the United States of America, as the world's leading power and a determining factor in financial services, have been put on a new footing. Claudia Fritsche, Liechtenstein's Permanent Representative to the United Nations, was accredited as the first (non-resident) ambassador in Washington in 2000 and moved there permanently in 2002. The frequency of ministerial visits to the USA has increased perceptibly: Otmar Hasler paid a visit in May 2002 as Head of Government and Ernst Walch, the present Foreign Minister, makes a point of going there twice a year.

Each year since 2001 a visit to Liechtenstein by US Congressmen has been organised by the Liechtenstein Chamber of Industry and Trade. The programmes include meetings with the manufacturing and financial services sectors, the Government and Prince Hans-Adam II or Hereditary Prince Alois. The conclusion of the Liechtenstein-US Treaty on Mutual Legal Assistance in Criminal Matters in 2002 and Liechtenstein's adherence to international anti-terrorist measures including the Agreement on the Suppression of the Financing of Terrorism have contributed to a positive atmosphere. The US Treasury Under-Secretary Jimmy Gurulé, in response to an erroneous British press report, was quick to emphasise the USA's satisfaction with Liechtenstein's support in combating the financing of terrorism (page 317 above).

Relations with the smaller European countries such as Luxembourg, Latvia and Lithuania are getting closer. Nor are Liechtenstein's fellow mini-states (Andorra, Monaco, San Marino), with which there is a natural community of interest, forgotten.

European Multilateral Co-operation

The significance of Liechtenstein's admission to CSCE, the Council of Europe, EFTA and the European Economic Area has already been described. In 2001 it

---

[4] "Liechtensteiner Vaterland" and "Liechtensteiner Volksblatt", 18 June 2003.

fell to the newly appointed Liechtenstein Foreign Minister to hold almost simultaneously the presidencies of the Council of Europe, EFTA and the EEA.

EFTA is important to Liechtenstein for several reasons. By its membership of EFTA, Liechtenstein is also a member of the European Economic Area. EFTA enables Liechtenstein to participate in free-trade agreements with some 20 third states. As a result of the Vaduz Convention, signed on 21 June 2001 during Liechtenstein's EFTA Presidency, there is now a closer, more dynamic element in the relationship between EFTA member states.[5]

The Council of Europe's role in fostering human and minority rights and the strengthening of democratic institutions has been important for Liechtenstein from the start. To this has been added the new dimension of the re-integration of the countries of central and eastern Europe into traditional European values. Liechtenstein is active at most levels of the Council's work, including the parliamentary and the governmental. At the end of the Liechtenstein Presidency in November 2001 the Secretary-General, Walter Schwimmer, said that it was due to Liechtenstein's "Alemannic tenacity" that two clear decisions on the campaign against terrorism had been achieved.[6] Liechtenstein has proposed a benchmarking system which envisages that financial institutions in all Council of Europe member countries should observe the same standards in combating organised crime and terrorism.

As an unarmed and vulnerable state Liechtenstein has a vital interest in peace and stability in Europe and, consequently, in the OSCE's roles of conflict prevention, early warning, crisis management and post-conflict rehabilitation. The role of the OSCE's High Commissioner on National Minorities also fits closely with Liechtenstein's concerns. It was for this reason that Liechtenstein opened its diplomatic mission in Vienna, the seat of the OSCE, in 1994. In 2003 Liechtenstein provided a person and financing for a place in the OSCE Conflict Prevention Centre.

These activities are complemented by Liechtenstein's membership of the Bank for European Reconstruction and Development.

Global Co-operation

At the United Nations Liechtenstein has chosen to concentrate on international law, human rights, social and humanitarian matters and the related question of self-determination. Its efforts were recognised at the 2002 General Assembly when its Permanent Representative, Christian Wenaweser,[7] was elected

---

[5] The Vaduz Convention brought up to date EFTA's founding document, the 1960 Stockholm Convention.
[6] "Liechtensteiner Volksblatt", 9 November 2001.
[7] Ambassador Wenaweser has remarked, "Since our financial contributions are comparatively insignificant and we provide no peace-keeping troops, we must make the most of brainpower – and there is a big demand for that. Since we are not bound to any group position, like the EU countries, we are free to develop our own ideas." ("Liechtensteiner Volksblatt", 2 October 2002)

chairman of the Third Committee, which is responsible for social, humanitarian and cultural affairs. This is the highest position that Liechtenstein has so far attained at the United Nations. In May 2003 Liechtenstein held its first-ever meeting of UN experts in its territory, to discuss ways of improving reporting under the UN human rights conventions.

Liechtenstein became a member of GATT in 1994 and, in the following year, a member of the World Trade Organisation. The WTO is of great importance to Liechtenstein in view of its dependence on international trade and the need for defence against any possible act of discrimination in future. At the WTO Liechtenstein concentrates on those areas which particularly concern it and in which it is not represented by Switzerland under the Customs Treaty. These include services, investment, intellectual property, public procurement and the future development of the WTO's work.

Regional Co-operation

Liechtenstein makes a full and varied contribution to its region. Since 1995 it has been party to the Alpine Convention of 7 November 1991, which is concerned with the protection of the Alps in its broadest sense including questions of traffic, environmental protection, agriculture, tourism and leisure. The convention's secretariat, CIPRA, which the Liechtenstein Government supports with 400,000 francs per year, is based in Vaduz. Germany, France, Austria, Slovenia, the EU, Italy, Monaco and Switzerland are also parties to the convention. The Liechtenstein communes bordering on the Rhine participate in the Rhine Frontier Community. The Government is a member of the Alpine Rhine International Governmental Commission, along with the governments of the Grisons, St Gallen and Vorarlberg. This organisation aims to find forward-looking solutions to the river's environmental problems in their widest sense.

Since their foundation in 1972 Liechtenstein has cooperated informally with the Working Community of the Alpine Lands ("Arbeitsgemeinschaft der Alpenländer", or ARGE ALP) and the International Lake Constance Conference ("Internationale Bodenseekonferenz", or IBK). ARGE ALP's membership stretches over eastern Switzerland, southern Germany, western Austria and northern Italy. It is concerned with transport, the environment, planning, agriculture, culture, health, family and social policies and trade and industry. The IBK, whose role is evolving, includes the Swiss cantons close to Lake Constance, Vorarlberg in Austria and Baden-Württemberg and Bavaria in Germany. Liechtenstein has had observer status with the IBK since 1995.

Diplomatic Resources

Liechtenstein belongs to many more international organisations than those listed above. The workload imposed by its increasingly pro-active and pre-emptive foreign policy is considerable. The Principality has eight diplomatic missions but only twenty diplomatic staff: nine at home and eleven abroad. They are supplemented as necessary both at home and abroad by the recruitment of qualified temporary staff (for example, for the strengthening of teams), partly as trainees, for periods of three to six months or longer.

Some 85 foreign ambassadors are currently accredited to Vaduz, but none resides there. Almost all of them are based in Berne. The main exception is the Austrian Ambassador, who by tradition is a Foreign Ministry official in Vienna. The Liechtenstein Embassy at Berne therefore continues to be an important post, both for representing Liechtenstein's many-sided interests with the Swiss Federal Government (though many issues may be dealt with directly from Vaduz) and for day-to-day diplomatic contacts with most of the bilateral missions accredited to Liechtenstein.

The mission at Brussels handles the full range of EEA and EU matters, under instructions from Vaduz. In addition, it serves in a largely representational function as the embassy to the Kingdom of Belgium and as the non-resident embassy to the Holy See.

The mission at Strasbourg, in addition to handling traditional Council of Europe business, serves as a useful point of contact with the central and eastern European countries. So, too, does the mission at Vienna, from the somewhat different perspective of the OSCE. The Vienna mission is increasingly busy with the UN institutions there. It is also accredited to the Republic of Austria. The Geneva mission looks after business with EFTA (to the extent that it is still conducted there rather than in Brussels), the WTO and the UN institutions there.

In addition to its chief role in United Nations activities, the mission at New York takes advantage as necessary of the UN as a clearing-house for world-wide diplomatic business. The bilateral work of the new embassies at Washington and Berlin has already been outlined.

Any foreign service runs the risk of paying insufficient attention to the longer term strategic perspective under the pressure of day-to-day business. The Liechtenstein Government therefore set up in 2002 an advisory council of senior experts from Germany, Austria, The Netherlands, Switzerland and Norway. Its purpose is to study likely scenarios for the future development of the EU and to consider Liechtenstein's own strategies as a small state. The Government is also considering setting up a network of honorary consuls who would, if the project goes ahead, help to supplement the work of its career diplomats abroad.

FOREIGN POLICY: INITIATIVES
AND DISAGREEMENTS

The Self-Determination Initiative at the United Nations

Prince Hans-Adam II chose to mark Liechtenstein's first appearance at the UN General Assembly on 26 September 1991 by delivering his country's speech himself. It was on this occasion that he launched his country's initiative on self-determination. Liechtenstein followed it up by putting it on the agenda of the 1992 General Assembly. The item was addressed at successive General Assemblies. It was also discussed in the Third Committee in 1992, 1993 (when Prince Hans-Adam himself took part in the debate) and 1994. The initial general comments were not too discouraging, but there were signs of strong opposition from some quarters, notably India and Pakistan (because of Kashmir) and Indonesia (because of its numerous secessionist problems). The opposition was not assuaged by Liechtenstein's emphasis on the gradualist and wholly voluntary nature of the concept. By 1993 the opposition had mustered solid regional support, so that a resolution in that year only "took note" of Liechtenstein's initiative and agreed to come back to it later at some unspecified date.

At that point Prince Hans-Adam decided that it would be more fruitful for the time being to develop the initiative within an academic rather than a political framework. Accordingly, he set up first a research programme at Princeton University and then, also at Princeton, the Liechtenstein Institute on Self-Determination. In developing the concept, the Institute has organised seminars and conferences and published collections of papers.

Self-determination and self-administration lie at the heart of so many actual and potential political disputes throughout the world that there is plenty of scope for the Institute's work. The example of the Red Cross, which is a private institution set up under Swiss law but which over time has become an international institution, could possibly be a precedent for the future of the Liechtenstein Institute on Self-Determination.

However, the Institute will at some point need to promote itself in the political and diplomatic worlds as well as in academia if it is to become the internationally acknowledged authority on self-determination and a general point of reference. Sponsors and supporters will have to be mobilised when in due course the initiative returns to the active UN agenda.

Liechtenstein and the Czech Republic

The Velvet Revolution of 1989 seemed to offer a chance to solve the long-standing differences between Prague and Vaduz. Liechtenstein was quick to indicate its wish to start negotiations with Czechoslovakia on the restitution of property in order to normalise bilateral relations. The first meeting took place in October 1990 during the UN General Assembly at New York between Hans Brunhart (Head of Government and Foreign Minister) and the Jiri Dienstbier (Czechoslovak Foreign Minister), at Liechtenstein's suggestion. Between the end of October 1990 and the end of 1992, there were numerous contacts at different levels in Prague, Berne, Vaduz and by correspondence. Both sides set out their positions in detail, sometimes with the assistance of delegations; but the Czechoslovak side appears to have had no mandate to negotiate and it resisted Liechtenstein's proposal to submit the matter to a neutral institution such as the International Court of Justice. By mid-1991 the privatisation of land had begun in Czechoslovakia. The Liechtenstein side asked the Czechoslovaks to halt the privatisation of Liechtenstein assets in order to avoid further complications, but the Czechoslovaks replied that their legal system would not permit this. At the beginning of 1992 Hans-Adam II concluded that these exchanges were fruitless. Liechtenstein decided to draw the international community's attention to the problem by blocking Czechoslovakia's admission to European institutions unless it agreed to start negotiations about the property. Not all of these blocking moves were successful, since at the time it was a high western priority to reintegrate Czechoslovakia into Europe.

However, Liechtenstein has still not ratified the agreement on free trade between EFTA and Czechoslovakia/the Czech Republic. After a gap in contacts that lasted nearly a year there was another meeting at the end of 1992, the last in this series, between Hans-Adam II and the Czech Minister of Culture in Vaduz Castle. It was friendly enough but showed no progress.

The greater part of the assets is claimed by Hans-Adam II as Head of the Princely House, but there are between 30 and 40 other persons affected who also hold Liechtenstein citizenship. The Czechoslovak position appears to have been that Liechtenstein should recognise Czechoslovakia unconditionally and establish diplomatic relations. Liechtenstein, made wary by years of delaying tactics, wanted a concrete indication that Czechoslovakia would be prepared to negotiate seriously about restitution before it would grant recognition. Czechoslovakia would not contemplate any concession that could even remotely be interpreted as bearing on the Benes Decrees. For Liechtenstein, however, the skein of issues (property, recognition and the development of relations) went back much further than 1945.

A new situation arose on 1 January 1993. After the Czech and Slovak Republics parted company, each had to seek recognition from other states and fresh admission to international organisations and institutions as the successor states to the Czechoslovak Republic. Liechtenstein now had to negotiate with two states which, as far as property was concerned, both based their positions on the Benes Decrees. On 15 March 1993, Liechtenstein replied to the Czech Republic's request for recognition by saying that it would recognise the existence of the new state on the basis of reciprocity and by suggesting the start of negotiations about diplomatic relations and other unresolved issues including property. In short, Liechtenstein was willing in principle to recognise both states, but the problem of expropriation without compensation had to be solved before proper diplomatic relations could be established. Although the Czech Republic presented itself for recognition as a new entity, Liechtenstein noted that it continued to hold to certain policies of its predecessor which Liechtenstein considered to be contrary to international law. Liechtenstein therefore raised objections to the Czech Republic's admission to, *inter alia*, CSCE and the Council of Europe. In the case of the Council of Europe, Liechtenstein abstained from voting on the Czech application. Hungary, which had its own problems with Slovakia dating from 1945, abstained on the Slovak Republic's application. In view of the wider issues at stake, such obstacles were unwelcome to the states that were not involved. The diplomatic formula that was usually found to overcome the immediate difficulty was that member states were invited to find solutions to open problems. However, a visit by a Czech delegation to Vaduz in April 1993 brought no movement.

The problem remains unsolved. Contacts at various levels have continued from time to time, including an informal meeting between Hans-Adam II and President Havel at Alpbach in 1994 and a private visit to Vaduz by the then Prime Minister Klaus in 1995. Without wishing to obstruct important business, Liechtenstein has patiently continued to remind international meetings that the problem exists. Liechtenstein will not cease to do so. The problem has not prevented industrial investment in the Czech Republic by Liechtenstein companies. Nor has it prevented a generous response by Liechtenstein to the Czech Republic in its hour of need. A Liechtenstein engineer joined the Swiss humanitarian help team after the floods in 2002.[1] Princess Maria Pia of Liechtenstein, who as her country's representative has several times had to criticise the Czech Republic at OSCE meetings, has presented to the Czech Minister of Culture a cheque for 340,000 francs for the restoration of flood-damaged cultural objects and bridges.

---

[1] "Liechtensteiner Volksblatt", 31 August 2002.

This money, like another 30,000 francs for a damaged school, was raised by private citizens and charitable organisations and was supplemented by the Liechtenstein Government.[2]

It is an anomaly in modern Europe that two partner states in various European and international organisations should not formally recognise each other or have diplomatic relations. A solution ought not to be beyond the wit of man. Although the problem has its roots in property, it extends beyond property. Liechtenstein is a much older state than the Czech Republic, its predecessor the Czechoslovak Republic and also Germany. Nevertheless, for its own reasons connected with property, Prague chose not to recognise it between 1918 and 1938. The Benes Decrees injected a new element in 1945, in that their application to the Liechtenstein assets appeared to deny the very existence of the Principality at that time. The Prince and his Government seek a retrospective (so to speak) recognition of Liechtenstein and an acknowledgement that the application of the Benes Decrees to Liechtenstein property was contrary to international law. The Czech and Slovak Republics for their part view the Benes Decrees as a vital line of defence against any possible Sudeten German and Hungarian minority claims. However, it is hard to see how a property settlement with Liechtenstein could lend substance to any such claims, since it would be based precisely on the fact that Liechtenstein citizens were not and are not German citizens and belong to an independent and neutral state.

If the problem of principle could be settled, various statements by Hans-Adam II suggest that he might be willing to be flexible about the property itself. Restitution, compensation or a combination of the two might be a matter for negotiation. The family would be likely to invest in the renovation and development of any buildings, land or forests that might be returned, to the benefit of the Czech economy.

Complaints against Germany

In 1991 the Brno Historical Monuments Office in the Czech Republic lent a painting for exhibition at a museum in Cologne. The painting, "Scene by a Roman Lime-kiln" by Pieter van Laer (1592–1642), was bought by one of Hans-Adam II's ancestors in 1767. It is from the castle at Feldsberg. It is not particularly important: its value is estimated at about 400,000 francs. However, its appearance outside Czech territory enabled Hans-Adam II, acting in his private capacity, to lay claim to it as his family's property. The case went to a succession of German courts, ending with the Federal Constitutional Court on 28 January 1998. The lower courts declared the case inadmissible. They argued that Germany

---

[2] "Liechtensteiner Vaterland", 29 January 2003.

was bound by Chapter Six, Article 3 (1) of the Convention on the Settlement of Matters arising out of the War and the Occupation, concluded at Bonn with the three Western Allies on 26 May 1952, to "raise no objections against the measures which have been, or will be, carried out with regard to German external assets or other property seized for the purpose of reparation or restitution or as a result of the state of war…". In the view of the courts, Benes Decree No. 12 of 21 June 1945 was a measure within the meaning of this article. The Federal Constitutional Court upheld this judgment, adding that the case referred to a time before the German Basic Law (Constitution) was in force and that the relevant clauses of the Settlement Convention had not been set aside by the 1990 Treaty on the Final Settlement with Respect to Germany. The painting was returned to the Czech Republic.[3]

Prince Hans-Adam, still in his private capacity, complained to the European Commission of Human Rights on 1 November 1998 about violation of his right of access to a court and fairness of the proceedings; breach of his right to property; and discrimination. On 12 July 2001 the Grand Chamber of the European Court of Human Rights rejected his case in all points. It upheld the German courts' interpretation of the Settlement Convention as depriving them of jurisdiction in the matter, since at the time Germany had not been a fully sovereign state. It considered that the Prince had been given a fair hearing by the Federal Constitutional Court. The Court, considering that it was not competent to examine the circumstances of the expropriation of 1946 or its continuing effects, found that the Prince could not, for the purposes of Article 1 of Protocol No. 1 of the European Convention on Human Rights,[4] be deemed to have retained a title to property nor a claim to restitution against the Federal Republic of Germany.

According to the former German Ambassador to Liechtenstein, the German courts reached a judgment of Solomon on the basis that owing to Germany's post-war agreements with the Allies it was beyond their competence to rule on the matter.[5] To Prince Hans-Adam II and his Government, however, the terms in which the Federal Constitutional Court's judgment was expressed meant that it required Germany to treat all Liechtenstein assets confiscated in Czechoslovakia as "reparations and restitution" under Article 3 (1) of the Settlement Convention: that is to say, as the property of the German State or of its nationals. This in turn implied a denial of Liechtenstein's independence and wartime neutrality.

---

[3] Summary based on the press release about the decision of the European Court of Human Rights, Strasbourg on 12 July 2001 (www.echr.coe.int).

[4] The first clause of this article says, "Every natural or legal person is entitled to the peaceful enjoyment of his possessions. No one shall be deprived of his possessions except in the public interest and subject to the conditions provided for by law and by the general principles of international law."

[5] Quoted in the "Liechtensteiner Volksblatt", 6 June 2002.

It had previously been understood between Germany and Liechtenstein that Liechtenstein citizens' property in Czechoslovakia was not subject to the Settlement Convention. It followed, in Liechtenstein's view, that German courts were not debarred from considering claims affecting such property, but also that there could be no question of compensation by Germany to the property's former owners under Article 5 of the Convention.

On 21 January 1997 Chancellor Kohl and the Czech Prime Minister Klaus signed a Joint Declaration intended to draw a line under more than six decades of hatred and injustice between their two countries. The German Government formally assured Liechtenstein at the time that any arrangement made by it with the Czech Republic would not affect the rights of third states and their nationals.

Against this background, the Federal Constitutional Court's decision of 28 January 1998 led to a protest by Liechtenstein to the German Government. After talking to the German Government for more than two years, the Liechtenstein Government concluded that the latter's position had indeed changed fundamentally in the light of that decision. In Liechtenstein's view, the matter had now become a question of defending state sovereignty and the interests of its citizens.

As a result, the VU government decided in January 2001 to make two complaints against Germany at the International Court of Justice that:

(a) by its conduct with respect to the Liechtenstein property, in and since 1998, Germany failed to respect the rights of Liechtenstein with respect to that property;

(b) by its failure to make compensation for losses suffered by Liechtenstein and/or its nationals, Germany is in breach of the rules of international law.

The successor FBP government presented the complaints at The Hague on 1 June 2001.

It is necessary to draw three distinctions in this legally and politically complex affair. First, the complaints to the International Court of Justice are not about Czechoslovakia's seizure of the property in 1945 as such; that is a separate matter. Secondly, Prince Hans-Adam's action about the painting in the German courts and the European Court of Human Rights was undertaken in his private capacity. Thirdly, and in contrast, the complaints to the International Court of Justice are by the State of Liechtenstein on behalf of all its citizens who have been affected.

LIECHTENSTEIN AND THE WIDER WORLD

Development Aid and Humanitarian Assistance

Liechtenstein is conscious of being a prosperous country that has been spared from war for over two centuries. It knows that it cannot change the world, but it takes its international humanitarian responsibility seriously. Its activities in this area may be divided into disaster relief, reconstruction assistance, co-operation with Eastern Europe and development co-operation.

As a general principle, the Government intends, step by step, to raise its Official Development Assistance (ODA) to 0.7% of Liechtenstein's Gross Domestic Product, as agreed at Rio de Janeiro in 1992 by the industrialised countries participating in UNCED.

International disaster relief is the responsibility of the Office for Foreign Affairs within the Ministry of Foreign Affairs. Apart from its participation in the Swiss Humanitarian Aid Unit (SHA), Liechtenstein does not operate directly in this field but contributes to the emergency programmes of international or national relief organisations such as the International Committee of the Red Cross (ICRC), the Office of the UN High Commissioner for Refugees (UNHCR) and the UN Children's Fund (UNICEF). Disaster relief also includes contributions to non-governmental organisations and the policy of doubling the proceeds of private fund-raising by the larger relief organisations in Liechtenstein such as the Liechtenstein Red Cross, Caritas Liechtenstein and the Hilfswerk Liechtenstein. This policy of doubling aims to promote humanitarian awareness in society as a whole. The budgeted provision for 2002 was more than 1.7 million francs. This sum does not include the Government's general contributions to the relief organisations mentioned above. Since disasters are often unforeseeable, it is not uncommon for the Government to ask Parliament for a supplementary credit when the budget has been exceeded.

Reconstruction assistance is the responsibility of the Foreigners and Passport Office. This office is subordinate to the Head of Government (Prime Minister) as part of his responsibility for government affairs in general. It supports and initiates reconstruction programmes in the regions of origin of those refugees who have found shelter in Liechtenstein. During the Kosovo crisis Liechtenstein was confronted with the largest inflow of refugees since the Second World War. Reconstruction assistance money has therefore largely been spent on programmes in the Balkans. Through the reconstruction of schools, medical centres or infrastructure in general, as well as through income-generating programmes, reconstruction assistance aims to create an environment that promotes the reintegration of the "Liechtenstein" refugees in their places of origin. The budgeted provision for 2002 was 3 million francs.

Co-operation with eastern Europe is the responsibility of the Office for Foreign Affairs. It is designed to help the countries of eastern Europe by promoting the rule of law, human rights, democratic and stable institutions, social and economic development based on market principles and sound environmental policies. For this purpose Liechtenstein supports programmes and projects of the Council of Europe and the OSCE as well as of non-governmental organisations and private persons. In 2002 the budgeted provision was 950,000 francs.[1] To this should be added Liechtenstein's contributions to the European Bank for Reconstruction and Development (EBRD) and, in part, the European Union's Cohesion Fund. As a result of the coming enlargement of the EU, Liechtenstein's contribution to this fund will rise in 2004 from 300,000 to around 1.5 million francs per year.

Development co-operation is the responsibility of the Ministry of Foreign Affairs. It is largely administered by the Liechtenstein Development Service ("Liechtensteinischer Entwicklungsdienst", or LED) and to a lesser extent by the Office for Foreign Affairs. LED was established in 1965 as an independent foundation and is chiefly concerned with supporting programmes and projects of non-governmental organisations or private persons. The Office for Foreign Affairs is in charge of development co-operation through regular contributions to international organisations or programmes such as the UN Development Programme (UNDP), the UN Development Funds for Women (UNIFEM) and the UN Population Fund (UNFPA).

LED is currently active in Central and South America and in Africa. Its projects are practical and businesslike. After carefully checking the feasibility and long-term value of the programmes LED carries them out either on its own account or, more usually, through its partner organisations. As typical examples, in six projects in Burkina Faso LED is working with a Swiss aid organisation, and in Mali with the German Development Service.[2] LED puts its emphasis on education, public health and the development of rural areas. In all its programmes or projects it aims at improving people's ability to help themselves and at promoting

---

[1] Article by Ambassador Roland Marxer, Head of the Office for Foreign Affairs, LED Magazine 2003.
[2] "Liechtensteiner Volksblatt", 21 May 2003 and LED Magazine 2003.

the empowerment of women. LED's budget is derived almost entirely from the State. It has risen from 92,000 francs in 1965 to more than 8.9 million francs (about £3.7m.) in 2002. As with disaster relief, LED encourages humanitarian initiatives by doubling the proceeds of private fund-raising for approved projects, up to a limit of 10,000 francs. In 2002 it spent more than 386,000 francs in this way.

Culture, Youth and Sport

Large international cultural manifestations by Liechtenstein are, naturally, rare. The great exhibition of the Princely Collections at New York in 1985 and the concerts in Vaduz, Munich and London by the London Symphony Orchestra in 2001 to commemorate the centenary of Rheinberger's death were exceptional events. However, the new Art Museum (which houses exhibitions from both the State Art Collection and the Princely Collections), the Stamp Museum and the Ski Museum attract visitors from all over the world. From 2004 the permanent and rotating exhibitions at the Liechtenstein Garden Palace in Vienna will be a standing reminder of the Principality in one of the most visited cities of Europe.

At a more day-to-day level, the Liechtenstein Government attaches importance to a steady programme of cultural, youth and sporting activities as a way of promoting the Liechtenstein identity abroad and giving fresh opportunities to its own people. It plays a full part in the various Council of Europe and EU programmes. Many of its activities are organised in conjunction with private organisations or individual citizens. It gives financial support to a range of events from the austerely intellectual to the unabashedly popular. Some of the cultural and educational establishments mentioned on pages 341–345 (in particular, the Theater am Kirchplatz in Schaan and the University of Applied Sciences ("Fachhochschule") in Vaduz) have won a regional importance that spreads well beyond Liechtenstein's boundaries. There is constant interchange with the German-speaking Swiss cantons and the Austrian and German federal Lands. Liechtenstein enthusiastically supports and takes part in the annual Small States Olympics with Andorra, Iceland, Luxembourg, Malta, Monaco, San Marino and Cyprus.

In addition to these programmed events, both official and semi-private, an unofficial Liechtenstein presence sometimes appears where it might not be expected.

In December 2002 the Peter Kaiser Memorial Foundation presented a new organ to the Sistine Chapel in Rome. The German Federal President was surprised to learn in August 2002 that the Director of the Max Planck Institute for History, Medicine and Natural Sciences in Berlin is a young Liechtenstein citizen, Professor Hans-Jörg Rheinberger. Recently the Liechtenstein-born landscape architect Günther Vogt, together with the late Professor Dieter Kienast, has contributed to the spectacular international success of the Tate Modern project in London by designing the green open space around the former Bankside power station in collaboration with the Swiss architectural partnership Herzog & de Meuron. The same team has worked with equal success on exciting designs for the new Laban Dance Centre in Deptford, south-east London.

PART V
THE FUTURE OF LIECHTENSTEIN

On 22 April 1939 Sir Alexander Cadogan, Permanent Under-Secretary of State at the Foreign Office, wrote to the British Foreign Secretary, Lord Halifax, "Liechtenstein is a historical curiosity, and only exists by mistake. It shouldn't, of course, exist at all as an independent state."[1]

How and why has it survived? In part, through chance. The country was too small, too poor and too much off the beaten track for most predators to find it worth making a determined effort to seize it. It was chance that the House of Liechtenstein should have bought the governance of that particular tract of land at the turn of the seventeenth century to further its political ambitions. It was chance that Johann I should have found enough favour with Napoleon to save his Principality's independence in 1806. It was Liechtenstein's good fortune that its Princes should have lived up to their responsibilities by helping to keep it afloat financially in the nineteenth century and the first third of the twentieth century.

But people also make their own luck. In the revolutionary period of 1848–1849 the Liechtensteiners were already conscious of their state identity. At that point some of them toyed with the idea of merging their country into a Greater Germany, but abandoned the idea when it became clear that it would bring them little say in German affairs and higher costs. In 1918–1923 the Liechtensteiners were determined to keep their political independence at a time when it might have been strategically and financially easier to give it up. Their choice of neutral Switzerland as a new economic partner was hugely important in saving them from Austria's fate before and during the Second World War. Yet even Switzerland could not have saved them from eventual Nazi rule if the great majority had not been determined to stand up for their freedoms and independence. In this, they were helped by having the Monarchy as a moral rallying point. Liechtenstein's entry into the Council of Europe and the United Nations, and the long, tough EEA negotiations followed by the difficult popular vote in December 1992, illustrate in a different way Liechtenstein's will to define and fight for its longer-term interests.

---

[1] FO 371/22969.

Liechtenstein has always been at the mercy of external political and economic forces. In difficult times it has occasionally had to survive by manoeuvring, adapting or simply hoping that it would not be noticed in the general mayhem. Yet at the root of its policies, whether active or passive, has been a stubborn determination not to be swallowed up and not to surrender self-government. Its people have wanted Liechtenstein to survive. That is the answer to the question underlying Sir Alexander Cadogan's comment. It is also the guarantee of Liechtenstein's future.

The Liechtenstein Identity

In Liechtenstein, as in many European countries, debate about the country's identity waxes and wanes according to the mood of the moment. The debate sometimes seems exaggerated. It is a mistake to think that national identity can be frozen at a particular moment in time. Like the Rhine (or the Thames), it is always changing but always there. The Liechtensteiners cannot be called a people in the sense of being a distinct nation or race. They are of Celtic, Roman and Alemannic descent. The Alemannic and Walser groups on Liechtenstein territory have long since mingled with people from neighbouring and more remote territories through centuries of foreign marriages. There is, nevertheless, a strong sense of continuity and community. It springs from several sources. Political identity since 1719 and 1806 is one. Cultural identity in the broadest sense, including the inherited traditions of local self-government, self-help and mutual help, is another. Politically, the sense of identity is now rooted in Liechtenstein's distinctive combination of monarchy and direct democracy. Less tangibly, it is rooted in pride in the country's survival and achievements and an awareness of its vulnerability. Liechtensteiners know that political survival and their new-found prosperity are not gifts from above: they are, and will continue to be, the result of internal unity, hard work, adaptability and alertness.

Liechtenstein and the Other European Mini-States

Liechtenstein is the fourth largest of the five mini-states on the European mainland. The others are the Vatican City (0.4km²), Monaco (1.9km²), San Marino (61 km²) and Andorra (464 km²). Of the five, and making allowances for the unique role of the Vatican City, Liechtenstein seems the most favourably placed. Unlike the Vatican City and San Marino, it is not an enclave within another state. Unlike Andorra, which has two co-sovereigns (the French President and the Spanish Bishop of Urgel), it has its own sovereign hereditary dynasty. Unlike Monaco, which is bound by treaty to have a French citizen as its Minister of State (chief minister) and whose future status depends in part on the survival of the House of Grimaldi, Liechtenstein's government is elected and appointed from within the country. Liechtenstein's balanced and highly diverse economy puts it in a different league from all the other mini-states. In that respect, it is closer to its larger analogue the Grand Duchy of Luxembourg.

Liechtenstein's Weaknesses

The country's most obvious weaknesses are its lack of natural resources, its small territory and population and its resulting lack of international political weight. Land is scarce and expensive, the labour market is tight and wages are high.

It is sometimes said that Liechtenstein has reached the limits of its ability to run itself as a fully-fledged state with the human resources of a small township. The Principality makes a virtue of small government. Sometimes this has gone too far, for example when inadequate supervision of the financial services sector provoked strong international criticism. Yet somehow Liechtenstein has always in the end been able to find the personal resources that it needs, whether from within its own population or by hiring them from abroad. That was the case when it met the FATF criticisms and more recently when it reorganised the national police. In the 1970s many Liechtensteiners and outside observers would have doubted whether Liechtenstein could run an active foreign policy or, in the 1980s, whether it could negotiate on its own behalf for entry into the EEA; but it did so. This suggests that it would be inadvisable to write off in advance Liechtenstein's ability to find the means to meet any future challenge. The country makes up for its lack of personal resources by concentrating on the priorities that matter to it and on the areas where it can make a distinctive contribution.

A small population also means a small pool of potential political talent. Politics in Liechtenstein is a part-time occupation, the politicians have to concentrate on their working careers, and the Principality's small scale cannot offer glittering political prizes. Nevertheless, the hour usually produces the right man (and, increasingly, the right woman) to match the international and internal situation.

There are two standing dangers in the political life of so small a country: factiousness and complacency. An unsympathetic German observer wrote in 1943, "The cramped conditions in Liechtenstein [help to] turn every small problem instantly into a matter of State of the first order"[2] The picture is recognisable today. Coalition governments are not necessarily the solution. Even in the "co-opposition" form practised in Liechtenstein between 1938 and 1997 they have the obvious advantage of drawing together the country's political talent, but they also have the disadvantage of tending to dampen debate. Whether or not there is

---

[2] Unsympathetic in every sense. He was SS Haupsturmführer (Captain) Dr Sichelschmidt, an official of the Volksdeutsche Mittelstelle. (Quoted by Jürgen Schremser in "Der Einzige Mann...", JBL 98, 1999, page 92.)

a coalition, closeness to the people and the imperative of consensus, which gives the country its stability, can lead to excessive cosiness and a reluctance to grasp nettles.

However, in practice it is almost impossible for a country to stagnate when it exports all over the world and is at all times exposed to external pressures. Its businessmen, financiers and lawyers, from among whom many of the politicians are drawn, are by their professions alert to what is going on in the region and more widely in the world. They are imaginative and resourceful. The Chamber of Industry and Trade, representing corporate Liechtenstein, helps to facilitate foreign policy. The Forum Liechtenstein and many other groupings and trade and professional bodies contribute their own thinking to internal and external policy-making. The Government's newly formed international experts' council is now adding its strategic perceptions. Not least, the Sovereign Prince himself, with his constitutional responsibilities in foreign affairs, has important insights to offer as Head of State, businessman and head of a large and cosmopolitan family. Liechtenstein therefore enjoys access to a much wider range of international information and opinion than its small size and limited personal resources might suggest.

It is possible that more could be done. The proposal to establish a network of honorary consuls abroad will, if it goes ahead and if the right people can be found, help to develop the country's antennae and promote Liechtenstein's public image. In addition, it might be useful if industry and the banks could be persuaded to second a few up-and-coming members of their staff for a couple of years at a time to the key diplomatic posts at Brussels, Washington and Berlin. Their accredited status would give them the entrée to official economic and financial circles which an honorary consul might not always enjoy. They would strengthen Liechtenstein's diplomatic resources abroad, improve the country's early warning system and on their return bring back valuable international expertise to their employers.

Liechtenstein's Strengths

The people and the politicians of Liechtenstein dislike arbitrary and unpredictable change; they set a high premium on continuity and stability in political, legal, social, economic and fiscal affairs. This is a commercial as well as a political asset: investors know where they stand. It is less clear whether old-style neutrality now matters very much as an asset in present-day Europe; but, to the extent that it does, Liechtenstein benefits from being a neutral country surrounded by neutral neighbours. Its customs and currency union with Switzerland gives it an economic hinterland with one of the most stable currencies and political systems in the world. Liechtenstein is lucky in being situated in the prosperous, high-technology region of Europe to which eastern Switzerland, Vorarlberg, Bavaria and Baden-Württemberg also belong. Membership of the European Economic Area gives Liechtenstein's manufacturing firms and financial institutions access to the European Single Market. Membership of EFTA gives them the advantage of trade agreements with other countries across the world.

There is little state intervention in business. The bureaucracy is small and readily accessible. Public finances are sound. There is no need for high taxes. Low taxes help to give Liechtenstein its competitive edge, for example by enabling high salaries to be paid to qualified staff and thus contributing to the retention of research and development facilities within the country. The banking system is efficient. The infrastructure is good. The remarkable variety of the country's business activity, which includes most kinds of manufacturing, large, medium and small enterprises, banks, trusts and insurance companies, makes Liechtenstein's economy resilient and elastic. The Principality is far from depending on any one branch of economic activity.

Many of the business leaders have an entrepreneurial spirit; but despite the European and even global activities of some of the companies, they continue to be rooted in Liechtenstein and to show commitment to the country. The labour climate and social climate are good. The population is generally well educated, multilingual and hardworking. The absence of long commuting makes their working time more productive. The proximity of some of the finest scenery and recreational areas in Europe adds to their quality of life. New educational establishments like the University of Applied Sciences are helping to recruit talent and ideas from the rest of the region. Among the various institutions of higher education one can begin to discern the possible outline of a future University of Liechtenstein.

The Image Problem

Liechtenstein has an image problem. There are two aspects to it.

The first is the insinuation that Liechtenstein is not a serious country: that it is a subject from an operetta. However, it makes no more sense to judge modern Liechtenstein by the admirable works of Franz Lehár than it would to judge the United Kingdom by the equally enjoyable operas of his near contemporaries Gilbert and Sullivan. If, as Aristotle would have recommended, one judges Liechtenstein by its capacity as a state, one sees that all the functions are there: a working political and administrative system, the rule of law, the administration of justice, internal security, an active foreign and regional policy, a strong economy and good provision for education, health and welfare. To this one might add a strong sense of public service and commitment within the population, which an ancient Greek would have approved. The only state function that is lacking is armed defence against external attack.

The second aspect concerns Liechtenstein's reputation in financial services. (The country's industrial success story is usually ignored.) The allegations usually revolve round past actual or suspected cases of abuse of financial institutions for criminal purposes; the assertion that banking secrecy gives cover to criminal and even terrorist activities; national and international campaigns against tax evasion; or even a visceral dislike of low taxes *per se*. Sometimes the stories have been whipped up in other countries for their own domestic political reasons. The resulting mixture of truth, falsehoods and clichés is hard to deal with, as Part III of this book has shown.

Every financial centre risks being abused. What matters are the measures, resources and persistence employed to deter criminals and to catch those who may nevertheless break through the defences. The smaller the centre, the bigger the damage to its reputation when a breach occurs. A major scandal in New York or London has to compete with other news; in a smaller centre, it may be the only news. Mud not only sticks; it is often re-cycled.

On the other hand, the smaller the financial centre, the easier it is to put the house in order. Liechtenstein's response to the FATF's strictures was fast and thorough. The legal and organisational reforms for combating organised crime and the financing of terrorism are increasingly acknowledged abroad, to the benefit of Liechtenstein's reputation. Liechtenstein is confident enough about them to cite them as an international benchmark. The IMF's recent praise for Liechtenstein's high level of compliance with international measures to fight money laundering and the financing of terrorism, for the "dramatic" improvement of its performance in Mutual Legal Assistance cases and for its determination to build on its successes in this field will go far to correct previous negative impressions.

The forthcoming negotiations with the EU on the taxation of income from EU non-residents' foreign capital will, if successful, dispose of the allegation that Liechtenstein wishes to make a one-sided profit from the EU. There is a strong principled and practical case to be made for tax competition. Those who may see high taxation as an egalitarian virtue in itself will never be appeased; but history can be left to look after them.

The foreign comment about Liechtenstein in 1999–2001 rightly pin-pointed failings in the country's financial regulatory and supervisory arrangements, but it also disclosed a good deal of international ignorance about the country and weaknesses in its public information policy. While measures to bring financial services regulation up to date were still in train in 2001, the Government set up a temporary (three-year) unit led by an Austrian expert to work out a realistic and credible communication concept in cooperation with the Government Press and Information Office. In the same year the Government established and helped to endow an "Image Liechtenstein" Foundation, whose board consists of the Head of Government and representatives of the business and financial communities. Its aim is to produce a quick, professional and better co-ordinated information service. A more active information policy is beginning to seize the initiative. False and damaging stories are being rebutted where previously they would have been tolerated with weary fatalism. The newly established Government internet portal www.liechtenstein.li offers access in German and English to a fund of governmental, economic, cultural, historic and tourist information about Liechtenstein, including links to other important web-sites in the Principality. In addition to its other information activities, the Government offers a full set-piece briefing once a year to the foreign ambassadors accredited to Vaduz.

The resolution of the constitutional controversy in March 2003 has settled an internal problem which hurt Liechtenstein's international image not only directly but also indirectly, to the extent that it must have distracted attention and energies from the solution of other pressing problems. Liechtenstein now has a freer hand to set its own active information policy agenda.

The Future of the Economy

Owing to the lack of a domestic market Liechtenstein's manufacturing companies, whether large, medium or small, will continue to be more exposed than those of most other countries to the fluctuations of European and global markets. The absence of state aid will, as in the past, keep them more agile than companies in more cosseted countries. If the Liechtenstein tax environment continues to be benign, if the State and the trade associations continue to foster life-long technical and vocational training at a high level, and if there is no discrimination against Liechtenstein products (which seems unlikely, given the international agreements to which Liechtenstein is party), there is every reason to expect that Liechtenstein's industry, with its high quality niche products, will continue to fight its corner successfully.

It is hard to assess whether, or how much, the financial services sector suffered from the international criticism and the measures taken as a result. So far as these things can be judged, there seems to have been no great material damage from the one or from the other. The volume of assets under management has been much more affected by the financial scandals involving conglomerates in the USA and Europe and by the continuing downturn in the stock markets in 2002. Nevertheless, the Liechtenstein banks have been able to avoid the significant dismissals of staff that have occurred in bigger centres. As the financial services sector moves into a counter-attack, there are signs that it is going to make Liechtenstein's high regulatory standards one of its selling points.

Liechtenstein will certainly keep bank secrecy, partly for cultural and constitutional reasons, partly because it remains a commercial asset. However, as an asset it is only part of the story, not the whole. The pressure on private banking in every financial centre continues to grow in terms of costs, competition, the search for qualified personnel, expensive technology and falling margins. There seems to be a growing consensus in Liechtenstein that the new generation of clients will look for performance, long-term strategic advice, sophisticated tax planning, continuity and protection from litigation rather than (as in the pre-war and post-war period) the mere protection of assets through confidentiality and tax evasion. Liechtenstein's offshore business will continue, like London's and that of other centres. In future, however, there is likely to be more emphasis on the management in foreign countries of assets that have been declared to those countries' authorities. There will be a constant demand for new and imaginative financial products. The remarkable success of Liechtenstein's new onshore insurance sector shows what can be achieved under tight anti-criminal regulation in a short space of time.

The Government's working group on the future positioning of Liechtenstein's financial services aims to define a new strategy autonomously, rather than have it dictated piecemeal by reactions to pressures from abroad. According to the present Head of Government, Otmar Hasler, the strategy will be based on a policy of openness to the outside world and will include a fresh look at the essence of Liechtenstein's advantages as a location, properly understood in the light of contemporary circumstances. It will include a continuing strict adherence to high regulatory standards: only in this way will it be possible to preserve the individual's legitimate privacy and a liberal economy.[3] It is too early to predict the results of this review, but the very fact that it is being undertaken shows yet again Liechtenstein's will to decide its own future within the limits of the possible.

Liechtenstein and Europe

Membership of the European Economic Area has suited Liechtenstein well. Although the EU has probably gained more immediate profit from the arrangement than the EFTA states, Liechtenstein sets much store by access to the Single Market and to EU programmes, free movement of people into the EU and a clear treaty and justiciable relationship with the EU.

There must however be a question mark over the EEA's future. Its elaborate structures were designed for a larger membership. After the forthcoming enlargement of the EU the quality of the EFTA component will continue to be as high as ever, but its size in relation to the EU component will become disproportionately small. It is just possible, though perhaps unlikely, that the EEA might grow. In one scenario, it could be a holding room for future applicant countries preparing

---

[3] "Liechtensteiner Volksblatt", 1 October 2002.

for EU membership. In another, it could be a retreat for member countries whose peoples were unwilling to accept the new constitutional arrangements now being discussed.

With so much already on its plate, the EU probably does not have the time and energy to take the initiative to abolish or adapt an arrangement that, although elaborate, seems to be working smoothly. The EEA could therefore continue indefinitely. If, however, Norway were to join the EU it is hard to see how the EEA could continue to exist with Iceland and Liechtenstein alone forming its EFTA pillar. If the EEA were to disappear, Liechtenstein would see the existing EEA Treaty as an important legal starting point for negotiating a successor relationship with the EU.[4]

Switzerland is another imponderable. There would be no problem for Liechtenstein if Switzerland were to join the EEA; but memories of the 1992 vote make that unlikely, and it is in any case the Swiss Government's policy to join the EU. If Switzerland were to join the EU, which looks unlikely in the near future, Liechtenstein could be faced with some historic choices. The economic relationship symbolised by the Customs Treaty and the Currency Treaty would be overtaken. Liechtenstein and Switzerland have already moved a long way towards EU norms and standards through EEA membership in the former case and bilateral agreements with the EU in the latter. But Swiss membership of the EU would entail further changes. Switzerland would surrender national responsibility for foreign trade policy, join the Common Agricultural Policy and, presumably, Economic and Monetary Union[5] as well (in which case, the Swiss franc would disappear). As a mundane but far-reaching practical example, Switzerland would be obliged to raise its Value Added Tax rate. If Liechtenstein had to follow suit as a consequence of the bilateral relationship, the extra tax would be superfluous as a source of revenue and the extra burden unwelcome economically.

For the time being, Liechtenstein can keep its options open and study all the possibilities – which it is doing. A good deal will depend on the direction that the EU takes in the coming years: whether it remains primarily a union of states or becomes more centralised, and in either case whether it retains the variety of interlocking internal memberships and external association arrangements that at present exists. The Head of Government, Otmar Hasler, has said that Liechtenstein has no intention of joining the EU.[6] This seems sensible on practical grounds: for example, in the way the EU is at present constructed and operates,

---

[4] Rita Kieber-Beck, Deputy Head of Government, quoted in the "Liechtensteiner Vaterland", 3 May 2002.
[5] When deciding the criteria for future applicants at Copenhagen in 1995 the EU ruled, *inter alia,* that "Membership presupposes the candidate's ability to take on the obligations of membership, including adherence to the aims of political, economic and monetary union."
[6] "Liechtensteiner Volksblatt", 1 March 2003.

it is hard to see how Liechtenstein could run a presidency. It also makes sense on domestic political grounds, not least because of the implications for direct democracy. One specialist on the subject has recommended, however, that the option of a membership application should not be foreclosed, if only to leave as much negotiating room as possible.[7] It could become necessary to bargain full EU membership against special status.

While Liechtenstein is analysing its options it has time to build alliances inside and outside the EU, which it is also doing. Most of these will be bilateral. It is for consideration whether it should apply to join OECD. As an advanced industrial country, it has common interests with the members of that body. There are differences of principle on taxation policy; but membership (if a realistic prospect) would allow Liechtenstein to make its case from within and so to win the better understanding from others that an outsider finds harder to achieve. Its membership of the Council of Europe and the WTO are already important assets, which in the latter case could be exploited further.

In the recent CEPS study of Liechtenstein's future challenges and options Peter Ludlow, among other useful ideas, suggested that the Liechtenstein authorities might consider establishing an independent, internationally staffed pan-European institute committed to encouraging debate and discussion about public policy issues of a European character, with a view to bringing the states and people of Europe closer together. This, he thought, would help to guarantee a continuing role for Liechtenstein in the European game at a moment when its access to European institutions might perforce become more restricted.[8]

One wonders whether yet another European think-tank in this already highly populated domain would be practicable. It would however be valuable for both Liechtenstein and the EU if some channel could be found, not necessarily via a specially created institute, for the merits and advantages of small states to be made better known. It is not always easy even in normal times for the smaller states to make themselves heard in Europe. It can be harder in more exceptional circumstances: the head of one of the larger member states recently advised the smaller candidate states to fall silent when their opinion on a particular issue differed from his, and one of the existing member states was sent to Coventry for a few months when it was deemed to have elected the wrong sort of government.

The European Council's Laeken Declaration on the Future of Europe[9] contained language which smaller states (and some bigger ones) may find encouraging:

---

[7] Dr Sieglinde Gstöhl, quoted in the "Liechtensteiner Volksblatt", 29 October 2001, on the occasion of the launch of her book "Flexible Integration für Kleinstaaten?"
[8] "Liechtenstein in the New European and Global Order", Centre for European Policy Studies, Brussels, 2000, page 34.
[9] 14–15 December 2001.

"Within the Union, the European institutions must be brought closer to its citizens. Citizens… want the European institutions to be less unwieldy and rigid and, above all, more efficient and open. Many also feel that the Union should involve itself more with their particular concerns, instead of intervening, in every detail, in matters by their nature better left to Member States' and regions' elected representatives. This is even perceived by some as a threat to their identity. More importantly, however, they feel that deals are all too often cut out of their sight and they want better democratic scrutiny."

Further on, the Declaration refers to Europe as "the continent of liberty, solidarity and above all diversity, meaning respect for each others' languages, cultures and traditions." It continues,

"National and regional differences frequently stem from history or tradition. They can be enriching. In other words, what citizens understand by "good governance" is opening up fresh opportunities, not imposing further red tape. What they expect is more results, better responses to practical issues and not a European superstate or European institutions inveigling their way into every nook and cranny of life."

A small state like Liechtenstein, which has been successful despite (or because of) being the abnegation of the "cult of the colossal", may provide some food for thought to its European partners. Its small scale, its history and its unique institutions could not, so to speak, be transplanted elsewhere. But it would be worth reflecting on whether there are any lessons that might be drawn from, for example:

– Liechtenstein's direct democracy. The EU, together with its member states, is rightly concerned about its democratic deficit. There is no easy answer either at the European or member state level, but some problems are more susceptible to solution than others. For example, the populations of some EU member states would envy the right of the Liechtenstein citizens to vote on new treaties.

– Liechtenstein's local government. The communes' "bottom-up" role contrasts with the centralised approach of many EU member states and of the EU itself, even when they apportion a certain measure of local autonomy in a "top-down" concept of subsidiarity.

– Liechtenstein's public finances. In Liechtenstein there is no feeling that taxation and governmental expenditure have run out of control. State taxation, expenditure and projects are subject to minute parliamentary and, ultimately, popular scrutiny. Auditing is strict. The same is true of local government finances. The result may be a lack of showy state projects, but the citizens get high-quality results in the areas that they want. The money left in the pockets of the citizens not infrequently produces in due course the grander initiatives such as the Art Museum or projects for humanitarian assistance.

- Liechtenstein's high economic performance against a background of low taxation, lack of state aids and relative freedom from red tape.
- The success of Liechtenstein's social policies in producing a high standard and quality of life for its residents, whether citizens or foreigners, while avoiding a benefits culture.

Analysis of Liechtenstein's political and economic culture might produce some practical conclusions to help make the EU and its member states both more efficient and more responsive to their citizens and businesses.

Liechtenstein's Bicentenary

In 2006 the Principality of Liechtenstein will commemorate the 200th anniversary of its full state sovereignty. It is younger than the USA but older than the modern states of Belgium, Greece, Italy, Germany and many others. In the heart of Europe, it is part of the diversity of Europe. Its people, its traditions, its institutions and its economy give it much to hope for. Amid their justified celebration of the past and their optimistic or solemn anticipation of the future, many Liechtensteiners will reflect on the much-quoted words of Peter Kaiser, their first historian, the country's representative at the German National Assembly in Frankfurt in 1848–1849 and one of those who defined the Liechtenstein identity:

"If we understand our advantage correctly, we may present ourselves as a small nation that endangers nobody but commands respect from all. Life is short; but an honourable name remains and serves down to the latest posterity for an example and for emulation."[10]

---

[10] Peter Kaiser (1793–1864), "An meine Landsleute!" (1848). (From the text reproduced in Europa Erlesen Liechtenstein, Wieser Verlag, Klagenfurt, 2000.)

A BRIEF CHRONOLOGY

1342 The County of Vaduz is established.

1434 The Barons von Brandis acquire the Lordship of Schellenberg in addition to Vaduz. Thereafter the Oberland and Unterland remain in the same hands except for the period 1699–1712.

1699 Prince Hans-Adam I of Liechtenstein acquires Schellenberg.

1712 Hans-Adam I acquires Vaduz and bequeaths both territories to his nephew Josef Wenzel.

1718 Prince Anton Florian, Ruler of the House of Liechtenstein, acquires the territories from Josef Wenzel and makes them inalienable within the House.

1719 Emperor Charles VI creates the Principality of Liechtenstein out of the two territories and makes it directly subordinate to the Holy Roman Emperor.

1799 The French General Masséna invades and plunders Liechtenstein in the spring. Liechtenstein's last direct experience of warfare on its territory. The Russian General Suvorov passes through in the autumn.

1806 Liechtenstein acquires full sovereignty by joining the Confederation of the Rhine.

1815 Liechtenstein is represented at the Congress of Vienna and joins the German Confederation.

1818 Johann I grants a very limited constitution. His heir Prince Alois pays the first visit by a member of the House of Liechtenstein to the Principality.

1836 The first factory (ceramics) is built in Liechtenstein.

1842 The first visit by a Sovereign Prince (Alois II).

1847 Publication of Peter Kaiser's "History of the Principality of Liechtenstein".

1848 Revolutionary unrest. Peter Kaiser represents Liechtenstein at the German National Assembly. Alois II grants, then revokes, a liberal constitution.

1852 Customs and tax treaty with the Austro-Hungarian Monarchy.

1861 The Savings and Loans Bank (later the Sparkasse, then the Liechtensteinische Landesbank) is founded. The first cotton-weaving mill is opened.

1862 Johann II grants a modern constitution. A decade of economic and social progress follows.

1866 The dissolution of the German Confederation leaves Liechtenstein politically isolated.

1868 The Liechtenstein Army is abolished. The first two of four fixed bridges across the Rhine are opened.

1872 The railway line across Liechtenstein is opened.

1880 Austria-Hungary undertakes the diplomatic representation of Liechtenstein.

1912 The first Liechtenstein postage stamps are issued.

1918 Collapse of the Austro-Hungarian Monarchy, its economy and currency. Severe hardship in Liechtenstein. Two political parties (the VU and FBP) founded. Baron von Imhoff forced to resign as Governor (7 November.)

1919 Liechtenstein denounces the Customs Treaty with Austria. Legations opened in Vienna and Berne. Switzerland undertakes the diplomatic representation of Liechtenstein.

1921 Postal Treaty with Switzerland. Josef Ospelt becomes the first native Liechtenstein Head of Government. On 5 October, after protracted negotiations, Johann II grants a new constitution which anchors power in the Prince and the people jointly.

1923 A Customs Treaty with Switzerland is concluded.

1926 The Persons and Company Act grants favourable conditions for foreign holding and domiciliary companies.

1927 The Rhine flood disaster.

1928 The Sparkasse has to be rescued from financial collapse.

1930 The people vote in favour of building the Inner Canal.

1933 Attempted kidnap by Nazis of the Rotter (Schaie) brothers.

1938 A coalition government is formed. Franz Josef II moves his official residence from Vienna to Vaduz.

1939 An attempt by local Nazis to seize power is foiled (24 March). The Prince, the Parliament and the people assert their will for continuing independence.

1945 Princess Gina founds the Liechtenstein Red Cross. Some 500 members of the "Russian National Army" cross the frontier and are interned in Liechtenstein.

1950 Liechtenstein becomes a party to the Statute of the International Court of Justice.

1960 The EFTA Convention is extended to Liechtenstein.

1972 Liechtenstein is an active participant in the CSCE talks at Helsinki.

1978 Liechtenstein joins the Council of Europe.

1980 Currency Treaty with Switzerland.

1984 Liechtenstein women get the vote at national level.

1990 Liechtenstein joins the United Nations.

1992 The "State Crisis" between Hans-Adam II, the Parliament and the Government (28 October). Unlike Switzerland, the people vote to join the European Economic Area (13 December).

1994 Liechtenstein joins GATT and, in 1995, the WTO.

1995 After negotiations with Switzerland and the EU, the people confirm their wish to join the EEA (9 April).

1997 The end of coalition government (February). Pope John Paul II separates Liechtenstein from the Diocese of Chur and erects a new Archdiocese on its territory (December).

1999 International criticism of the regulation and supervision of Liechtenstein's financial services leads to sweeping legislative and organisational improvements in 2000–2001.

2003 After more than ten years of debate, a popular vote approves constitutional proposals by Prince Hans-Adam II and Hereditary Prince Alois with a majority of 64.3% (14/16 March). On 15 August Hans-Adam II announces his intention to hand over the exercise of his political powers to Prince Alois as his Representative on 15 August 2004.

SOVEREIGN PRINCES OF LIECHTENSTEIN
(SINCE 1712)

Johann (Hans-) Adam I	Died 16 June 1712
Josef Wenzel	1712–1718
Anton Florian	1718–1721
Josef Johann Adam	1721–1732
Johann Nepomuk Karl	1732–1748
Josef Wenzel (again)	1748–1772
Franz Josef I	1772–1781
Alois Josef I	1781–1805
Johann Josef I	1805–1836
[Karl Johann, nominally reigned as an infant, 1806–1813]	
Alois Josef II	1836–1858
Johann II	1858–1929
Franz I	1929–1938
Franz Josef II	1938–1989
Hans-Adam II	1989–

THE PRINCES OF LIECHTENSTEIN:
A SIMPLIFIED FAMILY TREE

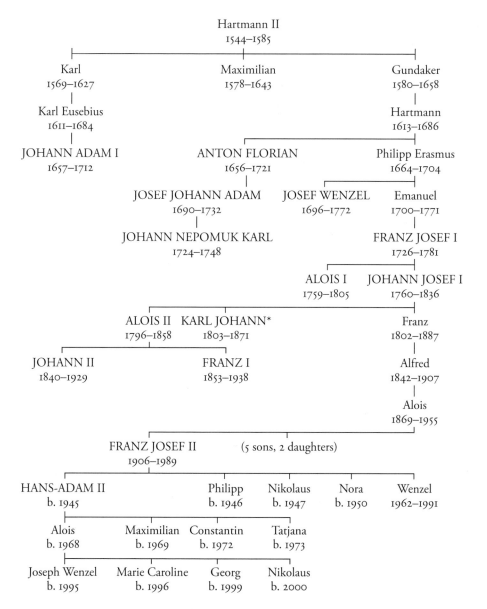

Hartmann II
1544–1585

Karl
1569–1627

Maximilian
1578–1643

Gundaker
1580–1658

Karl Eusebius
1611–1684

Hartmann
1613–1686

JOHANN ADAM I
1657–1712

ANTON FLORIAN
1656–1721

Philipp Erasmus
1664–1704

JOSEF JOHANN ADAM
1690–1732

JOSEF WENZEL
1696–1772

Emanuel
1700–1771

JOHANN NEPOMUK KARL
1724–1748

FRANZ JOSEF I
1726–1781

ALOIS I
1759–1805

JOHANN JOSEF I
1760–1836

ALOIS II
1796–1858

KARL JOHANN*
1803–1871

Franz
1802–1887

JOHANN II
1840–1929

FRANZ I
1853–1938

Alfred
1842–1907

Alois
1869–1955

FRANZ JOSEF II
1906–1989

(5 sons, 2 daughters)

HANS-ADAM II
b. 1945

Philipp
b. 1946

Nikolaus
b. 1947

Nora
b. 1950

Wenzel
1962–1991

Alois
b. 1968

Maximilian
b. 1969

Constantin
b. 1972

Tatjana
b. 1973

Joseph Wenzel
b. 1995

Marie Caroline
b. 1996

Georg
b. 1999

Nikolaus
b. 2000

NOTE: The names of Sovereign Princes are printed in capitals. Prince Karl Johann (denoted with an asterisk) was the third son of Johann Josef I and reigned only nominally as an infant between 1806 and 1813.

GOVERNORS AND HEADS OF GOVERNMENT OF LIECHTENSTEIN SINCE 1918

Governors

Baron Leopold von Imhoff		resigned 7 November 1918
Prince Karl von und zu Liechtenstein		1918–1920

Heads of Government

Dr Josef Peer (provisional)		1920–1921
Prof. Josef Ospelt	FBP	1921–1922*
Alfons Feger (provisional)	VP	1922
Prof. Gustav Schädler	VP	1922–1928
Prince Alfred von und zu Liechtenstein (provisional)		1928
Dr Josef Hoop	FBP	1928–1945**
Dr Alexander Frick	FBP	1945–1962
Dr Gerard Batliner	FBP	1962–1970
Dr Alfred Hilbe	VU	1970–1974
Dr Walter Kieber	FBP	1974–1978
Hans Brunhart	VU	1978–1993
Markus Büchel	FBP	1993
Dr Mario Frick	VU	1993–2001
Otmar Hasler	FBP	2001–

* Josef Ospelt was the first Liechtensteiner to serve as Head of Government.

** Between 1938 and 1997 each government was a two-party coalition, led by the party which had gained the most parliamentary seats at the last general election.

A NOTE ON SOURCES

There is a great deal of specialist literature about Liechtenstein, much of it in German. The Liechtenstein National Library ("Landesbibliothek") regularly publishes up-dated selective bibliographies. A useful but now somewhat older bibliography is to be found in "World Bibliographical Series: Vol. 159: Liechtenstein", by Regula A. Meier (Clio Press, Oxford, 1993).

There is, however, relatively little literature that seeks to pull together the threads of Liechtenstein's history, constitution, politics, economy and society. Pierre Raton's "Le Liechtenstein, histoire et institutions" (Paris, 1949) was an important new contribution in this field. It was up-dated, revised and published in English in 1970 as "Liechtenstein: History and Institutions of the Principality" (Liechtenstein-Verlag, Vaduz). Alphons Matt, in "Unbekannter Nachbar Liechtenstein" (AT Verlag, Aarau), provided a perceptive overview of the Principality in 1986. Among official publications, successive editions of the staid but informative "A Documentary Handbook" in German and English are now being succeeded by a series of handsomely produced and illustrated slim, large-format productions, each covering its own group of themes. (Presse- und Informationsamt, Vaduz.)

Most of the author's printed sources are mentioned in the text or in footnotes. While he cannot claim to have covered every possible source (and he apologises for the inevitable oversights and omissions), he has found the following publications particularly useful.

History of the House of Liechtenstein

The traditional source is the weighty and reverential "Geschichte des fürstlichen Hauses Liechtenstein" by Jakob von Falke (three volumes, Vienna, 1868, 1877 and 1882, reprinted in Vaduz, 1984), which takes the story down to the death of Johann I in 1836. More accessible to a modern reader is Harald Wanger's "Die Regierenden Fürsten von Liechtenstein" (Frank P. van Eck Verlagsanstalt, Triesen, 1995). "Klar und Fest", by Gerald Schöpfer (Karl-Franzens-Universität, Graz, 1996), includes material about less senior members of the family as well as many photographs. Franz Kraetzl's "Das Fürstentum Liechtenstein und der gesamte Fürst Johann von und zu Liechtensteinische Güterbesitz" (Brünn, 1914, eighth edition) gives an overview of the Liechtenstein properties just before the First World War. Gustav Wilhelm's genealogical tables (Vaduz, undated but evidently published about 1980) are excellent but need to be brought up to date. Graham Martin has researched the many references to the House in German literature ("Das Haus Liechtenstein in der deutschen Literatur", JBL Vol. 88, 1990).

History of Liechtenstein

Among more general works, Otto Seger's "A Survey of Liechtenstein History" (Liechtenstein Government Press and Information Office, Vaduz, 1984) gives a good short overview in English. At a more specialised level, the successive Yearbooks of the Liechtenstein History Society (JBL) contain valuable studies of Liechtenstein's political, archaeological and natural history from earliest times up to and after the Second World War by many of the Principality's leading historians. They are too numerous to list here, but those used are referred to in the text. Three volumes of well-focussed essays, "Das Fürstentum Liechtenstein" (Konkordia, Bühl/Baden 1981), "Fürstliches Haus und Staatliche Ordnung" (Liechtensteinische Akademische Gesellschaft, Vaduz, 1987) and "Der Ganzen Welt ein Lob und Spiegel" (Verlag für Geschichte und Politik, Vienna, 1990) together cover a great deal of ground from the seventeenth to the twentieth centuries, as does "Liechtenstein Gestern und Heute" (Adulf Peter Goop, Liechtenstein-Verlag, Vaduz, 1973).

Prince Eduard von Liechtenstein's "Liechtensteins Weg von Österreich zur Schweiz", published at Vaduz in 1946 towards the end of his life, gives a vivid personal account of the hectic period immediately after the First World War (and, one senses, settles a few scores along the way). Veronika Mittermair's "Die Neutralität Liechtensteins zwischen öffentlichem und fürstlichem Interesse" (Chronos Verlag, Zurich, 1999) provides a well researched analysis of the effect of the First World War on Liechtenstein and the interaction between the State, Princely House and Czechoslovakia after it. Rupert Quaderer's "Neutralitäts- und Souveränitätsprobleme Liechtensteins im Umfeld des Ersten Weltkriegs" (Basel/Frankfurt am Main, 1993) also analyses the dilemmas of that period. The two volumes of Peter Geiger's "Krisenzeit" (Historischer Verein für das Fürstentum Liechtenstein, Vaduz, 1997) contain a full and masterly account of Liechtenstein's often dramatic political and economic problems during the 1920s and 1930s up to and including the outbreak of the Second World War.

"Liechtenstein 1938–1978" and "Liechtenstein 1978–1988" were produced as records of Franz Josef II's reign on the occasion of his Ruby and Golden Jubilees respectively. They are year-by-year compilations of press reports and photographs and, as such, provide a valuable chronicle of events as seen by contemporaries. A successor volume would be welcome.

Constitution, Government and Politics

The Speeches from the Throne and at the National Day ceremonies are an important source for the views and policies of the Sovereign Prince of the day. The Speeches from the Throne of Franz Josef II from 1939 to 1983 (together with some other major ones) and of Hereditary Prince Hans-Adam from 1984 to 1989 were printed and published by the Liechtenstein Government in 1986 and 1990 respectively. Again, a successor volume would be welcome.

The Government's annual report to Parliament ("Rechenschaftsbericht") is a full and important official source for the administration's policies and activities. So, too, are the reports which accompany and explain the Government's legislative proposals to Parliament on specific issues. The VU government's comprehensive report of July 1997 on foreign policy objectives continues to hold good as a general framework. The annual Statistical Yearbook is a mine of information about Liechtenstein. The main data are distilled from it into conveniently sized booklets in German or English ("Liechtenstein in Figures"). The Government's internet portal www.liechtenstein.li gives access to the main websites in the country.

Paul Vogt's "125 Jahre Landtag" (published by Parliament, Vaduz, 1987) gives not only an account of the working of the Liechtenstein Parliament at the date of publication but also a history of that institution, short biographies and many photographs of members of Parliament since 1862, together with annotated accounts of the results of general elections since 1862 and of popular votes since 1919.

The Liechtenstein Academic Society ("Akademische Gesellschaft") has since 1972 and 1974 respectively published two important series of study and analysis: "Liechtenstein Politische Schriften" (here referred to as LPS) and "Kleine Schriften". Some of the LPS are monographs; others are collections of essays or records of symposia. The author has made particular use of LPS Vol. 18, Arno Waschkuhn's study of continuity and change in Liechtenstein's political system (1994); Vol. 21, on the 1921 Constitution (1994); vol. 12, on local government (1987); and vol. 26, on State and Church (1999).

The Economy

The Government's statistical data and other reports are prime sources, as are the annual reports of the major companies and banks, the annual reports of the Liechtenstein Chamber of Industry and Trade and the Liechtenstein Bankers Association and the published histories of the major companies and banks. There are numerous occasional articles and other publications. Among these might be mentioned the studies in the series "Wirtschaftsfragen", published by the Verwaltungs- und Privat-Bank at least once per year and sometimes more frequently. Alexander Meili's "Geschichte des Bankwesens in Liechtenstein 1945–1980" (Frauenfeld, Stuttgart, Vienna, 2001) is a useful history of the Liechtenstein banking system up to and including the 1980 Currency Treaty with Switzerland. Heinz Klaus's "Das Bankkundengeheimnis in Europa" (BHW Trust Reg., Vaduz, 2001) is a comparative study of the bank secrecy regimes in force in Germany, Austria, Luxembourg, Switzerland and Liechtenstein.

The Price Waterhouse Information Guide "Doing Business in Liechtenstein" (1991, up-dated in 1996) is still a good general guide to the subject. Bryan Jeeves' "Liechtenstein Company Law" (2nd edition, Liechtenstein-Verlag, Vaduz, 1999) provides precise translations of the legislation in force at that time and a helpful glossary.

Peter Ludlow's "Liechtenstein in the New European and Global Order" (CEPS, Brussels, 2000) is a trenchant study of the challenges facing the Liechtenstein economy (in particular, the financial services sector) at that time and of possible options for the future.

Diplomatic Documents and Archival Material

The published Swiss and German diplomatic documents contain important material about Liechtenstein. Time and distance have prevented the author from consulting the Liechtenstein Princely and national archives. The British National Archives (formerly the Public Record Office) hold a good deal of relevant material, mostly of British origin but also in the form of photocopies of captured German documents. The references to these should be clear from the context and the footnotes. This book is not a history of British-Liechtenstein relations. However, the British documents (mostly, but not entirely, from the Foreign Office) serve to illustrate the problems facing a small and defenceless state trying to keep afloat in the turbulence of history, and offer insights into how it was viewed by one of the major powers. Some of those documents are used here for the first time.

GLOSSARY AND SELECTED ACRONYMS

Anschluss. A union between states, either voluntary or forced.

bn. Billion. Here used in the American sense of thousand millions.

CHF. The Swiss franc.

FBP. Fortschrittliche Bürgerpartei. Progressive Citizens Party.

Freie Liste. "Free List". The smallest of the three parties represented in the Parliament.

Federal Council. The Swiss Government (Bundesrat).

Gemeinde. The unit of local government in Liechtenstein, equating to a civil parish or township.

GWK. Gewerbe- und Wirtschaftskammer. The Liechtenstein Chamber of Commerce and Trade. (For small and medium enterprises.)

Hausgesetz. The House Law. (The Princely House of Liechtenstein's internal governing code.)

Hofkanzlei. The Prince of Liechtenstein's Court Chancery in Vienna, from which Liechtenstein was governed until 1918.

KYC. "Know Your Customer".

Landtag. Parliament.

LANV. Liechtensteiner Arbeitnehmerverband. The Liechtenstein Trade Union movement.

LGT BiL. Founded in 1920 as the "Bank in Liechtenstein". Now wholly owned by the Prince of Liechtenstein Foundation.

LIHK. Liechtensteinische Industrie- und Handelskammer. The Liechtenstein Chamber of Industry and Trade. (Liechtenstein's "Patronat".)

LLB. The Liechtensteinische Landesbank. Founded in 1861 as the State-owned savings and loans bank.

Oberland. The "Upper Country". The southern of the two electoral districts, equating to the former County of Vaduz.

Princely Titles. The English word "Prince" uniformly translates a variety of German styles and titles. The German title of the Head of the House of Liechtenstein is "Fürst". He is often referred to as the "Landesfürst", or Prince of the land. His consort is the Fürstin or Landesfürstin. The Heir Apparent is styled "Erbprinz", usually translated as "Hereditary Prince". His consort is the Erbprinzessin. All other members of the House (descendants of Johann I and their wives) are styled "Prinz" or "Prinzessin". All members of the House have the title of Serene Highness ("Durchlaucht"). However, Hereditary Princess Sophie and Princess Margaretha (wife of Prince Nikolaus) are Royal Highnesses ("Königliche Hoheit") by virtue of their descent from the Royal Families of Bavaria and Luxembourg respectively.

The Head of State of Liechtenstein is variously described in documents as "souveräner Fürst" (as in the 1921 Constitution), "regierender Fürst" (now the most frequently used title, usually rendered into English as "Reigning Prince") and "Fürst und Regierer des Hauses von und zu Liechtenstein" ("Prince and Ruler of the House of Liechtenstein – a title and role that date from well before the foundation of the Principality). The official English translation of the Constitution styles him "Prince Regnant". In this book he is styled "Sovereign Prince".

Putsch. A coup d'état.

Rechenschaftsbericht. The Liechtenstein Government's annual report to the Parliament.

Regierungschef. Head of Government (Prime Minister).

Regierungschef-Stellvertreter (-Stellvertreterin, if female). Alternate or substitute Prime Minister

Regierungsrat (Regierungsrätin, if female). Government Councillor (Minister).

Regierungsrat-Stellvertreter [-in]. Alternate or substitute Minister.

SMEs. Small and Medium Enterprises.

Unterland. The "Lower Country". The northern of the two electoral districts, equating to the former Lordship of Schellenberg.

VDBL. Volksdeutsche Bewegung in Liechtenstein. National German Movement in Liechtenstein. A pro-Nazi movement lasting from 1938 to 1945.

VPB. Verwaltungs- und Privat-Bank. The third of the bigger Liechtenstein banks to be founded, in 1956.

VU. Vaterländische Union. Fatherland Party

INDEX OF NAMES